Illuminate Publishing

AQA

Media Studies

for A Level Year 2

Stephanie Hendry • Elspeth Stevenson

Published in 2018 by Illuminate Publishing Ltd,
PO Box 1160, Cheltenham, Gloucestershire GL50 9RW

Orders: Please visit www.illuminatepublishing.com
or email sales@illuminatepublishing.com

British Library Cataloguing-in-Publication Data

A catalogue record for this book is available from the
British Library

ISBN 978-1-911208-09-9

Printed in the UK by Cambrian Printers, Aberystwyth

8.18

The publisher's policy is to use papers that are
natural, renewable and recyclable products made
from wood grown in sustainable forests. The
logging and manufacturing processes are expected
to conform to the environmental regulations of the
country of origin.

This material has been endorsed by AQA and
offers high-quality support for the delivery of AQA
qualifications. While this material has been through
an AQA quality assurance process, all responsibility
for the content remains with the publisher.

AQA examination questions are reproduced by
permission from AQA. AQA has not approved the
suggested reading sources.

Editor: Dawn Booth

Design and layout: Jon Fletcher

Cover design: Nigel Harriss

Cover image: Shutterstock / Dinga

Thank you to Kelly Markham and Luke Donlan
who kindly offered their `work in progress'
practical productions to be published here. Thanks
also to Damien whose patience and willingness to
chat about the media has proved invaluable.

Approval message from AQA

This textbook has been approved by AQA for use
with our qualification. This means that we have
checked that it broadly covers the specification
and we are satisfied with the overall quality. Full
details of our approval process can be found on
our website.

We approve textbooks because we know how
important it is for teachers and students to have
the right resources to support their teaching and
learning. However, the publisher is ultimately
responsible for the editorial control and quality
of this book.

Please note that when teaching the A level
Media Studies course, you must refer to AQA's
specification as your definitive source of
information. While this book has been written
to match the specification, it cannot provide
complete coverage of every aspect of the course.

A wide range of other useful resources can
be found on the relevant subject pages of our
website: www.aqa.org.uk

Contents

How to use this book   4

Chapter 1 Media language   6

1.1   What you learned in Year 1   6
      about media language

1.2   Developing your   12
      understanding of media
      language

1.3   How media language   21
      constructs and incorporates
      values and ideologies

1.4   Postmodernism   25

Chapter 2 Media representations   32

2.1   Year 1 mastery: what   32
      you already know about
      representations

2.2   The relationship between   37
      representation and reality

2.3   Discourses around   47
      representation and ideology:
      gender studies and the mass
      media

2.4   Ethnicity and postcolonial   59
      theory

Chapter 3 Media audiences   65

3.1   Understanding the   65
      relationship between
      media products and media
      audiences

3.2   Developing your   69
      understanding of media
      effects debates, cultivation
      theory and reception theory

3.3   How audiences use media   81
      in different ways, reflecting
      aspects of demographics,
      identity and cultural capital

3.4   The role of specialised   88
      audiences, including niche
      and fan (Jenkins)

3.5   'End of audience' theory   94

Chapter 4 Media industries   99

4.1   Introduction   100

4.2   The media and technological   103
      change

4.3   The rise of 'digital' producers   115
      and distributors

Chapter 5 Applying the   128
      framework: CSPs

5.1   Introduction   128

5.2   Case study one – targeted   129
      close study product case
      study: the *Daily Mail*

5.3   Case study two – targeted   147
      close study product case
      study: 'Letter to the Free'

5.4   Case study three – in-   157
      depth close study product
      case study – Tomb Raider:
      Anniversary (2007)

Chapter 6 Media for non-   170
      mainstream audiences

6.1   Introduction   170

6.2   Media products produced   171
      for non-English-speaking
      audiences

6.3   Case study: *The Killing*   173

6.4   Independence and the mass   192
      media

6.5   What do we usually mean by   193
      alternative media?

6.6   Case study: *Oh Comely*   194
      magazine

Chapter 7 Making media   206

7.1   Print production   206

7.2   Producing and working with   214
      still images

7.3   Moving image production   220

7.4   Audio production   228

7.5   Approaches to e-media   231
      production

Chapter 8 The NEA   234

8.1   Introduction to the NEA   234

8.2   Working on the NEA   237

8.3   A sample brief   241

Glossary of key terms   252

Glossary of key thinkers   258

Further reading and references   259

Index   261

Acknowledgements   272

How to use this book

Since 2015, English A levels have moved from a modular to a linear structure. From September 2017, A level Media Studies has, like all other A level subjects, become a two-year course. Assessments for this qualification will be undertaken at the end of the second year and will consist of two written examinations and one practical based non-exam assessment (NEA).

In addition to the full A level qualification there is an AS level in this subject. This is a one-year course that is assessed at the end of the year. AS Media Studies is a standalone qualification; marks awarded for the AS do not contribute to the final grade at A level.

The A level examinations test your knowledge and understanding of the theoretical framework of Media Studies.

This framework is divided into four areas:

- media language
- representations
- audience
- industry.

You will demonstrate your knowledge and understanding by applying the theoretical ideas to close study products (CSPs) named by the exam board. You will also be asked to apply your knowledge of the theoretical framework using media products that you have not studied. There will be one 'unseen' media product included on each examination paper.

> The AS exam does not contribute to the A level mark but the subject content for 'AS Media Studies' will be assessed in the A level examinations.

The AS & Year 1 book covers the following:

Media language		
The practical choices made by media producers when creating media products You need to be able to identify and analyse the way media producers communicate meaning in the way they use media language choices. You will need to understand how codes and conventions of form and genre are used and how narratives are constructed.	Required for the AS exam	Introductory knowledge for A level students
Representations		
The way the media portrays events, issues, individuals and groups You will need to consider how representations are constructed and how meanings are created by them. You should be able to critically evaluate how ideologies can be communicated through representations.	Required for the AS exam	Introductory knowledge for A level students
Audience		
How the media targets and attempts to reach audiences and how audiences respond and interpret media products You will also need to consider the way audiences can become producers of media products themselves.	Required for the AS exam	Introductory knowledge for A level students
Industries		
The way media industries produce, distribute and circulate media products You should consider the relationships between audience and producers, the economic issues that motivate media industries and the way industries are responding to changes in the media landscape.	Required for the AS exam	Introductory knowledge for A level students
Skills development		
There is a free downloadable chapter also available, which offers practical tips on building the skills that are required in Media Studies. You can find this on the Illuminate website: http://illuminatepublishing.com/AQA_Media_AS_Yr1_ExamChapter. The chapter looks at the skill of analysis as well as using media theory and terminology in formal written work. These will help you develop the skills that will be assessed in examinations, so will need to be practised over the course over one (AS) or two (A level) years. **NB This exam chapter is not approved by AQA.**	Provides examples of the underpinning skills required in Media Studies for both AS and A level students	

Close study products	
A number of media products have been selected and are identified as 'close study products' (CSPs). These are the products you must study before taking the AS examination at the end of the first year and/or the A level examination at the end of year two. Chapter 8 offers some examples of detailed analysis using the theoretical framework and some of the CSPs. It is possible that CSPs may change in the future, so you must check with the most up-to-date information provided by the exam board to make sure you are using the correct products for the examination you are sitting. The analytic methods found in Chapter 8 can be used as a model for a detailed and considered analysis using aspects of the theoretical framework for other or, if applicable, newer CSPs. Chapter 8 offers examples of media products that cover all three platforms (broadcast, e-media and print) and three of the nine media forms (magazines, television and media) identified in the specification. The analysis of these products also uses many of the ideas and much of the language identified in the key terms features of earlier chapters as well as the ideas from the key thinkers. The examples here can help you prepare your CSPs or could be used to develop your analysis skills and your ability to apply theoretical ideas prior to engaging with some of the more advanced A level theories and ideas.	Provides examples of the application of the theoretical framework to media products for both AS and A level students

This book develops and extends the ideas covered in the AS & Year 1 book and has been constructed to support the second year of study with a view to taking the A level examinations and non-exam assessment at the end of the two-year course.

This book covers the following:

Chapter 1 Media language
Development of ideas regarding the analysis of media language choices made in the production of media products including the application of genre and narrative theories, structuralism and postmodernism.

Chapter 2 Media representations
Development of ideas related to media representations, including feminist, post-feminist and postcolonial theories.

Chapter 3 Media audiences
Building on ideas about audience that include discussions on changes in audience behaviours, fandom and 'end of audience' theories.

Chapter 4 Media industries
Case studies considering the impact of technological changes and globalisation to the way media industries produce, distribute and circulate media products. This chapter engages with the way traditional media industries' dominance of the media landscape is being challenged.

Chapter 5 Applying the framework: CSPs
Case studies demonstrating approaches to analysing targeted and in-depth CSPs using the theoretical framework. CSPs have been chosen to cover different media forms, and examples of close analysis and application of theoretical ideas are offered.

Chapter 6 Media for non-mainstream audiences
Further CSP case studies are provided with a focus on independent and foreign language CSPs. These products are in-depth CSPs and need to be studied for A level Paper 2.

Chapter 7 Making media
This chapter looks at the codes and conventions of a range of media forms that you may need to create for your NEA.

Chapter 8 The NEA
This chapter offers advice on the practicalities of production covering all three media platforms – print, broadcast and e-media.

Chapter 9 The examinations
There is a free downloadable chapter also available on the Illuminate website: http://illuminatepublishing.com/AQA_Media_Yr2_ExamChapter. This chapter breaks down the two A level examination papers and offers advice and guidance on approaching the different types of questions you may encounter. **NB This exam chapter is not approved by AQA.**

The two books combine to provide a detailed overview of the key ideas from each area of the theoretical framework and offers EXAMPLES from a range of different media areas and forms. Each chapter offers several APPLY IT features which offer activities to help you develop your knowledge and understanding.

The nature of Media Studies is that it is dynamic and things change fast but these books offer you ideas and examples of approaches to the CSPs and ways to engage with and think about the contemporary media world we live in.

Chapter 1 Media language

What you will learn in this chapter

- Year 1 Mastery: recap of the theoretical framework from Year 1
- Year 2 Development: narrative, genre, structuralism and post-structuralism
- Year 2 Development: how media language constructs and incorporates values and ideologies
- Year 2 Development: post-modernism and media language

1.1 What you learned in Year 1 about media language

In Year 1, you explored the key methods and theories used to explore media texts. This helped you to understand how they communicate with their audience, and that there are many different approaches we can use when you try and understand the significance of media texts in contemporary culture. You learned the terminology that describes the technical codes associated with decoding audio-visual, print and digital media texts, and the contribution made by semiotic theory to this process. You applied some important theories associated with studying narrative and genre to the texts you studied. This section provides a quick reminder of your learning from last year and some examples of that learning in action, as well as some activities getting you to apply your knowledge to ensure you've really mastered it.

You should be able to use some of the principles and terminology of semiotic analysis with confidence and be aware of the contributions made by key thinkers to the field, including understanding the process of signification (Saussure and Barthes) categories of sign (Peirce) and denotation/ connotation /myth (Barthes).

By now, you'll be confident in your ability to decode a range of print media texts, such as magazine covers and features, advertisements, newspapers and promotional posters, with confidence and using appropriate terminology. You'll also be happy decoding a range of audio-visual and audio texts, including television, advertisements and trailers, radio, podcasts, and contextual material embedded in digital media forms, such as web video content.

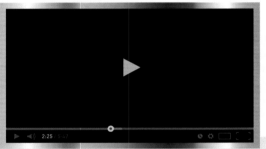

EXAMPLE: Analysis of technical codes in the trailer for *A Series of Unfortunate Events* (Netflix, 2017)

In the case of technical codes, you may have a specific focus you are looking at – or you may be looking for what is interesting about the technical codes you see and using the codes themselves to find a focus for something to say about the text. In this situation, you definitely don't need to comment on everything – this example shows how picking out just five points per type of technical code gives you plenty of evidence you can use to support a solid response to this kind of analysis.

In this example, let's imagine that the focus in the form of a question is:

- How do technical codes in the trailer contribute to our understanding of what life is like for the children after the death of their parents?

Camerawork

- An extreme close-up of the Count's eye through the peephole signifies suspicion, along with the anti-social tendencies of the character and his lack of suitability as a guardian.
- The whip pan that follows the bird from the beautiful neighbourhood to the gloom of the house signifies the rapid change in their circumstances and loss of the children's freedom.
- The frequent framing of the children in two-shot (plus Sunny held in Violet's arms) reinforces the strength of their bond.

Mise-en-scène

- The ashen desaturated tones of the interiors in Count's house signifies that their situation will not improve as long as they remain there.
- The Count sits in long shot at a huge table, with a plate of food before him, on a chair that is throne-like. In terms of proxemics, the children are right at the opposite end of the frame, and their non-verbal communication is hunched and intimidated; nothing is placed before the children.
- The light source in every frame shot in the Count's house is externally sourced, connoting that there is no hope for the family as long as they remain inside – but that escape could offer them a chance.

Editing

- The montage of bleak situations the children find themselves in at the Count's home is shown in rapid succession – cleaning the filthy bathroom, preparing food in a cluttered kitchen, sitting on a single bed in a leaky attic, all emphasising their bleak prospects.
- The mise-en-scène of the exterior neighbourhood is colourised to highlight the soft tones of pastel pink cherry blossom, green turf and blue sky, which is swiftly juxtaposited with the filthy and grey interior of the house.
- The abrupt change of soundtrack from jazzy upbeat lyrical song to the sound jerks of the score signify again the abruptness of their change in situation.

Audio codes

- The selective use of certain diegetic sounds above the score contributes significantly to meaning because they are used so sparingly – for example, the ominous tone of the doorbell.
- The quality of the Count's vocal performance signifies dislike of the children from the moment of his greeting, as he sneers the word 'children'.
- The full orchestral score borrows from the intensity and scale of a cinematic production, signifying the dramatic nature of the disaster that befalls the children.
- Lemony Snicket's reverent vocal performance and the verbal codes he uses in voice-over quickly signify that the tale is to be filled with misfortune.

APPLY IT

Choose a current TV show that has an interesting or extended title sequence. Practice using the terminology of sound, camerawork, editing, mise-en-scène and other relevant technical codes to identify key meanings in the text.

Although the range of forms in which they appear makes the decoding of various digital media forms quite challenging, you should by now be feeling more confident about how to use technical codes and adapt them to the form you're exploring. Websites, games, apps and social media, including emerging and experimental texts should all form part of your exploration and growing familiarity with the ways in which texts work, even when these are not as common or confined to a specific use in digital media production.

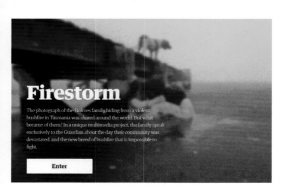

EXAMPLE: Analysis of a multi-media parallax story – *Firestorm* (*Guardian*, May 2013)

Multi-media texts can provide an immersive dimension to online journalism. These hybrids between magazine and newspaper journalism and documentary form borrow conventions from both and are becoming more common. They are marked out by limited hypertextuality and an absence of plugins. They may have interactive elements to them, but these are usually rather simple and are more about the control over pace of consumption experienced by the user of embedded content. This is defined by the **parallax design**, which allows items to scroll and appear at different paces, creating a 2D effect rather than the more traditional flat appearance of websites. The kinds of stories commonly given this treatment are those that might have traditionally appeared in the weekend supplements of newspapers.

The example you explore here focuses on a story that appeared on the *Guardian* website in May 2013. Although the story is quite old, there has been very little change in how storytelling like this works and is a good example that exploits the full potential of the form. It focuses on the story behind widely distributed images of the Holmes family sheltering under a jetty during a major bush fire in Tasmania. It walks the reader through the events of the day, as well contexualising the fire in a climate context.

The story itself is told in six chapters, accessible from the right-hand side of the screen if viewed on a desktop. This allows the user to quickly review or jump to the sections they might find the most interesting in a non-linear way. Scrolling through the story, we experience in the first chapter a series of white text narrative segments overlaid on video that uses the diegetic sound of the landscapes to signify nature, tranquillity, the remoteness of the community and so on. These function in the same way as an establishing shot in a conventional audio-visual documentary. This is followed by the appearance of a short video, a close-up talking heads shot of Tim and Tammy Holmes. Graphical elements are used to show the conditions, activated by scrolling and set over a map of Tasmania, which allowed the bush fire to spread. As the story builds in Chapter 2, background video of the landscapes fills us with foreboding as the white text narrates the action. This is interspersed again with the recurrent headshots of the two main subjects of the story narrating alternately the events of the day.

We hear a voice recording of two further subjects – a fire service officer and a local resident who captured footage of the fire. In the first case, the voice is set to a backdrop of the journey he describes filmed by a point-of-view (POV) shot on a dashcam, gathering pace to the narrative. The second uses the actual footage of the fire approaching the town filmed on a camera phone, a good integration of citizen journalism into the experience. There is some use of extradiegetic soundtrack to act as a signposting device, signifying the rising tension as the fire progresses.

Once the iconic photograph itself is reached, we hear a short recording of Tammy's voice, together with a mournful piano track, and the sounds of both water lapping and fire. A slideshow then plays of the key photographs taken by the family at the scene.

Organisationally, the text follows Todorov's theory in a conventional way, with the movement between the two equilibriums of life before the fire ('a cloudless sky') versus life after its devastation ('the Holmes family rebuilds'). There is therefore a time-based element to the chronology, but most of the narration is in analeptical form – the whole story is driven by powerful binary oppositions that speak to our very primal fear of fire, which acts as a symbolic code (SYM). The vulnerability of the family versus the raging fire is focalised, with all aspects of the narrative pivoting on their need to survive. Barthes' five codes are, in fact, all present and very much active in the text. We have proairetic codes (ACTs) of the individual actions taken by the firefighters and the family members as they make their life-or-death decisions. We have the referential codes (REFs) of the overall context of Australian bushfires and our knowledge of these from news reporting. Overarching hermeneutic codes (HERs) frame the story for us – what will become of the town? Will everyone survive? What will be the extent of the damage? Strong use is made of the semantic codes (SEMs) arising from the photographs themselves, which the narrative centres on – the huddling together of the family and the non-verbal communication of their facial expressions as they bear the heat and experience the approach of the fire as they stay on the jetty.

The whole experience of the story is seamless and immersive, allowing the viewer to control the pace at which the narrative unfolds, and to spend as much or as little time as is necessary experiencing different segments of the story. Hero images are used throughout, frequently overlaid by text, foreshadowing their more contemporary use in modern web design.

(Source: *Guardian*, 2013)

APPLY IT

Choose a news-based or documentary multi-media parallax story, and decode it using any relevant technical codes and the language of semiotics. You may need to draw not only on terms specific to the study of digital media codes, but also those from print and audio-visual media, depending on the content and stylistic presentation. Identify key meanings in the text.

In studying narratives in media texts, you should be able to apply relevant terminology commonly used in discussion of narrative organisation. More of this will be introduced in this chapter to help deepen your understanding of ways in which you can write about narratives.

By now, you will be able to discuss how narratives are organised in texts and how audiences make sense of narratives, using appropriate terminology and the specific theories of Todorov movements between two equilibriums (Todorov), five codes (Barthes) and binary oppositions (Lévi-Strauss).

EXAMPLE: Narrative analysis of Green & Black's Velvet Edition television advertisement (2017)

Even a 30-second television advert can be very fruitful for testing your understanding of the range of narrative theories you have learned so far on the course. This Green & Black's chocolate advert features a girl in a red velvet cloak on a bicycle, who is pursued by wolves. The end of the advertisement reveals a twist – they are playing hide and seek, and now it's the wolves' turn to hide. The slogan is, 'Not everything is as dark as it seems'.

1 Todorov's five stages of narrative

Equilibrium	The girl is on her bike taking a break from a journey (enjoying a bite of chocolate).
Disruption	She hears a twig snap.
Recognition	She realises someone is watching and possibly following her.
Attempt to repair	She cycles away at speed, she leaves the road for the cover of the trees, then hides behind a rock.
New equilibrium	Found by the wolves, she despatches them to take their turn to hide and takes her time to enjoy the chocolate.

Verdict on usefulness of theory?

This text is very short, but, nonetheless, Todorov's model still works to describe the advancement of the action through a series of stages.

2 Lévi-Strauss' binary oppositions

Rest versus motion	The advert offers us the contrasts between the symbolic action of the chase, and the more languorous moments when the chocolate is being consumed.
Traditional tale v modern interpretation	Everyone knows the wolves are bad in the original tale, but the bicycle already signifies to us that we might expect an updating in some way. The advert uses the traditional tale as a reference point then subverts our expectations, suggesting that our preconceptions of a dark chocolate as 'bitter' may in fact be unfounded.
Red Riding Hood v the wolves	This opposition is used to signify danger and threat, drawing readily on our understanding of the wolf signifying danger in this story and many other European folk tales. The threat is then resolved in an unexpected way – this is pleasurable for the audience.

Verdict on usefulness of theory?

The theory works well and is an interesting one to use, since Lévi-Strauss' original work explored traditional tales and myths in different cultures. There are potentially more oppositions to be found, or the ones selected could be redefined or restructured in different ways.

3 Roland Barthes' five codes

Hermeneutic code (HER)	What has Red Riding Hood heard? Will the wolves find and catch her? What will she do when cornered?
Proairetic code (ACT)	Units of action can be defined, such as Red Riding Hood hears the noise, and pedals away as fast as she can. She drops the bike at speed and runs through the wood to hide. She meets the gaze of the wolves, begins to count. The wolves turn and run.
Semantic code (SEM)	Red Riding Hood's fast breathing is heard as a selective sound, signifying that she is exerting herself and possibly in fear.
Symbolic code (SYM)	The redness of Red Riding Hood's cloak signifies that she is in danger in the natural background of the woodland.
Referential/ cultural code (REF)	The advert relies on our understanding of the traditional European tale of Little Red Riding Hood.

Verdict on usefulness of theory?

The theory works well and is in fact underexplored here – this is a rich text for Barthes' codes given its length.

In terms of genre studies, your confidence should be increasing in your ability to identify codes and conventions for yourself of any genre, and be aware of the limitations of any genre analysis that relies purely on convention identification.

By now, you will be able to use the terminology of genre analysis (Neale) and understand some of the different ways in which genre can be understood as a concept by both audience and industry (e.g. Andrew).

APPLY IT

Choose a 30-second advertisement for a confectionary product, food or drink. Can you apply all of the theories you have learned so far on the course? Critique the theories as you use them. Do they all work equally well?

The Keepers is a Netflix Originals web-television documentary series. The documentary focuses on the murder of a nun decades ago in a small American town. Documentaries focusing on a crime investigation of cold cases or suspected miscarriages of justice are currently a popular genre, spanning both audio and audio-visual production. Netflix's *Making a Murderer* performed extremely well in the video-on-demand (VoD) market in 2016, perhaps forming a blueprint for further additions to the corpus. *Serial*, featured in the Year 1 book, topped podcast charts. In the UK, Radio 5 Live broadcast their own answer to *Serial: Beyond Reasonable Doubt*.

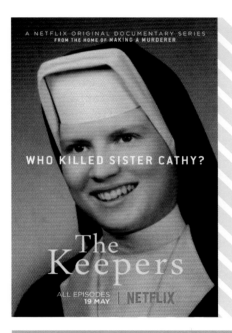

🔗 For more on *Serial* see page 246 of the Year 1 book.

Conventions common to many texts in the corpus of investigative crime-based documentary include:

- **Linear narrative chronology based on the investigation of a crime and/or its prosecution** – there is the suggestion that this documentary may vary this convention, and that the focus will not be on the death of Sister Cathy, but its alleged cover-up.

- **A miscarriage of justice or unsolved case at its heart** – it is implied that her killer has not been successfully found, fitting with the audience's generic regime of verisimilitude and forming a structure that audiences can relate to and expect contractually from the genre.

- **New insights or fresh evidence, witnesses or documents associated with the case** – many documents are seen – photographs from the time-period, newspaper headlines viewed on microfiche, a medical report – and form part of the iconography of the genre. One subject in particular makes a statement claiming their father confessed to burying the body. These contribute to the manipulation of the audience's expectations and hypotheses.

- **Passionate commitment to the case and determination to find 'the truth'** – in this case, there appears to be a team of amateur investigators who knew Sister Cathy or were taught by her: seems to be a variation of the single investigator model.

- **Engagement with mainstream ideologies about crime and punishment, although not necessarily about law enforcement and the justice system** – this documentary engages with our sense of fair play: Sister Cathy is represented as epitomising kindness and Christian values. She is young and innocent. The Catholic Church, on the other hand, is represented as the villain of the piece. This might run counter to conservative Catholics' values, but resonate with the wider community's experience of news stories and sex abuse scandals involving the Catholic Church, fitting with our cultural regime of verisimilitude.

- **Documentaries of this kind have a ritual and ideological function** – they serve to remind us that, even when justice has not been done by the system, a wrong may yet be made right.

Repertoire of elements common in documentary trailers:

- **Soundtrack** – a dramatic score punctuates the montage, emphasising proairetic codes encoded in the intertitles and pausing dramatically for witnesses to utter key phrases.

- **Use of intertitles** – these help to cultivate a narrative image for the series'; examples include 'a story buried for fifty years' and 'abuse, murder, conspiracy'.

- **Soundbites from participants** – a positive representation of the team is generated by their collaborative efforts to pursue the case.

- **Locations** – places around Baltimore, mainly exteriors, are used as iconic signs of place.

- **Archive footage** – in this case, of a separate investigation relating to the murder.

APPLY IT

Choose a trailer for a film or television release. Explain what you think the conventions are both of a trailer for that type of product and the signifiers of the genre itself. Explore whether your example conforms to these, making sure you integrate some of the key terms used to present discussions about genre.

See 'Postmodernism and media language' in Section 1.4.

- **Hand-held camerawork** – used to create a sense of immediacy and spontaneity.
- **Re-enactments** – a priest viewed from the back in close-up, suggesting he is up to no good; two nuns walking together lend atmosphere; however, it is unclear how much of a role re-enactments will play in the actual documentary.
- **Voice-over/narration** – in this case, the narration is created using the soundbites of participants, and meanings anchored by footage of locations, reconstruction and so on.
- **Montage editing** – the technique is used in a conventional way in this trailer.
- **Clear binary oppositions** – those that will drive the investigation are established as 'abuse, murder, conspiracy', 'Fear, lies, corruption' v 'strength, hope, justice'.

KEY TERM

parallax design	a graphics technique where separate elements scroll at different rates on the screen, making the resulting text feel as though it has more depth

1.2 Developing your understanding of media language

For the full A level, there are some aspects of your understanding of media language that will benefit from further development and a deeper understanding. These include your understanding of some topics, ideas and aspects of key thinkers and the theoretical framework you have already encountered in the Year 1 book.

You will be increasing your awareness of the significance of genre to media producers and audiences, which in this section will be explored more fully. The historical changes and developments you have seen in a number of specific media genres will be considered, so that you can understand how to research and apply this process for yourself. The importance of non-genre texts and those that subvert genre rules to create particular effects will also be considered, as well as considering genre as a vehicle for other ideas and purposes.

APPLY IT

During Year 1, you became confident in applying some of the terms used in semiotic analysis. To check your understanding, choose an example of each of the following texts:

- a newspaper front page
- a magazine front cover
- a print advertisement.

Annotate them, interpreting the meanings of each sign using some of the following terms from semiotic analysis:

signifier signified sign
icon indexical sign code
symbolic sign anchorage
paradigm syntagm
denotation connotation
myth

In the Year 1 book, you were also introduced to some structuralist and post-structuralist theories such as semiotic theory and the concept of myth, and the key thinkers behind these theories – during the full A level you will build on this knowledge and ensure you understand its historical placement and uses in critical theory. You will be thinking in a more sophisticated manner about the ways in which media language is constructed to convey particular values and ideologies.

During the first year of the course, you also encountered intertextuality. You will be adding to this understanding and connecting it more powerfully with a new area of the theoretical framework – postmodernism.

Structuralism and post-structuralism

Two of the key thinkers you have used in understanding how to analyse media texts have been structuralist thinkers. Saussure's semiology is an example of early structuralism, and Lévi-Strauss is renowned as being a structural anthropologist. Strauss's work in this field was considered revolutionary for its time and had strong implications for anyone studying culture, including how narratives function in media texts. Barthes is usually considered a post-structuralist, and his ideas about denotation, connotation, myth and the signification process have already been embedded into your understanding of how you read the media.

Barthes' study of the codes of narrative and work on narratology have also been a significant part of your studies so far. Structuralists attempt to find meanings in human cultural production and interaction by analysing the frameworks that support it. They believed there was an intermediary point between 'reality' and abstract concepts of it, and this was what they sought to understand – the process that connects the two. This could be understood by the **deconstruction** of the text – using the tools of structural analysis to find its meaning.

Saussure was one of the founders of structuralism, and semiotic theory in its earliest forms is a structuralist theory. Lévi-Strauss is also a key structuralist thinker. Later developments in structuralism, which took some of the original ideas but also rejected others, became known as post-structuralist approaches. Barthes is the best-known post-structuralist thinker you have learned about on the course. You will notice that Barthes progressed, for example, the idea of the signifier and signified, and the way they combine to form a sign into the idea that there were orders of signification – a first, a second and a third that related to ideology and myth. You can think of post-structuralism as being both an evolution of structuralism but also a rejection of some of its aspects, which may be considered in later thinking as either underdeveloped or too rigid.

In the Year 1 book, you have already encountered some structuralist and theories. Lévi-Strauss' theory of binary oppositions is a crucial one. In the process of using his approach, an **ideological reading** could be obtained from a text – a conclusion that aims to expose how power relationships between social groups operate and manifest themselves in cultural production, and therefore normalise certain ways of thinking, attitudes and values so powerfully that they become part of a person's identity. This process was described by Althusser as interpellation – the creation of a subject of ideology.

For more on binary oppositions see page 20 of the Year 1 book.

The Force Manchester interpelates the viewer as a subject of an ideology which favours law enforcement and naturalises the Police Force as an ideological state apparatus.

Mytheme

Another important aspect of Lévi-Strauss work involves the analysis of **mythemes**. Mythemes are small units of myths that he identified in the traditional stories of tribes he studied. Another term he gave to them was gross constituent units. In this way, a narrative could be understood as being comprised of units of relationships between characters, actions they undertake and the themes that result. Lévi-Strauss was interested in the relationships between these units. Each element of a narrative does not therefore have its own fixed meaning but operates within a framework of ideas and cultural meanings. It is in relation to other elements of the story that a mytheme takes on its role in the production of meaning – mythemes are part of the functioning of binary oppositions. They cannot be read in isolation but have a meaning when the whole overview of the narrative is taken into account.

Lévi-Strauss called mythemes 'bundles of meanings', clearly showing the interconnectedness of the individual units in creating meaning. Oppositions are played out in myths because they help to resolve contradictions that a culture may experience in day-to day living. They are therefore meaningful to the context of the cultural codes that produce them, and although myths may be similar across cultures, the way in which mythemes are organised will vary according to the function of the myth in that culture. The relevance of this work to studying narratives in contemporary media is still considerable, since media texts arguably have the same role in contemporary culture – they render the world comprehensible to us.

Revisiting narrative

In the Year 1 book, you spent some time looking at how narrative codes operate, specifically Barthes' five codes. If you remember, Barthes envisaged his five codes – the hermeneutic, proairetic, the semantic, the symbolic and the referential – all functioning together like a braided rope. You also looked at the ideas of Lévi-Strauss and Todorov. You reviewed narration styles and explored how some of these functioned within the diegesis – the story-world, the sphere of action inhabited by the characters. Also, you explored narration styles, including omniscient narration and restricted narration.

Character types can have an important role in narratives. These should be studied alongside representations in order to understand how certain types can have function in a narrative. Their roles can help to advance the story or promote **causality**. Causality can almost be thought of as the way in which the story runs itself, the way in which the events, usually driven by the desires and motivations of characters and the events that impact on them, drive the logic of the narrative forwards. Each event or action acts as a trigger for further actions – one thing causes another in a complex chain that can encompass subplots as well as drive surprise endings. One technique associated with an unresolved aspect of causality is known as a **dangling cause** – an action, event or motif, the inclusion of which remains unclear until later in the narrative when its purpose and connection with cause and effect is made clear. Causality is also associated with narrative progress and delay, and can be used to control the pace at which a narrative unfolds.

Archetypes are shared across cultures and in human stories all around the world. They are basic, rather simple character types who appear over and over in narratives. Heroes are archetypes, but so are jesters and sages. Note that most significant characters based on archetypes are male in classical stories and much of the canon of Western literature, and that this bias can still be seen in many media products – although their roles may of course be taken on by a person of either gender in contemporary texts. Tropes, on the other hand, are quite often gender-specific, or, where they have a male and a female equivalent, may have

For more on Barthes' five codes see page 20 of the Year 1 book.

The way in which Barthes' five narrative codes operate – braided together like a rope.

distinctions in how the trope is expressed depending on gender. Archetypes often give a recognisable but simple grounding for a character, but tropes can be more developed.

Tropes can be thought of as taking an archetype and placing it in a relevant contemporary context specific to the culture that produces the media text. Although many have their origins in archetypes, they are more modern – a single archetype, for example, might spawn more than one trope.

Although tropes are used to tell stories and are therefore usually quite harmless, they often rely on the audience's understanding of stereotypes for their impact. Although tropes are often created primarily to serve the narrative, they can end up being ill-considered repetition of stereotypes. Tropes are also not limited to characters – they can also describe set-ups or conflicts in narratives and even locations where certain predictable or familiar plot points or events take place.

Another term you may come across is **stock characters**. Many people use the term stock character and trope interchangeably, but, again, crucially their function is driven by narrative, their existence perpetuated by repetition in popular cultural products. Their purpose is to entertain us by providing a familiar framework of actions, behaviours and attitudes. A stock character is not intended to be sophisticated, and the writer of a stock character is not duty bound to make them new or refreshing. Stock characters are interesting to Media Studies students because their presence can tell us about the symbolic function they have in our culture – the manic pixie dream girl, for example, often enables the hero to find his true self – while she may appear to be a free spirit, she is still a form of princess subservient to the hero's greater need.

Three archetypes in traditional tales include the sage, the magician and the fool.

Tom Kirkman is the ultimate 'everyman' stock character, thrown into the role of US President in a moment in *Designated Survivor* (Netflix, 2016).

There will be times when you come across characters in fictional or non-fiction media texts who genuinely surprise you. They may be represented in a way that seems to run counter to dominant representations of similar people. There may be a counter-hegemonic purpose to these representations, or they may have been created purely to surprise the audience. They may form part of a concerted effort to contribute to the process of signification in a deliberate way, changing our minds and opinions about a group of people or an issue, and affecting the course of the narrative in surprising or unconventional ways.

APPLY IT

Choose a fictional TV series or a reality TV show you know well. American television series with ensemble casts work particularly well for this activity, but any programme with a good range of characters or participants is suitable. List the main characters in the show – you can use a site such as IMDb initially if you wish. Can you identify any stock characters or archetypes without researching them?

Look online to find a source of stock characters, archetypes and cultural tropes. There are many such sites online – a particularly good one is http://tvtropes.org.

Prepare a cast list for your show that gives a short description of the character and the trope they fulfil.

When considering these components of a narrative, it is worth also thinking about what you mean by the terms plot and narrative. Although the term narrative is commonly used to describe any aspect of the story, the easy way to remember narrative is that it is the way in which a story is told. Think of the word narration – it tells you something about the style and perspective of the story and many other nuances. Plot is a term more commonly used in industry writing practice, but also has a function and meaning for audiences – it is the 'events' of the story in chronological order that constitute the 'backbone' of the story. The plot is what someone will often tell you if you ask them what a television programme or film is about.

A **masterplot** refers to an overarching narrative that is meaningful to a particular culture. It may be comprised of particular character types, plot events or conflicts that are explored over and over again. Many of these plots have universality to them – you can recognise elements of them in many popular texts. So established are masterplots that many writers have published checklists to use as a source. These tend to be rather more detailed and prescriptive than the backbone function most masterplots have on the organisation of narratives that are influenced by them.

The quest narrative, for example, is summarised as follows in Ronald Tobias's (2012) book on masterplots:

- Something must happen which triggers the hero's journey/quest.
- The journey should involve travel and movement.
- The protagonist should have a companion.
- They should discover something about themselves and mature as the journey goes on.
- The plot should end up geographically back close to home.
- The hero should realise that what they learned is not necessarily what they thought they were setting out to learn.
- The hero should mature and grow.
- The hero should pronounce his/her insight into their growth.

EXAMPLE: *American Gods* and the influence of the quest narrative (Amazon Prime, 2017)

Elements of the quest narrative elements of the plot can clearly be seen in this narrative of a young man whose life is thrown into disarray by tragedy but regains meaning through his journey.

- Shadow, an ex-convict, is released from prison, only to find his wife, Laura, has died. He is devastated to learn that she has also betrayed him with his friend.
- Unable to stay in their former home, he takes up the offer of a work as a bodyguard from the enigmatic character Mr Wednesday.

Shadow and Mr Wednesday undertake their quest in *American Gods*.

- Mr Wednesday is on a journey to meet various people across America to recruit them for a cause – Shadow joins him.
- Wednesday can qualify as a companion, since, although he is a powerful agent in the narrative, the narrative perspective focuses on Shadow as protagonist.
- As he journeys, Shadow discovers strengths he was not aware he possessed, including forgiveness as he meets his wife Laura once more, now a zombie.
- He discovers knowledge about his environment that casts aside his perceptions of reality rather than himself – the people Wednesday takes him to meet are all rather unusual. Shadow begins to realise his travelling companion and his old acquaintances have supernatural powers. He loses his naivity about his relationship with Laura.
- Far from the journey being a distraction from Laura's death, Shadow discovers it is an unveiling of the supernatural dimension; the old gods brought to America by its immigrants are still surviving in some surprising places
- Shadow admits his belief in the old gods and in Wednesday, who is revealed as the god Odin. He has a new purpose and an important role in Odin's battle against the new gods of Media and Technology, although we are not yet sure why he is so significant.

APPLY IT

Some other familiar masterplots in Western culture include revenge, transformation and forbidden love.

a Can you source a fiction media text as an example that makes at least partial use of one of these?

b Can you see evidence of them in any fact-based texts, such as interviews with celebrities? Journalists as well as fictional writers are aware of the existence of masterplots and the audience's receptiveness to them as cultural tropes.

Revisiting genre

In the Year 1 book, you explored Stephen Neale's ideas about genre. One of Neale's most influential ideas about genre is that they are not stable – they fluctuate over time because they are always responding to a crucial tension between sameness and repetition, variation and change.

These tensions give rise to hybrids and sub-genres. Hybridisation is becoming increasingly common in television. The huge investment by production companies in well-funded, long-lasting drama series means even more experimentation and stretching of what you expect from genre. Sub-genres, where a group of conventions identify a sub-group within an overall generic category, can sometimes develop to an extent that they can outgrow the genre that spawned them. They then become something which is well-defined category in its own right. This is what we mean by genres as cultural categories – we love to categorise things and new genre labels are as likely to spring up from audience participation and response to media texts online as they are in media marketing or critical circles.

For more on Stephen Neale's theories on genre see pages 43–44 of the Year 1 book.

EXAMPLE: *Outlander* (Amazon Prime, 2017) as an example of generic hybridity

The television series *Outlander*, which began in 2014 with the third series being broadcast in October 2017, defies generic categorisation, but simultaneously draws on conventions, themes, modes and tropes from a range of cultural categories. Listings across the internet attach a whole host of generic and sub-genre categories to the programme. These include science fiction, time-travel, adventure, drama, historical drama, fantasy, war and romance. This resistance to categorisation, while simultaneously showing the audience's desire to categorise, makes it an interesting example of the fluid nature of contemporary genre and the playfulness with which it may be exploited by its producers.

Genre conventions change over time in response to two main factors. These can be separated into two broad influences: technological change and social and cultural factors, although this is a slightly artificial division. In this section, you'll be breaking these down a little further and exploring them in more detail.

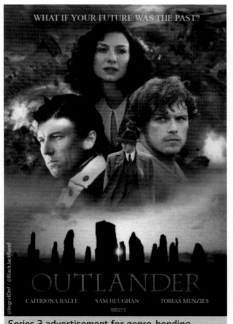

Series 3 advertisement for genre-bending programme *Outlander*

Genre and technological change

One of the factors that impacts on genre is technological change. Factors affecting genre transmission vary across media forms.

The way in which VoD services categorise and label genres is a study in its own right.

The development of video-on-demand and increasing international reach of big audio-visual content providers through subscription packages, cable and satellite services has meant a big increase in the reach of certain television genres as part of the impact of globalisation on the mass media. New genres can spread from culture to culture more rapidly than at any other time in the history of the mass media.

Like television, radio has gained more of an international audience with the advent of the internet. The technology of podcasting distribution and the distinct way in which podcasts tend to be listened to when compared with radio listening has meant the emergence of new genres and transmission of genres that work well on television but may be heard less on radio, specific to the form. The comedy podcast and insight into other cultures are good examples of these.

Most newspapers have made the leap from print to digital platforms, but at the same time new news-based sites have emerged. An almost entirely new genre is the satirical news website, providing a constant almost real-time social commentary on world and domestic affairs. News websites such as the *HuffPost*, which exist only online and are designed to be experienced through other social media feeds as much as through the main site, have also become commonplace.

Magazine genres have remained fairly stable, since their digital versions are consumed in similar ways and they use similar subscription models to print editions. However, comics – in decline over the years in print form – have exploded in genres online. Fan comics have emerged, as have other genres.

The emergence of genres in digital media

Digital video, especially in the short forms it appears in embedded into social media sites and on YouTube, demonstrates an almost constant emergence of new genres. Prior to the digital age, the only short forms in existence tended to be animations, children's programming and short film. In the age of mass media proliferation, short video forms are everywhere. Vlogging is often used as broad generic term, but in fact it is a complex genre with many sub-generic hybrids and variants. Because digital video is so heavily viewed, and because of the huge global reach

The emergence of new gaming technologies brings new genres to audiences as well as developing familiar ones.

of a platform such as YouTube or other social media networks, new genres can be spawned over a matter of days rather than the years or even decades it could take, for example, for a film or television genre to evolve.

Computer game genres move incredibly fast, and gaming is one of the forms where genre is closely integrated with the technological experience of the game. In some cases, the development of new gaming technologies, such as virtual reality (VR) headsets, may simply change the way in which a genre is experienced – other changes, such as augmented reality, may spark new genres for which there are no real antecedents.

Blogs and websites also have their own genres. The lifestyle blogger, for example, may also be a vlogger on YouTube and be followed on Instagram, with each manifestation of their digital persona appearing in different platforms.

EXAMPLE: Vlogging as an emergent new media genre

The vlogger has been one of the surprising success stories of YouTube. Vlogging is one of the main genres that has led to the phenomenon of the YouTube 'personality', a world that is dominated by amateur enthusiasts in a wide range of fields, who share their thoughts and experiences on a massive range of topics. The comparative ease by which digital video can be produced quickly in the home has hugely benefited vloggers, who can upload their instalments almost daily if they wish to do so. This lends a freshness and immediacy to their content, which is very gratifying for the audience.

Vloggers might be vlogging about their life – a kind of confessional online diary. There are still vloggers who do this. However, there are numerous vlog sub-genres that exist. Take, for example, computer game walkthroughs – people might initially come to a particular subscriber looking for knowledgeable support about a particular aspect of gameplay but come to see the vlogger as an opinion leader on other game-related topics, the release of new hardware and so on. The game vlogger may have started out just posting their own simple walkthroughs but ended up featuring much more prominently in their vlog as a personality, covering a far greater range of topics as they gather more subscribers.

The overlap between vlogging and the mainstream media is almost non-existent, except in cases where a vlogger's status as an opinion-leader is used by companies who may use them to market their goods in a covert way, as well as the advertisers whose products appear before we view the episode. This means that the primarily youth-based audience and creators of vlogs are not entirely beyond the reach of mainstream companies and their ability to exploit new markets.

YouTube success story *Smosh Pit's* Squad Vlogs showcase an ensemble cast for their comedy vlog.

APPLY IT

Can you think of a digital media text where hybridity occurs?

Identify a sub-genre of vlogger:

- What characterises their posts?
- What conventions are there?
- What parent features from the overall genre of 'vlogging' are apparent in your chosen sub-generic text?

Genre and social and cultural change

Most genre theorists admit that there is a connection between the popularity of genres at particular times and the social and cultural conditions that produce them. Although they may disagree about the way in which genres grow and change, with the notion of evolution as borrowed from scientific principles being particularly contentious, you need to remember that genres are always a product of the relationship between audience, industry and text. This relationship is a dynamic one – social and cultural conditions can almost be seen as a force that gently exerts influence over this relationship.

The appearance of some genres and the decrease in popularity of others cannot always be explained in a straightforward way, and when studying texts in relation to others you should think carefully about what social and cultural influences could account for their increased presence or absence.

EXAMPLE: The soap opera and reality television

A great example of how rapidly one genre might take over another can be seen in the movement of television audiences, traditionally female, of soap operas, towards reality television. The two genres may initially appear to be unrelated, but actually share a number of pleasures in common, which might account for the relatively easy poaching of audiences from one genre to the other, despite one being a fictional text and the other non-fiction.

Soap operas rely on loyal audiences, and this may in fact be their greatest weakness when faced by competition from reality television. Let's look at how the two genres measure up to one another.

Soap opera	Reality television
• High investment in regular viewing – loyal audiences – time to get to know characters and families, and familiarity with their quirks and histories, compulsive with viewers afraid of missing out. • Single platform – some dedicated soap magazines for fans who watch most – appeals to mainstreamers. • Older audience. • Long history born out of early advertising in America and began in the UK on radio with *The Archers* in 1950. • Different tones to different soaps, but some notorious for treating controversial subject matter in a responsible way. • Offers utopian solutions of community, intensity. • Offers uses and gratifications of social relationships and personal identity. • Single genre with stable boundaries and with repetition and sameness. Few sub-genres – medical soap – high investment in set and salaried cast. New examples of the genre rarely appear – sustained drops in viewers can be catastrophic.	• Binge viewing – shorter seasons which have a narrative resolution. • Synergy with tabloids, celebrity magazines and gossip websites, aspirational lifestyles which may have cultural resonance and appeal to aspirers. • Youth audience. • Genre exploded in around 2000 and quickly became considered to be low-brow TV. • Producers unafraid to push boundaries of taste and decency and court controversy. • Offers utopian solutions of community, intensity, abundance. • Uses and gratifications of social relationships and personal identity. • Huge array of genres and opportunity for variation and change – easily exploited by producers and low investment costs. Failures can easily be cancelled.

Theorist Thomas Schatz (1981) proposed that there are only really two types of genre – **genres of order** and **genres of integration**. This is an idea that foregrounds the social and cultural uses of genre and attempts to address some of their ideological dimensions. The first is considered to be a 'male' mode of genre, where order is threatened and a power struggle must take place. Genres of integration are thought of as more 'female' and offer more exploration and resolution of emotional conflicts. Although his work relates to Hollywood film genres, it's a useful idea to bear in mind if you're thinking about the **ideological reading** of the nature of genres as a site for conflict and resolution.

Some genres certainly endure across media, with their popularity standing the test of time – although their conventions may change to reflect social and cultural attitudes and values.

 APPLY IT **Choose a television genre that has been around for a long time. Research the genre and create a seven-slide presentation covering the inception of the genre including early examples, its conventions, key changes in the genre, its present-day examples and what you believe the future holds for it.**

Action films are considered to be a classic example of a genre of integration.

One final word about genre – some texts do genuinely resist generic classification. Others subvert the conventions of genres for their own ends or parody them in a way that could be considered as postmodern.

See Section 1.4 Postmodernism.

Be careful not to apply genre labels just for the sake of doing so, and if the genre conventions are not immediately obvious to you when studying a text, you might want to consider what the reasons are for this – or is it simply that genre is not as important an aspect of studying the text as other elements of media language? Neale himself cautioned against the idea of mechanistically using conventions as a checklist – in reality, many genre texts are quite subtle and make interesting use of their conventions beyond merely signifying categorisation.

KEY TERMS

archetypes	basic, rather simple character types who appear over and over in narratives	genres of order and integration	systems of genre categorisation that foregrounds the social and cultural uses of genre and classes them as essentially male or female	interpellation	the normalisation in media texts of certain ways of thinking, attitudes and values so powerfully that they become part of a person's identity
causality	the way in which the events, usually driven by the desires and motivations of characters and the events that impact on them, drive the logic of a narrative forwards	ideological reading	a conclusion that aims to expose how power relationships between social groups operate and manifest themselves in cultural production	masterplot	an overarching group of bare narrative elements that are meaningful to a particular culture
cultural categories	a way of understanding genre labels as products of both industry and audience			mytheme	small unit of myths that Lévi-Strauss identified in the traditional stories of tribes he studied
dangling cause	an action, event or motif, the inclusion of which remains unclear until later in the narrative				

1.3 How media language constructs and incorporates values and ideologies

Politics and the mass media

See Chapter 5.

You are already aware from our Year 1 studies that all media texts contain ideologies, messages about society and culture. Learning about politics and the mass media helps you to be able to identify and decode messages. Many media texts contain a political bias, meaning they promote either a left- or right-wing political stance. Many media texts also engage with a single political agenda or issue (such as *women's rights*, *racial equality* or *climate change*). Political bias is most evident in the news agendas of national newspapers, but fictional media texts can also engage with political ideas and be a powerful tool for promoting political thought and engagement. There are many links between politics and the mass media and alternative media, which are explored in more depth in Chapter 5.

EXAMPLE: The treatment of political figures in lifestyle magazines

Lifestyle magazines sometimes feature coverage of politicians, but often focus on the 'person' and tend to represent them in such a way that, although their status in society is linked clearly to a specific political party, the reader's assumed interest is neutral rather than politically engaged. This is important so as not to alienate a section of the readership, since, distinct from a newspaper's readership, a lifestyle magazine's audience might be expected to constitute a cross-section of political viewpoints. This can serve the interests of the politician also – the magazine can act

Jeremy Corbyn features on the *Grazia* website to coincide with the print issue in January 2018.

as a platform to bring their ideas to a new audience in a way that tends to represent them in a positive light.

In January 2018 editions, both *GQ* and *Grazia* magazine featured interviews and photo-sessions with Labour Party leader Jeremy Corbyn, a figure of interest to the British public given his increase in popularity particularly among the younger section of the electorate during the 2017 election. Corbyn is often represented in a negative way or under-represented by the mainstream conservative press, so appearances in such magazines circumvent the loaded political agendas readers associate with conventional news outlets.

Most political standpoints on key issues can be seen as a series of oppositions. Centre politicians such as the Liberal Democrats tend to adopt a middle way though these, selecting from them on an 'issue-led' basis. Conservative, right-wing politics can be summed up as supporting the wealthier in society and 'conserving' traditional values/promoting traditional morals. Labour, left-wing politics are more about supporting the working classes and being tolerant of difference/diversity in society. Some of the ideologies associated with left- and right-wing thinking are summed up below, but there are many more issues you could add to the list. Be aware that some of these ideologies have contradictions within them – for example, right-wing ideologies might seem to be anti-class mobility, but in fact it's important that Conservative voters (many of whom are working class) feel that class mobility, e.g. through small business ownership or entrepreneurship, is available to them.

Left wing	Right wing
Embracing social and political change	Conserving traditions
Secular approach to all aspects of society	Christian values, especially Church of England (C of E)
Anti-monarchy or ambivalent; republicanism	Pro-monarchy
Social equality and reduction of class differences	Maintenance of the status quo, preservation of social class
Supportive of non-traditional families and relationships	The 'family' as traditional unit
Less focused on morals, more on social equality	Traditional moral values for all
Global citizenship	Domestic affairs come first, patriotism
Workers' rights	Employer protection
Protection of people	Protection of property

The Political Compass Test, with its additional authoritarian/libertarian axis, is more complex than the more conventional way of viewing the political spectrum. This can be visualised as a line going from left to right, with the extremes of political thought at either end. At the extreme left, there is Marxism, then socialism. A little further towards the centre there is Labour, then 'New Labour', the centrist relaunch the party experienced under Tony Blair's leaderships, which still holds sway in some sections of the party despite its return to more Old Labour values under Jeremy Corbyn. Towards the centre, there is centrist politics – many of the politics of the Liberal Democrats as a political party can be found clustered around here, before we move onto Conservative Party territory. Moving along to the right, there are far-right parties, with strongly patriotic and anti-immigration agendas before reaching fascism – the political manifestation of the extreme right, just as Communism is on the extreme left.

Looking at the history of any societies that have existed under either of the regimes at each end of the spectrum, there are many similarities, including the tendency for these systems to produce dictators and be politically corrupt. Both systems will heavily promote their ideologies at the expense of any others in education systems and tend to severely punish anyone who expresses dissent. The mass media in such societies has news agendas that are subject to a high level of political influence and control, filled with propaganda, and with personal liberties repressed.

Your Political Compass

Economic Left/Right: 0.75
Social Libertarian/Authoritarian: -0.56

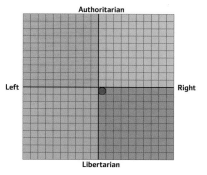

How the result displays on the two axes in the Political Compass Test.

If you are studying texts produced from outside the UK – for example, in the USA – it's worth considering the political climate and views that might make a difference to how ideologies are expressed in the text.

In the US, for example, you might initially assume that the Democratic Party could be thought of as equivalent to Labour, and the Republican Party to the Conservatives. To do so, though, would be an over-simplification of the system, as you would be comparing two systems that have each grown out of different cultural traditions and some quite different influences. The 'centre' of the political spectrum model you looked at to describe the UK is further right, meaning the main opposition party in the US is far more centrist in its policies than the one in the UK.

In the US, gun control and the right to bear arms under the constitution have an important role to play, and they may shape ideologies relating to conflict and war. The influence of the Christian right and the blurring of religious and secular ideologies is much more of a feature of right-wing political thinking in the US. Strongly capitalist ideologies are more prevalent in mainstream thinking and much more embedded into culture, and there is a historical suspicion of 'Communist' thinking that affects how more socialist views might be expressed in the media.

Last year, you looked at two broad approaches to understanding the mass media that are rooted in political theory – ways of reading the media that use political approaches to expose the ideologies of the text. You looked at cultural hegemony, a left-wing way of thinking that tended to regard mass media texts as created by the wealthy and powerful and dominated by ideologies that served their agendas and naturalised roles of many kinds in society. One of the key theorists who explored these ideas was Antonio Gramsci, but more contemporary thinkers such as Noam Chomsky are also very influenced by them.

An approach counter to this was the more centrist/right-wing approach: liberal pluralism. One of the theorists you have already met on the course, David Gauntlett, typifies this approach with his 'pick and mix' theory, whereby he suggests that media consumers are largely in control of their own media consumption and will select or reject ideologies according to their own belief systems. In general, Gauntlett's ideas borrow from both approaches – pluralism with some acknowledgement of hegemony.

Take the Political Compass Test, which can be found at www.politicalcompass.org/test.

It's quite important that you don't read too much about the test before you take it, as it could skew your results – equally, if there are some questions you don't understand, its better just to guess rather than discuss the question too much with other people.

Once you've done the test, make sure you print out your result. You can then see how you compare with key figures from history, and it's an interesting activity to compare your results with the rest of the class.

- Can you remember which of the questions on the Political Compass Test you felt most strongly about?
- Were you at all surprised about your own personal result?
- Were the results of other people in the group similar to your own, or was there a range of views?
- Do you think most young people share the political views of the group, or would you expect to see more variation? If so, why?
- Why do you think many people become more conservative in their politics as they age?

See Chapter 5 for more discussion of approaches to studying world media.

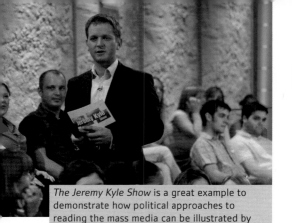

The *Jeremy Kyle Show* is a great example to demonstrate how political approaches to reading the mass media can be illustrated by audience responses to the programme.

EXAMPLE: Applying a liberal pluralist and a hegemonic approach to two UK television programmes

Trying to sum up how a liberal pluralist or a neo-Marxist theorist might view a text is a really interesting activity, and can sometimes throw up contradictions in how texts are read and understand the ideologies that operate within them. You will notice in the following examples that the liberal pluralist reading in each case feels much more optimistic and the hegemonic reading is pessimistic. This is because we exist in a Capitalist society that makes the liberal pluralist reading the preferred/ hegemonic one – the neo-Marxist reading will tend to be oppositional since it tries to expose the operation of hegemony and critique the way in which media texts naturalise capitalist ideologies.

Television programme	Liberal pluralist reading (centre/right wing)	Neo-Marxist hegemonic reading (left wing)
The Jeremy Kyle Show	• Entertaining viewing – the feel-good factor comes from seeing people who have got themselves into difficult personal circumstances through foolish behaviour. • Opportunity to feel superior to others who have brought the media attention on themselves by taking part in the show.	• Kyle promotes a conservative view of the world in his criticism of guests' lifestyle choices. • Selects people from disadvantaged backgrounds and makes them appear foolish for mass entertainment purposes. • Distracts people from real problems such as inequalities in social class, access to education, etc.
Channel 4 News	• Offers a different news agenda from mainstream news, which either appeals to you or it doesn't. • Quality journalism supported by the licence fee – doesn't patronise its viewers – simplicity lower as a news value. • Makes you feel better informed about single news issues, a more left-wing bias. • Shows that there is a range of ideologies on offer across the media.	• News agenda still selected from the main stories being covered by other channels because of market forces. • May promote thinking about political issues, but does not encourage action – people may simply feel reassured that their world view on current affairs aligns with at least one broadcaster. • In-depth coverage of issues relating to foreign policy distracts from home affairs.

How might you see political standpoints evident in the media language used in texts?

Following is a list of the ways in which media language can be used to advance a political perspective. It isn't exhaustive and you should always be on the lookout for the nuances in media language used whenever you have identified the presence of a particular political ideology. The examples given are hypothetical, but you will easily be able to find real ones of your own by using these as a starting point.

• Images selected to portray an issue or person in a positive or negative light.

• Lexical or verbal coding taken out of context, content juxtapositioned in a particular way or heavily edited.

• Agendas in coverage of issues – selection, focusing and combination.

• Emotive content included to sway the audience's feelings.

• Soundtracks used to underscore particular moments in fictional texts.

1.4 Postmodernism

Post-modernism and media language

Post-modernism is an approach to reading media texts that is useful to consider in relation to media language. It is often through aspects of media language that you can most clearly identify the post-modern characteristics of a text and use these to consider different possible meanings or ways of understanding it. It explores a media-saturated world, and concludes it to be a fragmented world of signs that have little meaning and are ephemeral. Post-modernism isn't confined to media language as an area of the theoretical framework, since it considers the nature of how you read representations and the role of the audience in making meaning as crucial factors. There is some overlap between theorists who are regarded as post-modernist and post-structuralists.

Post-modernism is a famously ambiguous critical area, with poorly defined boundaries and a resistance by some of its main theorists to being categorised as post-modern at all. It is a critical approach that has been applied to almost every aspect of intellectual pursuit, art and culture, but in this section you will be trying to apply its overall precepts to a media-specific context.

In his introduction to his anthology, *From Modernism to Postmodernism* (2003), Lawrence Cahoone draws out some of the ideas in post-modernism as 'themes', which is a good way into understanding it. He presents these as oppositions, showing us some of the interesting overlap you sometimes see between post-modernism and post-structuralism. These form part of the way in which post-modernism critiques as aspects of culture and society.

Presentation v representation and construction: postmodernists generally agree that in a sense there is no originally 'present' idea or image. Everything is represented, mediated and interpreted in various cultural, social and historical ways that may be interpreted differently from person to person. This doesn't mean that postmodernists don't believe that the real world exists, but that everything you encounter is subject to the various ways it has been mediated and represented to us in our experiences.

Origin v phenomena: postmodernism denies the validity of any approach that tries to identify a definite, original, contextual meaning to a media text. In rejecting the idea of an original meaning that holds some kind of 'truth', postmodernism deals instead with the idea of phenomena that do not have any kind of permanent relationship to a deeper 'reality'.

Unity v plurality: postmodernists propose that there is no single unified definition or meaning of any text that is understood by everyone in an identical way. Postmodernism, like post-structuralism, focuses on the plurality of meanings offered by media texts, where everything is related to everything else. It does, however, push this idea to its very limits. This includes our understanding of the self and it has interesting implications for the study of identity. Theories of identity that view identity as fragmented are influenced by postmodernism.

'Truths' that we hold to be universal, such as goodness, justice and courage, are all seen as serving other social or intellectual agendas rather than having inherent qualities which mean the same thing at different points in history.

Postmodern analysis means resisting all the hierarchical organisational structures by which we usually recognise cultural products, and instead seeing them as subjects of systems that attempt to define one thing by privileging it over another. Postmodernism makes no distinction between popular culture and high culture because it makes no value judgements about texts. Representational systems will always work to actively maintain hierarchies. Because of this, postmodern theorists try and look beyond the commonly studied aspects of texts, and look at what is marginalised or absent, rather than obvious.

Some of these ideas may be difficult to grasp, but that is the nature of postmodernism – it is a completely different way of reading media language. However, there are some aspects of texts that are most easily recognisable as postmodern. It is more likely you will need on the course to be able to recognise texts that have postmodern features than to critically apply a complex postmodern approach to a text. You are now going to look at some key terms and their associated ideas, which are useful when identifying techniques used in a postmodern text.

Intertextuality

For more on intertextuality see pages 25–26, 46, 48, 51, 57, 65 and 186 of the Year 1 book.

In the Year 1 book, you spent some time looking at examples of intertextuality. It is the easiest aspect of postmodernism to identify in a text and refers to the process where a media producer consciously or even subconsciously references another text. This may be deliberate and a conscious attempt to repurpose the connotations of that sign in a new order of signification, or a subtler interaction of signs and symbols from the referenced text and the newly created one. You not only need to be able to recognise where intertextuality is present in media texts, but also to understand why it has been used, the meanings it borrows and how audiences might respond to the its uses.

Pastiche

Pastiche involves the making of a new media text from components of another. In the case of pastiche, this is done in a positive and respectful way to bring new meanings, rather than in the case of parody, where the original text is mocked and derided.

Although it borders on parody because it is slightly humorous, there are numerous visual recreations online of the famous Beatles album cover, which are examples of pastiche since they are reverential.

Bricolage

Bricolage describes a product made from other media texts or borrowing signs from them. It literally means 'DIY' in French and means that the product made has been assembled with what was at hand to create something new. Many fan products, however, use bricolage in a productive way within their own semiotic productivity, re-appropriating signs to give them meanings that are not oppositional but alternative. Bricolage is therefore an interesting element of some practices in fan culture and highly participatory. Internet memes often also use bricolage.

Implosion

Implosion may be seen as part of bricolage – it is the media's constant recycling of itself and its signs, because it has no new material to feed it. Meaning 'implodes' – we have information circulating through communication, but this is more of a process for recycling rather than the creation of new meanings. Cultural forms and structures emerge, flourish briefly, then collapse in on themselves.

Although Baudrillard saw implosion as something that affects wider social structures worldwide – business, politics, even law – he saw the media as playing a role in implosion and a place where it can be seen to manifest. For example, TV news, crime dramas and television series all reassure us that the real violent world out there is at a distance or confined to a fictional realm. Presented alongside these genres and content are light entertainment, a bombardment of advertising and product consumption that make us feel secure and removed from the threats of the world.

Jean Baudrillard: *Simulacra and Simulation*

Jean Baudrillard wrote *Simulacra and Simulation* (1981) in which he explored philosophical ideas about the relationship between human understanding of existence and the role of culture and the media in constructing those ideas. There are three key terms you will need to be familiar with to apply Baudrillard's ideas: simulacrum, simulation and hyperreality. All of these aspects of the world and human condition today Baudrillard believed to be related to our increased urbanisation and culture of consumption. These established the pre-conditions of the simulacra because they remove us a step away from the reality of the production of goods, made thousands of miles away, and the experience of the natural world – which we may just now perceive as another part of the simulacrum. His ideas have even more implications for the evolution of gaming technologies and ways of navigating our environment such as augmented reality apps, which literally overlay the landscape of our existence with the signs of consumption.

Simulacrum

The simulacrum is a state of semiotics where a sign no longer refers to any original meaning but refers to other signs, like a hall of mirrors. It no longer represents a thing itself but means nothing more. Baudrillard saw this process as happening in stages, like a game of Chinese Whispers where the original message becomes something else entirely.

Europe return from
99€

My God, France is so cheap these days.

www.lufthansa.com   There's no better way to fly.   Lufthansa
A STAR ALLIANCE MEMBER

Advertisers frequently appropriate existing artworks or cultural references in a bricolage style. In this case, the painting of the Mona Lisa is given the Moulin Rouge treatment. The effect is irreverent, as is often the case with bricolage – remember that postmodernism does not recognise hierarchies of high or mass culture.

APPLY IT

It can be hard to distinguish between different forms of postmodern media-making techniques and styles. Many of these techniques can also be referred to as intertextual as well as being more specific about the way in which this intertextuality manifests itself at a textual level.

Research an example of pastiche and bricolage. Source images and write a short case study of each text and the text it refers to in order to help you see the mode or style of connection between them and the differences between those connections.

A hall of mirrors – the idea of multiple reflections and distortions is commonly used when trying to understand the relationship between objective reality and the simulacrum.

This is known as the **precession of the simulacra**:

- Firstly, a basic copy is made of something that exists in the real world, in which we have trust because we can see a resemblance to the original.
- Secondly, a corrupted second is made which obscures the 'truth' of the first copy – which we no longer trust.
- Thirdly, the sign presents us as representing something that did not exist to begin with.
- Finally, we arrive at the signs and symbolisation processes of contemporary culture and late capitalism; we accept signs as part of the simulacra, where there is no longer any reference to reality.

EXAMPLE: The precession of the simulacra and scripted reality television

Baudrillard's ideas can be applied in all sorts of interesting ways to contemporary culture. We could see the development of scripted reality television shows as an analogy for the precession of the simulacrum.

1 Firstly, we have the origin of the genre in *fly-on-the-wall documentaries* with an observational mode, which could be seen as the basic copy. They seem to bear some resemblance to reality – we trust the copy and believe it stands in for something that has actually occurred in the real world.

2 Over time, programme-makers offer us mock documentaries – the parody that obscures the truth of the first. Because it is 'malevolent', in that a mock documentary is often satirical and perverts the meanings and the 'truth' apparently offered by the earlier predecessors that it parodies.

3 Perhaps emboldened by the acceptance of the mock documentary and its deliberate posing as reality despite being a falsehood, programme-makers offer us a third stage – 'reality' television, the very name of the emergent genre making a claim about the relationship between the show and reality. Scandals initially appear about the relationship between the shows' content and 'reality', but these quickly die down as audiences lose to some extent the expectation that there is a straightforward relationship between representation and reality in the text and come to a new contractual understanding of the genre.

Distinct from its documentary predecessors, there is often a competitive aspect to these shows, which is purely driven by the product, is highly constructed and does not refer to anything outside itself as imitator spawns imitator. This takes us back to the idea of the hall of mirrors, where we no longer perceive a true original but simply accept distortion itself. The contestants become short-lived d-list celebrities, perhaps with their own associated product lines and feeding other media products for subject matter. Reality television purports to offer us a version of reality, but this is a pretence the audience quickly comes to accept.

4 The fourth stage is the endless making of scripted reality shows, where the participants are part actor, part participant, and the whole genre has become improbably self-referential. The audience accepts and no longer cares how much of the show's content is scripted, because the scripted reality is a sign that does not refer to anything else, and the d-list celebrities it makes of its contestants or participants are empty signifiers in a hyperreal world – another simulacra within a web of simulation. Viewers may accept the hyperreal representation of the participant characters and their narratives as 'real' even though they bear little resemblance to reality.

 For more on the relationship between documentary modes and reality, see Chapter 4 Representations.

APPLY IT

Source examples of the genres and sub-genres mentioned in the example. To what extent do you think they fit the idea of the precession of the simulacra? Use them in the following discussion:

1 Can you see any problems in using this genre as an example? Is it too simplistic?

2 Does the precession of the simulacra, for example, need to happen in a specific order – since media genres don't always behave in this way?

3 Since postmodern approaches are fragmentary, how might you be able to relate this to existing genre theory we covered earlier in the chapter?

4 Could the ideas in simulacra and simulation be used to understand other media genres?

Simulation

This is the end product of the precession of the simulacrum. In the simulation we no longer perceive any difference between representation and reality. Consumers of cultural products inhabit this world without need to refer to reality, because all of us are so far removed from its original reference points.

Baudrillard uses a fable to explain simulation, of an empire that created a map to be laid over the physical space it occupied. When the empire crumbled, all that was left was the map. Baudrillard suggests that the hyperreal world, the simulation that is the end point of the precession of the simulacrum, is like living on that map despite the land having crumbled away beneath it. It is this world that he suggests we all inhabit. We continue to draw our culture onto the map, but there is no longer anything beneath it to which it refers.

EXAMPLE: Augmented reality and simulation

Consider the way in which augmented reality apps and digital navigation/mapping systems, full of signs relating to consumption, literally overlay the ground beneath our feet, the homes we live in and the cities or spaces we walk around, with cultural signs in a composite that combines the real and the virtual. Even the term, 'augmented reality' is fascinating – it suggests that the world we overlay with its cultural signs is somehow 'better' than the world without it, and that we are dependent on the apps to navigate this world.

In 2017: Spectrek is a game which lets you capture ghosts as you walk around your environment; apps allow you to try out new tattoos or hairstyles without the bill or regret; and Yelp Monacle allows you to overlay real maps to see reviews of goods and services. Quiver allows children to see their colouring pages in 3D; artists can use I Art view to showcase how their work would look in real spaces; and Star Chart allows you to see constellations mapped over the night sky.

Spectrek allows you to 'see' ghosts in your environment.

APPLY IT
Search for an augmented reality app that is free to download on your phone. Try it out. In what ways does it 'augment' an experience? How much use does it make of the 'real'?

In 'Nosedive', an episode of *Black Mirror*, a person's advantages in life and work are all impacted on by their social media rating.

APPLY IT

Can you think of any other examples of the ways in which hyperreality can be seen manifesting in individual cultural signs?

On a computer, create an A3 collage or moodboard of a young person's media consumption, showing visually the numerous ways in which their reality could be viewed as the cultural simulacra they encounter and interact with every day.

Hyperreality

The term **hyperreality** relates to a state of living in Western culture populated by simulacra, inhabiting a simulation where we no longer have any connection to a 'real' world but live instead through a commodified world that never existed to begin with. This merging of the real and media is constructed from a merging of consumerist signs and meaningless cultural practices which we feel are 'real' but do not connect with reality or have true meaning – a 'simulation' of human experience.

EXAMPLE: Disneyland and Disneyfication v *Black Mirror*

The gap between the aspirational images projected to us in the simulacrum and the real world of austerity today, defined by globalisation, war, terror, it's no wonder we are comfortable in hyperreality and the diversions it offers us. Think about the way in which Disney culture is such as huge part of childhood, especially for many young girls. They know the films and songs by heart, they wear the costumes and they sport the brands on their personal effects. Baudrillard uses the example of Disneyland to show how the supposed boundary between representation and reality is voided in hyperreality. For many families, the ultimate dream is to visit Disneyland itself, arguably one of the biggest symbols the world has of commodification of childhood, in order to immerse themselves fully in the experience.

An interesting feature of hyperreality is its ability to offer us critiques of itself as part of its network, embodying the often problematic issues we come across when trying to apply postmodern interpretations. *Black Mirror*, a television series of one-off stories which has run from 2011 to the present, is a fascinating representation of our relationship with technology, media images and materialism, and its impact on our culture. Incredibly pessimistic and dark in tone, it savagely critiques our increasing social and cultural dependence on media technologies.

KEY TERMS

bricolage	a product that is made from other media texts, or borrows signs from them
hyperreality	merging of the real and media worlds to the point where it is difficult to distinguish between them
implosion	the media's constant recycling of itself and its signs
pastiche	the making of a new media text from components of another

precession of the simulacra	the series of stages between simulacrum and simulation
simulacrum	state of semiotics where a sign no longer refers to any original meaning, but to other signs, like a hall of mirrors
simulation	end product of the precession of the simulacra. In the simulation we no longer perceive any difference between representation and reality

KEY THINKER

Jean Baudrillard	(1929–2007) French philosopher who contributed the key ideas of simulacra, simulation and hyperreality often debated in relation to postmodern thinking. Baudrillard is sometimes also regarded as a post-structuralist thinker because of his interest in semiotics and new ways of understanding how signs are interrelated in a complex web of meanings

CHAPTER SUMMARY

• The language of semiotics continues to be important and confidence in using it accurately should be in place by Year 2. An understanding of types of sign and the signification process as described both by Saussure and Barthes is central to the way in which we decode texts, and needs considering as a contributory factor in the creation of meaning whatever further methodologies and critical frameworks you may then go on to apply.

- Technical codes of the different media forms you are studying all have their own associated terminology, which by now you will have gained confidence in using. You'll be continuing to develop your confidence and familiarity with these throughout the remainder of the Year 2 Media Studies course.

- The narrative theories you learned in Year 1 of the Media Studies course, including Barthes' five codes, Lévi-Strauss's binary oppositions and Todorov's movement between two equilibriums, should now be well established in the way in which you approach texts. The study of narratology involves an understanding of some other concepts that you were introduced to briefly in Year 1, but have learned more about in this chapter, such as archetypes and tropes, causality, the quest narrative and masterplot. Understanding narrative perspective and how this impacts on the audience was also studied and should be viewed as an integral part of your narrative studies.

- The study of genre has been considered in more depth this year. You revisited Stephen Neale's work on genre and added more to your understanding of his approach, as well as considering how genres respond to technological change, and new genres which have emerged as a result of the digital age and internet.

- You considered how genres evolve to keep up with social and cultural change, and also considered the genres that have endured. Central to your understanding here was the idea of genres of order and genres of integration.

- Having learned about cultural hegemony and liberal pluralism last year, you connected these ideas with politics in the UK. You learned why it's important to be able to recognise political ideologies in media texts, and how the hegemonic (left-wing) approaches to studying the media might result in different perspectives from liberal pluralist approaches, which are more centre right.

- Political ideologies in media texts, like all messages and values, are embedded at the level of media language. Some of the ways this might happen were suggested, and you need to be looking out for examples in your close study texts and be able to pinpoint the codes responsible for the construction of that particular ideology.

- Having encountered some of its key thinkers such as Barthes and Saussure last year, you learned in this chapter the distinction between structuralist and post-structuralist approaches to media texts, and more about the ways in which these theories came about and their usefulness to you as Media Studies students.

- Adding to your understanding of Lévi-Strauss' work on binary oppositions, you looked more closely at his ideas relating to the mytheme, the story-elements and the way in which meaning is derived from the ways they interrelate.

- You considered the contribution of postmodern thinking to the ways in which you might read some contemporary media texts and the way audiences make sense of them. You considered postmodernism as being characterised by a resistance to fixed and finite readings, without inherent truths and only shallow meanings and fragmentary forms, often borrowing consciously or unconsciously from other sign systems.

- You looked at three important ways by which you might recognise postmodern features in a media text – bricolage, pastiche and implosion. You discussed that there that there may be cross-overs in these techniques.

- Jean Baudrillard's ideas were explored as one of your key thinkers for the postmodern study of texts. You were introduced to the idea of the precession of the simulacrum, by which the process of representation becomes such that there is no longer any real-world reference point for media representations and everything becomes simulation. You explored the idea of modern living being a hyperreal experience. According to Baudrillard, we live in a world saturated by the media that we no longer have a connection with reality but only with signs that construct a version of it but bear no relation to it.

FURTHER READING AND REFERENCES

Claude Lévi-Strauss (1974) *Structural Anthropology.*

Jean Baudrillard (1981) *Simulacra and Simulation.*

Guardian (2013, 23 May) 'Firestorm', www.theguardian.com/world/interactive/2013/may/26/firestorm-bushfire-dunalley-holmes-family.

Lawrence E. Cahoone (2003) *From Modernism to Postmodernism: An Anthology.*

Ronald Tobias (2012) *20 Masterplots: And How to Build Them.*

Thomas Schatz (1981) *Hollywood Genres: Formulas, Filmmaking, and the Studio System.*

Chapter 2 Media representations

What you will learn in this chapter

- Year 1 mastery: what you already know about representations, revisiting representations and why they matter, and reconsidering the significance of stereotypes and countertypes

- Year 2 development: the relationship between representation and reality and how industry contexts impact on representations

- Year 2 development: discourses around representation and ideology: gender studies and the mass media

- Year 2 development: discourses around representation and ideology: ethnicity and postcolonial theory

APPLY IT

Using the Year 1 book, create a revision card on each of the key thinkers.

- Which aspects of their work were important to your studies?
- What are the key ideas they contributed to the field of representational study?

2.1 Year 1 mastery: what you already know about representations

In the Year 1 book, you learned about the process of representations. You explored representation as a process whereby meanings are mediated. You also explored the role of both media language and the audience in creating representations and making meanings from them. Crucial to your understanding was being able to identify who or what was being represented, how they were being represented, and why those representations are the way they are. Key thinkers used to support your ideas included Stuart Hall, David Gauntlett and Richard Dyer, all of whom contributed different ideas to the field.

Another dimension you explored was the way in which both qualitative and quantitative approaches could be taken to representational study, and the benefits of each method. We learned some of the key aspects of media language that are the most significant in constructing representations in different media forms. We also considered some of the ethical reasons why representations matter, and this will inform your study in your second year as you learn more about gender studies and the mass media, and postcolonial studies.

A critical aspect of your learning also focused on stereotypes and counter-types, and developing an understanding of in-groups and out-groups. You looked at how exploring these frequently repeated representations could contribute to our understanding of how minority groups in society are represented by the mass media. You considered the possibility that there might be a connection between these representations and the way in which they could contribute to real-life perceptions and treatment of actual groups in society by perpetuating myths. You also looked at how they could help to challenge stereotypes by the use of counter-types. Related to this was your study of the link between globalisation and the representational issues brought by cultural imperialism and a globalised mass media.

Men are usually considered to be an in-group because of their role in patriarchy. Women, despite being demographically more or less equal in number, are an out-group because they are subject to the norms of patriarchal society.

Lastly, you considered the ideological nature of common media representations. This allowed you to understand why it matters what values and messages are conveyed by media texts. You began to explore some of the ideas relating to how the mass media might affect or even partially construct the way our own identities and place in the world are understood.

You also considered the political nature of some media representations, using neo-Marxist and liberal pluralist ideas, including reference to Louis Althusser, Antonio Gramsci and Noam Chomsky. In the next two sections of this chapter, you will be revisiting some of these ideas so that you can master them and ensure you feel secure in applying them before moving on to extend some of these ideas.

Year 1 mastery: the process of representations and why they matter

In the Year 1 book, you looked at Stuart Hall's work on two systems of representation. Hall looked at the process of representation as being comprised of sign systems themselves, and what we do with those signs when we read them. This can be understood as the encoding of a preferred reading by a media producer, and the subsequent decoding of it by the audience. We explored the idea that media texts are polysemic signs that can never accurately depict reality, since people interpret them using their own conceptual maps. Hall concluded that a constructionist approach rather than an intentional or reflective one to understanding how the mass media creates a version of reality in its representations was the clearest way of understanding this process. Hall suggested that the makers of sign systems and the people who read representational systems both play a part in how that representation achieves a meaning. This is vital to our understanding that meanings in media texts are not fixed – media producers can attempt to anchor them as much as they like, but there is no guarantee audiences will all respond in the same way.

For more about Stuart Hall's work on systems of representation see page 74 of the Year 1 book.

The image above is a great example of the way in which a sign can be polysemic. Although the broader third level of signification of 'hell' as a cultural myth might be agreed by most people reading it, its actual meaning will vary from person to person depending on their conceptual map.

You looked at some of the key areas in which significant representations might be constructed. Because media products are complex signs, representations of individual people, places and events are highly significant and are used by us, constantly cross-referencing with our conceptual maps, to understand the bigger picture – the overall nature of the ideologies and values contained in the text. Modifying any single aspect of these can make a big difference to the nature of that

Ariel Levy's (2006) influential book on raunch culture.

🔗 For more on raunch culture and post-feminism see Section 2.3.

Nicki Minaj's video for 'Anaconda' divided commentators and the different potential readings of the text illustrate well the issues posed by raunch culture.

representation – already not a given, since we know that meanings cannot be wholly or permanently fixed in any case.

You also considered why it actually matters how people are represented, an assumption that underlies Media Studies but is worth stopping and considering for a moment. In looking at people, we note key categorisations that could be factored in when reading representations, and these broad social groupings could be seen in some cases as having real divisions, in others as a sort of sliding scale.

EXAMPLE: Intentional, reflective and constructionist approaches to reading contentious female representations in music videos – raunch culture

Some music videos have come under scrutiny in recent years for representing women in an overtly sexualised way. These are a sign of raunch culture.

Media critics as well as social pressure groups have noted that in some genres or individual examples of music videos, women are represented as accessories to the male ego, decoration, prizes or commodities. This can even be the case in videos made by female artists. We can use Hall's three definitions of ways in which the relationship between representations and reality works to approach the debates around these texts.

Look at these statements and the attitudes they suggest:

> *Music videos and the artists who appear in them create sexist attitudes to women and normalise female subordination in our society.*
>
> *Music videos reflect the demeaning attitudes towards women that exist in a society that doesn't value them beyond a sexual and aesthetic role.*
>
> *Music videos are understood by their viewers as genre texts with certain conventions, including some stereotypical roles of women. Some argue that the women in these videos have sexual power and are being celebrated for their beauty – in a post-feminist society, women are powerful owners of their own destinies and free to express themselves as they wish. Others may feel that although these videos are light entertainment, they could be more socially responsible but that most viewers should be aware of their narrow range of representations of female identity.*

The first two statements are very polarised and seem to suggest a quite simplistic view of the relationship between representations and reality.

The first view loosely conforms to an intentional view of representations. According to this approach, the mass media constructs representations that perpetuate the low value of women in our society in every sphere except sexual desirability and availability. It fails to represent women in music videos in any kind of complex way, and this in turn affects how attitudes to women will be formed by young men in the audience, and also how young women see themselves and their worth. This connects very much with conservative effects arguments which perpetuate the idea of the mass media as a powerful negative influence.

The second view absolves the media of any active role in the representations it creates. It suggests a reflective approach – that the version of reality we see in this video simply reflects the low status of women in our society and the attitudes of young men towards them.

The third view is more complex, and represents the beginnings of a constructionist argument, which takes into account the polysemic nature of the texts and factors in many more complex arguments which see the media both as a partial reflector of reality and a possible influence. Media texts as cultural products are in dialogue with our ideologies and cultural values. There is a process of exchange between texts and the values they reflect and possibly perpetuate.

Gender, sexuality, race, ethnicity and membership of a religion are all factors that warrant closer contextual investigation when reading a text. These aspects are considered so important by media theorists that sections of this chapter will be dedicated solely to exploring specific critical approaches that help you to better explore these representations. Social class, age and whether someone is able-bodied or disabled can also be important. Portrayals of illness – and particularly mental illness – are also quite significant. For almost every structural group in society, there are pressure groups who watch media portrayals of people similar to themselves and may try to hold producers of media texts to account or applaud them when they get it right.

The role of media language in constructing representations is highly significant, but it is not just the individual signifiers themselves that are significant – it is the way in which the elements are selected, focused and combined that makes a big difference to the construction of a representations. If we forget to look at what is absent from a text as well as what is present, then we completely miss the significance of quantitative representations.

The relationship between the dominant ideologies that circulate in our society, and how these shape all of our ideas about almost every aspect of politics and everyday life, is of huge significance. If those who have the power in our society are responsible for the larger part of the production of meanings in media texts, what implication does this have for us all, and the way we think of ourselves and each other? How does it affect how we may vote, and the issues we care about in everyday life? By the end of your Year 1 studies, you were hopefully confident with the idea that mass media effects cannot be easily measured but that most theorists accept, at least in some form, that they exist. As such, we cannot afford to ignore them.

Year 1 mastery: stereotypes and countertypes

In the Year 1 book, we looked at the idea that in-groups and out-groups could be applied to describe the way in which a dominant culture stereotypes people from minority groups and creates stereotypes which focus on difference, rather than focusing on people's essential humanity. Stereotypes of out-groups could potentially be damaging to that group if they are frequently reinforced. This idea is connected also with George Gerbner's cultivation theory, which you read about in Chapter 5 of the Year 1 book, and which is also explored further in this book.

For more on in-groups and out-groups see pages 80–81 of the Year 1 book.

For more on George Gerbner's cultivation theory see pages 104–105 of the Year 1 book.

Cultivation theory suggests our attitudes are partly formed by repeated exposure to certain types of media representations.

APPLY IT

Identify two out-groups that are sometimes negatively defined in British culture. Find an example of a front-page tabloid newspaper story which seems to support the assumption that the majority of its readers will share the stereotypes of the group being perpetuated by the headline article. Google image search for tabloid newspapers is a good way to begin this activity, as it may help you to select the out-groups to begin with.

This advertisement, which can be watched on YouTube, was produced by Danish television channel TV2 to promote its products and the notion that the channel is inclusive of all Danes. The advertisement has been widely shared on social media internationally, as it speaks to more than just people of Danish origin. It is filmed in a studio space in the style of black box theatre, with boxes painted on the floor indicating initial groupings of people according to some common societal groupings that are also stereotypes, such as 'those we trust and those we try to avoid' and 'the new Danes … and those who've always been here'. Intertextually it could also reference the set design of *Dogville*, a 2003 avant-garde film by Danish director Lars Von Trier, which uses white markings on a floor space to delineate locations and actions.

A screenshot from the video short 'All That We Share'.

The video features a mixture of people who are representative of the make-up of Denmark's population – predominantly white European with some people from different ethnicities, a range of social class, age, gender and occupations. These comprise both in-groups and out-groups. The video aims to break down prejudices rooted in stereotypes and the distinction between in-groups and out-groups by showing that these boundaries are artificial.

A man with a clipboard appears and asks the groups to regroup based on other factors which anyone from the original grouping could belong to – who was the class clown, and who is a step-parent, for example. Initially suspicious, people are shown as welcoming each other when they realise what they have in common. This is reinforced by positive non-verbal communication, the diegetic sounds of chatter and laughter, and the dispersal of initial tensions and suspicions into camaraderie. The black box setting naturally emphasises the atmosphere, along with the lack of focus on individuals and the message that social cohesion is a collective act for which we should all take responsibility. Although some hierarchies and oppositions are initially established, by the end these have dissipated entirely.

The English language version of the video was posted to YouTube on World Holocaust Day to promote a message of acceptance and tolerance across the English-speaking world.

For more on 'Rethinking stereotypes' see page 83 of the Year 1 book.

In the Year 1 book, you explored Tessa Perkins' article 'Rethinking Stereotypes' (1997). You looked at the groups we hold stereotypes about, such as major structural groups or pariah groups. Perkins' method of dividing up who we hold stereotypes about helps us to understand why they exist, and how they help us to make sense of our world. Similarly, her division of stereotypes into the broad categories of pejorative or laudatory helps us to consider what impact the stereotype might have if it is often repeated and is borrowed by media texts.

2.2 The relationship between representation and reality

In the Year 1 book, you studied Hall's overview of the relationship between representation and reality. You studied how semiotic analysis alongside other structuralist and post-structuralist models can be used to understand how people make meaning from signs, and the role of language in contributing to representations. We know that there is no single reality or truth mediated by the media. We know now that every media text has its own agenda and an investment in conveying a preferred reading. This might be in order to entertain, promote a social or political standpoint or to encourage consumers to buy a product – all processes essential to the maintenance of hegemony and continue to drive the processes in the capitalist economy – or provide people with a range of entertainments, services and viewpoints, depending on whether you adopt a neo-Marxist or liberal pluralist approach to reading the media.

This is best considered through a range of media forms and genres which many people feel have a closer link with representations of real life or 'reality' than others.

For more on Hall's overview see page 74 of the Year 1 book.

Newspapers

In the Year 1 book, you looked at the idea of news values: a framework for understanding how news organisations determine their agendas. This is worth learning when you are considering the nature of the relationship between news reportage and reality. The way in which tabloid newspapers select their front-page news in order to sell their copies has been referred to a number of times, and that the profit motive will naturally dictate that the most sensationalist stories will tend to feature higher up the news agenda. The problem is that we know many people do assume some of their values and belief systems from the ideologies perpetuated by the selection and focusing behaviours of newspaper editors. There is an assumption on the part of many that what is reported on in newspapers is the important issues of the day – we rely on news outlets to select our news for us without really considering the processes and influences behind this. We also know that the representation of news is affected by political bias.

For more on news values see page 96 of the Year 1 book.

For more on framing and agenda setting, both concepts linked with this section, see Chapter 3.

EXAMPLE: Climate change as a news story

Many scientists agree that climate change is one of the biggest threats to human life and the sensitive ecosystems we depend on for the quality of the air we breathe, the pollination of crops, ocean resources and so on. In a way, it should be the biggest news story of our generation since it could have a huge impact on the quality of all our lives in the future. However, climate change itself doesn't appeal as front-page news. There is a number of reasons why, which we can understand by comparing it with news values:

- It's a vast, complex subject that can be difficult for a lay-person to understand, so it lacks SIMPLICITY. When covered, it tends to be as a result of individual weather events, which are selected for their dramatic nature, such as the series of hurricanes that affected the US (ELITE NATIONS) as well as many poorer island communities that regularly have to deal with storm surges and violent weather events, and on whom the effects can be much more long lasting and powerful.

- Its effect are currently felt most by those in poorer countries, so it lacks PROXIMITY.

- It does have CONTINUITY but lacks CURRENCY.

A climate change news story on the *Guardian* website

Poster for the documentary, *An Inconvenient Truth*.

 APPLY IT

Source three examples of news stories about climate change and/or threats to the environment. Prepare a short verbal presentation in note form, accompanied by images, exploring their relationship with news values and the wider contexts discussed in the example.

Other possible reasons for a lack of prioritisation in the news agenda include pressure from big businesses. This is less of a factor in the UK media, but in the US, where climate change denial exists openly at the highest levels of governmental office and influence, there is clearly a bigger problem. This issue was famously brought to public attention worldwide in the documentary *An Inconvenient Truth* (David Guggenheim, 2006), an excellent example of counter-representation of a social issue – global warming – in action.

So, do we see climate change reported on? The answer is yes – every time there is an unusual weather event it makes front-page news, particularly in the tabloid papers. In terms of sensationalism, the bigger picture of climate change is a pattern of events caused by human agency is a less interesting angle. When there is an unseasonal or particularly dramatic weather event in this country, this domestic nature of events is interpreted as a purely domestic news story – the severity of event, SIZE (amount of people affected) and PROXIMITY suddenly push it up the agenda.

The *Guardian*, as a left-wing newspaper, is more likely to report on issues relating to the environment. The news story shown on the previous page, on the collapse of insect populations, was widely shared.

'Reality' television

If a show features ordinary people, do we tend to trust that they are just being represented in a way that reflects who they 'really' are? Reality television, as one of its appeals, has people 'just like us' – people who come from ordinary backgrounds are as likely to appear as any other social strata. Reality television is particularly known for its blurring of the line between representing aspects of reality with the need to provide entertainment values, and its overt commodification of its celebrity factory. Many shows feature their participants being transformed in some way, growing into a new identity or escaping the everyday in a fulfilling way that is highly pleasurable for the audience. That most of these situations are set up matters little to the audience.

Contemporary 'scripted reality' shows may be the most extreme example, but in fact most reality television is heavily edited, and the formats of the shows designed to cast participants in certain stereotypical roles and to elicit certain behaviours from them. Both participants and producers are highly conscious about the identity they are projecting for the cameras. We should question, though, how far the audience is actually concerned by whether their 'reality' TV shows are heavily manipulated 'versions' of reality that create narratives or not. Incidents can be set up regularly, and there tends to be a less strong ethic surrounding reality TV about how it represents the people and events in the show compared with the documentary forms they emerged from.

Graeme Turner and the demotic turn

Graeme Turner is well known in academic circles for his research into the role of ordinary people who are thrust into the limelight as participants, mainly in entertainments programming such as talent shows, reality television and other contexts. His work also explores YouTube and considers what he believes to be the subservience of the apparent blogger star to the advertising on the platform and the need to generate clicks. Turner considers that there is little connection to 'reality' in these forms and that representations are as highly constructed of these people as any other text, but that the 'ordinariness' they bring to their roles is as much of a construct and a gimmick to attract audiences as anything else.

In his book *Ordinary People and the Media: The Demotic Turn* (2010) he explores the nature of how ordinary people are represented in ways that make them appealing without the contextual factor of star appeal, which is explored in more detail later in this section where we look at Richard Dyer's theory of stardom. Turner also explores how the industry can generate its own celebrities and make use of ordinary people for entertainment at a rate never previously seen. He uses the phrase **demotic turn** to describe the frequent appearances by 'ordinary' people across a range of media forms and genres. Some genres, of course, are entirely built on the participation of members of the public.

Turner makes the following points:

- He is critical of the ubiquitous use of ordinary people as participants in popular entertainment today, seeing it as exploitative.
- He argues that far from benefiting in terms of representation from an increased visibility in the mass media, audiences as participants are treated as just another commodity by the industry.
- He explains that audiences are represented in a way that simply fits the tightly controlled agendas of media producers, even when the content appears to have been generated by the participants themselves.
- He considers the demotic turn to be ultimately an illusion – people feel that they see an increase in people 'just like them' on screen and in the digital sphere, but in fact these appearances are just as manufactured and the representations tightly controlled by media producers as with any other content they consume.

Susan Boyle's demotic turn on *Britain's Got Talent* became extraordinarily famous and a global news story.

Documentary

Documentaries have long been the source of controversies over the way in which they represent the issues they explore. The problem is a basic misunderstanding on the part of an audience of what a documentary does. Documentaries cannot be free from bias, since they always serve an agenda, tell a story or aim to offer a perspective. Documentaries are no less subject to the issue of selection and focusing when creating representations than any other genre – in fact, documentaries are a great place to begin when studying how representations work.

Bill Nichols: documentary modes

Nichols identified six 'modes' of documentary form. Many contemporary documentaries are a mixture of these, and they should not be used in too rigid a way. Nonetheless, they are a useful way into considering not only the aesthetics of documentary form in a 'pure' sense, but also how representations are being constructed through media language – how is the particular version of a 'reality' they offer us being constructed according to the various techniques being used. Three of the modes you will most often see are given here:

- **Observational mode**: these kinds of documentary do not reveal the filmmaker and rely on our trust that what we are seeing is 'real'. This is reinforced by the rough feel to the camerawork and often the pace of editing, which implies events are recorded almost incidentally. It is the form of documentary that we perhaps feel is the least 'contrived' since events appear to have simply unfolded as we watch. The term 'fly on the wall' is sometimes used to describe documentaries that have a strongly observational element to them. Today, there are few pure examples of the form, with many using techniques such as interviews with subjects interspersed with the long takes and spontaneous feel and apparent lack of awareness of the camera's subjects.
- **Expository mode**: this is the mode we most associate with documentaries about the natural world, although it is used also for other subject matter. Expository documentaries feature heavy use of narration in the form of a

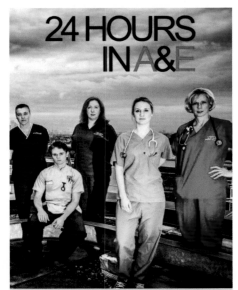

24 Hours in A&E is a long-running Channel 4 documentary still in production in 2018.

APPLY IT

Choose a documentary you have seen recently that had an impact on you.

- What did it represent?
- How did it represent this?
- Why did it have an impact on you?
- How did the media language combine with any elements of the modes of documentary to create these representations?
- Could another story have been told from a different perspective which might have been quite different using the same subject matter, and even some of the same footage?
- What kinds of documentary techniques could you see being used? (See Chapter 1 for a reminder of these.)

Write a 500-word case study of your chosen documentary considering relevant aspects of the link between documentary from and reality using the pointers above and creating your own subheadings to structure your ideas.

voice-over. This may be someone well known, an authority on the subject matter – or use the star status of an actor with a familiar voice. The direct mode of address leaves little room for ambiguity in interpretation of events, so it feels very didactic.

- **Participatory mode**: in this mode, the filmmaker is a visible part of the narrative and has a role to play within it. These presenters come across as being more subjective, but the ambiguity built into their work can be quite powerful, deliberately leading the audience to feel as though they are taking part in the building of a conclusion. There is some cross-over between this mode and **performative mode**, which is similar in style but elicits much stronger emotional effect on the part of the audience, so can feel more manipulative. Makers of performative documentaries in particular are often charismatic and use disappointment and failure as part of the emotional journey they take their viewers on, as well as representing themselves as champions for their cause and seekers of 'truth'.

EXAMPLE: Two documentaries in which these modes predominate

24 Hours in A&E: this Channel 4 documentary follows the nurses and doctors, as well as unfortunate patients who visit accident and emergency units of hospitals around the country over a 24-hour period. It features observational sections intercut with pieces to camera spoken by accident victims, their relatives, and the doctors and nurses themselves. This combination of techniques results in some highly emotional storylines based on life and death situations.

Giants of the Ocean: this documentary series about whales was first broadcast in 2011, and is still widely available on VoD services. As with many nature documentaries, it uses scientific research to create a scripted narration, voiced over by Stephen Fry.

Soap opera

Since soap operas purport to represent ordinary people who undergo a range of human experiences, some of them common and some of them far more extreme, they frequently come under scrutiny for their excessive portrayal of the negative end of the spectrum of human experience. As the years have gone by and censorship relaxed, so soap operas, despite their pre-watershed broadcast slot, have often played with some challenging subject matter such as still-births, rape and murder. Ridiculed by many for their ludicrous plotlines and the apparent liveliness of their characters' lives, many forget that soap operas do not represent reality at all but have a ritual function in exploring dimensions of real-world experiences through a range of familiar characters and locations in a sort of microcosm for society.

Also, crucially, their primary audience is women, bringing another question into your study of the relationship between representation and reality – whose reality do we mean? It is no coincidence that many of the scenarios played out have a hegemonic quality to them, and the way in which this might be used overtly for educational purposes was discussed in the coverage of the Sabido method in the Year 1 book. Fans of soap operas may demand generic verisimilitude, but they are little concerned with the cultural regime of verisimilitude. So, fans of *EastEnders* may not care that the region of London they see is far less ethnically diverse than it is in reality, or that the cast of *Hollyoaks* appear to live their lives largely free from the interference of parents.

For more on the Sabido method see pages 103–104 of the Year 1 book.

Christine Gledhill on the soap opera

In *Representation: Cultural Representations and Signifying Practices* (Hall, 2013), Christine Gledhill contributes a chapter called 'Genre and Gender: The Case of Soap Opera'. Although primarily interested in soap opera as a vehicle for understanding gender representations, Gledhill makes a number of interesting points about the nature of the genre itself and its relationship with 'realism'.

Neighbours is a long-running Australian soap opera that continues to be popular with some sectors of the UK audience despite its different cultural context, suggesting that the pleasures of soaps go beyond national or regional identity.

1   The soap opera genre has been such a presence in everyday life for countless people over a number of generations, that the fictions they offer and our own lives become 'intertwined'. Gledhill points out that soap opera events and their reception often become national news.

2   Real-world issues such as domestic violence form part of what Gledhill describes as a circulation between issues we see reported on in fact-based media such as the news or documentaries and their fictionalised play-out in soap narratives.

3   Soap operas do often repeat out-dated ideologies, but the continual serialised nature of their narratives and the influence of what Gledhill refers to as modes of expression (generic influences such as comedy and melodrama) mean that it is difficult to pin down these ideologies to work out what meanings they have for their audiences in terms of their depictions of community lives, relationships within families and the tendency of plots to resolve themselves in favour of mainstream values.

4   Soap operas, as a genre with quite established conventions, make an interesting study when reflecting on Neale's notions of cultural and generic verisimilitude. Gledhill points out that these can be used in soap operas to assess their relationship with 'realism' – so soap operas can respond to pressure for social change from a range of outside influences, very much based on the assumption that because they are set in the 'everyday' they must therefore have a duty to reflect some of the emerging experiences of real people in real community settings. It is notable that soap operas often preserve a detachment from real-world events, which is part of the generic regime of verisimilitude, and usually accepted by audiences. It is quite rare for soap opera storylines to reference specific real-world events within their diegesis.

5   Because of the significance of cultural verisimilitude to the genre as a whole, Gledhill notes that soap operas are an interesting site of negotiation for cultural hegemony in action, as the mainly conservative mainstream values reflected in their narratives struggle to resolve this tendency with contested space and pressure to represent things that have not been seen before, such as child abuse, a gay kiss or a character who is transgender. These, however, rapidly become absorbed into soap narratives, meaning this regime of verisimilitude is under constant renegotiation in terms of signifying practices.

Kyle Slater did not retain a long-running role in BBC soap *EastEnders*.

APPLY IT

Search for three online news articles from the UK relating to storylines in UK soaps.

- How do they demonstrate some of Gledhill's ideas about realism and cultural verisimilitude in the soap opera?

- In terms of cultural hegemony, do these media sources decry the social change or storylines being depicted, or are they broadly supportive?

- What do they then contribute to our understanding of the positioning of their audience and the audience of the soaps and the progressive nature or otherwise of some soap opera representations?

🔗 See Chapters 5 and 6 to help you connect up ideas about how industry contexts affect representations.

🔗 For more on public service broadcasters, see Chapter 6 and pages 126–128 of the Year 1 book.

In 2015, the BBC news website announced in a positive article the upcoming inclusion of a transgender character in its flagship soap, *EastEnders*. The article about the announcement can be found online (BBC Newsbeat, 2015).

The character did not become established as a long-running member of the cast and was written out of the series after a year. This could be read as an attempt to reflect real-world gender diversity within the series without long-term commitment to inclusivity.

How industry contexts impact on representations

Who produces a media text and why it is produced can have a significant effect on the representations it contains. The nature of media companies as powerful purveyors of mainstream ideologies or counter-hegemonic organisations is explored in much more depth in Chapter 5. You will also find discussion in Chapter 6 of the historical nature of media texts and the impact this can have on representations, which is again closely connected with industry values as a part of the societies that produce media texts.

The commercial drive to make a profit, coupled with political pressures, doubtless has a significant impact on the nature of the representations produced by newspapers in the UK. Public service broadcasters such as the BBC and to some extent Channel 4 are far more likely to represent minorities or offer a wider spectrum of more complex representations of different groups than a commercial broadcaster such as ITV or Channel 5. They may also be more willing to tackle more complex representational subject matter. This willingness to tackle complex representational issues can sometimes backfire.

EXAMPLE: *My Week as a Muslim* (Channel 4 documentary, 2017)

Channel 4 has a long history of not only serving the interests of minority groups but also creating original content which may counter mainstream representations.

In this controversial documentary, a white British woman, who held stereotypical views about Muslims, experienced a week living with a Muslim family and dressing as a British Pakistani. The programme was deemed offensive by many in the Muslim community, particularly as the participant was made up physically to have a Pakistani appearance, complete with brown make-up and a prosthetic nose. There is a long tradition of racist comedy which involves 'black face' in Western cultures – parodying the physical appearance of non-whites for entertainment. Because of this, the programme-makers were accused of being exploitive, falling far short of their stated intention to reveal prejudice and to show someone who was casually prejudiced against Muslims to be exposed to that prejudice from the other side, transforming their opinions and renouncing their former views. This example shows just how easy it is for programmme-makers to begin in a well-intentioned way in constructing a

representation, but to entirely miss the mark, with a large section of the community they intended to validate taking an oppositional reading to the approach used in the documentary.

The Muslim Council of Britain was quoted in an article for the *Guardian* as follows:

> *The use of brownface and blackface has a long racist history and it is not surprising that it has caused deep offence amongst some communities. Had we been consulted, we would not have advised this approach ... We do, however, laud the apparent goals of the documentary – to better understand the reality of Islamophobia, which has become socially accepted across broader society.* (Sherwood, 2017)

Globalisation and the problems of representation was another factor considered in the Year 1 book – cultural imperialism can result in the homogenisation of cultural content, and much of this takes place at the level of representational processes and the repetition of a narrow range of cultural representations which do not reflect the real diversity of the cultures where these products are consumed. Connected with this is the idea of **cultural relativism** – the idea that we tend to judge other cultures based on the values and ideologies of our own. Reframing other cultures in this way is potentially very damaging to them.

For more on reframing cultures see Section 2.4.

There is a number of other significant aspects of industry practice that do have an effect on representations. In studying representations, we should be careful that the methodologies we use do not overemphasise the content of those representations identified through semiotic analysis. They must also take into account broader contexts of study, considering issues relating to audience reception and industrial production, and how these shape the way representations manifest.

One issue that easily acts as a factor in the globalised nature of media representations we mentioned briefly in the Year 1 book, but is worth exploring more here, is the relationship between the industry, audience, and the stars and celebrities who populate many of our media texts.

Stars in the media

There is a huge co-dependency within the mass media industry – both domestic and global - between producers of media texts and the stars whose careers they forge. One reason people consume some media texts is because of the appeal of certain celebrities. Role models in the media are thought to have some influence over our identities – this might be in fashion, media consumption practices, outward expression of our tastes, etc. One way in which we can link stars and identity is through Barthes' third layer of signification – that of the cultural myth – the values and ideologies that circulate in our society.

Contemporary audiences love celebrities and stars, and mass media proliferation has resulted in the proliferation of celebrity culture. In the Year 1 book, you looked at the phenomenon of film magazines, which showed that this appetite for them goes back at least as far as the early days of cinema. Audience members can feel an emotional affinity with or attachment to particular celebrities, and they enjoy the sociability of discussing them with others. This links well with the active theories of audience you studied last year, including the social relationships aspect of Blumler and Katz' uses and gratifications theory and community in Dyer's utopian solutions.

For more about the 2017 UK election campaign see pages 22–23 of the Year 1 book.

This screenshot from the video physically demonstrates solidarity with the Corbyn campaign.

APPLY IT

In a small group, create a list of prominent people from a range of the mass media. Sort them into those you consider to be stars and those who are celebrities. What sorts of discussions did you have? How did you apply the terms?

EXAMPLE: Celebrity endorsement and the 2017 election campaign

One of the interesting aspects of the 2017 UK election campaign was the increase in youth voter turnout. It is difficult to separate out the complex factors in play that lead to this, but one factor may have been the campaigning and high visibility of some celebrities who endorsed Jeremy Corbyn, who received a high proportion of the youth vote.

Celebrities who may have held particular sway for sections of the youth vote include Stormzy, Novelist and JME. JME made a video in which he interviewed Jeremy Corbyn that was widely shared on platforms such as YouTube which have a huge reach. JME's video can be viewed on YouTube by searching for 'When JME Met Jeremy Corbyn'.

This is one example of ways in which the mass media can play a positive role in engagement with democracy.

Many 'stars' of the media today can be seen as brands who seemingly infiltrate large areas of the mass media to their gain.

It's also worth distinguishing between a star and a celebrity – one way of understanding the difference between the two is the level of fame they have achieved. Global and domestic celebrities recognisable to the majority of consumers are stars – people who rise to fame in more of a niche arena can be thought of as celebrities and will not be as widely recognised.

We are living in the age of the celebrity. The explosion of the mass media in the digital age has given more and more opportunities for celebrity generation. It's worth, then, taking a closer look at the ways in which some theorists approach the study of stars in mass entertainment. We can consider at a more complex level the relationship between their representations and the contributions they may make to our own identities through the only way we access these celebrities – the mass media.

Stars can be actors in television series – but the media creates many other stars and celebrities: those from the music world, the world of sport, reality TV and vloggers. Whenever you are considering the meanings signified by a particular star, you should always be evaluating the relationship between the celebrity and the industry that produced them. How carefully is access to the star controlled? Are you seeing paparazzi shots that may or may not have been set up by that star? Is the level of control of the star's image very high – such as in the case of a vlogger – or is it tightly controlled by layers of PR agency, as expected for a domestic television star?

Richard Dyer's theory of stardom

A reason people consume some media texts is because of the appeal of particular celebrities or stars to them personally. Star theory is a discipline that comes from Film Studies but can be readily adapted to suit your needs as Media Studies students. One of the first theorists to create an 'anatomy' of stardom was Richard Dyer. In his book *Stars* (1998), Dyer identified a way of understanding how star images were constructed. Dyer understood star image as a complex signification system, and that **star image** – a star is perceived – is highly polysemic.

In Dyer's original theory, he identified two main parts to a film star's image – the **reel persona**, a sum of all the roles an audience member has seen a star perform in, and the **real persona**, their image outside of role, which might include TV interviews and appearances, celebrity gossip magazines, awards ceremonies, newspaper entertainments coverage and sensationalist tabloid stories. He suggested that the audience's reading of the star as a cultural sign was a combination of these factors. Stars as signs are highly polysemic, because a film star's presence across their medium through time and in other mass media is so omnipresent that no two people in the audience are likely to have viewed all their appearances.

Dyer then went on to identify these aspects:

- **Love**: we are fascinated by the love lives of stars and can also feel a romantic affiliation with them.

- **Ordinariness**: we like to see that although they're super-rich and live lifestyles beyond most of our dreams, stars still do routine things and have ordinary aspects to their lives just like us.

- **Success**: the myth of success is very important to star image. Success myths take different forms. As consumers, we like overnight success stories. They make us think that there is little difference, except luck, between ourselves and a star. This is one of the main appeals of reality television stars. We also like stories of failure before success –the idea, for example, that a star might have been turned down for numerous roles but worked hard until their dreams came true. This appeals to our sense of fair play.

- **Conspicuous consumption**: since early Hollywood and the first star magazines that showed off their luxurious homes, we have been fascinated by the huge material wealth brought by media success. This goes beyond material possessions and into other lifestyle factors – strict dietary regimes provided by nutritionists, the physique of stars who can pay for personal trainers, their lavish holidays, etc.

- **The dream turned sour**: just as we celebrate their successes and their fabulous lifestyles, so we love to gloat when things go wrong for celebrities. Many soft news tabloid stories and the whole industry of the celebrity magazine exploit this pleasure we feel at the misfortunes of those more privileged than us.

You will probably have noticed that some of these elements within the anatomy are contradictory. This is not an issue – star images are full of contradictions that can co-exist quite successfully in the mind of the audience. However, the way in which star image is signified and the codes and the generic codes which are often the vehicles for this signification will vary according to the nature of the celebrity and the media in which they appear. Some of these variations are explored below:

- **Music stars**: the 'reel' persona is mainly presented in music video and concert performance as well as promotional materials such as album artwork. Usually it draws on audience understanding of musical genres too. The 'real' persona may be seen in interviews in music magazines or media reportage, and is often also quite artificial and deliberately controlled by the artists' managers. Flamboyant and eccentric behaviour and complicated private lives often add to the appeal of music stars – 'sex, drugs and rock and roll'.

- **Sports stars**: the 'reel' persona of a sports star can be seen mainly in their conduct and performance at sporting events and post-event interviews. It is constructed in part by commentators and mass media coverage of their participation in these. A cross-over area with the 'real' includes TV show appearances such as quizzes. Male sports stars may be 'heroes' or 'bad boys' – David Beckham has been both in his time. Their 'real' persona is harder to separate out, but it may include information about their private lives they have not controlled the reporting of.

- **Television personalities**: this category covers a whole range of people who appear in the media – celebrity chefs, comedians who appear on panel shows, presenters of reality TV shows, etc.

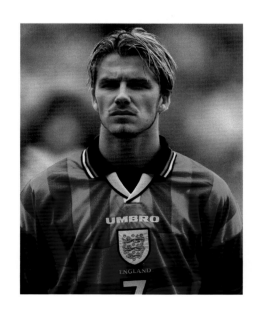

- **Love**: in his younger incarnation, Oliver was represented as a young, approachable but sexy personality. The first television series was called *The Naked Chef*, which was about simple/bare ingredients and stripped-back cooking.
- **Ordinariness**: Oliver uses ordinary working-class language and tries to demystify high-end cooking techniques. Interactions with his wife and family, who sometimes have a visible presence in the show, and his long marriage emphasise his status as a 'regular guy'. Politically influenced campaigns, such as heathy eating in schools and being on a tight family budget, have grown this aspect of his star image in the audience's minds.
- **Success**: people enjoy the supposed narrative of Oliver as a young chef from an ordinary background challenging the stuffier image of his contemporaries in the industry.
- **Conspicuous consumption**: filming locations at the Oliver family home offer a pleasurable insight into a wealthy and stylish family existence complete with glamorous parties.
- **The dream turned sour**: so far so good for Jamie Oliver – not applicable.

Jamie Oliver's Christmas cookery programmes often include segments with his family and powerfully signify the aspects of his celebrity persona mentioned in the example.

APPLY IT

Choose a sporting, television or music star and apply the anatomy of stardom to their star image.

KEY TERMS

cultural relativism	the idea that we tend to judge other cultures based on the values and ideologies of our own
demotic turn	the appearance by ordinary people in mainstream media
expository mode	style of documentary featuring heavy use of narration in the form of a voice-over
observational mode	style of documentary where events appear to simply unfold as we watch
participatory mode	style of documentary where the filmmaker is a visible part of the narrative and has a role to play within it
performative mode	style of documentary similar to participatory but frequently more emotive
real persona	the star's image outside of role, often also highly managed and constructed
reel persona	the sum of all the 'roles' an audience member has seen a star perform in

2.3 Discourses around representation and ideology: gender studies and the mass media

A **discourse** in academic terms means a discussion in academic thinking, often taken in different directions and explored from different angles by different theorists. Some of these theorists may disagree, others develop and reinforce each other's ideas. It's important to understand that no theory can ever be all-encompassing – in Media Studies, you are expected to be able to apply and outline the differing ideas expounded by different key thinkers, but you should also maintain your own critical autonomy – be aware of the criticisms of some theories and other perspectives that may counter them.

The fields of queer theory and studies in masculinity are relatively small when compared with feminist theory. The reasons for this are complex. Feminist thinkers were the first to question how patriarchal society shaped our values as a society, and how media texts might contribute to the maintenance of this hegemony. As society has changed so much in terms of the position and rights of women, so thinkers have studied the manifestations of these changes in cultural products – not just those produced by the mass media, but also those in in art, photography, cinema and almost every area of public life. Since women have historically been treated as inferior in legislation as well as elsewhere, it is natural that a swell of critical theory should develop in response to that.

Queer theory also developed as a critical field, as the visibility of lesbian, gay bisexual and transgender (LGBT) people and awareness of the qualitative nature of their representations has increased in our society. Following behind are studies in masculinity, which evaluate the role of men in this changing society, as their superior status under traditional patriarchy and older modes of representation of traditional masculinity fade. There have been many interesting individual writings about masculinity in cinema, and David Gauntlett undertook some very interesting work in researching contemporary images of masculinity in *Media, Gender and Identity* (2008) – but there is not yet an equivalent body of rich discourse on masculinities, as is the case with feminism.

Rupaul is a good example of a popular television personality outside the heterosexual 'norm' whose audience goes beyond the gay community.

Feminist approaches to media representations of women

Feminism is a huge field of study in critical thinking. Its relevance to our subject is significant, because it doesn't only allow us to consider the nature of female representations, but also to question who makes and owns the media we consume and how this might affect the text being produced at a representational level. One way of understanding the progress of feminist thinking over the past few decades is to understand it in terms of waves – patterns of thinking and analysis that have distinctive characteristics which change noticeably over time. It is an enormous and complex field, with distinct movements having very specific views on identity and schools of thought emerging in various countries worldwide at different times, some of which influenced others and some that remained more domestic in their influence.

All feminists are united in their ideological opposition to patriarchy, a system where men exert control at every level within the power structures in society. Under patriarchy, men are over-represented in almost every sphere where power is wielded – politics, business, etc. Feminists argue that power structures in society need to be more inclusive of women and, until women are equally represented in every sphere, they will still continue to be oppressed by the system. Feminists challenge every aspect of male domination in society. They seek to expose the nature of society as serving the rights of men rather than women, and to counter many traditional ideologies about the role of women in society.

Some critics have even identified what is known as the post-feminist era. Some even disagree on whether there are three, four or even five waves. Some, inevitably, are thought of as more radical than others. You need to be aware that there is some disagreement about the ways in which waves in feminism are defined, including their timescales and defining qualities. The summaries offered here are necessarily broad and quite generalised so as to offer non-specialist Media Studies students new to the field a way of contextualising the movement. In a sense, the picture is complicated by the way in which the aims of each movements become progressively more ideologically complex and diverse as time goes on.

The first wave of feminism originated with women — as well as some men — who campaigned for women's political rights and equality with men in law. It grew out of more liberal views and left-wing trends in thinking that were nascent in this time period, and is often considered to have been most active during the second half of the 1800s and the early part of the 1900s. The concerns of women during this period were mainly about political equality, but also began to look at some of the other ways in which women's rights were less than those of men in a whole range of nuanced socio-political issues.

APPLY IT

Collect six examples of suffrage posters, UK or US, using an online image search.

- What is the issue or focus of each poster?
- What is the mode of address in terms of both images and any lexical coding?
- What messages do they send about the problems facing women in society at the time?
- If men or children are represented in any of the posters you chose, how are they represented?
- How does the poster draw on aspects of real women's lives to persuade the audience of the political message?

EXAMPLE: Political suffragette poster, UK, 1913

The 'Prisoners Act' ('cat and mouse' act) of 1913 was a move by the government of the time to defeat hunger-striking suffragettes in prisons and prevent them from dying there and becoming martyrs. The act worked by releasing them when they became too ill through refusal to eat, then sending them back to prison when they were considered to have recovered sufficiently.

The second wave was in part a response to World War II and the huge impact it had on gender roles in society. There was an attempt to reinvent women's place in more domestic roles and place them firmly back at the heart of the family, following their engagement in many traditionally male spheres' during the war, particularly in work. In the 1950s, women were also being freed up by developments in technology from much of the drudgery of household maintenance and were beginning to look beyond the traditional values of home and family for fulfilment. The 1960s and its explosion of counter-cultural values coincided with women seeking more equal status with men in society and other movements that were anti-war and pro-civil rights. Another issue very important to women in this time period was reproductive rights and this tended to exclude men. This wave is generally considered to last until the early 1990s.

A typical household product advertisement targeting 1950s women.

This iconic shot of Gloria Grahame in *The Big Heat* demonstrates a classic cinematic example of the male gaze as defined by Mulvey.

In the 1970s, a feminist named Laura Mulvey, who was heavily influenced by psychoanalytical film theory, wrote a hugely influential essay called 'Visual Pleasure in Narrative Cinema' (1975). In this essay, Mulvey argues that women are there to be looked at by men, and that women who view films are forced to see themselves in the same way – as 'looked at'. She identifies a voyeuristic way of filming women which she said appealed to fetishistic scopophilia – an obsessive love of looking at women. We can still see this today in the way women are filmed, and even in the poses women are placed in on film posters. The camera frequently lingers on the female form, pans over it languidly, or fragments it into close-ups and extreme close-ups – lips, legs, feet. Mulvey coined the term the male gaze to describe the way we all are positioned to look at women in film. She also noted that powerful female characters, perceived as potentially threatening by the male audience, have to undergo punishment.

Today, some argue for the existence of a female gaze. It is certainly true that men may now be filmed in a similar way.

From the 1990s to the present day is often referred to as third wave feminism. Having achieved a great deal of recognition for women and creating lots of social change, feminists began to develop more niche interests that reflect the concerns of more diverse groups of women. The idea of feminism as a unified movement with similar values and aims finally broke down, as some progress had been made towards gender equality, at least superficially. The third wave of feminists began to challenge all kinds of notions held by the second. Many rejected the term 'feminist' altogether, viewing feminism as more of a struggle for rights for all, not purely women. Third wave feminism is closely associated with the digital age, and the refusal to categorise based on traditional notions of gender identity. It also seeks to champion the different interests of marginalised groups. The arguments about the expression of women's sexuality in the third wave are not all in agreement, with many third wave feminists seeing women as powerful owners of their own sexuality rather than vessels for male desire. Much of the third wave is about ownership of gender expression and the right of women to manifest it as they please. Another aspect to the third wave is the ownership of media representations and challenging stereotypes of women.

Some theorists believe that a fourth wave of feminism is now underway, with other critics suggesting that this isn't the case, showing the difficulty of defining the movement, which is in constant flux, with any real precision. The fourth wave of feminism is considered by some to be an extension of the third, incorporating a highly visible online presence and use of social media for discussion of sexual politics and maintaining social activism about gender inequality.

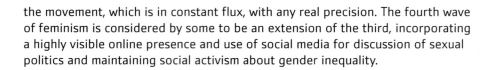

EXAMPLE: Media coverage of the Harvey Weinstein scandal and the #MeToo

Following a spate of accusations of sexual misconduct against Hollywood producer Harvey Weinstein in Autumn 2017, the hashtag #MeToo began to trend on social media, as women shared their stories of sexual assault and male intimidation. The consequences of the Weinstein scandal and its coverage were huge, with ramifications not just for the film and media industries, but in UK politics and business. For a time, accusations were made almost daily against high-profile figures. The empowerment of ordinary and well-known women to feel there was a groundswell of unity among women with these experiences was widely reported.

Raunch culture and post-feminism

Raunch culture is the sexualised performance of women in the media that can play into male stereotypes of women as highly sexually available; whereas its performers believe they are powerful owners of their own sexuality.

In her book *Female Chauvinist Pigs* (2006), writer Ariel Levy proposes that the sexual objectification of women in images, once confined to the private male sphere in areas such as erotic art, has become a dominant representation of women across the mass media. Raunch culture plays into the same dated objectification of women under patriarchy while positioning it critically as female empowerment. It began to emerge in the 1990s and was possibly a backlash (sometimes referred to as **post-feminism**) to the perception that earlier feminists were dismissive of female sexuality and saw sexual agency as being the province of men and part of the exploitative nature of patriarchy.

Closely linked to the idea of raunch culture is lipstick feminism, which is also seen as a brand of third wave feminism that allows women to portray themselves as equal to men in terms of their sexuality by expressing it in any way they choose. This is seen as a counter-ideology which challenges notions of decency and purity demanded of most women and policed by other women in a patriarchal society. It also takes ownership linguistically of chauvinistic terms for women, which can be seen in political protests, asserting the right of women to look or behave how they wish without fear of male reprisal or abuse. The validity of third wave feminism's ownership of sexuality through control of their image as sexualised is one that still divides feminists and is an on-going debate surrounding raunch culture. The term post-feminist is sometimes used to suggest that, because feminism has tended to form schisms in debate and take on many fragmented new forms, it is in some way weakened, when in fact these new, more diverse feminisms could be taken as evidence that feminism is actually thriving.

Critics of raunch culture suggest that it may position women as powerful owners of their own sexuality in posturing, but it does so in a way that validates chauvinistic attitudes to women and continues to commodify them. Its pervasiveness in the mass media can impact on male expectations of female sexual availability and it pits women against each other in competition to be the most sexually appealing and therefore powerful. Post-feminism is a term used to define any critique of feminism at any point following a particular manifestation of feminist thinking, so it is a difficult concept to explain in a definitive way, since it is more a collection of critiques of feminism which may be contradictory rather than a single ideological stance on gender equality.

APPLY IT

Create an A3-size digital collage of news headlines, images and extracts from social media and the internet about the Weinstein scandal and the #MeToo campaign.

- What impression do you get from this of the scale and reach of the reportage and sharing?
- What are the messages conveyed by seeing all these extracts together in terms of third or fourth wave feminism and its relationship with the mainstream?
- Which groups or perspectives are neglected? Is it global or a white Western issue? Is it just about women?

EXAMPLE: Female musical artists and raunch culture

Miley Cyrus is a well-known performer whose acts can be classed as raunch culture, with hyper-sexualised dance moves, and suggestive narrative and lyrical themes and dress code. Other performers include, to varying degrees, Rhianna, Nikki Minaj and Beyoncé.

Many critics of raunch culture believe that the only benefit to women of the proclaimed 'liberation' of overtly sexual musical performance and expression by these artists is the financial one to themselves. In reality, their message is far from empowering for women but simply a repackaging of the traditional commodification of women's bodies in the media and in society as a whole.

Miley Cyrus in the video for 'Wrecking Ball' – powerful owner of her own image or sexualised subject of patriarchy?

 APPLY IT Analyse a video track by one of the artists in the example. Try applying both perspectives – one reading the video as an empowering example of lipstick feminism, the other viewing the performer as a subject of patriarchy. Can you use semiotic evidence to justify both perspectives from the audio-visual, generic and narrative codes and what they signify?

An overview of some key aspects of the perspectives of the key thinkers named in your specification on the topic – van Zoonen, hooks and Butler – are offered here, but it is recommended you take your reading beyond this book to gain a more developed and contextualised understanding of what these theorists have to offer you in your study of gender representations.

Van Zoonen

Liesbet van Zoonen's book *Feminist Media Studies* (1994) is an influential collection of explorations into a range of issues connecting dominant modes in feminist thinking, specifically with issues of media representation. Van Zoonen gives us a close look at the main issues affecting female representation in the media and assesses the usefulness of feminist approaches to the study of the mass media. Van Zoonen acknowledges the complexity of a 'feminist' approach to studying the media, arguing that there are many different ways it can be approached, all with their own strengths and weaknesses. Although mainly focusing on traditional media, van Zoonen's ideas are readily transferable to the study of contemporary media in the digital age. She feels that feminist discourse is still very much dominated by a symbolic conflict about definitions of femininity. She suggests that the mass media has a huge amount of power in constructing gender representations that are broadly stereotypical, but also that no-one has really been studying closely what women actually do with these messages when they receive them. At the end of Chapter 3 (page 42) she asks some important questions which can help to shape your own reading of gender in media texts. Following this way of enquiring into gender representations will give you thoughtful and engaged interpretations of your close study texts:

Liesbet van Zoonen

*   *How are discourses of gender encoded in texts?*
*   *Which preferred and alternative meanings of gender are available in media texts, and from which discourses do they draw?*
*   *How do audiences use and interpret gendered media texts?*
*   *How can these processes be examined and analysed?*

Van Zoonen broadly agrees with Stuart Hall's ideas about the process of signification in media texts, the encoding and decoding model you are already familiar with. In looking at his model, however, she argues that although media texts are polysemic, their means are not infinite. They are constrained by the producers of texts. She is an interesting writer because she draws on and finds connections with the ideas of both bell hooks and **Judith Butler**, both of whom are key thinkers on the course.

These are some of the issues van Zoonen identifies in the way feminists have attempted to make sense of discourse surrounding meaning in the mass media:

*   All feminist debate is in some way about gender and power. Women, though, are not a homogenous group. Feminists therefore struggle to agree on a definition of femininity. Approaches to understanding how women are represented need to be aware of differences between women and their real-world experiences who come from different social strata and ethnic backgrounds. Gender is not the defining quality alone for women, and intersects with race, sexuality and class.

*   The practice of constructing gender identities is constantly being constructed not only symbolically in media texts but also in everyday life. Gender is seen by van Zoonen as a vital aspect of culture at all levels, and one that is institutionalised by factors such as genre and the domination of the industry by rich, white men on the level of mass mediation, but is also evident in all the ways in which we interact with others in our daily lives.

*   Stereotypes and socialisation by the mass media have often been an important component in understanding how the media represents gender. They were historically accepted as the norm, and it is only in more recent decades that anyone began to question how stereotypes about gender developed, were reinforced or how they continued to circulate. The mass media tends to reflect the real-world issues women face and as a result, *'symbolically denigrate women, either by not showing them at all, or by showing them in stereotypical roles'* (page 17). This, however, does not factor in the uses women make of the media – their understanding of it, and other complex factors such as narrative and generic contexts.

*   Feminism has come from left-wing thinking because it offers a cultural critique – it asks us to question the signs we see all around us. Strongly socialist feminists use the ideas of Gramsci and Althusser to support their view that gender is an important construct in ideology – since the media is the primary source of cultural hegemony in our society which allocates a place to women economically and socially, and whose messages strive to maintain that status quo.

*   The concept of **distortion** is very significant in understanding just how difficult it is for feminists to come to an agreement as to what needs to change in terms of female representation in the mass media. Most people would agree that the way in which the media usually represents women's lives does not reflect the reality of many real women. There are plenty of women living complex and interesting lives who see no-one like themselves from day to day on television. Stereotypes, however, do reflect the reality of some people's lives. Because many women really are housewives, for example whose main

Rupert Murdoch typifies the domination of the media industry by wealthy white men commented on by van Zoonen.

For more on Gramsci and Althusser see page 85 of the Year 1 book.

role is child-rearing and domestic duties, we can ask whether this is really so problematic. There is no universal agreed replacement for these stereotypes, so constructing counter-types that satisfy everyone who wants to see more progressive representations of women is always going to problematic.

This image demonstrates well the problem of distortion.

- Gender has always been dynamic, varied across cultures and full of contradictory meanings. In our own popular culture in recent years, there are plenty of examples of stars and personalities who draw on more androgynous or ambiguous notions of gender identity. It seems, then, that the mass media can be open to the transgression of traditional notions of gender boundaries between male and female. If the mass media could begin to reflect this possibility and go beyond the socially constructed paradigm of how we see men's and women's roles in a binary way, distortion would no longer be an issue.

EXAMPLE: Verizon 'Inspire her Mind' digital video advertisement (2016) advert and John Lewis 'She's Always a Woman' television advert (2010)

Both advertisements use similar techniques, with each offering a montage of moments in a girl or woman's life, but with quite different perspectives – one challenging the way girls are often raised in Western culture, the other reinforcing dominant ideology.

In this US-produced advert, technology company Verizon seeks to challenge our attitudes about what girls can do and encourage their involvement in science, technology, engineering and mathematics (STEM) disciplines. The advert seems to play out van Zoonen's idea that the construction of gender identities does not just happen symbolically in media texts but is a key aspect of our cultural exchanges every day. This is contrasted here with a historical advertisement for John Lewis department store, which shows a woman's life from babyhood to old age compressed into a cleverly edited sequence in which she experiences some of the defining romantic notions of womanhood, another area van Zoonen cites as being most frequently explored by feminist critics of the mass media.

Image from the John Lewis advert

The John Lewis advert was very popular with its female target audience, despite its restrictive portrayal of a woman's life as revolving solely around the (luxurious) domestic setting, marriage, pregnancy, childrearing and the nurturing of family ties and grandchildren. This suggests that many women accept the preferred reading that women should be proud of their centrality to family life.

APPLY IT

Find two contrasting examples of advertisements that feature women. How clearly do they seem to act as examples of such symbolic reflection of women's real lives? Use them to explore some of van Zoonen's ideas about a feminist approach to reading the roles of women in media texts.

In the Verizon advert, a single girl's life from toddler to teenager is compressed into a minute, during which we hear but don't see parental voices discouraging her from showing curiosity in the natural world, doing model making or trying to use power tools. In the final scene, she sees a sign for the science fair at her school. We then realise that instead of reading the poster, she is actually checking her own reflection in the window it is placed in – which she then uses to apply her lipstick. The advert is a hard-hitting critique of the way in which girls are socialised by the world around them into disbelieving that they are scientifically and academically capable. It attempts to use the mass media to promote this message, counter to van Zoonen's observation that advertising is a prominent purveyor of stereotypes about women and their roles in society. It draws on the absence of portrayals of 'ordinary' women taking on disciplines such as science without being turned into stereotypes of geeks.

The advertisements can be watched online by searching YouTube for 'John Lewis Ad 2010 – Fyfe Dangerfield "She's Always a Woman"' and 'Inspire Her Mind – Verizon'.

bell hooks

bell hooks

Gloria Jean Watkins is a prominent African-American feminist thinker. She has written many books, all under the pen name **bell hooks**, which she does not capitalise in order to emphasise her ideas rather than her persona. She is a very interesting theorist for an A level Media Studies student to learn about, as her ideas not only are central to many issues of gender representation, but you can also apply her ideas to issues of race representation and postcolonial thinking as well as political theory relating to social class.

hooks has been preoccupied throughout her career by the **intersectionality** of race, social class and gender issues, which she believes work together in differing power structures to limit the opportunities available to black women. Her writing is important as a reaction to the predominantly white middle-class concerns that preoccupied early feminists, some of which seemed to have little relevance to the lives of black American women struggling with issues relating to other aspects of their oppression in American society. Many of her ideas translate equally well to the treatment of women from ethnic minorities in predominantly white European culture, and as a feminist who dislikes the separating out of different schools of feminist thought, her work is of interest when looking at any female representation.

hooks believes that equality of the sexes is not possible without the participation of men in feminist thinking. In real terms for you as Media Studies students, this means you need to consider not just whether the imbalance of men to women in key roles of the media industry affects female representations, but also whether the men who are there are thoughtful and engaged with issues that affect women when they create representations in texts. hooks has written many books and is still writing – it is not necessary to read all of these to be able to apply her ideas to media texts at your level of study.

A highly readable account of many aspects of popular culture, which gives insight into hooks' mode of critical thinking that can help to align you with her ideas, is given in the lecture transcript on 'Cultural Criticism & Transformation' (1997), which is available online.

Although the lecture was given in 1997, many of the points she makes are still relevant in today's media climate and still reflect her thinking about the role of the media in people's lives:

- Studying popular culture is hugely important as it is where the politics of difference manifest – that popular culture is a site of interplay between the various power relationships which exist in the real world.

- The individual, whatever their gender, social class or racial background, is responsible for thinking critically about the world they live in and the media they consume.
- There may not be a direct causal link between portrayals of sexual violence in the media and real-world actions, but seeing these images can contribute to both men and women's perceptions of what is acceptable behaviour in the real world.
- The conscious construction of representations, and that media producers should be held to account by all of us for lazy stereotyping.
- Mass media representations in the late 1990s reflected a conscious backlash against feminism, and a deliberate attempt by a patriarchal business and power structures to put women back in their place.
- Her deliberate use of the term 'white supremacist capitalist patriarchy' to remind us of the links she sees between all these oppressive factors in society.
- The media industry is permeated at all levels by the prioritisation of the profit motive over fair representation of women or people from ethnic minorities. She believes that the profit motive gets the better even of those who begin with good intentions.

EXAMPLE: Michael Burnham in *Star Trek: Discovery* (Netflix, 2017)

Michael Burnham, played by Sonequa Martin-Green

Star Trek: Discovery is the latest in a series franchise that stretches back to the 1960s. The first series was famous for featuring an inter-racial kiss between a white man and a black woman on American television. Many critics have dismissed this moment in televisual history because of its dubious narrative context, which implied that Captain Kirk was not in control of himself when the kiss took place. However, it was widely seen as signifying the beginning to reflect the wider changes which were taking place in attitudes to race in US society. Uhuru herself was represented as a curiosity, able to occupy the position she did on the bridge because of the futuristic context of the series. In reality, her portrayal was somewhat exoticised and her role little more than the science fiction equivalent of secretary to the male crew.

The new series shows clear progress in attitudes to women from ethnic minorities. The main protagonist, Michael Burnham (played by Sonequa Martin-Green), is a powerful black female lead, around whom all the series narratives are centred. Writer and co-creator Bryan Fuller said,

> *We want to carry on what* Star Trek *does best, which is being progressive. So it's fascinating to look at all of these roles through a colorblind prism and a gender-blind prism.* (Goldberg, 2016)

hooks' ideas seem to have come to fruition here – a positive, complex black female character who resists many of the more habitual stereotypes. It is doubtful whether this series or any of the others in the *Star Trek* franchise can be said to be truly 'gender and colour-blind', but the aspiration from someone with the control over representations in the series is at least a start.

Judith Butler

Judith Butler has become a very well-known theorist, primarily for her book *Gender Trouble: Feminism and the Subversion of Identity* (1999). In this book, she challenges the notion that gender is a biological fact that places masculinity and femininity in binary categories. It became highly influential not only for the impact it had on feminism, but also its contribution to the field of queer theory. Her work is exciting because of the way in which it opens up arguments about how

APPLY IT

Source and read a copy of bell hooks' lecture transcript. It is conveniently sub-sectioned into different areas of discussion and debate relating to black and female representations. Pick out all the examples of popular cultural products, and research them to make sure you understand her points. Can you find any examples of more recent texts that have similar issues, or can you find examples where you believe representations of class, gender and race are more progressive? Aim to collect five examples of texts and prepare notes on them to discuss in class.

we perceive masculinity and femininity in society and how they manifest in media representations. It also helps to account for the free-floating gender characteristics we have seen in some musical artists and comedians.

Butler proposes that sex may be biologically defined, but that gender is learned through society – and proposes the view that gender is a performance.

Her original book is a highly complex read, but her overall challenge to traditional ways of thinking about gender politics is not too difficult to grasp. Some points you can gain from reading her work are as follows:

Ian Alexander as Buck Vu in *The OA* (Netflix, 2016)

- Many traditional approaches to gender and the way we understand it in society are governed by the notion that 'heterosexuality' can only be defined in a binary way by the existence of an 'other', 'homosexual' state.
- Feminist strategies that identify men and patriarchal structures as oppressors mimic the divisions and creation of barriers in society they would like to see removed.
- 'Women' are a huge array of people. Traditional feminism focuses on unity and tries to suggest that the sharing of biological sex is a trans-cultural phenomenon dictated by reductive qualities such as sexuality and child-bearing, which excludes a whole range of other aspects that influence the formation of gender identity.
- Most previous work on identity politics requires a known, categorised identity to be fully formed in order to be included in debate.
- Exclusion and hierarchies are present in almost every debate about gender and identity.
- Transformative approaches to identity politics can only emerge if we resist categorisation and open up debates about gender and politics, which remove a preconceived notions of gender an accept less 'stable' manifestations of gender identity.

EXAMPLE: Case study of a transgender character, Buck in *The OA* (Netflix, 2016)

The OA is a science fiction series that was shown on Netflix in 2016. It is based on the premise of a young blind woman, Prairie, who reappears after seven years missing and has recovered her sight. The character of Buck and the actor who plays him, Ian Alexander, form an interesting case study because it shows just how far media producers can go to represent characters from minority groups in a positive and thoughtful way. The show's writer/producer team, Brit Marling and Zal Batmaglij, were determined that the character should be cast as written – a young, female to male transgender character, with mixed Asian heritage. Initial casting calls were unsuccessful, so the producers put out a call on social media. Ian Alexander recorded his audition tape on his phone in his bathroom. The 15-year-old actor was immediately cast in role despite his lack of formal acting experience and has been critically lauded for his performance.

Crucially, the character of Buck is not written to exploit his transgender status. He is a secondary character, one of four boys, who just happens to be transgender. Although he has his own contextual story arc – that he is supplied testosterone illegally by local drug dealer Steven because his father will not accept his transitioning from female to male – Buck's status as a trans boy is never focused on in a gratuitous way. Alexander himself posted in advance of the programme's premiere on his Tumblr account:

> *Buck's character is not reduced to his trans-ness ... Buck is a well-rounded, lovable character.*

> ***reasons to watch the oa, a Netflix original series***
>
> * Note: it isn't out yet
>
> 1) buck vu, an asian-american transboy
> 2) buck's character is not reduced to his trans-ness
> 3) buck is a well rounded, lovable character
> 4) did i mention buck vu
> 5) buck is the oa's #1 biggest fan
>
> thank you for your time. watch the oa
>
> sincerely,
> the actor that plays buck vu
>
> SOURCE:
> 1 YEAR AGO   + 285
> this is silly sorry   self promo   its gonna be out before
> the end of the year that's all i know

Ian Alexander's Tumblr post about the character of Buck Vu.

Studying representations of masculinity in the mass media

In the Year 1 book, we touched briefly on the notion that representations of traditional masculinity still persist in the mass media, but that they have also come to be more diverse. Many social commentators and some academic theorists have suggested that changes in gender roles in the last decades have led to what is sometimes termed a 'crisis' in masculinity. Certainly, this has become a popular cultural trope, with angry emasculated men seeking revenge on women or society in general being a popular device in cinematic and crime narratives. Some theorists, however, suggest that in reality there is no crisis in masculinity, and that the majority of modern men are perfectly equipped to deal with the changes in their roles and those of the women around them.

Studies that explore the nature of masculinity in media texts may be fewer than those that look at the role of women, but it is a very interesting line of study. Masculinity used to be considered a monolithic single set of traditional representations with qualities that varied in their proportions and way they were expressed but very little in other ways. Any deviation from these models was offered in a binary way as a negative. Portrayals of male emotion have to be properly contextualised historically, such as limited expression of grief being appropriate if a comrade has fallen.

Today, masculinity is generally expressed in a plural way. Many media texts are more progressive and diverse in their exploration of masculinities, but others still remain that draw on conventional archetypes. The following example explore two advertisements in this interesting range.

EXAMPLE: Two television advertisements depicting masculinity in 2017

Lynx 'Find your Magic' advert

The Lynx advertisements, which were famous for their depiction of regular-looking men who suddenly attracted the attentions of hordes of adoring women, became so well-established in popular culture in the 1990s and 2000s that a 'lynx effect' became a byword for anything that enhanced perceived popularity with women. In 2017, Lynx has to a degree kept its central message – that you don't have to be conventionally attractive to attract women – but updated it to fit with more contemporary representation of masculinity while downplaying the sexist overtones of the womanising men of previous decades.

APPLY IT

Choose a representation of a transgender person or character from anywhere in the media. Explore the qualitative nature of the representation in around 300 words.

- To what extent does the representation accept that gender is just a performance? How inclusive is the treatment of the person or character?
- If the text is fictional, is the transgender character played by a transgender person?
- Is the representation centred on their perceived 'difference' from social norms of gender, or does it have other more complex aspects to it?

For more about representations see page 76 of the Year 1 book.

In the advert, a range of men with their own quirks, which might not be associated with traditional masculinity as appeals, display their 'talents' in a positive and uplifting way. It's worth noting that a feminist might argue that the advert would be hardly likely to work were the gender roles reversed.

Hugo Boss aftershave advert featuring Chris Hemsworth

This is a much more traditional portrayal of masculinity rooted in the English gentleman stereotype, which has in turn much older roots in the archetype of the knight and the chivalric code in Western culture. The colour codes of the mise-en-scène are cool and masculine, and the significance of good physique and designer clothes signify the image of a businessman who has as his core values 'integrity' and good behaviour towards others.

 APPLY IT

Choose two television adverts for products aimed predominantly at men. Try and identify how the media language draws on codes relating to traditional and new masculinities. Which cultural myths are present about the role of men in our society?

KEY TERMS

discourse	an academic discussion or debate about a subject embodying a range of perspectives around a similar subject	lipstick feminism	a brand of third wave feminism that allows women to portray themselves as equal to men in terms of their sexuality by expressing it in any way they choose
distortion	the phenomenon by which the way the media usually represents women's lives does not reflect the reality of many real women	male gaze	describes the way we all are conventionally positioned to look at women in film in an inferior, and often sexualised, way
female gaze	the subversion of the male gaze in which men become the subject to be looked at by women	queer theory	critical approach that explores LGBT perspectives on culture and the media
fetishistic scopophilia	an obsessive love of looking at women	raunch culture	specifically associated with music video but with cultural resonance seen elsewhere – the overt sexualisation of female artists
intersectionality	the acknowledgement that issues of power relating to gender, race and social class all intersect		

2.4 Ethnicity and postcolonial theory

Postcolonialism as a field is closely allied with race representations and can be used to help you consider how power structures between groups are represented, as well as to evaluate the significance of who has created a representation of a particular group or individual. It describes a collection of ideas that come out of the legacy of colonialism. It attempts to define attitudes and values that can often still persist, including an assumption of the superiority of Western values in relation to other cultures.

Colonial attitudes still remain influential in Western culture, long after the withdrawal of most colonial occupations. They are a deeply ingrained part of the legacy of the historical Western economic, social and political exploitation of other cultures. Historically, there has been a tendency for Western cultures to ignore the complexity of other cultures when studying them, holding them up for scrutiny against Western values that label them as strange, primitive or deviant. This imposing of what we might think of as an external value system onto other cultures suggests that Western culture and societal values represent a kind of 'norm' from which other cultures deviate.

Edward Said's 1978 book Orientalism describes how Western cultures have always sought to define countries in the East – but also more broadly outside 'Western' culture in ways that seem to justify Western values and attitudes to them, including political agendas and narratives of exploitation and colonialism, which could be justified if a culture was seen as sufficiently different and, by default, inferior or strange. This is apparent historically in high cultural artefacts such as art and literature, which depict these places and people in a subservient way and patronise their heritage. These ideas dominated the approaches of scholars in the 18th and 19th centuries and shaped the ways in which these cultures were studied, always from a point of difference and comparison with Western society. Said's work was a turning point in attitudes to the study of other cultures and their artefacts, and is a key text for anyone studying postcolonialism in higher education.

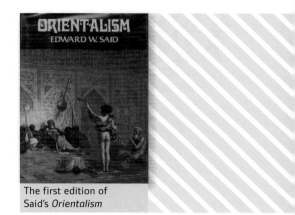

The first edition of Said's Orientalism

The idea of otherness is central to postcolonial studies. Attitudes to race in media consumers can be in part shaped by the consumer's experience of them as 'alien' to white westerners rather than being represented as having things in common with them. Difference can be emphasised in a voyeuristic way. 'Otherness' in media representations can result in the eroticisation of ethnic minorities and other demeaning stereotypes or reductionist portrayals. It can also be used negatively in cases where ethnicity is made to seem more important than other dimensions of a character, public figure, star or criminal. It can romanticise aspects of a culture, highlighting a kind of purity of spirit and naivety – the 'noble savage' stereotype, which has a long legacy in the European imagination. However, there are occasions when 'otherness' can spark interest and cultural understanding in a positive way by engaging a majority white audience with issues and insights relevant to other cultures, such as through comedy or by emphasising commonalities between races and cultures rather than differences.

Postcolonial studies have been a popular approach in literary theory and criticism, but many of the ideas can readily be applied to any cultural product. The approach allows you to ask fundamental questions about cultural identity and meanings in media texts, and the power relationships between who is doing the representing and who is being represented. It allows you to review narratives and power structures, particularly when considering historical and present-day racial stereotypes that persist in the mass media. Different Western countries may have distinctions in the ways in which they represent different cultures due to their own colonial histories and associations with them. It is a good idea when studying postcolonialism to think about how globalisation and cultural imperialism have brought some of these issues even higher up the social agenda – if we are **transnational** media consumers, how does that impact on consumers in other countries, and the way they see themselves being represented in media texts?

Representing race in multi-cultural Britain today

Why does postcolonialism matter if it's connected with power structures that have long since been dissolved or with centuries-old values? It matters because colonial relationships mean that many of these countries have a mixed ethnicity, with people whose cultural heritage may be deeply intertwined with the colonial past, either recently or generations ago. These British citizens have every right to see fair representation of themselves in the media texts they consume, and better cultural understanding could be reached if media representations could be more carefully considered.

Public service broadcasters in particular have taken deliberate measures to improve the quality and diversity of their representations of people from ethnic minorities in recent decades – progress has been made. There has been an increase in the presence in the mass media of people from ethnic minorities and their casting/presence in more significant roles or high-status broadcasts signifies a quantitative improvement. More diversity in the niche media market shows recognition that mainstream media products may not always cater well for people from different cultural backgrounds or racial groups.

EXAMPLE: Niche media products for ethnic minorities in the UK

There has been an increase in media products that cater for the specialist interests of ethnic minorities in the UK, such as the BBC's *Asian Network*, *Black Beauty and Hair* magazine, *Eastern Eye* and *The Voice* newspapers. *The Voice* website is one of your close study products for 2019.

APPLY IT

Source a print copy or view the website for a niche publication other than *The Voice*.

Analyse a single article from it, exploring the way its perspective differs from mainstream media in a case study of around 300 words.

Today there is more awareness of the language used to discuss race across media forms to show more consideration for consumers from ethnic minorities. Greater awareness of racial stereotypes and more caution in referencing or repeating these, coupled with a greater effort to portray people from ethnic minorities in a positive light or in more significant roles, means that qualitative representation has improved.

Racial representations have often historically seen men in particular as threats to the dominant white culture, as criminally deviant and so on. This is still the case today and can be seen in the abrupt rise of Islamophobia in the UK in response to the global terrorism threat.

For more on the link between race representations and moral panics see Chapter 3.

EXAMPLE: Situation comedy: *Citizen Khan* (BBC2, 2012–present)

Citizen Khan is an interesting example of a text made for a public service broadcaster for a diverse audience, and attempts to light-heartedly explore cultural tensions and build bridges between elements of British culture. Written by and starring comedian and presenter Adil Ray, the sitcom features the larger than life character Mr Khan who was first created as a comic entity outside of the series.

The series exaggerates to comic effect the lives of an ordinary Pakistani-Muslim Birmingham family, making numerous cultural references to values and lifestyle and in-jokes relevant to that community. However, it is in many ways a very traditional British family-based sitcom, complete with familiar family tensions, stock characters and comic set-ups a white British audience can easily engage with. The series could be seen as creating understanding between communities, in that it uses a typically

British genre with a longstanding history of a corpus that has been dominated by white characters in UK media history, but imbues it with cultural distinctiveness relevant to another social group.

Paul Gilroy: Double consciousness

In **Paul Gilroy**'s book, *The Black Atlantic: Modernity and Double Consciousness* (1993), Gilroy explores the idea of **double consciousness** first proposed by American academic and civil rights activist W.E.B Du Bois in 1903. Du Bois described a vision of black identity that has been explored by numerous writers and critical thinkers since. Double consciousness describes two aspects of black experience. The first of these is living within a predominantly white culture and having an aspect of identity rooted somewhere else. Secondly, it can also refer to the experience of living in a white culture that consistently represents black people from a white, often racist perspective and the experience of being essentially forced to look at the self though other eyes.

Gilroy explores this idea further arguing that black experience is transnational, a hybrid of multiple influences and cultural forms that come from the movement of black people around the 'Atlantic', which he uses as a term to encompass diverse experiences of black people in the US, UK and Caribbean. He suggests that cultural production across networks is relevant to and contributes to the making of black experience that is international and does not fit with pre-defined notions of cultural or national boundaries to black experience. He also, importantly, sees cultural and artistic production by black artists and practitioners as politicisation – a way of resisting white Western capitalism. The legacy of slavery is seen by Gilroy as highly significant in the double consciousness of black experience. The movement of people and the cultural mixing and influencing of people who were displaced without any deference to their roots or original cultural identity is seen as crucial to the notion that black identity is complex and heterogeneous.

The term **diaspora** means a scattering or spread of people, and it is not exclusive to the history of black populations in the US and UK – for example, the Jewish diaspora has been written about a great deal. Gilroy advanced the use of the term critically to describe the experience of black people in the UK in his influential book, *There Ain't No Black in the Union Jack* (2002). In Chapter 5, Gilroy makes the following points, which are useful to help a Media Studies student understand his concept of the diaspora:

- The terms race, ethnicity, nation and culture are not interchangeable. They all have very specific politicised meanings.

- The black British experience can be seen as diasporic – its culture is a blend of different experiences from different places and includes influences from black America. Black culture in the UK is in constant flux, being 'actively made and remade' (page 202).

- He rejects what he refers to as **cultural absolutism** (sometimes also called **racial essentialism**), which relies on linking a person's cultural and racial heritage to a place of national or ethnic origin.

- The culture of black Britain can be understood as a critique of capitalism – as you saw earlier with feminism, oppression of any social group can be linked to white patriarchal structures endemic in Capitalist society.

- 'Contingent and partial belonging' and 'ambiguous assimilation' are both phrases he uses to describe the black experience in Britain.

- **Cultural syncretism** is the blending of different influences to form a new means of expression.

Watch an episode of *Citizen Khan*. Compare it with a historical or more recent example of an all-white family sitcom, such as *2 Point 4 Children*, *My Family* or *Outnumbered*.

Draw up a list of similarities and differences between the two episodes. What elements of cultural distinctiveness make *Citizen Khan* unique, and what does it borrow from more established examples?

Paul Gilroy

- The idea of cultural exchange and commodification – new ideologies through distribution of music, for example, worldwide, including back in the directions artists have their roots – and new uses being made of these ideas and their reappropriation and absorption into other geographical spaces.
- Gilroy's exploration of cultural products produced across the diaspora focuses mainly on black musical genres and artists and their relationships with a predominantly white industry.
- He also explores the political power and influence of black culture and music in responding to events worldwide, and the way in which these function within the diaspora, as a call to action for people with diverse black heritage.

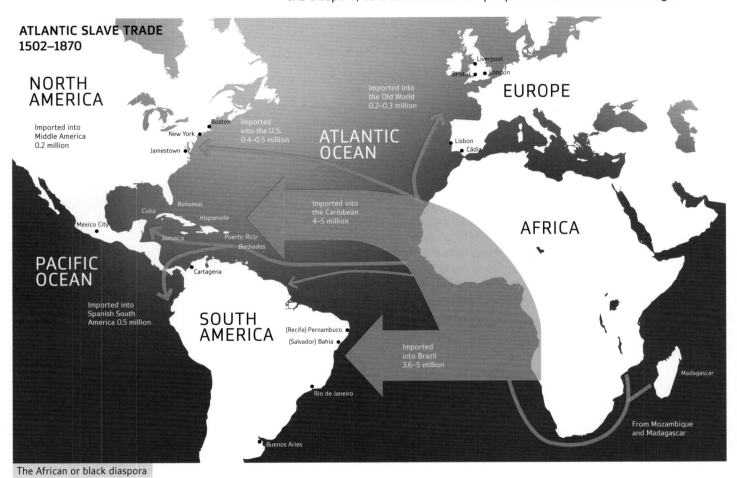

The African or black diaspora

Gilroy's ideas about double consciousness and the diaspora can be used in a number of ways when applying a postcolonial reading to a media text and in exploring race representations. It can be used to look at ways in which different black identities merge in representations. It can also be used to understand the polysemic way in which race representations may be read by different social groups, and can be used to understand how power relationships in society manifest in media representations.

KEY TERMS

cultural absolutism/ racial essentialism	the linking of a person's cultural and racial heritage to a place of national or ethnic origin
cultural syncretism	the blending of different influences to form a new means of expression
diaspora	a scattering or spread of people
double consciousness	two aspects of black experience; living within a predominantly white culture and having an aspect of identity rooted somewhere else
orientalism	prejudiced Western view of other cultures, which defines them as inferior
postcolonial theory	the study of the many ways in which the legacy of colonialism affects race representations
transnationality	in the case of text, having a presence or value that crosses cultural and geographical divides

KEY THINKERS

bell hooks	(1952–) an important contemporary American feminist and social activist, bell hooks has written extensively about issues relating not only to gender representation but also its connections with race and social class, so is considered an important thinker on intersectionality
Edward Said	(1935–2003) Palestinian-American postcolonial theorist whose ideas about how we perceive the Orient in the West transformed cultural studies in the second part of the 20th century
Judith Butler	(1956–) American feminist and author of *Gender Trouble: Feminism and the Subversion of Identity* who is well known for her theory of gender and performativity

Liesbet van Zoonen	(1959–) Dutch author of feminist media studies, van Zoonen developed a wide-ranging theory of the importance of looking at all aspects of media production and content in exploring representations of women
Paul Gilroy	(1956–) Gilroy is a contemporary British cultural theorist who writes about race relations in the UK and US

CHAPTER SUMMARY

- You should now feel secure in having mastered the basic processes by which representations are constructed, and understand the significance of representations to society as a whole.

- There are many different ways into debates about representations and reality. Factual media in particular contain many approaches to understanding the issues.

- Reality television is anything but reality and is contrived to prioritise entertainment values. The authenticity and feeling of ownership we gain from seeing ordinary participants is questioned by Graeme Turner in his work on the demotic turn, which suggests the relationship between the media industry and ordinary people can only ever be exploitative.

- Documentary programmes today are widely trusted by audiences but should be viewed as just as full of constructed viewpoints and representations as any other media text. Documentary modes are characterised by aspects of media language and aesthetic style that have influenced the way in which modern forms present, and often influence how much we trust or accept the authenticity of the messages and values a documentary-maker seeks to convey.

- Soap operas, which in some ways reflect aspects of real life, are a genre form that has an ambiguous relationship with 'realism', best understood through Steve Neale's division between the two regimes of verisimilitude – the generic and the cultural.

- The effect of industry contexts on representations and the mass media is explored in more detail in Chapters 5 and 6, and you should read these carefully in preparing to study the historical, world and alternative media texts that are included in your close study products.

FURTHER READING AND REFERENCES

Ariel Levy (2006) *Female Chauvinist Pigs: Women and the Rise of Raunch Culture.*

BBC Newsbeat (2015, 9 October) '*EastEnders* Cast Transgender Actor in Transgender Role on UK Television', www.bbc.co.uk/newsbeat/article/34479713/eastenders-casts-transgender-actor-in-transgender-role-on-uk-television.

bell hooks (1997) 'Cultural Criticism & Transformation', www.mediaed.org/transcripts/Bell-Hooks-Transcript.pdf.

Bill Nichols (1991) *Representing Reality: Issues and Concepts in Documentary.*

Christine Gledhill (2013) 'Genre and Gender: The Case of Soap Opera', in S. Hall (ed.) *Representation: Cultural Representation and Signifying Practices.*

David Gauntlett (2008) *Media, Gender and Identity.*

Edward Said (1978) *Orientalism.*

Graeme Turner (2010) *Ordinary People and the Media: The Demotic Turn.*

Harriet Sherwood (2017, 19 October) 'My Week as a Muslim Documentary Sparks Racism Row', *Guardian*, www.theguardian.com/media/2017/oct/19/my-week-as-a-muslim-documentary-sparks-racism-row.

Judith Butler (1999) *Gender Trouble: Feminism and the Subversion of Identity.*

Laura Mulvey (1975) 'Visual Pleasure and Narrative Cinema', *Screen*, 16(3), 6–18.

Liesbet van Zoonen (1994) *Feminist Media Studies.*

Matt Goldberg (2016, 23 June) 'Exclusive: New "Star Trek" Showrunner Bryan Fuller on Progressiveness, Number of Episodes, Filming Details, and Much More', Collider, http://collider.com/new-star-trek-series-details/.

Paul Gilroy (1993) *The Black Atlantic: Modernity and Double Consciousness.*

Paul Gilroy (2002) *There Ain't no Black in the Union Jack: The Cultural Politics of Race and Nation.*

Richard Dyer (1998) *Stars.*

Stuart Hall (2013) *Representation: Cultural Representation and Signifying Practices.*

Tessa Perkins (1997) 'Rethinking Stereotypes', in T. O'Sullivan & Y. Jewkes (eds) *The Media Studies Reader.*

- Celebrity and star study is a significant aspect of your study of the relationship between industry context of representations and audience appeal.

- Feminist approaches to reading gender representations are very important on the course. Feminism is not a single movement, but rather a collection of approaches with a long history, which are sometimes loosely connected together into 'waves' by thinkers wanting to make sense of how feminist approaches have changed and developed over time.

- You are expected to have a working knowledge of some of the preoccupations of three key thinkers on the subject of feminism and mass media representations: Judith Butler, Liesbet van Zoonen and bell hooks.

- Butler's main ideas concern the idea that biological sex and gender do not necessarily coincide, and that gender is a performance, a construct that society imposes on men and women and that culture replicates.

- Liesbet van Zoonen collated a range of contemporary thinking about feminist approaches to your subject in her book, *Feminist Media Studies.*

- bell hooks' brand of feminism looks particularly at black female representation but sees gender in the context of much broader ideas about social class, patriarchy and so on. She is one of the most significant modern feminists to write about this intersectionality.

- Studies in masculinity have less emphasis on the course, but it is important to be able to distinguish, for example, between traditional masculinities and more contemporary representations, as well as to be aware of the concept of plural masculinities.

- You should be able to analyse representations of people from LGBT groups in a thoughtful way and be aware of some of the political aspects to the representation of out-groups defined by more fluid gender identities.

- Postcolonialism is an important field when considering race representations and any depictions of other cultures.

- Edward Said's ideas in his book *Orientalism* helped to define postcolonialism as a field, and to bring about widespread changes in the way other cultures are studied by academics in Western societies.

- Paul Gilroy's notion of double consciousness is central to your understanding of representations of race, and how those representations are read by those who consume them. His development of the concept of diaspora has also been very significant in the field of postcolonial theory and helps us to understand the complex networks of exchange in black culture internationally.

Chapter 3 Media audiences

3.1 Understanding the relationship between media products and media audiences

What you already know about media audiences

In Year 1, you learned about how audiences are targeted by various media producers. You discovered some of the ways in which media producers can be understood to be actively constructing audiences, researching and profiling them to refine their products. You explored the uses of techniques such as demographics, and how media producers are using increasingly sophisticated ways through digital media of researching their audiences. There are many overlaps here between the study of audience and industry, and it's really important that you don't try and draw artificial boundaries between them when actually writing about media texts.

Age and gender are useful broad categories used by media producers to target products, but many other subtle factors are used by media producers to help them better focus their targeting. Social class, ethnicity, income, the region of the country in which audiences reside, and even their political persuasion are all dimensions of audience composition which are valuable to producers.

What you will learn in this chapter

- Year 1 mastery: understanding the relationship between media products and media audiences

- Year 1 mastery: developing further your understanding of media effects debates, cultivation theory and reception theory and Year 2 development: how media organisations reflect the needs of mass and specialised audiences

- Year 2 development: how audiences use media in different ways, reflecting aspects of demographics, identity and cultural capital

- Year 2 development: fandoms and participatory culture and the role of specialised audiences, including niche and fan

- Year 2 development: end of audience theories

The use of techniques such as celebrity endorsement is also a part of audience targeting. Psychographics and lifestyle profiling were explored, and you also found out about well-established advertising agency Young and Rubicam's influential cross-cultural consumer categories. Other ways of understanding how specific sectors of media production have their ways of constructing audiences were modelled by looking at news agendas. All of these approaches continue to be relevant in the second year of the course, and in some cases will be developed in more depth.

APPLY IT

Collect a total of nine print advertisement from three contrasting print publications. Choose either newspapers or magazines for this activity. Learn how profiling techniques such as those used by advertisers, e.g. psychographics and lifestyle profiling, may have been used to target audiences. Make three points for each advert, linking your findings to evidence from semiotic analysis.

For more on technological determinism see Section 3.2.

The Year 1 book took you through how news technologies have changed patterns of media consumption. You considered the major changes undergone in the ways in which we consume traditional media, and you also looked at the growth of gaming and video on the web, as well as the emergence of completely new media such as social media. This category covers a huge range of popular sites including those such as YouTube, whose primary aim is to share content of a particular type such as image or video. You had an early introduction to the idea of technological determinism, as well as globalisation, both of which will be explored in greater depth later in this chapter. The personalisation of digital content, very much linked to the semantic web, was also explored as a very significant factor in the way in which media producers can now actively construct audiences.

After you had considered some of the ways in which producers actively target their audiences, you started to consider the specific ways in which audiences read the media – the reasons why they make the consumption choices they do. You gained an overview of the development and history of the group of approaches known collectively as effects theory. These range from the simple model of the hypodermic syringe, to two-step flow. This model has regained some credibility in recent years for its uses in explaining ways in which social media networks can work.

From this starting point, you began to explore some slightly more complex theories such as social learning theory and cultivation theory. Although it was acknowledged that some effects approaches have their limitations, they also have aspects that can contribute a great deal to the continuing exploration of how much the mass media potentially influences our daily lives. It's important that you remember the contributions that can be made by effects discussions when thinking about the ethical dimensions of the mass media, such as being able to recognise when effects debates are being hijacked to suit specific political agendas.

Having considered some of the more passive theories of audience, you considered more active theories. These theories tend to put the audience's reception of the

Snapchat's shares sank in 2018 following this Tweet from celebrity Kylie Jenner – evidence of anticipation of a contemporary two-step flow response in action.

text at their heart – to consider not only how the media might impact on people's lives in a negative way, but also whether it might be contributing something that actually supported them in modern living and social situations. Uses and gratifications theory, utopian solutions and reception theory are all considered as approaches to understanding the differing ways in which audiences might make use of media texts – to actively use them for a range of purposes that leave them feeling more fulfilled, and the reasons why audiences don't all respond to media texts in the same ways. It's important to understand this year that although we refer to 'active' and 'passive' theories, in fact all can be critically grouped under the umbrella term 'effects debates'.

Lastly, you began to consider the ways in which media audiences are becoming more interactive, and the breakdown of the traditional barrier that exists between media producers and media audiences. This chapter will explore in much greater depth this issue, as you find out more about **participatory media**.

Reaching specialised audiences through different media platforms and technologies and ensuring products fulfil their needs

In the Year 1 book, you considered some of these issues across both the audiences and institutions chapters. One of the huge changes to the ways in which media consumption practices have changed is the way in which the media is no longer 'here today, gone tomorrow'. Today's news was once quickly forgotten. Television broadcasts were similarly ephemeral. This is certainly no longer the case. Internet searches will now easily allow access to digital archives containing hundreds of thousands of old news stories that have been published since the advent of the internet. Television content and films now have an extended life through video players and VoD services, meaning their ratings may increase slowly over a much longer period of time.

The phenomenon of continued access to older media products was referred to in 2004 by Chris Anderson, editor of technology magazine *Wired*, as the **long tail effect**. Media producers are now much more aware of this when they choose which products to create in the first place and what to cover. The long tail may be good news for consumers as it increases the likelihood that niche products, which might never have been made, on the assumption that they wouldn't sell or attract large ratings, are now more likely to be commissioned. This does lead to a fragmentation of popular culture, and it could be said that this fragmentation is actually one of the defining emergent trends of the impact of the digital age on the output of large media organisations in almost every platform. In terms of media audiences, more choice is good news, and could even leads to us to question eventually what we mean by the term 'popular' culture.

APPLY IT

Choose a recently released computer game and collect a range of promotional materials associated with it, including reviews from magazines and YouTube. Write a 300-word case study of the materials, explaining how two-step flow theory could be used to understand the influence of both industry and the intermediary prosumer in promoting games.

YouTube gaming influencers such as Tom Cassel of The Syndicate project can have a measurable impact on sales spikes of the games they choose to showcase.

For more on the development of approaches to audience theories, see Neuman's six stages of effects theory in Section 3.2.

VoD services have contributed hugely to the long tail effect, bringing archived content to new audiences.

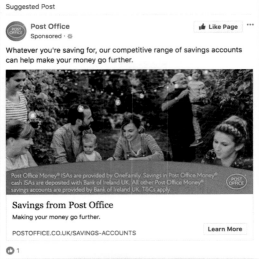

Mainstream companies use social media to advertise as a matter of routine.

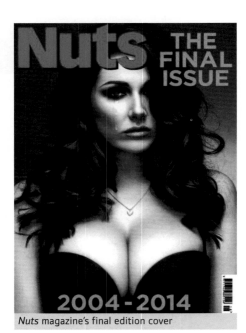

Nuts magazine's final edition cover

In the Year 1 book, you also considered how media producers are increasingly becoming multi-platform, both in terms of diversification in their actual businesses and in harnessing technological convergence. It is much easier now for producers to target specific audiences, as information about their digital behaviours can be easily gathered, sold and exchanged. On the other hand, there is less desire on the part of consumers to part with money for entertainment or information they can obtain elsewhere for free. Faced with the choice of parting with money for a health and lifestyle magazine in print or following a vlogger for free, many young people would choose the digital option today. It is a constant challenge for big media business to ensure that their audiences are targeted in the right platform through digital marketing and guided towards the products that still generate revenue.

Some of the ways in which producers might try to reach specialised audiences include:

- Advertising using social media platforms, where paid-for ads can be tailored to reach some quite specific demographics and focused using clicks for similar products or content.
- Using Google analytics to track who visits their sites and how they interact with content in order to refine it.
- Profiling audiences using statistical information about their use of a service then cross-referencing it with similar consumers who have accessed that content to make targeted suggestions.

Many media producers are also conscious that a move in platform may not be the only change they have to make. Shifts in cultural thinking about issues such as race, gender and sexuality mean that media producers often need to rethink their strategy regarding content. Competition from other leisure activities and forms of media consumption have also taken their toll on some publications, with audiences abandoning some platforms or dropping their consumption to a point where production is no longer economically viable.

This is evident in the case of defunct genre of 'Lad mags' such as *Zoo*, *Nuts*, *FHM* and *Loaded Magazine* that were at the peak of their popularity in the 1990s and early 2000s. They were impacted on by competition from smartphones, internet access and the movement in men's interest towards social media and online content. They also faced social pressure in the form of campaigns to have them withdrawn from sale in some locations or sold with plain wrap over the images of the scantily clad women who often appeared on the front covers. At time of writing there are few men's lifestyle titles left in print that do not explicitly focus on a hobby or interest, such as fitness, sport, gaming or technology. The women's lifestyle magazine sector has also faced challenges, with some titles choosing to go online only and others facing continued decline in circulation.

EXAMPLE: *Vogue*'s recent changes in address to various audiences

Even the best-established brands in the magazine sector have had to adapt with changes in tastes and media usage. *Vogue* magazine has been at the forefront of high-end fashion since its early days as a weekly paper, originally targeting both male and female middle-class New Yorkers.

The British edition of *Vogue* for December 2017 featured a 14-page article about diversity and black Britishness, after being taken over by new editor Edward Enninful. The new editor pledged in this a commitment to representing a more diverse range of women in the magazine itself. The front cover features British model Adwoah Aboah – have a look at it online. Inside the magazine, we find an article by Zadie Smith, 'Mrs Windsor', about the Queen. The issue also features Naomi Campbell interviewing London Mayor Siddiq Khan. In his editor's letter,

Enninful harmonises the ideology of multiculturalism with Britishness and positions the audience to accept it. This is a challenge in an era when debates about cultural integration of a range of ethnic groups are particularly prominent, and Enninful also refers to the divisions caused by the Brexit vote:

> Whatever your views are on Brexit, there is surely one thing we can all agree on: we're a talented bunch. We are also diverse. I hope you will be as gratified as I am to note how many of the amazing names featured on these pages didn't necessarily begin their lives here ... Regardless of where they were born or how they got here ... they all share a huge pride in their homeland, with an outlook that is pleasingly global. (*Vogue*, December 2017, page 69)

In November 2017, Condé Nast also announced that the print edition of *Teen Vogue* would be going and it would be online only. Although reflecting similar economic decisions by other major publishers, *Teen Vogue*'s migration seems more natural as it has a firm online presence already, which is heavily integrated with social media use, forming an ideal intersection with its target audience's tastes and consumption preferences. The US-based magazine has received positive critical attention in recent years for its engagement with issues beyond fashion and beauty, exploring gender politics and issues of inequality as well as retaining some lighter entertainments-centred focus and the core values of style and beauty features.

KEY TERMS

long tail effect/theory	in marketing, the idea that increased accessibility to media for a longer duration due to changes in distribution mechanisms means a product can continue to be consumed beyond its previous marketable shelf-life

participatory media	media that allows not only interaction but also contribution by audience members, blurring the traditional distinction between audience, producer and even 'text'

3.2 Developing your understanding of media effects debates, cultivation theory and reception theory

Mastering media effects debates

One of the issues surrounding some media effects theories is their presumption that audiences are not really aware of media effects but are passive subjects of them. It is therefore very important that you begin to factor in the idea of **media literacy** when understanding how aware of media messages audiences really are. It's important you consider how able they are to properly reflect on and understand their content in context. Media literacy can mean, in the most obvious sense, being taught to read and to critically evaluate the meanings of the media as we do in our subject.

The *Grunwald Declaration on Media Education* was written in 1982, long before proliferation and technological convergence of the digital age or the advent of the internet and social media. It was the outcome of a UNESCO (United Nations Educational, Scientific and Cultural Organisation) summit on Media Education from over 30 years ago. There was an awareness that the world was on the cusp of a media revolution without the knowledge of just how significant that would be for all

In the digital age, high levels of 'screen time' increasingly dominate our leisure time from an early age.

of us. The *Grunwald Declaration* is only a page long, and it can be found at on the UNESCO website (UNESCO, 1982).

Its main points promoting formalised media education are as follows:

- The media is 'omnipresent', with some children spending as much time consuming the media in a week as they do at school.

- The media should neither be denigrated as a pernicious or applauded as a positive influence, but rather appreciated as a key aspect of cultures worldwide.

- New technologies bring more choice in terms of consumption – people need to be able to make sense of what they consume in order to be responsible citizens.

- The mass media has a huge role in the shaping of cultural identity

- Media education should be the collective responsibility of the school, the family and media policy-makers.

- We all need to be prepared for 'living in a world of powerful words, images and sounds. Children and adults need to be literate in all three of these symbolic systems ...'.

Media literacy is vital because it enables people not to take mass media content at face value, but to see it in a broader cultural context and to understand media production as a business, often driven by a profit motive.

In small groups, discuss the following contemporary issues, which all require some level of media literacy to understand. Reflect on your own media literacy and that of people you know. For each one, record two or three of the points which came up in your discussion to share in feedback to the class.

ISSUE 1

Does everyone understand that news agendas mean that some issues attract more coverage than others? Do they understand that the profit motive is driving what appears on the front page of their newspaper? Can they distinguish between real and fake news on social media?

ISSUE 2

Are both male and female consumers aware of the extent to which images of women's bodies and are digitally manipulated to achieve an ideal body shape and perfect skin and hair? Are they aware that some of the body weights or proportions depicted by models are not only rare but can even be unhealthy?

ISSUE 3

Is everyone who plays computer games aware of issues relating to violent content, desensitisation and compassion fatigue? Are gamers really aware of the highly immersive properties of some gameplay modes?

ISSUE 4

Are we aware of the echo-chamber qualities of social media, that we will tend to connect with people with similar views to our own? Do we fully understand that complex algorithms are at work all the time to present us with a world-view and products which align with what we already believe and are likely to like or buy, rather than giving us other perspectives or offering alternatives?

Kim Kardashian herself posted this comparison of raw and doctored images from *Complex* magazine on her personal website.

Many people argue that there is a more general 'literacy' relating to media consumption that can be linked with a broader level of general education, and skills in critical thinking. Do we really have a proper understanding of how the media is constructed and to what end? If we don't get our media literacy from education, where do we get it? How do most media consumers become media-literate? Is it through comparing some media sources with other, more 'legitimate' media? Through an understanding of history, psychology or other academic subjects that foster critical thinking which can then be accessed in an abstract way? These are all important questions in thinking about whether audiences have the critical ability to understand the media-saturated world they inhabit.

Technological determinism and its connections with media effects debates

Technological determinism is an interesting area to explore in relation to media effects, because it considers the relationship between human society and the ways in which it may shape technologies, including media technologies. We can all agree that the effects of internet and digital technologies on our lives have been wide-ranging. Because of this, some subscribers to the theory believe that technology has grown so fast out of capitalist production processes that there has not been sufficient time for societies to adjust to its proliferation. This has been seen before, during a time of huge human social change. The Industrial Revolution brought many social problems and hardships as well as the changes and benefits to lifestyles. These changes and benefits tended to be felt initially by the owners of the means of production, and not the skilled and unskilled workers who performed the labour.

The last huge change our civilisation saw was the Industrial Revolution.

Technological determinism is therefore a controversial theory, and tends to see human society as quite passive in its acceptance and incorporation of technologies into lifestyles. Critics of the theory argue that this is not a simple one-way process. They argue that technologies co-evolve alongside human uses, and there is perhaps a more subtle interplay between technological advancements and the uses to which these are put than the theory appears to suggest. Social uses of technology can be powerful in shaping its effects. The democratisation of the mass media and advent of participatory culture does seem to suggest that the relative ease with which technologies can be harnessed by ordinary people and used in such diverse ways is a benefit, and it has brought many advantages.

Nonetheless, the idea that technologies can powerfully determine aspects of our society and the way we live continues to influence thinking. Dominant ideologies, which may be pro-capitalist, pro-consumption and emphasise the benefits we stand to gain from technology, promote the appearance of increased and more diverse leisure time. Counter-hegemonic ideas and moral panics alike tend to focus on the negative aspects of technology and see it as harmful to our ethical thinking. There seems to be a contradiction at the heart of this – that so many people on all sides of the political debate see technology as a potential threat to so many aspects of our lives, but everyone seems to enjoy using it.

Weekend magazine technology special

'Our minds can be hijacked': the tech insiders who fear a smartphone dystopia

The above-the-fold start of this feature article.

EXAMPLE: Two negative representations of digital media – from the media

Because social media is such a new phenomenon, there is little guidance for any of us on how to use it in a way that is beneficial to us without pitfalls. When compared with traditional media, there is a huge lack of information and knowledge about how social media usage can affect our lives. This example explores how two interesting texts both play on the potentially negative aspects of digital technologies.

The first, an article from the *Guardian*, can be found by searching for 'Our Minds can be Hijacked: The Tech Insiders Who Fear a Smartphone Dystopia' (Lewis, 2017).

The article describes how the tech programmer who invented the Facebook 'Like' button, Justin Rosenstein, is so aware of the addictive properties of social media usage that he has asked his assistant to operate parental controls on his own phone to prevent him from downloading social media apps. He uses the phrase *'bright dings of pseudo-pleasure'* to describe the experience of receiving feedback on a post.

The article describes smartphone usage in very negative terms, raising issues such as *'continuous partial attention'*, also commonly referred to as 'digital distraction' to describe the way in which smartphone usage has impacted on interpersonal communication. It even cites a study that suggests that smartphone usage has a negative impact on levels of intelligence. The term, the *'attention economy'* is used to describe the huge industry that has grown up around social media use, but also its cultural influence and potential impact on identity.

The second text is Moby's video for the song 'Are You Lost in the World Like Me?', animated by Steve Cutts it can be viewed on YouTube. In the video, a small, helpless character styled like a 1920s cartoon is buffeted from one desperate scene to another. Dating apps are represented as shallow and entirely based on looks. A young girl, depressed and miserable, is filtered and becomes smiling and happy as she takes a selfie and uploads it. An accidental bump into someone on a crowded train leads to an explosion of hatred. A young woman is bullied on social media for her dancing and is finally goaded to jump from a building by tormentors who in turn video her leap.

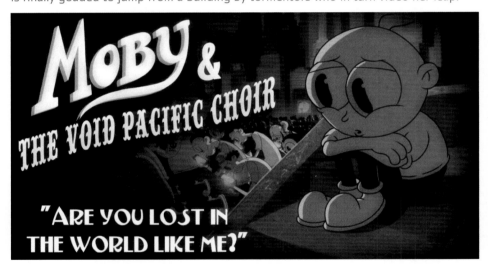

It is hard to watch the video without feeling that digital media has indeed made the world a very frightening place, so strong is the impact of its montage of negative connotations.

The attribution of violent acts to media consumption is a simple social learning model link popular with tabloid front pages.

🔗 For more on models of media effects see pages 102–109 in the Year 1 book.

Models of media effects

In the Year 1 book, you looked at the simpler models of media effects.

If people have lower levels of media literacy, perhaps you might find that they are, in theory, more susceptible to media effects. Early sociological models, such as the simple hypodermic syringe model and Albert Bandura's social learning theory, can be problematic to apply. Nonetheless, the media probably does have some effect on people in all kinds of subtle ways every day. The problem is that these effects can only really be reported as a possibility unless we find examples of large numbers of people who are willing to admit they have been affected by the media. Some effects are always going to be more readily admitted to than others.

Just because media effects are difficult to measure, it doesn't mean that we should dismiss or ignore them. The media is such a large part of our lives it would be naïve to think it doesn't affect us at all – it's just that those effects are very difficult to measure in an objective way. For this reason, many theorists try to find a balance by proposing that short-term exposure to a particular type of media or a certain text is unlikely to cause an effect – but that with long-term exposure the likelihood of an effect occurring increases. This obviously also has issues. Where do we draw the line, at how many hours of exposure, for example? It is almost impossible to design a methodology for such an experiment that could control for other influences. These ideas that consider longer-term exposure are called the cumulative effects theory. Looking at an overview of developments in effects theory is helpful for understanding how different trends have evolved over time, and to help you understand that different elements of effects theory can co-exist.

In Media Studies, you have often drawn a distinction in between 'passive' and more 'active' models of audience theory. In fact, all of them try to identify some kind of effect, even if the effect is that people 'use' the media to some end, such as integrating some of its messages into their own identity or using them in some way to benefit them socially or personally.

The six stages of effects theory: W. Russell Neuman

Neuman attempts to make sense of the progression of effects theories in his essay, 'The Evolution of Media Effects Theory: A Six-Stage Model of Cumulative Research' (Neuman & Guggenheim, 2011). In his article, Neuman argues that many approaches to understanding effects theory tend to oversimplify it. His model is a response to this over-simplification, which makes the development and grouping of the ideas comprehensible for a Media Studies student. His table, originally published in that essay, has been simplified here and an explanation supplied at the level of awareness of their development needed for A level. You will notice that there is overlap between some time periods – many of the theoretical approaches overlap with one another and functioned as concurrent schools of thinking about the issues.

Neuman's six stage model:

APPLY IT

Discuss the six broad categorisations given in the model. Write out a prompt card about each one. You could set these up as six presentation slides, and then print them off six per page and cut them out. Provide:

- Your own definition of the category.
- Its key characteristics (in your own words).
- An example of the theory.

Choose five of the full CSPs you have studied so far on the course. Draw a card at random. Try applying the approach. How suited is it to each of the texts? Draw another and try again. This will help you to gain confidence in understanding not only the different approaches to reading audiences, but variations in their usefulness when applied to real-world examples.

Historical stage	Example	Characteristics
1 Persuasion theories 1944–1963	Social learning	• Audience modelling of behaviours • Direct effects
2 Active audience theories 1944–1986	Uses and gratifications [Utopian solutions also fits well here, although it is later in origin – 1990s]	• Still assume direct transmission of messages • Don't really account for social position of audience members
3 Social Context theories 1955-1983	Two-step flow	• Focus more on social contexts of consumption • Take into account individual social interactions and how messages are diffused
4 Societal and media theories 1933–1978	Cultural hegemony Cultivation theory	• Cumulative media effects over a long period of time • Associated with political views and perspectives
5 Interpretative effects theories 1972–1987	Agenda setting Priming Framing	• Assessment of media effects and research into responses to media messages • Assess attitudes thought to result directly from media influence
6 New media theories 1996–	Computer-mediated communication [Jenkins and Shirky could also be potentially grouped here]	• Focus on new technologies and their interactive properties • Still evolving as a field

Stanley Cohen: *Folk Devils and Moral Panics*

Cohen's influential book, *Folk Devils and Moral Panics*, was first published in 1972. Since then, the preface has been updated a number of times by the author. In the 2002 edition, he cites a number of contemporary moral panics that can be explored using his idea which were not around at the time of the first edition.

Cohen discusses an interesting dimension to the relationship between the mass media's coverage of an issue (this was at a time when the mass media had arguably an even greater influence than today) and perceptions of risk in society. This is relevant to our understanding of newspaper coverage, because it describes a negative dimension to the relationship between people's understanding of the nature of how newspapers represent reality.

Cohen explores the ways in which the mass media can create 'folk devils' – people who act as a locus for people's fears in society. These folk devils in a contemporary sense can be located in a single personality – for example, Kim Jong-Un. The way in which they are represented often borders on the grotesque, and is overly-exaggerated and simplified. They might also be more generalised – a section of society who are perceived as threatening to mainstream values or actual physical safety, such as terrorists.

Cohen also identifies what he termed a 'moral panic' that could be in part instigated or perpetuated by the tabloid press in particular. In the case of a moral panic, the population as a whole or in part may become hypersensitive to an issue. Its currency then leads to further reporting in the press, which appears to make the risk or threat posed by the original story greater in people's minds than the real-world risk posed by the source of it. The stages of a moral panic were identified by Cohen as:

1 Something or someone is defined as a threat to values or interests.
2 This threat is depicted in an easily recognisable form by the media.
3 There is a rapid build-up of public concern.
4 There is a response from authorities or opinion makers.
5 The panic recedes or results in social changes.

Moral panics are also significant because they involve not only the media and public perceptions, but also the response of authorities to an issue. Aspects of a moral panic were defined by Erich Goode and Ben Nehuda in *Moral Panics: The Social Construction of Deviance* (1994) in the following way, and this update is acknowledged by Cohen in the preface to the 2002 edition of his original book:

• Concern – an issue is identified as a problem for society.
• Hostility – the issue is perceived as a threat to the fabric of society.
• Consensus – the story is presented in such a way that suggests everyone agrees the issue is a threat.
• Disproportionality – the facts relating to the issue may be distorted, misrepresented or fail to be properly contextualised.
• Volatility – the issue is seen as one that can flare up at short notice – the idea also that it can happen anywhere and affect anyone.

There is a sense, then, that moral panics are a very influential and important consideration when assessing the effects of the media both on people's views of the society they live in. They may also have a powerful effect on institutions and governing/policy-making. This is similar to George Gerbner's findings about television, which you explored in your study of cultivation theory in the Year 1 book, which is worth revisiting at this point.

Kim Jong-Un is a contemporary example of a folk devil.

For more on Gerbner's findings see pages 104–105 of the Year 1 book.

A double-page spread moral panic over games addiction from the *Sun* newspaper shown in an online counter-article at Den of Geek.

EXAMPLE: Reportage of shark attacks – modelling a moral panic

Shark attacks globally are considered to be newsworthy, partly because shark attacks resulting in death or life-changing injuries are thankfully rare. Although not an example of a 'moral' panic, looking at one story about such an event shows exactly the kinds of problem that can be encountered when news sources demonise a particular threat to society. Sharks are represented as monsters – there is a synchronising between cultural myth of the shark as a threat to luxury water-based lifestyles and a rise in its negative media image and exaggeration of the threat it poses to humans.

Sharks are a convenient axis of a narrative that asserts the right of humans to control the sea and to use it for leisure. Much as the wolf was first persecuted and then eradicated from large parts of mainland Europe, so legislative approaches such as the use of shark nets and culling have tried to keep areas of the sea which are used for leisure in countries like Australia shark-free.

A Sky News interview with a shark attack victim available to watch on YouTube, called 'Surviving a Shark Attack'.

Here is how the issue can be used to model the stages of a moral panic:

1 The shark is identified as a threat to humans' water-based leisure activities such as surfing, diving, spearfishing, etc.

2 The media reports on shark attacks where serious injuries or deaths occur.

3 People who visit holiday destinations or live near the areas are put off using the water, potentially damaging tourism and the local economy.

4 Local authorities respond with measures such as barriers, culling and surveillance programmes.

5 The panic relating to sharks recedes in that area, only to be revived when another high-profile media story breaks.

On 23 October 2017, the BBC News site reported on a UK tourist's apparent lucky escape from a predatory tiger shark while on a boat trip in Australia. The story is not even the story of a shark attack – but of a spearfishing diver who is represented as having had a narrow escape from injury or death. It is ironic that spearfishing itself is probably a far greater threat to sharks than sharks pose to humans. The article, called 'UK Diver Swims to Safety after Australia Shark Scare', can be found on the BBC News website.

The article concludes:

> *Tiger sharks are responsible for the second-highest number of reported attacks on humans, according to the International Shark Attack File.*

APPLY IT

Identify three moral panics and/or folk devils you think are prevalent in contemporary culture. Find at least two front-page tabloid news articles or internet news stories from tabloid news sites that cover the issue.

1 How is it represented?

2 Can you think of any problems of representation in the way in which the issue is reported?

3 How does the mode of address and other aspects of semiotic analysis support a preferred reading that suggests consensus and signifies concern?

4 Which wider societal values seem to be connected with the issue?

Present your ideas in a gridded format, using the questions above as headings.

APPLY IT

Consider another issue where a cultivation effect of cumulative exposure might in theory affect perceptions or world view.

However, clicking on the link included at the end of the article takes us to the Florida Museum's website, which could be regarded as a reliable factual source as it specialises in record keeping relating to shark attacks. The number of recorded attacks by tiger sharks is 111. This sounds quite dramatic, until we realise that the record keeping goes back to 1580. This means that there have been fewer than 0.2 injuries per year worldwide – this does not even count fatal attacks – caused by tiger sharks since recording of these events began. In this case the media reporting of the story, while not inaccurate, represents the tiger shark as posing a serious threat to human safety when the statistics do not bear this out.

The problem with both moral panics and folk devils is that they can lead to vigilantism and grossly exaggerate the threats posed. They may come from highly conservative ideological standpoints and can often be considered to be moralising, and frequently misrepresent the facts of a complex issue which deserves serious exploration by simplifying the aspects of it that best fit a narrow, sensationalist news agenda.

Mastering cultivation theory

In the Year 1 book, you explored Gerbner's cultivation theory. This included the idea of a **cultivation differential** – how much someone's world view and perception of their social reality aligned with television is based on how heavy their consumption was. You looked at mainstreaming, the gradual aligning of ideologies based on shared media viewing, and resonance – the magnification of the impact of television when events it depicts seem to mirror the social reality of viewers. This in turn could lead to an increase in mean world syndrome – the impression that the world is a far more dangerous place than it actually is. Gerbner's original work was based on crime reporting and people's perceptions of the world as a place fraught with danger. However, cultivation theory can be applied much more broadly to explore other issues and identify possible effects from these.

EXAMPLE

Female nutrition, wellness and fitness bloggers are an example of how both moral panics and cultivation effects can be observable in social commentary and news articles based on this genre of contemporary digital media. These personalities are accused of a range of social ills, from promoting imbalanced diets and unrealistic body image to outright fraud.

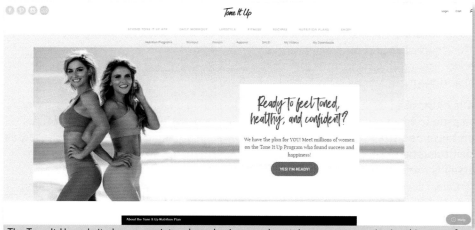

The Tone It Up website has grown into a huge business and contains numerous aspirational images of its founders to promote its products and services.

Associated with a cultivation approach are some other ideas that we can explore more here – the role of the media in socialisation and enculturation. Since most of us are exposed to the mass media from birth, it is assumed that it plays a contributory role in shaping our values and ideas about our culture alongside other influences such as family, education and peer groups. The media can provide role models for identity formation and circulate cultural myths in ways we are receptive to.

John Fiske, who you will be learning more about later in this chapter, identifies what he referred to as a **bardic function** played by television in our culture. He argues that television simply fulfils an ancient role in society but in technological guise. He likens the role of television to that of a medieval bard, whose function was to tell stories in poetic form for their patrons, and to structure and organise ideas about what was relevant to people living in that time. Bards were influenced by all kinds of sources. They blended conflicting ideas, scraps of mythology, with nods to present fashions and trends. Through these texts, ideas which engrossed the audience could be produced and old content made to feel relevant. Crucially, the bard was not a representative of authority but a mediator, in the way we might view television today.

Fiske also used the term **clawback** to define the way in which television can give a sense of recognition of the self and cultural identity, the way in which television can function to make issues relevant once again to our own individual reality and experience of our culture. Texts that use clawback may take a character whose situation or aspects of identity might make them lack power in the real world, and then represents them as significant in the text, therefore 'clawing back' their place in society.

Fiske found television to fulfil the equivalent modern role of the bard in the Middle Ages.

Agenda setting

Agenda setting is connected with the conditions of reception, since it attempts to steer the reader towards the hegemonic reading of the text. If expectations are established in the mind of the audience about what they expect to see, this makes the conditions of reception more fertile. The theory of agenda setting was first applied to the political uses of the mass media in covering election campaigns. This suggests that the media appeared to have an influence over people's perceptions of the campaign. Its creators, Maxwell McCombs and Donald Shaw, compared news coverage of election campaigns with research into what people when interviewed perceived as the most important aspects of the campaign. They found a high degree of correlation between the two.

Since most people's only source of information about politics is the news media, it could be proposed that the media was literally setting the agenda of what is important. This theory therefore views the media as actively selecting certain issues and shaping public opinion of these by reporting on them more frequently. This aggregative effect happens because only a small proportion of people who encounter political stories pay much attention to them – the rest is picked up by the majority simply because it is something they've seen or heard frequently.

It is interesting to correlate agenda setting with news values, since people will tend to pick up more stories that affect them – and news producers will tend to report on these because they encourage more sales or improve ratings if people feel that the issues being covered in the news – particularly political news reporting – actually affect them.

Framing

Framing is a concept that is linked with agenda setting. Framing is more about the content of a story – its bias and the way in which it is read by the audience according to their own interests and situation. Rather than the ease of accessibility that agenda setting focuses on, framing shifts this focus to how the individual can make sense of the issue or story – and how it is presented to them in a way that easily facilitates this. Framing means that we tend to interpret news stories according to factors which have already shaped out life experience. They determine how applicable it is to them rather than just how accessible the story is.

Lastly, we need to consider the **conditions of consumption**. It matters whether the media is being used in a social way, or if it is consumed alone. When we consume media with others, we subconsciously modify our view of it when discussing it with others. This effect may also be seen on social media. We need to think about whether we are giving a media text our whole attention, as in the case of solus media use – this is becoming a rarer condition of consumption – or not. For example, we might decide to sit down and 'devote' our evening to watching an episode of a favourite television programme – the reality for most of us, however, is that we might be engaging with or interrupted by social media while we do so. Does the divided attention we experience mean we miss the complexity of some media texts – or miss out on some layers of meaning? Is it different watching something on different devices? In the case of radio or podcasts, are listeners giving them their whole attention or dipping in and out of texts while doing other things? Does it matter what kind of device we view texts on? If 24-hour news is always on in the background on a screen in a workplace, are employees more susceptible to cultivation effects? Are people watching something because it's a scheduled broadcast, or have they sought the text out specifically to view at a time suited to them – and how many of the texts will they consume in one sitting. Do we watch something because it was advertised to us, or because we know others are watching it? Think about how this affects the level of power media messages have to potentially influence us.

EXAMPLE: How much do the public trust their news sources?

In 2013, a poll was conducted for the BBC by Ipsos Mori. A thousand 'nationally representative' people were questioned about the trustworthiness of the BBC as a news source compared with other sources.

The BBC scored significantly above any other news outlet available in the UK, with 58% of the population trusting the news they saw reported on BBC programmes. It's an interesting survey, because perhaps rather than showing the comparative trustworthiness, it actually shows the wide consumption of BBC news by a range of individuals who also consume other media but would not necessarily take those other media at face value.

Since 'one source' is stated alongside 'trustworthiness', this does not mean that people are not taking away messages from other news sources and absorbing other media organisations' agendas – it just means that when reliability is at hand, the BBC is the most popular choice. You also need to bear in mind that the access to BBC content is free, and universal in the UK to anyone who has a television set or internet connection.

So, does this tell us anything about agenda setting? The BBC clearly has a great deal of power to set political agendas, and this was seen in the 2017 election, when rows erupted time and time again over perceived political bias at the BBC in favour of the Conservative Party. If people are not conscious of agendas being set, then they are only able to take their news at face value – the effect of the presentation of a story may be cumulative, but if it comes from a trusted source, this may make the message that bit more powerful.

Interestingly, if we look at the issue of bias and partiality, the BBC also scores the lowest for perceived bias, with tabloid newspapers and social networking at the other end of the scale. However, on a scale of 1–10 there is only around three points of difference between the highest and lowest scores, meaning that while people tended to rate the level of bias as less from television news outlets, there was not a huge gap in perceptions, and that there was an awareness of the issue of bias across the board. Again, if we're thinking about agenda setting, this matters very little. The news issues have to be selected first before people even get a chance to consciously consider how those stories are being presented to them – so, regardless of whether they 'believe' news stories or not, they have already had the content of their media consumption selected for them.

The BBC is the news source that the public say they trust the most.

Of all the news sources, which one are you most likely to turn to for news you trust the most?

- BBC: 58%
- ITV: 14%
- Sky News: 6%
- Guardian: 2%
- Channel 4: 2%
- Al Jazeera: 1%
- Daily Telegraph: 1%
- Google News: 1%
- Independent: 1%
- The Times: 1%
- Channel 5: 1%
- Daily Mail: 1%
- Other: 4%
- Don't know: 3%
- None: 6%

Source: Ipsos MORI. UK adults 16+ who follow the news (1,873) interviewed face-to-face, February 2013. Newspapers include Sunday editions.

APPLY IT

A good way of understanding both framing and agenda setting is to look at the front pages of a range of news sources on a single day. These might include two or three newspapers, two different news broadcasts (e.g. Sky News and Channel 4) and two news sites, such as the BBC and *HuffPost* (UK). Explore the way in which different news stories are sequenced in the agenda, positioned and framed. Consider what assumptions are being made about issues such as the audience's political views, their prior knowledge of the story, their understanding of international events and so on.

Mastering reception theory

In Year 1, we looked at the idea of a preferred reading (sometimes called the dominant or hegemonic reading) of a text, and the negotiated and the oppositional readings. This theory, written about by Stuart Hall, explores the possibility that different audience members make different meanings from the texts they consume. It considers the processes that can happen and the space between the encoded meaning of the text and the decoding that happens on 'reception'. It's an excellent way into understanding the polysemic nature of texts, and to explaining differences between audience tastes and choices in media consumption. It's important that you continue to use reception theory as a way of differentiating between different attitudinal readings of texts and to align these ideas with semiotic theory.

Hall's theory is relatively easy to grasp but using it sensitively and appropriately can be tricky as, for some students, there is a tendency to over-simplify or to misapply the negotiated reading. Since there can be all kinds of negotiated reading, you need to make sure that you really understand what's going on and are not too definitive, since the polysemic nature of texts dictates that there could be a wide variation in possible negotiated readings.

Reception theory states that a range of responses to a text is possible depending on the conceptual map of the person consuming the text.

APPLY IT

Find an interesting example of an advertisement, in any media platform, which has proved controversial for their producers. Why do you think the preferred reading was not accepted by so many of the audience? Try to link your ideas to semiotic evidence.

Now find an example of an advertisement that sets out deliberately to shock, as these tend to have been read in the preferred way – although the impact may be greater than was anticipated by the producers of the text. How do issues of taste and decency impact on whether we accept a preferred reading or cross the line into a negotiated or oppositional reading?

EXAMPLE: Gap Kids online advert, April 2016 and Alex Upton, a historical Barnardo's print advert

The Gap advertisement caused a great deal of public debate when it appeared online and many users used social media to express their oppositional reading of the text.

The hegemonic reading of the advertisement, argued that Gap Kids was a message of diversity and inclusivity. However, the 'inclusion' of only one child from an ethnic minority and her positioning, being leaned on by a much taller white girl, were both read in an oppositional way by many in the audience, who accused the company of both tokenism and racism.

Barnardos' advertisements have historically been controversial and often used shock tactics to draw attention to their message. In the Alex Upton advert, an implied link between child abuse and neglect and adult criminality is made. A young boy is dead in the street, a sawn-off shotgun lying beside him, apparently killed in an armed police response to an event. The hegemonic reading of the advert sends a strong message of empathy for the child and positions the audience to believe that bigger problems that affect many in society could be tackled if children were better cared for. An oppositional reading might reject the link between the two issues, with some audience members perhaps feeling that criminality is more connected with individual morality than social problems. A negotiated reading might fall somewhere between the two positions, or perhaps accept the ideological link but feel the tactics of the advertisers are manipulative. The sensitivity of the use of a child model in such grim circumstances could also lead to another unintended oppositional reading – rejection of the message due to issues of taste, decency and even exploitation.

KEY TERMS

agenda setting	theory relating mainly to news media that views the media as actively selecting certain issues and shaping public opinion of these by reporting on them more frequently
bardic function	the modern role of television in our lives as an aggregator of many different ideas and cultural influences
clawback	the way in which television can give a sense of recognition of the self and cultural identity, our experience of our culture
conditions of consumption	a wide range of factors that can affect how a media text is interpreted by the audience, both in terms of ideological reception and physical consumption practices

cultivation differential	how much someone's world view and perception of their social reality aligns with television is based on their level of consumption
cumulative effects theory	collective term for audience theories that consider longer-term exposure to media texts
framing	a news story's bias and the way in which it is read by the audience according to their own interests and situation
media literacy	the level of awareness of the audience about factors affecting the production of meaning in media texts

3.3 How audiences use media in different ways, reflecting aspects of demographics, identity and cultural capital

Demographics and psychographics

In the Year 1 book, you considered demographics and psychographics as profiling tools that are used by media producers. You looked at how media producers use organisations such as the National Readership Survey to gain insight into who is buying their magazines and to sell their advertising space to the right kinds of advertiser. You learned about the ways in which audiences for other sectors of traditional media such as the Broadcasters' Audience Research Board (BARB) and Radio Joint Audience Research (RAJAR) measure the performance of individual programmes and channels or stations with audiences.

Demographics means the simpler measures of difference between audience members such as where they live, their gender and their age.

Psychographics was also explored as a way of understanding some of the more complex ways in which consumers can be understood. In this book, we'll be looking more closely at some of the more subtle and complex ways in which audiences may identify themselves, rather than focusing as much on how they are constructed, categorised and targeted by producers.

So, how do audiences view their own participation in media consumption? How do they see the relationship between the media and their own lives? It's likely that demographics play a role in this – the perception, for example, that a media production is made for a particular gender may either actively discourage or encourage someone to feel it's addressing them. But what other factors might be at work?

David Gauntlett and identity

The issue of media identities forms an overlap between two of the areas of the theoretical framework, audiences and representations. In the Year 1 book, you considered the ideas of **David Gauntlett** in terms of representations and how people read these in relation to their own identity. Here you'll be considering his ideas with more of an emphasis on the audience themselves, and how they negotiate their identities in relation to media content.

A great introduction to a more developed understanding of David Gauntlett's ideas is to repeat his Lego experiment. This experiment asked people to construct a version of their identity in order to challenge the notion that people perceived their identity as a fragmented concept. He aimed to show that people had little difficulty in perceiving their identity as a whole comprised of differing elements. You may wish to try out the Apply It activity that follows before reading on, in order to get the most from the experiment.

Gauntlett's Lego experiment uses the building toy as a way of understanding how people represent themselves, and to establish how they see their identity through their own explanations. What they actually build is not particularly important – it is the accounts of the model-makers that are most valuable in understanding how people perceive their own identities. Gauntlett uses the activity as a springboard to test not only his own ideas about identity, but those that have gone before. In the Year 1 book, you had a brief introduction to some of these.

For more on demographics see Chapter 5 of the Year 1 book.

For more on David Gauntlett see pages 105–106 of the Year 1 book.

If you have access to some Lego or building bricks, you could try out Gauntlett's activity for yourself. Allow one hour to build a model of your own identity. Photograph your model and keep it in your notes. Reflect on what it says about your own identity.

If you don't have access to Lego or building bricks, try writing an introduction to yourself in the third person as a character in a book – or creating a collage of images and words that represent your identity. There are many ways of exploring the aspects of cultural and personal identity that are meaningful to you.

Which aspects appeared on the model, image or in the writing? Which didn't? Why? Was it because they were too hard to recreate, or because they were less important aspects of yourself? What made it into your symbolic projection of your identity? Personality? Personal history? Hobbies? Hopes and dreams for the future?

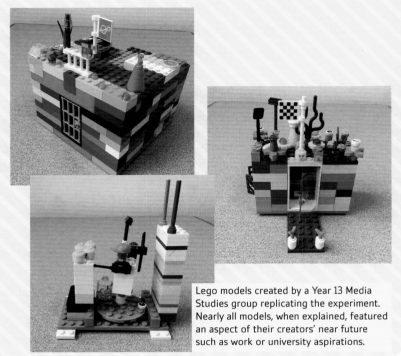

Lego models created by a Year 13 Media Studies group replicating the experiment. Nearly all models, when explained, featured an aspect of their creators' near future such as work or university aspirations.

Gauntlett found the experiment appeared to disprove the idea that identities are a fragmentary phenomenon and that we don't have a single clear idea of what our identity is. People taking part in the Lego experiment almost always build a whole model with different parts or dimensions, for which they are able to explain the links between without any difficulty. This is the case even when elements of their lives seem contradictory, and this is relatively easily absorbed into the task as a whole.

People do not encounter difficulties in building an outwards representation of their identity, suggesting that the concept of identity is readily understood by anyone. Gauntlett compares this with the familiar practice of sticking posters, mementoes and photographs on bedroom walls, a pin board or a fridge. It's interesting that teenagers traditionally have particularly enjoyed using bedroom walls and pin boards to express their identity at a time when doing so is a crucial statement of who they 'are', or who they wish to become. This habit could logically be progressed to understand how many teenagers display their identity on social media.

The relevance of the experiment to studying the relationship of the mass media with identity was that the mass media is less of a direct influence than we might think on identity formation, although it is likely the media provides us with a set of narratives that we use alongside other information to express them. Since audiences are made up of individuals and individuals are complicated, you need to be careful about how much we believe media representations actually affect our sense of identity compared with other influences – the participants in the study made little reference to the mass media when exploring their own sense of self in relation to the outside world. This means that media texts on their own cannot be read without understanding what people actively 'do' with them in the real world, which seems to support a constructionist view of media texts as well as a range of active theories of audience.

Teenagers' bedroom decor has always been a common place where expression of identity can be seen.

Interestingly, Gauntlett himself has reflected on how his ideas about identities and their complexity have changed in a summary of the final points of a presentation he gave at the BFI Media Studies conference in July 2017. This was published on his blog, and was called '"Theories of Identity" in the New Media Studies A & AS Level'. In it he says:

> *Theories of identity* [associated with representation] *from me would be the ideas around:*
>
> → *People having a route to self-expression, and therefore a stronger sense of self and participation in the world, through making & exchanging online*
>
> → *Media* [made by all of us] *... can be places of conversation, exchange, and transformation*
>
> → *a fantastically messy set of networks filled with millions of sparks – some igniting new meanings, ideas, and passions, and some just fading away.*
>
> → *The need for better 'platforms for creativity'*
>
> *So it's still the idea of people building their own sense of self-identity, but through everyday creative practice.*
>
> *I say it's 'still the idea of ...' because I mean that in* Media, Gender and Identity, *a decade or more ago, I was talking about people building their own sense of self-identity in the ways they selected and used different kinds of media in their lives; and then, what we are talking about now is still the idea of people building their own sense of self-identity, but through everyday creative practice.*

This shows you how you must always consider changes in the mass media and how the changes impact on broader notions of the relationship between media representations and identities, which are subject to flux and are a constantly changing means of technological expression.

There are a number of key terms in identity theory you need to be confident in using when discussing issues relating to representation and identity:

- **Fluidity of identity**: this idea, currently a key component of critical thinking about identity, suggests that people do not have a fixed identity that is wholly and permanently a part of them, with only superficial changes being constructed by that individual. Where this seems to be the case, this is perhaps because people have willingly chosen a part, for example, of their cultural identity and subsumed it as a dominant feature of their personal identity. There is a strong groundswell of critical thinking from a range of disciplines that suggests there is a big influence from society as a whole that affects how aspects of our identity are expressed according to mainstream norms and values. The idea that identity is fluid informs a lot of contemporary critical thinking about gender.

For more on gender fluidity and gender as performance see Judith Butler, page 55.

- **Constructed identity**: the mass media constructs identities in the representations it offers us – many theorists believe that we then assimilate various aspects of these in building our own identities, which we may then display in various ways – for example, through online group memberships or mainstream social media. In his 2008 book, *Media Gender, Identity*, Gauntlett is particularly interested in the ways in which gender identities are constructed in media texts that target one gender in particular – for example, men's and women's magazines. He considered that these constructed identities may have a subtle influence through repetition on people's sense of self and the way they express their identity.

- **Negotiated identity**: refers to the ways in which we negotiate the various influences on our composite identities and relate to others in relationships – how we perceive ourselves in relation to others. The idea of identity negotiation is active in the fields of sociology and psychology, but has currency also in

Media Studies because you can use it to try and understand how we relate not only to real, present 'others' in society but also the constructions of other identities seen in the media, whether fiction or fact-based.

- **Collective identity**: media representations and fandoms, or the sense of belonging to a sector of a media audience, form just one factor in the construction of individual identity. In general, in media theory the phenomenon of collective identity is widely accepted as the sense of belonging to an audience for a media product, drawing on ideas often repeated in active theories of audience such as Dyer's community pleasure within utopian solutions, or the social relationships aspect of uses and gratifications. Gauntlett believes that people easily navigate the identities available for them to choose from in the media – assuming some and rejecting others – but that the media is only one influence of many on their lives.

Pierre Bourdieu and cultural capital

Bourdieu's model works on two axes and is closely allied with the idea of social privilege attained through capitalist class system. It is a neo-Marxist theory, as it critiques the way in which capitalist society allows the movement of some people up social rankings within the class system, while others are held back. Essentially, Bourdieu see what he refers to as cultural capital as the ability to mix in higher levels of society because education has given you qualifications, ownership of cultural products or access to works of culture – a frame of reference that includes familiarity with and appreciation of aspects of high culture such as music, art and literature.

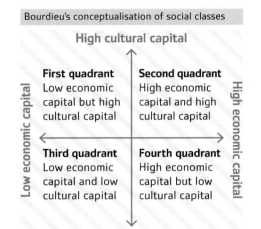

Bourdieu's conceptualisation of social classes

High cultural capital

Low economic capital / High economic capital

First quadrant
Low economic capital but high cultural capital

Second quadrant
High economic capital and high cultural capital

Third quadrant
Low economic capital and low cultural capital

Fourth quadrant
High economic capital but low cultural capital

Low cultural capital

Source: F.P.A. Demeterio III (2003) The Grammar of Class Conflicts in Philippine Electoral Process and the Task of Filipino Philosophy

Bourdieu identified three types of cultural capital:

- **Embodied cultural capital**: the acquired knowledge of culture experienced and outwardly presented by a person.
- **Objectified cultural capital**: can be classed as something like a work of art or some other cultural artefact, such as a valuable musical instrument, which confers status on the person who owns it, and can be transferred to someone else. Its significance must be understood by way of embodied cultural capital by the other person if the material symbol is transferred.
- **Institutionalised cultural capital**: recognised qualifications that symbolise someone's worth in terms of cultural capital, and can be used to gain higher employment status or accumulation of material wealth.

John Fiske, who you will read more about in the next section, argues that Bourdieu's categories of art, music and literature can be expanded to include art house film and cultural practices such as fashion, elite brand awareness and choices of travel destination/types of holiday, food and so on. We could, in a sense, think of Bourdieu's cultural capital in modern terms as middle-class 'tastes' and education.

The way in which a person displays their cultural capital is the habitus. The habitus is the way in which a person has been socialised and interacts with the world according to their education, social class and so on – ways of expressing the self or engaging with the world. These are acquired and passed on in culture from those around us, so are important as signifiers of social class and tastes and also act to reinforce these. The habitus can be a combination of the presence or lack of all three types of cultural capital – embodied, objectified and institutionalised. It's really interesting to cross-refer Bourdieu's ideas and the later discussion we'll be having about fan culture with what you have already learned about identity. In a sense, your media consumption forms part of your habitus and therefore your identity.

TRADITIONAL WORKING CLASS: contains more older members than other classes but also scores low on all forms of the three capitals. They are not the poorest group.

TECHNICAL MIDDLE CLASS: a less culturally engaged new class with high economic capital. Small in numbers, they have relatively few social contacts.

ESTABLISHED MIDDLE CLASS: not quite elite but members of this class have high levels of all three capitals. They are a gregarious and culturally engaged class.

PRECARIAT: the poorest and most deprived class in Britain. With low levels of economic, cultural and social capital, everyday lives of members of this class are precarious.

EMERGENCY SERVICE WORKERS: young and often found in urban areas, this new class has low economic capital but has high levels of 'emerging' cultural capital and high social capital.

NEW AFFLUENT WORKERS: generally young and active, members have medium levels of economic capital and higher levels of cultural and social capital.

ELITE: this is the most privileged class in Great Britain who have high levels of all three capitals. Their high amount of economic capital sets them apart from everyone else.

The *Independent*'s illustration of new British social classes expressed in terms of the varying levels of social, economic and cultural capital.

Cultural capital is important because it allows people to move freely in the upper levels of society where those tastes are shared – where people have similar cultural capital. Economic capital, the accumulation of material wealth, is described as falling into different sectors – so someone can have low cultural capital – be a professional person but disinterested in the arts and high cultural products, and this person would be distinguished from someone who possesses both economic and cultural capital. It is possible to have low economic capital but still be higher in cultural capital.

EXAMPLE: BBC4 and cultural capital

There are ways in which cultural capital is promoted through two niche BBC services: BBC Radio 4 and BBC4 television, which is available on Freeview. Both these stations aim to cross Bourdieu's cultural axis by making higher cultural capital available for free at point of access to anyone. Since anyone can watch its scheduled content, it is accessed by people who fit into both the first and second quadrant in Bourdieu's model. There are some drama series and comedy shows with higher entertainment values than the documentaries the channel is particularly renowned for, which might encourage viewing by those from the third and fourth quadrants. Historically, the BBC was associated with quality programming, and commercial television – represented by ITV – was seen as more entertainments-driven and therefore lower in its address to high cultural capital.

Hedd Wyn, subject of one of the BBC4 documentaries

BBC4 Schedule, Sunday 12 November 2017, 7pm till late:

Time	Programme	Description of programme from website
19.00	*Only Connect*	Quiz show presented by Victoria Coren Mitchell. The Meeples and Belgophiles return for tonight's round-two game.
19.30	*University Challenge*	It is the last of the two highest-scoring loser matches tonight when two teams get another chance to make it to the second round. Jeremy Paxman asks the questions.
20.00	*Hedd Wyn: The Lost War Project*	The story of Hedd Wyn is one of Wales's enduring tragedies. A young man with little or no education succeeds in winning The Chair, one of the main literary prizes at the National Eisteddfod, but is killed in WWI before he could claim his prize. To mark the centenary of his death, National Poet of Wales Ifor ap Glyn reassesses Wyn's life and work.
21.00	*Shark*	The first programme shows how sharks are the ocean's great predators, living in every ocean and hunting in every way. Blacktip sharks hunt in huge packs and herd fish into baitballs, tasselled wobbegongs are ambush hunters, Greenland sharks live under the arctic ice, and whitetip reef sharks are the masters of hunting at night.
22.00	*The Sky at Night*	This month The Sky at Night explores this world of transient phenomena. We hear more about the explosive event that created the recently detected gravitational wave – the collision of two neutron stars. And Chris spends 24 hours at the SWIFT space telescope base in Leicester in an attempt to detect a gamma ray burst – the most powerful and extreme short-term event known.
22.30	*Horizon: Strange Signals from Outer Space!*	For decades some have suspected that there might be others out there, intelligent beings capable of communicating with us, even visiting our world. It might sound like science fiction, but today scientists from across the globe are scouring the universe for signals from extraterrestrials.
23.30	*I Was There: The Great War Interviews*	In the early 1960s, the BBC interviewed 280 eyewitnesses of the First World War for the series, The Great War. Using never-before-seen footage from these interviews, this film illuminates the poignant human experience of the war, through the eyes of those who survived it.
00.30	*War of Words: Soldier-Poets of the Somme*	The 1916 Battle of the Somme remains the most famous battle of World War I, remembered for its bloodshed and its limited territorial gains. What is often overlooked, however, is the literary importance of the Somme: more writers and poets fought in it than in any other battle in history.
02.00	*Ballet-boyz: Dance film about Young men Brought Together by the Brutality of War*	A group of young men brought together by the indiscriminate brutality of war struggle to maintain their humanity in an unending cycle of combat and death. A potent combination of music and choreography, this film without words is an immersive emotional journey into the reality facing young men at the extremes of human experience.
03.00	*Shark*	*See previous entry.*

APPLY IT **Can you think of any other media products whose consumption is associated with people who have higher cultural capital? Create a case study of a media product or outlet that you believe appeals to consumers who have high cultural capital, regardless of whether they fit into the first or second quadrant. Consider too the interplay of social class and politics here – for example, the *Guardian* might be more likely to be read by people in the first quadrant, whereas the *Telegraph* might have a higher readership among the second quadrant.**

Bourdieu's theory refers primarily to high culture, as mass or popular culture is not seen as part of cultural capital. Mass entertainment is produced for a mass audience, the majority of whom will have a low to middle socio-economic status. However, there are numerous interesting ways in which we can see his ideas could be adapted to interpret modern audiences – some theorists argue that models of popular cultural consumption actually replicate this model.

Objectified cultural capital could be seen as being present in ownership of technologies, particularly higher-status brands of electronic goods and services, which allows a differentiation in level of access to differing degrees of 'quality' in popular culture. It is apparent that there is a divide in ownership between technological haves and have-nots in UK society, with economic poverty in particular producing a divide in access to digital culture and the information age. Henry Jenkins referred to this idea as the participatory gap.

Connected with this is the issue of cultural poverty – where people may have access to material goods and high-status technological gadgetry, but have little connectivity to traditional cultural capital in the way in which these devices are used. These people could have been placed in Bourdieu's model in the fourth quadrant, but this is not necessarily the case – consumer culture is a powerful influence in our society, and many families will spend a high proportion of a lower-end income on access to technology, partly perhaps due to an awareness of the participatory gap.

Institutionalised cultural capital can be seen in the level of knowledge needed to access some aspects of modern technology – the technological literacy and knowing of the digital native. These are all interesting debates and ideas for you to try out in thinking about how media audiences are being constructed by producers – is there a prestige associated with the consumption of some media products? Does this demonstrate the view that popular culture and fan culture have hierarchies that replicate the principles of cultural and economic capital as described by Bourdieu?

⊃ See more in Section 3.4 about participatory culture

KEY TERMS

collective identity	sense of ownership of media representations and fandoms or the sense of belonging to a sector of a media audience	cultural poverty	social condition where consumers may have access to material goods and high-status technological gadgetry, but little connection with traditional cultural capital in the way in which these devices are used	institutionalised cultural capital	recognised qualifications that symbolise someone's worth in terms of cultural capital
constructed identity	the view that the mass media constructs identities in the representations it offers us			negotiated identity	ways in which we negotiate the various influences on our composite identities – how we perceive ourselves in relation to others
cultural capital	the ability to mix in higher levels of society because education has given you qualifications, ownership of cultural products or access to works of culture	embodied cultural capital	the acquired knowledge of culture experienced and outwardly presented by a person	objectified cultural capital	a cultural artefact that confers status on the person who owns it
		fluidity of identity	the concept that people do not have a fixed identity which is wholly and permanently a part of them	participatory gap	the effect of economic poverty, in particular, producing a divide in access to digital culture and the information age
		habitus	the way in which a person has been socialised and interacts with the world according to their education, social class, etc.		

3.4 The role of specialised audiences, including niche and fan (Jenkins)

Fan culture is one of the most interesting and dynamic aspects of studying popular culture, and since going online the visibility of fan culture is growing; it's an area of study that is becoming increasingly important. In this book, we'll be exploring fan culture through the idea of two theorists: John Fiske and **Henry Jenkins**. Both have written prolifically about the relationship between fans and cultural products.

Central to contemporary thinking about fandom and participatory culture is the concept of the **prosumer**, the media audience member who also makes their own media. This development in society was being predicted as early as the 1970s by futurologist Alvin Toffler. Toffler perceived prosumption as a positive move in society, which he believed meant people would feel less alienated. This is really interesting in the light of contemporary research into the effects of social media usage, where we are constantly connected with others but that connectivity – if not meaningful – can still give rise to a sense of alienation.

People who support prosumerism, seeing it as a positive contribution to human expression and industry, argue that it has given increased ideological and creative freedom and modes of expression to some people who before may have lacked a voice. Its critics argue that it merely supports the consumer economy, and that the freedoms it gives are actually illusory. These critics argue that prosumerism is a veiled part of the exchange mechanisms of capitalism that has made the most of sales of technological goods, and to the promotion of brands.

Somewhere between the two arguments, there is a compromise. Perhaps there is a harmony overall between the sense of identity, self-esteem and connection with others gained from engaging with capitalist production in a way that benefits the consumer. Perhaps it reconciles their place as part of the commodification of internet users, and allows them to feel they are participating in a shared culture over which they feel ownership and participation. The prosumer, although a concept first mooted a long time ago, is intimately connected with the development of Web 2.0. You looked at the characteristics of Web 2.0 in the Year 1 book, and you should review this section of the Industries chapter alongside this one.

🔗 For more on Web 2.0 see Year 1 book, pages 116–117.

Make-up artist Jaclyn Hill demonstrates techniques – and promotes products – on her YouTube channel.

EXAMPLE: Make-up tutorials and game walkthroughs on YouTube

Both these prolific YouTube genres are good examples of products made by prosumers. The platform itself is a mass media institution, but content may be anywhere from very amateur to very professionally produced. On the level of the individual text producer, they may or may not have a formal relationship with business linking them to the products they test out, demonstrate or promote – but their activities can be seen as promotional whether or not a formal agreement, such as exchange of material goods for positive reviews, exists. Advertising revenue may also be accumulated from clicks views and external content may also appear on individual posts. All these issues make the status of the prosumer and their positioning within the media industry difficult to place with precision. But the further question is, do audiences really care about the distinction?

APPLY IT

How much actual content is genuinely creative and detached from economic activity in the prosumer content you consume yourself? Choose an example, either of one of the genres above or another from YouTube, and explore the transparency and other dimensions of your chosen producer's relationship with both YouTube as a platform and business and the wider media industry.

When Fiske was first studying fandom in the 1970s and 1980s, the fan behaviours people might have demonstrated included wearing T-shirts with images of idols emblazoned on them, the writing of fan mail, attending events where the object of the fan's attentions might be present, the creation of fanzines and membership of fan clubs – either official or unofficial. Collecting memorabilia and objects such as signed photographs was a real expression of fandom.

In the 1990s, the internet allowed fans to become more organised. Conventions began to appear for fans, places where they could get together with other fans. Television fandoms used to be associated with geeks – now they are considered to be a mainstream cultural practice, with conventions such as Comic-con attracting thousands of devoted visitors with a huge range of interests. Fandoms have almost always historically been associated with youth culture – and closely linked with the expression of identity.

Badges collected by a Sex Pistols fan – an outward expression of fandom from the 1970s.

John Fiske: 'The Cultural Economy of Fandom'

In Fiske's (1992) essay, 'The Cultural Economy of Fandom', he describes fan culture as something that people who are otherwise marginalised by society can take part in and achieve status and a sense of belonging as a result. He discussed the ways in which fans can become producers and distributors of their own texts, which, although rooted in popular culture, stand largely outside its conventional forms. He describes the space in which fan culture exists as the shadow cultural economy.

Fiske finds that fan culture exists alongside and in dialogue with mainstream cultural practices. He refers to the idea that fandoms produce a sense of self-esteem and social prestige. Interestingly, Fiske identifies those participating in fan culture as lacking in what he calls official cultural capital – that they are seeking a way of gaining it through alternative means. He also points out that many young people who participate in fandoms may not lack cultural capital, but use their affiliation with fandoms as a way of exploring their identity and setting themselves apart from parental influence or societal expectations of them. Importantly, Fiske sees the shadow cultural economy as rejecting the values of the official cultural economy. He points out that it exists purely to validate the interests and receive feedback from peers within the fan community, and that this is its end gain.

Fiske characterises fandoms using three perspectives. These are summarised briefly here.

Discrimination and distinction

The tendency of fans to strongly define themselves as a group, and the tendency of others to also be able to identify that group, is a significant characteristic of fandoms. Fans also like to establish and debate the content of their fandoms in hierarchical ways – to create their own canons relating to aspects of the dominant, popular culture that is the subject of the fandom. These in a sense legitimise the fandom, and promote the aesthetic, in particular, of the cultural product. Fiske noted that white male fans were more likely to do this than other groups 'subordinated' by gender, race or class.

Productivity and participation

Fiske identified different forms of fan productivity, while acknowledging that there can be cross-over between all three categories:

1 Semiotic productivity: the meanings made from the source texts by the fan.
2 Enunciative productivity: sharing these meanings and ways of talking about the text – 'fan-speak' and wearing clothing, or styling hair or make-up in a particular way.
3 Textual productivity: fan-made texts and the sense of ownership of the source text. This can also be known as textual poaching.

Cosplay at conventions is an example of enunciative productivity.

Capital accumulation

Fiske points out that fan-based acquisition of cultural capital cannot be translated into economic capital, since the subject of fandom – popular culture – is excluded generally from mainstream education and the qualifications that can advance economic status as part of it. Fan knowledge does, however, still confer privilege, and sets the fan apart from wider consumers of popular culture, therefore still replicating a hierarchy.

Fiske uses the example of a Shakespeare play compared with the script for the *Rocky Horror Show* – a Shakespeare expert uses their knowledge to differentiate between performances of a text, whereas a fan uses their knowledge of a script to 'participate' – to feel part of the performance and the fandom associated with it. Fan collecting behaviours are also addressed by Fiske – the memorabilia associated with popular culture are often cheap to collect and do not require a high amount of economic capital, compared with the collecting of works of art, so the emphasis is on volume of artefacts rather than their individual worth. Again, there are times when fan culture coincides with the traditional intersection of cultural with economic capital, such as in the status that might be gained by owning a rare comic – an objectified part of cultural capital.

Owning a rare comic is an example of objectified cultural capital, an intersection between the mainstream and shadow cultural economy.

So far, you have considered fans to be a specialised sector of the audience. You have observed the ways in which, through Fiske's uses of Bourdieu's theory of cultural capital, fans can be distinguished from audiences and the ways in which fandoms can be seen to model some of the patterns of behaviour seen in the acquisition of conventional cultural capital within the shadow cultural economy.

What is participatory culture?

Participatory culture has fundamental differences from consumer culture, a model of culture where the audience receives texts but does not 'interact' with them. The study of consumer culture does take into account the meanings of texts and the ways in which audiences relate to brand identities and particular media products, but it lacks visible evidence of action on these meanings. In some ways, the digital age has relegated the status of purely consumer culture as the primary mode of consumption, but it's important to acknowledge that it does still persist. We can therefore think of consumer and participatory culture as co-existing. One is controlled by industry but subject to the dynamics of trends and consumer tastes, the other with many more dimensions and complexities to the dynamic between producer and audience. Audience power in consumer culture is limited to economic expression – the decision to purchase or otherwise.

In their introduction to *The Participatory Cultures Handbook* (2012), Aaron Delwiche and Jennifer Jacobs Henderson identify four phases of participatory culture. They are summarised in the following table.

Phase 1: *Emergence* (1985–1993)	• Personal computers begin to find their way into homes • ARPANET and other connected networks began to appear • Laser printers and DTP software • Nascent computer sub-culture and the hacker ethic • Academic research into *textual poaching* (Jenkins); increased interest in what fans do with products
Phase 2: *Waking up to the web* (1994–1998)	• Graphical browsers allow people to start making their own web pages and navigate the web more easily • Huge increase in speed of transformation in digital technologies • Increase in academic interest in human connectivity online, including studying gaming • Recognition that online cultural expression was important and worth studying
Phase 3: *Push-button publishing* (1999–2004)	• User-friendly web publishing services arrive, so participation reaches a much wider audience • Platforms appeared that were early social media, and the iPod revolutionised the portability of some media content • Both lead to the increased ability of audiences to publish, share and 'remix' • Studies began to focus on fandoms more and the collective uses and sharing of information
Phase 4: *Ubiquitous connections* (2005–2011)	• Changes in broadband technology brought video-sharing platforms • Transmedia publishing • The increased take-up and rapid development of the smartphone • Academic recognition of some of the critiques of the networked era as well as Jenkins' *Convergence Culture* (2008), a hugely significant work

Henry Jenkins: *Participatory Culture and Convergence*

The ideas of Henry Jenkins have been considered enormously important since people really began to study participatory culture. He has written extensively on convergence culture and participatory culture. It is highly recommended you take your reading of Jenkins beyond this book – his style is accessible, and his writing is full of interesting examples from popular media that help to embed his ideas.

Henry Jenkins and 'Textual Poachers'

In his 1992 article, 'Textual Poachers: Television Fans and Participatory Culture', Jenkins begins by exploring the popular stereotype of the *Star Trek* fan in other media, summarising the perception of them as as desexualised social misfits who cultivate worthless knowledge, are unable to separate real life from a TV show, and are emotionally immature. This is the starting point for a number of points he makes about fans and fandoms:

The ability to share a pop cultural artifact, news story or meme at the touch of an icon defines the age of ubiquitous connections.

- Fans are often stereotyped as mentally unbalanced in news media and in fiction as psychopathic. Fans are represented as an 'other' in popular media because their *cultural preferences and interpretative practices ... must be held at a distance so that fannish taste does not pollute sanctioned culture*.
- Referring to Bourdieu, Jenkins points out that fan culture is seen as distasteful because it values pop cultural artifacts over more traditional signifiers of cultural capital.
- Much of the condescension surrounding fan culture is actually symptomatic of our anxiety around issues of the 'violation of dominant cultural hierarchies', which are transgressed by fans. Fans do not have the 'aesthetic distance' experienced by consumers with high cultural capital, and readily transgress and blur boundaries between fact and fiction.

- Fan culture challenges cultural hierarchies partly because they often seemingly possess cultural capital and come from middle-class, educated backgrounds. They are active producers of meaning who are able to manipulate the texts they encounter for new social bonds and transform the meanings of television shows into a rich and participatory culture.

- Fans are aware of their perilous position on the fringe of the original texts and the meanings encoded by their producers, and sometimes react with anger at narrative decisions taken by the programme-makers.

Dr Who is an example of a television programme with a very active fan community going back many decades.

Jenkins explores the meanings of the term textual poaching, originally suggested by Marcel de Certeau. If you were to apply Hall's model, then this would be the process by which fans encroach without authorisation on the hegemonic meaning encoded by the producers of a text. In this way, we can see the notion of a received meaning passively being accepted by the audience being challenged by fans. Jenkins suggests that textual poaching is an even more complex process than this. It resists the idea that there are identifiable meanings somehow already present in the text, and accepts that there are multiple positions in the meanings fans make which are not necessarily oppositional ones. Instead, they are alternatives to the dominant reading, ones that subsume the dominant reading and repurpose it to fit their own ideologies, since fans like a text in the first instance because it appeals to their way of interpreting the world. He suggests that because fans cannot (in terms of television production – in the 1990s) own the means of production or direct it themselves, they are culturally marginalised. Jenkins believes that this creates a sense of dependence that is rejected by some, who then reappropriate cultural products and use them for their own, alternative purposes. His chapter ends:

> *Fans possess not simply borrowed remnants snatched from mass culture, but their own culture built from the semiotic raw materials the media provides.* (page 49)

Contemporary fan art for the television series *Sherlock*.

EXAMPLE: The enduring appeal of Sherlock Holmes

Jenkins refers to the example of Sherlock Holmes fans, who wrote to Sir Arthur Conan Doyle to beg him not to retire his character. It's an interesting coincidence that the modern television updating of *Sherlock* has also inspired passionate fandoms.

Between these two texts, one published in 1993 and the other in 2016, Jenkins continued to explore participation in his book *Convergence Culture*. Written in 2008, this book looks at the ways in which traditional media has not been entirely replaced by new media, but co-exists with it, and the myriad of interesting ways audiences can use new media to interact with old. It considers the old media's attempts to harness the power of new media for its own purposes, and the rise of huge media conglomerates that are multi-platform in their reach. Collective knowledge and play are considered as important aspects of the power that media consumers are able to express.

In *Participatory Culture in a Networked Era* (2016), Jenkins joins forces with two other key theorists in the field, Ito and boyd, to explore and debate some of the key ideas active in the field of participatory culture study today. It is a very readable book, with chapters that are themed in which each theorist presents their ideas in a conversational way, as suggested by the title. The most relevant chapter to you is the first, debating, for example, the differences between participation and interactivity. Jenkins identifies the key questions that the debate hinges on as follows:

- Can meaningful participation take place when the nature of contributions is controlled by big media and technology businesses?
- Is participation exploitation where clicks generate not only access to content, but generate money for advertisers?

Jenkins makes clear that his first usage of the term in 1993 was about describing the dynamics between fan, producer and text, and their relationships with other fans. All three academics agree that what is meant by participatory culture has changed enormously and acknowledge that participatory culture may have started out as a study of fans, but that it now has academic usefulness in exploring networked connections way beyond these.

Jenkins says that he does not believe that technologies are participatory, but that cultures are. This is a great argument to use to counter the technological determinist view of the internet. He believes that people are doing with social media and sites such as YouTube what people have always sought to do – to connect social experience through their use. He feels that interactivity itself is not participatory – it is the use of interactive tools that makes them so. Participation means to take part, to share experiences and creative production. Technology therefore facilitates participation – it is not participation itself.

Jenkins does not believe that participatory culture necessarily stands in opposition to mainstream cultural values or that they resist them – but they do offer alternative sources of status and social belonging to people who may otherwise feel that they are low status in the world beyond their use of networks. Participatory culture exists alongside mainstream culture but does not necessarily challenge it.

APPLY IT

Choose a television series that inspire fandoms. Search online for evidence of fan activities based on the show. What kinds of products can you find based on the 'semiotic raw materials' sourced by fans from the shows? Try and find three solid examples of contrasting fan-made artifacts. They might be costumes, videos, fan-fics, artwork, comics and so on. How do they use the original material in their own ways? What do you think appeals about the show to fans, based on both the fan materials you found and the dominant messages contained in the original?

KEY TERMS

consumer culture	a model of culture where the audience receives texts but does not 'interact' with them	prosumer	media producer who spans the categories of both audience and producer of media texts in variable proportions	textual poaching	the act of reappropriating a cultural product which may result in new meanings
enunciative productivity	sharing the meanings and ways of talking about the text – 'fan-speak' and wearing clothing, or styling hair or make-up in a particular way	semiotic productivity	the meanings made from the source texts by the fan	textual productivity	fan-made texts as sense of ownership of the source text
		shadow cultural economy	the space in which fan culture exists		

3.5 'End of audience' theory

The changes in the producer/audience relationship have been so extraordinary over the last couple of decades that it is not surprising the way in which we conceptualise audiences and understand how we should even define audience has come under scrutiny. A term for some of these collective ideas is **end of audience theory**. Most theorists do not literally propose that media audiences, in the sense we used to understand them, no longer exist. Instead, they suggest that we need to re-evaluate almost everything we assumed to be true about them because they no longer engage with the media on the same terms that we understood historically. A lot of thinking about the end of audience focuses on the **digital native**, the community of media users who have grown up with the internet rather than **digital immigrants**, the older generation who have had to acquire the skills to participate in the digital world more consciously.

Digital 'immigrants' may be happy using technology, but it's a habit they have acquired rather than it being an integral part of their upbringing.

A thorough introduction to this issue is 'The End of Audience?' (2009), an article by Sonia Livingstone and Ranjana Das. In their writing, the authors ask whether we can still define media audiences in the same way now, as the way in which they consume the media has changed so radically. The change from receiving mass communication to belonging to networks impacts enormously on *'the mediation of identity, sociality and power'* (page 1), yet some aspects remain a constant. Livingstone and Das caution us to reject the notion that the audience is 'dead', but point out that the conditions of consumption and the ways in which we interact with texts have changed the way we need to explore audiences, and perhaps the way we understand what audiences are doing with texts when they interact with them, form networked communities based on them or become prosumers.

Here are some concise points taken from the essay, although it's well worth reading yourself for its depth of exploration of the issue, and the full text is widely available online:

- In the age of digital media it's important we continue to recognise the *'mutuality of text and reader'* – in other words, texts are still open to different readings and what audiences do with those meanings can and does vary from person to person.
- We have reached a point in time where we are bombarded by media exposure, just as representational issues are higher on the political agenda than ever before, and we are a part of the constantly circulating messages in our culture.
- Because content is spread across media platforms, there is no neat boundary by which we can define a 'text'.
- Audiences are situated between text and context, with the technology that supports it and the text itself becoming increasingly indistinct from each other.
- Many theorists writing about the end of audience focus on the idea of a consumer becoming a citizen, and a lot of debate surrounds just how much power this new relationship with the media actually brings the consumer.

Livingstone and Das conclude that both social and semiotic approaches need to continue to work in tandem if we are to understand the complexity of the audience's new relationship with media. Audience theorists still face the same problems today that they did in previous generations – that we struggle to join up the meanings people make from what they see on screen with the context of the society that shapes those views. This continues to be a very difficult argument to grasp.

In addition to older models of reception, the digital age brings with it the audience as makers of not only meanings but also texts – that we should neither privilege the audience nor the text but try and acknowledge the duality of approach needed to really understand the relationship between the two.

Dan Gillmor: *We the Media*

Dan Gillmor's 2004 book, *We the Media: Grassroots Journalism by the People, for the People* was an assertion of the changes that were happening in news media, where the impacts of a more participatory culture were just beginning to make themselves felt and shaping the future of news. In his book, he proposes that the de-professionalisation of the news industry and increased participation of the semi-professional or amateur 'grassroots' journalist is to be welcomed rather than perceived as a 'dumbing down' of the profession of journalism.

In his introduction, Gillmor talks about the changing roles of news providers; he views the evolution of journalism as the difference between moving from being in a lecture to being in a conversation. He puts the point quite strongly that news should not be a commodity solely owned by the most powerful media organisations. Gillmor discusses three groups of people who are changing in response to the rise of citizen journalism – journalists, newsmakers, and the former audience. Now that access to publishing technology has become democratised, there are implications for all. Journalism is no longer the hierarchical profession it once was, newsmakers have to be aware of the treatment of the subject matter they create by new more grassroots news providers, which may not follow the old 'rules' and the audience, who are no longer the passive recipients of news but are in dialogue with it or even reporting it and contributing to it themselves.

Clay Shirky

Clay Shirky is an influential contemporary thinker who specialises in the field of how digital media and communications may be shaping our society. He has written and lectured extensively about the new dynamic between media producers and audiences. Shirky has given numerous talks as well as writing two books – *Here Comes Everybody: The Power or Organising Without Organisations* (2008) and *Cognitive Surplus: How Technology Makes Consumers into Collaborators* (2010). Two of his key ideas applicable to your studies are outlined in the following section, but it is worth seeking out these books and reading for yourself some of what he has to say about how we are learning to engage as audiences with a new, far more participatory media world.

Mass amateurisation

Shirky's work centres on the premise that the audience–industry hierarchical relationship of old, where professionally made media was consumed by audiences in a fairly simple model, no longer predominates. He sees this new world as not yet full-fledged, and full of issues as the cross-over and blurring of lines between audiences and producers is not yet completely resolved.

An important aspect of Shirky's work centres on the idea of **mass amateurisation**. Shirky, in exploring this aspect of mass media change in relationship between audience and industry, treads similar ground to the ideas we have encountered already – the prosumer, citizen journalists, the fan producers of texts.

Shirky sees the shift in roles and the loss of distinction between producer and audience as one of the most significant changes in media consumption and production history. He defines this shift as being from 'Why publish this?' to 'Why not?' He points out that the selection of what can be published is no longer as highly structured and regulated as it was within the old media 'profession'. Amateurs simply don't need to follow any rules since there is no cost or low cost involved in

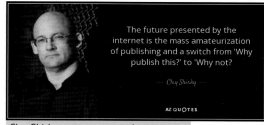

The future presented by the internet is the mass amateurization of publishing and a switch from 'Why publish this?' to 'Why not?

— *Clay Shirky* —

AZ QUOTES

Clay Shirky quote presented as a meme.

APPLY IT

Watch one of Clay Shirky's TED Talks online:

- How Social Media can Make History
- Institutions vs. Collaboration
- How the Internet will (One Day) Transform Ggovernment
- How Cognitive Surplus Will Change the World.

Make notes as you view your chosen talk. Look back over your notes, and do the following:

1 Write a summary of the talk. In one sentence. What was its subject?

2 What were Shirky's main points?

3 Did you feel he was optimistic or pessimistic about social change brought about by media technologies?

distributing their content. He also explores the idea that, although the individual small producer of a blog or minor social media alternative news outlet may not individually be held in high esteem by the audience, there is an amplifying effect to their repetition in numerous places.

Shirky does not necessarily imbue the term 'amateur' with negative associations. At the end of his third chapter, 'Everyone is a Media Outlet', he points out that the profession of scribe was once hugely important in an age where mass reproduction of texts was not yet available from the printing press, and the majority of people were illiterate. Being able to read and to write was imbued with huge significance and status. The advent of movable type and the increased literacy of the population meant reading and writing became commonplace tools that were available to all. Shirky sees this as a metaphor for the transformation of the relationship between people and the media.

Cognitive surplus

In his second book, Shirky uses the term cognitive surplus to describe the way in which people globally now use their free time to develop collaborative online projects that demonstrate diverse collective creativity. Two main perspectives seem to drive this use of time – the desire to be recognised and respected as a contributor to a project, and to join with a group who share interest and common goals.

Game of Thrones fans' wiki homepage

Choose a website that demonstrates Shirky's notion of cognitive surplus being put to use. It could have as its focus environmental activism, a fan wiki or science project – there are all kinds of different texts and a huge range in subject matter.

Take screenshots of your site, and include them when preparing a five-slide presentation on how the collaborative nature of the site is apparent in its mode of address, its statement of intent (this often can be found in the 'About' section) and user interactivity/contribution mechanisms.

The purposes of these groups might vary from pure entertainment to the formulation of groups who are serious about social activism of some kind. Fan wikis and online media archives are good examples of this in media terms, but Wikipedia and Kickstarter could also be seen as examples of how technology can be used to get momentum together by using the collective knowledge and intellect of a large number of contributors.

KEY TERMS

cognitive surplus	the way in which people globally now use their free time to develop collaborative online projects
digital immigrant	the older generation who have had to acquire the skills to participate in the digital world more consciously
digital native	community of media users who have grown up with the internet
end of audience theory	changes in the way in which we conceptualise audiences and understand how we should even define audience
mass amateurisation	state of the media today, where professionally made media that was consumed by audiences in a fairly simple model no longer predominates

KEY THINKERS

David Gauntlett	(1971–) Gauntlett is a British writer and academic who was well-known for his influential exploration of a range of critical approaches to reading gender and identity in media texts, as well as contributing his own research into the field to test out some established ideas
Henry Jenkins	(1958–) Jenkins is a notable contemporary American academic theorist whose work has focused on fandoms and participatory culture, as well as the impact of digital connectivity on society and the cultural artifacts it produces

Clay Shirky	(1964–) Shirky is an influential contemporary thinker who specialises in the field of how digital media and communications may be shaping our society. He has written and lectured extensively about the new dynamic between media producers and audiences

CHAPTER SUMMARY

- Media audiences are becoming increasingly fragmented, and media producers are having to find more and more creative ways of reaching them in light of increasing specialisation of audiences whose experience of consumption reflects the fragmenting of popular culture.

- The expression 'the long tail' describes the increased longevity of some media products and the continued or revived interaction of some audience members with these products in addition to their continued consumption.

- Media literacy is a key idea when thinking about how equipped people are to make sense of the messages in the mass media.

- Although many social commentators recognise media literacy as an important issue, formal media education is still not accessible to many, so consumers are reliant on the development of critical thinking skills in a piecemeal way depending on their exposure to a wide range of other cultural and social circumstances. This means there are sometimes considerable variations in the ability of people to read the media in an informed way.

- Technological determinism is an area of sociological study which is related to media debates because of the huge growth in the individual's use of a more varied range of media for increased amounts of time.

- Neuman described six stages of effects theory, which aimed to identify different ways of thinking about media influences. His model is useful to help you see the distinctions between some approaches studied on the course, as well as place them in a broad historical timeframe. Neuman's model is not a perfect account, and does not consider the cycles of popularity and potential adaptation of older theories to uses in evaluating the impact of new media.

- Cohen's theory of folk devils and moral panics is an interesting piece of research relating to media effects and people's perceptions of the world as affected by news media. It could easily be considered alongside cultivation theory (Gerbner) as well as framing and agenda setting.

FURTHER READING AND REFERENCES

Aaron Delwiche & Jennifer Jacobs Henderson (2012) *The Participatory Cultures Handbook.*

BBC News (2017, 23 October) 'UK Diver Swims to Safety after Australia Shark Scare', www.bbc.co.uk/news/world-australia-41717024.

Chris Anderson (2004) 'The Long Tail', www.wired.com/2004/10/tail/.

Clay Shirky (2008) *Here Comes Everybody: The Power or Organising Without Organisations.*

Clay Shirky (2010) *Cognitive Surplus: How Technology Makes Consumers into Collaborators.*

Dan Gillmor (2004) *We the Media: Grassroots Journalism by the People, for the People.*

David Gauntlett (2017, 6 July) '"Theories of Identity" in the New Media Studies A & AS Level', http://davidgauntlett.com/making-media-studies/theories-of-identity-new-media-studies-a-as-level/.

David Gauntlett (2008) *Media, Gender, Identity: An Introduction.*

Edward Comor (2010) 'Digital Prosumption and Alienation', *Ephemera*, 10(3), 439–454.

Erich Goode & Ben Nehuda (1994) *Moral Panics: The Social Construction of Deviance.*

Henry Jenkins (1992) 'Textual Poachers: Television Fans and Participatory Culture', *Journal of Fandom Studies*, 2(1), http://williamwolff.org/wp-content/uploads/2015/01/lbennett_1-libre.pdf.

Henry Jenkins (2008) *Convergence Culture: Where Old and New Media Collide.*

Henry Jenkins, Mizuko Ito & danah boyd (2016) *Participatory Culture in a Networked Era.*

John Fiske (1987) *Television Culture.*

John Fiske (1992) 'The Cultural Economy of Fandom', in Lisa A. Lewis (ed.), *The Adoring Audience: Fan Culture and Popular Media.*

Maxwell E. McCombs & Donald L. Shaw (1972) 'The Agenda-Setting Function of Mass Media', *Public Opinion Quarterly*, 36(2), 176–187.

Paul Lewis (2017, 6 October) '"Our Minds can be Hijacked": The Tech Insiders who Fear a Smartphone Dystopia', *Guardian*, www.theguardian.com/technology/2017/oct/05/smartphone-addiction-silicon-valley-dystopia.

Sonia Livingstone & Ranjana Das (2009) 'The End of Audience? Theoretical Echoes of Reception and the Uncertainties of Use', paper presented at 'Transforming Audiences', University of Westminster, 3–4 September, www.researchgate.net/publication/292135601_The_end_of_audiences_theoretical_echoes_of_reception_amid_the_uncertainties_of_use.

Stanley Cohen (2002) *Folk Devils and Moral Panics.*

UNESCO (1982, 22 January) *Grunwald Declaration on Media Education*, www.unesco.org/education/pdf/MEDIA_E.PDF.

W. Russell Neuman & Lauren Guggenheim (2011) 'The Evolution of Effects Theory: A Six-Stage Model of Cumulative Research, *Communication Theory*, 21(2), 169–196.

- Cultivation theory was highlighted as an area to revisit from the Year 1 book. We explored the idea of the mass media as part of the process of socialisation and enculturation, as well as thinking about John Fiske's proposal that television can have what he referred to as a bardic function, weaving together cultural attitudes, values and ideas.

- Agenda setting and framing are interpretative effects theories that seek to understand the extent to which news media influence people's perceptions of political and social agendas and issues. Although complex academic ideas, it is possible at A level to apply elements of these complex theories in a relevant way to the texts you are studying.

- Hall's reception theory, which you first met in the Year 1 book, still forms an important part of how you approach the relationship between the encoded message and the decoding process, as well as the idea of a hegemonic, negotiated or oppositional reading.

- You developed more extensively some of Gauntlett's theories about identity, first looked at in Year 1. In relation to these, you considered the ideas of fluidity of identity, constructed identity, negotiated identity or collective identity. The nuances of each of these terms was discussed.

- Bourdieu's theory of cultural capital is useful to contextualise work on fandoms. We learned the distinctions between the forms of cultural capital – embodied, objectified and institutionalised, and the way in which people express their cultural capital as habitus.

- You considered the arrival of the prosumer, who both creates media and consumes it. You explored briefly the relationship between the prosumer and capitalist society in the light of Web 2.0, the characteristics of which were explored in more depth in the Year 1 book.

- Fiske's concept of shadow cultural capital was contextualised in light of Bourdieu's ideas, and seen as a system that shares much in common with the structure of and engagement people experience with the official culture. Fiske highlighted the differences and similarities by exploring discrimination and distinction, productivity and participation, and capital accumulation as aspects of fan behaviour, which might be expressed in variable ways depending on the nature of the fandom.

- Delwiche and Henderson helpfully described four phases in the development of participatory culture: emergence, waking up to the web, push button publishing and ubiquitous connections. These delineations help us to understand the speed with which participatory culture emerged as part of the digital revolution, and the technologies and academic thinking that defined each phase.

- Gillmor described the changes happening in the relationship between journalists, audiences and traditional news outlets, viewing the de-professionalisation of the news industry as not necessarily being a negative move but one that allows more voices to be heard from grassroots journalism, as hierarchical barriers disrupt traditional gatekeeping protocols.

- Shirky explored for us the related ideas of mass amateurisation, integrating ideas about the prosumer with commentary on the changing relationship between audience and industries brought about by new technologies, and the shifts in power and accessibility to the means of media production that have resulted.

Chapter 4 Media industries

Year 1 mastery

Chapter 6 in the Year 1 book provides a wide-ranging introduction to a range of different aspects of the study of media industries, including the history of many of the main media forms, a consideration of the way media products are **distributed** and **circulated**, and how their reach is measured. The chapter also looks at issues regarding the ownership, control and regulation of the media and some of the contemporary issues that modern media industries are having to contend with. The importance of advertising to media industries is discussed and the chapter offers information about the way media industries are regulated.

Year 2 development

Some of the ideas found in Chapter 6 of the Year 1 book will be developed further and this chapter will discuss issues and debates related to:

- the impact of digitally convergent media platforms on the production, distribution and circulation of media products
- the current position of cultural industries
- the role of regulation in **global** production, distribution and circulation
- the effect of individual producers/media industries.

How to use this chapter

The areas of study listed above are all interconnected so, rather than create false separations, this chapter will engage with each idea by providing examples of the ideas in action across a number of media industries. A summary of key terms and definitions is provided at the end of each section. The **Apply It** activities can be used to develop your understanding of the issues raised and will help you to consider how these issues and ideas relate in media areas other than the ones discussed here. The contemporary media context is dynamic and it is in a constant state of change; this can make the study of the industrial aspects of the media frustrating. More important than the facts and figures of an industrial study are the issues and ideas that relate to the way the cultural industries (Hesmondhalgh, 2012) operate in the contemporary context.

Central to this discussion will be ideas on the cultural industries as presented by Hesmondhalgh in his book *The Cultural Industries* (2012). This book is a wide-ranging overview of issues and debates about the current state of the media, and his work offers research and analysis from a number of different sources.

Similarly, Lunt and Livingstone (2012) offer a range of ideas and case studies related to regulation and the globalisation of contemporary media in their book *Media Regulation*.

Ideas raised by these writers will be integrated into the discussions in this chapter and you will find them used throughout this book, as industrial issues can influence all other areas of the theoretical framework and the analysis of media products.

4.1 Introduction

The study of media industries is to engage with the structures and economics that support the production of media artefacts. It is an important part of the study of media, as understanding the industrial context of the production of media products gives an insight into why media products are the way they are. At the heart of this is the culture of commercialisation (Hesmondhalgh, 2012), which leads to the commodification of both media products and audiences.

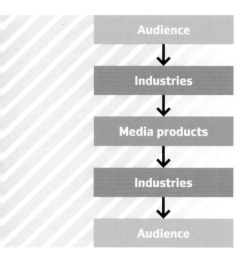

Put simply, Media Studies is the study of the relationship between audiences and industries. At the centre of this relationship are the media products themselves.

Traditional media industries

Traditionally, the cultural industries produced the media products that audiences read, watched, played and listened to. This was because production, distribution and circulation was so expensive that companies that had access to money and resources were able to create media products with any chance of finding a large audience. Traditional media industries still produce a lot of media content but since the mid-2000s more and more media products have been produced and distributed by independent and amateur content providers. Traditional media institutions and industries are under enormous pressure, as they are increasingly competing for audiences and advertising revenue. In addition, technological developments have created new audience behaviours and expectations. Shirky argues that the internet 'challenges existing institutions by eroding the institutional monopoly' (Hesmondhalgh, 2012, page 328).

The relationship between audiences and industries is primarily economic. As they exist within a capitalist framework, cultural industries seek to find a way to commodify their product or service and then attempt to attract an audience to buy or buy into whatever they are selling. Most media industries exist to serve their shareholders. Companies such as Sky, BMG, Columbia Pictures, YouTube, Global Radio, Rockstar Games, etc. all exist to create profit. In a neo-liberal, free market environment, all media industries are in direct competition with one another for our time, attention and money.

Rockstar Games

New media industries

In 2006 YouTube was acquired by Google and soon afterwards the video sharing site bought in advertising which generated an income for the platform as well for the content creators. Some amateur content producers began creating Instagram accounts, blogs or videos for fun or just to create a record of their ideas. Popular amateur content providers could begin to generate an income based on the numbers of views per video and subscribers to their channels. This commodification of their products has created millionaires out of high-profile YouTubers such as Zoella and PewDiePie. As their popularity has grown, amateur content providers have branched out and many have become small cultural industries in and of themselves by offering feature films (e.g. *Smosh: The Movie* (2015) and *Joe and Casper Hit the Road* (2016)), books and all sorts of merchandise connected to their brand. Many YouTubers appear on each other's vlogs and some have worked with a traditional broadcaster such as the BBC. This diversification (Hesmondhalgh, 2012) allows the content provider to provide a range of products for their fans to buy into and also helps them appeal to new audiences. The synergy (Hesmondhalgh, 2012) created by the products enables each one to promote the others.

The digital divide

The rise of the amateur can largely be put down to changes in technology that allow more people access to **the means of production** (Marx, 1867), distribution and circulation. It is worth noting that this access to smartphones, editing apps and internet connections may feel universal but there are still barriers to the access to these technologies. According to the Office of National Statistics (ONS), as of March 2017, 89% of adults in the UK had recently used the internet with 99% of adults aged 16–24 being recent users compared to 41% of adults over 75. However, 22% of disabled adults had never used the internet.

Outside of the UK, Europe and North America, the internet is not as freely available. Some nation states place limitations on their citizens' access to and use of the internet. According to *USA Today* (2014), only 4% of North Koreans have direct access to the internet, Saudi Arabia blocks access to websites that 'discuss political, social or religious topics incompatible with the Islamic beliefs of the monarchy' and bloggers in Iran have to register with their government. In Turkmenistan, the government is the only internet service provider available to its citizens. *USA Today* (2014) identifies China as the most restrictive state when it comes to online information:

> The [Chinese] *government filters searches, block sites and erases 'inconvenient' content, rerouting search terms on Taiwan independence or the Tiananmen Square massacre to items favorable to the Communist Party.* (USA Today, 2014)

According to internetworldstats.com, as of March 2017, 45% of the population of Asia and 28% of the population of Africa use the internet. This causes a digital divide (Hesmondhalgh, 2012) as, globally, there are inequalities in access to and use of digital technologies. This means that most ideas about the democratising nature of the internet and the freedom it offers are coming from a very specific Euro–US perspective, which cannot be applied globally.

New ways to produce, distribute and circulate to new types of audiences

However, 80% of the UK's population currently own smartphones (cbrononline.com, 2016). Smartphones come with moving image cameras and free editing apps are available, so most people in the UK have access to the technology required to **produce** their own media content. There is no charge to upload a video to YouTube or Vimeo, or a photo to Instagram, so content can easily be distributed by anyone with an internet connection. Circulation is the most difficult part of the process. Just because a video is on YouTube doesn't mean anyone will watch it. Hesmondhalgh (2012) notes that some early viral successes were reliant on 'old media' for circulation. Arctic Monkeys were early adopters of the internet to distribute their music, as well as information on and images of the band. However, their success

Smosh the Movie

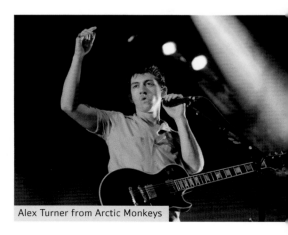
Alex Turner from Arctic Monkeys

'owed much more to their repeated exposure on traditional media, notably radio'* (Hesmondhalgh, 2012).

YouTube offers marketing tools to help content providers circulate their material. Social media strategies can be used to promote content on YouTube and other social media sites but only a small percentage of the total number of YouTubers or Instagrammers achieve wealth and fame. Social media celebrities are the exception rather than the rule but new technologies do mean that amateur content producers now have the potential to generate a direct connection to an audience in a way that was not possible before. Not many vloggers will achieve the level of success of PewDiePie but many will be able to access an income and retain creative control that may not have been possible when production was the sole province of media institutions.

Online success is not always limited to the country where the content is generated, as the sharing of media products can go global (e.g. the success of the video for 'Gangnam Style' by Psy in 2012). Recent technological changes have altered audiences' behaviours and expectations, and have challenged the ways that the media industry approaches its business. Previously reliable income sources have been decimated (e.g. the decline of the sales of newspapers, DVDs and music) and traditional approaches to the regulation of the media are currently being challenged as the media context changes. Traditional media producers need to diversify, so contemporary products usually exist across platforms, forms and for multiple audiences. Media producers often consider their content's potential appeal to both global and local audiences, as the internet has created a potential global audience for transnational cultural products (Lunt & Livingstone, 2012). All of this creates an environment where audiences appear to have more choice than ever before.

New media institutions are rising (e.g. platforms such as Twitter, Netflix and YouTube), while other more traditional ones are in decline (print newspapers and magazines, broadcast TV). The fact that the development of digital technologies occurred relatively recently and is still ongoing means that the context of modern media industries is in a constant state of change. However, the older cultural industries still exert a lot of power even though they are under threat from newer production and distribution methods.

In Chapter 6 of the Year 1 book, we learned that media industries are engaged in making media products (**production**), distributing those products (providing access to the products) and circulating them (getting them to the target audience). The way that products are created is in part influenced by production technologies and technological developments in **distribution** and **circulation**.

Japanese rock group, Babymetal

KEY TERMS

circulation	the act of getting media products to an audience
commercialisation	the practice of running an institution or creating media products specifically with an aim to generate financial gain
commodification	to turn something into something that can be sold
content providers	individuals, groups or organisation who create the content of media products; they may or may not be media producers
convergence	the use of different technologies and/or platforms to produce and distribute media products
cultural industries	the industries that are involved in the production, distribution and circulation of cultural artefacts, including media products
digital divide	the term used to describe the fact that there are disparities in power between those who have access to digital technologies and those who don't
distribution	methods used to make media products available to audiences

diversification	the act of producing different products or targeting different markets
early adopters	individuals who take advantage of technological developments before they become mainstream
globalisation	the economic and/or technological removal of nation state boundaries
monopoly	when one corporation dominates the provision of a specific product or service so there is no choice for the consumer
production	the manufacture of media products

regulation	a term used to cover the legal and/or voluntary rules that are used to offer guidance and, in some cases, control the actions and output of media producers
shareholders	groups or individuals who are part owners of a company, as they have invested money by buying shares
synergy	the way different media products can act to promote one another
transnational	working across national borders

4.2 The media and technological change

The history of the media is the history of technological change. From the invention of the printing press to today's virtual reality headsets, we can see that methods of production, distribution and circulation have developed with the technologies that are available.

Print

The printing press (invented in 1440) made possible the mass reproduction and, consequently, the distribution of the written word and images. This enabled information and ideas to be communicated and become widespread. Literacy used to be limited to members of the powerful institutions of the time (the Church and the legal profession) and then to a wealthy, educated elite. The invention of the printing press led to a rise in literacy, and, slowly, more and more people learned to read. A literate population wanted to be informed and entertained and could be encouraged to pay for written media, so pamphlets and newspapers were developed to meet audience demand and to make money for the producers.

Printing and distributing written materials was, however, a costly endeavour:

- Writers and journalists offer a specialised skill and a professional approach that traditionally attracted a professional salary.
- Print media businesses needed to have access to specialised equipment to be able to produce the materials and distribute them across the country.

This meant the power to produce was in the hands of large companies or individuals with personal wealth, or ones who could attract large amounts of investment. This paradigm of industrial production and ownership can still be seen in UK newspaper industries. Most national titles are owned by members of the English aristocracy (Jonathan Harmsworth, the 4th Viscount Rothemere, is the Chairman and majority shareholder of the *Daily Mail*), multi-national media businesses (the *Sun* and *The Times* are owned by the global company News Corportion) or entrepreneurs (the *Telegraph* and the *Independent* are owned by the Barclay Brothers and Russian Oligarchs Alexander and Evgeny Lebedev, respectively). The only national British newspaper that is not a simple for-profit business is the *Guardian*. This newspaper is run by the Scott Trust Limited, which has no individual owner and does not pay dividends to shareholders.

The distribution of hard-copy newspapers requires a delivery network to ensure 'today's paper' arrives in newsagents and supermarkets early in the morning. All of this is labour intensive, costly and time-consuming, and means that daily newspapers need to recoup their substantial costs if they are to survive. There are two ways newspapers can make money:

- by selling advertising space and
- by selling the newspaper itself to its audience.

In recent years both of these income sources have been hit. Newspapers have found that the competition provided by free online news sources has meant that fewer people are prepared to pay for their news and, as circulation has dropped, the amount a newspaper can charge advertisers has also steeply declined, reducing their income even further. All British print newspapers have an online edition and in 2016 the *Independent* became the first newspaper to go 'internet only'. The *Independent* closed its print edition as the cost of production and distribution became unsustainable. The survival of the newspaper title could only be possible if costs were reduced by limiting the distribution of their content to their website and social media.

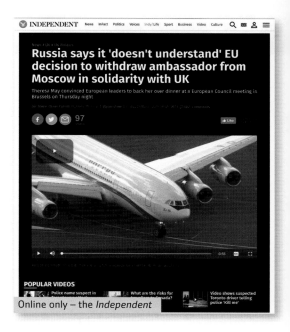
Online only – the *Independent*

Of all the platforms for distributing media products, print is one that is most steeply in decline. Circulation decreases have meant that longstanding newspapers and magazines have had to abandon selling hard copies. As more people use smartphones, tablets and computers to access media content, print media becomes less appealing to media institutions and audiences alike. Print is costly and largely less convenient for the reader.

Radio

Radio bought mass communication into everyone's home. The technology required to be able to access radio broadcasts was relatively cheap and audiences needed no special skills to access broadcast material. The BBC was set up in 1922 to create radio programming to be broadcast to the UK public with a view to inform, educate and entertain, and, as the use of radio spread, it became the first electronic mass media form. It was an important technology that allowed audiences to hear the voices of their leaders. Two of the most famous UK radio broadcasts in the early 20th century are King Edward VIII's abdication speech in 1936 and Chamberlain's declaration of Britain going to war with Germany in 1939. In this period radio could be seen as a unifying force, as it formed the first consensus audiences with people accessing the same programming at the same time. This in turn led to a shared culture, bringing people together through their shared media experiences.

This idea of the BBC being a central cultural force is still with us today. Although now there are many BBC radio stations providing different programmes for different audience groups as well as multiple TV stations, magazines and e-media resources provided by the BBC, the idea of the consensus audience can still be seen as many people still turn to the BBC for information when there are major events or national tragedies.

Radio's popularity reduced with the advent of television and, more recently, the internet offering audience more varied ways to obtain information. But, when driving to work in the morning, five million people listen to the Radio One *Breakfast Show* every week and over seven million to Radio 4's *Today* programme. *The Archers*, on Radio 4, is the world's longest running radio soap opera and has over four million listeners per week. Many TV programmes struggle to attract audiences of this size. Radio has always been a relatively mobile form of media but internet radio shows and podcasts mean that 'radio' programmes can be accessed via phones and tablets anywhere and at any time, and access is not limited to specific broadcast times, which has the potential to increase the circulation of radio programmes or podcasts.

Serial (2014) was a massively successful podcast. Discussions on social media created viral interest in the show and its audience grew over time. As the episodes were available to listen to (or download) online, audiences could access the show when they heard about it and listen to it at their own convenience. This is crucial for programmes such as *Serial* as it has an extended, ongoing narrative. In the old system, where access was restricted to broadcast times, an audience member who missed early episodes would be excluded from enjoying the programme properly.

Television

Like radio, TV became the centre of popular culture. It became the primary source of media from its introduction in British households in the 1950s. TV offered information and entertainment across, at first, a limited number of channels. Through the 1960s, 1970s and into the 1980s there were only three UK channels. Channel 4 was launched in 1982 and Channel 5 in 1997. Twentieth-century TV audiences for single programmes could be massive. For example, as many as 27 million people watched *Coronation Street* at any one time. This figure was recorded for the marriage of the popular character Hilda Ogden, which was broadcast on Christmas Day in 1987.

As most people watched mainstream mass-market television this created a shared cultural knowledge and experience. The shooting of a character in the soap opera *Dallas* became an important discussion point in 1980. T-shirts were printed and songs were recorded all asking the question 'Who Shot JR?' The question became a talking point in the US and the UK, and the episode that revealed the killer was the most watched TV episode of all time at that point.

Television is still very popular today, but distribution methods have changed. Beginning with the introduction of domestic video recorders/players (see below), distribution methods have developed to such an extent that audiences no longer need a television set to access 'television shows'. Streaming, video-on-demand and digital downloads allow audiences to watch programmes created for TV on phones, computers and tablets, making the programmes more accessible than ever before and more portable. Streaming services such as Netflix provide programmes over the internet, allow downloads for offline viewing and are making a massive library of film and TV programmes available to subscribers. Many of the programmes available on Netflix are old programmes that may find new audiences as well as appealing to existing fans. Netflix also provides access to shows produced in countries other than the UK and the US, giving audiences the choice to access shows from other cultures and in other languages. These shows are likely to be a minority interest but Netflix's business model doesn't need individual shows to attract large audiences. Netflix is based on a subscription model, so the more people that subscribe the more money the company makes. Providing services for minority interests is one way to expand the number of people who subscribe, making Netflix freer to invest in programmes that may not attract advertising revenue on more traditional channels.

Vinyl records

The phenomenon of late 20th-century pop music owes its existence to two communication technologies: radio and vinyl records. Records allowed music to be recorded and then distributed to be played at home. Radio played and, therefore, promoted music allowing audiences to select the music they wanted to buy. Radio could provide musical entertainment based on choices made by radio stations or DJs. Buying a record meant that the audience could play their chosen song whenever they wished.

From the middle of the 20th century, media companies saw the potential for profit in creating and selling music for young people. Record companies marketed rock and roll to young people in the 1950s. This generation of teenagers had a disposable income and soon bought music to express their individual and collective identities. Record companies have attempted to engage and attract new audiences in these ways ever since.

Music was distributed to audiences through radio at first and then record shops where the music was bought. TV was also part of the marketing and distribution of music, and a music press grew around the industry. The music press offered interviews with artists and reviews of singles, albums and live shows. The journalists for publications such as *Melody Maker*, *Sounds*, *The Record Mirror* and *New Musical Express* became self-appointed experts offering opinions of what and who was 'in'.

Later pop music was discussed in *Smash Hits* – a fortnightly magazine that had a circulation of up to 500,000 in its early 1980s heyday. Pop musicians were promoted on children's TV and in more general magazines – all of which fed into the distribution and circulation processes.

As technologies changed, the music industry offered audiences new experiences to meet their changing behaviours. Cassettes were a popular format for music and their popularity rose when audiences started using mobile technologies such

as the Sony Walkman. The introduction of CDs as a format for music encouraged audiences to update their existing collections by re-purchasing classic and favourite recordings on the new format.

The music industry also invested increasingly large sums of money into video, using the popularity of MTV and the audience's desire to watch music on television as a new way to market and promote their artists. The music industry saw sales of music rising throughout the 20th century but the rise of digital downloads and, later, YouTube saw changes in audience behaviour that impacted on the music industry's business model. People stopped paying for music, so the old models of distribution and circulation of physical products became increasingly irrelevant.

Music sales today are much smaller than in the past so record companies look to other sources of income such as merchandise sales, live shows, corporate sponsorship and licensing agreements to generate an income. This has led to changes in the relationship between record companies and musicians too. Traditionally, record labels would recoup the expenses accrued when recording, promoting and distributing music from the money made via music sales. The record companies had no claim on money made by musical artists in any other way. New contracts (called 360-degree contracts) mean that artists have to pay record companies a percentage of their income from any and all sources, including performances and merchandise.

Video players/recorders

Video players/recorders revolutionised the distribution and circulation of films and television programmes. The introduction of domestic video players in the late 1970s also led to two major changes in audience behaviour:

- audiences could choose to record TV broadcasts and watch programmes when they chose rather than at the time determined by the broadcasting institution
- audiences could also rent films (and later buy them), so had access to a wide range of film releases available to them outside of the cinema or to broadcast schedules.

In the early days of film rentals, most of the films available to the public were low-budget genre films or films that had had a limited release in cinemas. Video rentals gave films a second chance to find an audience. For example, the first *Terminator* film had some success on its release in the cinema in 1984 but, through word of mouth and ease of accessibility, the film became a big success on video and went on to be a major Hollywood franchise.

At first Hollywood feared that videos would impact on its ability to attract audiences to the cinema – the primary source of income for the film industry. Sony was sued for providing technology that could allow people to pirate films and TV shows, but the court ruled that the inventor of a technology could not be held responsible for it being used in a way that broke the law. However, the film industry soon realised it could tap into the audience demand for home video by making more titles available.

At first, audiences rented videos and later a market for the sale of films was established. TV companies found that audiences liked the freedom from TV schedules that home recording provided. They were slower to pick up on the market potential in renting or selling videos but by the mid-1990s cult shows such as *The X Files* and *Star Trek* led the way in the video box set, which, of course, became the DVD box set by the end of the decade. By the early 2000s, DVD sales had become a crucial part of the film and TV industry's business model.

The X Files seventh season

Although the physical technology has become less relevant, the DVD box set and the way audiences are able to access programmes when they choose, as well as having the ability to binge-watch multiple episodes at a time, is mirrored in the methods of circulation used by streaming services such as BBC iPlayer, Amazon Prime and Netflix, which regularly make full seasons of programmes available at the same time, giving audiences total freedom as to how programmes are accessed.

It is clear that technological changes have influenced the way media industries act. The technologies led to changes in audience behaviour and expectations, and media industries have to respond to these changes.

New ways to think about media industries

Not only have technological developments impacted on the way industries produce distribute and circulate media products but they have also altered the way we think about what (or who) a media industry is. The traditional media industries were 'industrial', churning out lots and lots of media products for **mass consumption**. As identified earlier, these industries were expensive to run but could make huge profits if their products proved to be successful. Most modern media industries are moving away from this model with perhaps Hollywood cinema being the best example of the traditional model working (some of the time) today.

APPLY IT

1 **Access BBC's iPlayer.**

   In what ways do you think iPlayer is responding to the competition provided by streaming services such as Netflix and Amazon Prime?

2 **Access Spotify.**

   What advantages does Spotify have over conventional music radio?

EXAMPLE: Marvel

Marvel produces superhero TV programmes. It was initially a comic-book publisher that introduced audiences to hundreds of superhero related characters such as Spiderman, Captain America, Iron Man and Daredevil. It is now a subsidiary of Disney and Marvel Studios produces superhero films. Marvel TV produces superhero TV shows, while comic books, merchandise, games and a host of other media all combine to make Marvel one of the great media success stories of the 21st century. Its films have become the most profitable films of all time with *Avengers Assemble*, *Age of Ultron*, *Iron Man 3* and *Captain America Civil War* all making over a billion dollars. It has programmes on TV and creates products for diverse audiences. The company minimises financial risk by producing products that follow conventional genre and narrative conventions (with a few twists here and there). It creates an interconnected universe where characters can mingle and interact, and it bases its stories on characters and situations that have already proven popular with audiences. Marvel has created a brand identity. Audiences can rely on Marvel's products being well written and produced. The products feature famous actors and have high production values, using the most up to the minute digital technologies and special effects. Marvel products are fast paced and exciting. This branding also minimises the financial risk for the audience. If you know Marvel, you know what to expect, and, if you like what Marvel offers, you'll probably not mind spending money on a cinema ticket, a digital download or a Netflix subscription.

Avengers Assemble

Although Marvel is a traditional production company, it is not an 'old-fashioned' media institution. As well as still making and promoting traditional media forms, it uses social media extensively. From creating sophisticated online marketing campaigns, to exploiting its avid and active audience base, Marvel uses new and digital media to help promote both the primary media products (films, TV programmes and comic books) and the secondary products it generates (merchandise, soundtracks, etc.).

The film industry, like other traditional media industries, has seen changes in technology and audience behaviours impact on its profits. Marvel's great strength is that it bases its productions on existing intellectual properties (the comic books) that it owns. The film industry is keen to make films that will immediately attract an audience. One of the best ways to do this is to create films based on stories and characters that already have a following, which is why so many films today are adaptations of books, comics, TV shows or other films. If something has already proved itself to be popular and successful, the logic is that it will not only bring existing fans into the cinema but also will have the potential to appeal to new audiences. The brand for an existing **intellectual property** is usually already established and this makes marketing the product easier. Marvel is a prime example of an institution that produces traditional media forms in a traditional film studio set-up but is still immensely successful despite changes to media production and consumption practices. By using existing intellectual property and revisiting its own older ideas, Marvel uses audience familiarity with the characters and situations while also maintaining audience interest in the new titles it creates. It uses new distribution and circulation methods (e.g. Netflix) and uses the internet to market and promote its products.

Even trailers are now an income source rather than just a marketing expense, thanks to platforms such as YouTube. Trailers can attract huge numbers of views online and this explains why a Marvel marketing strategy will include teaser trailers, TV spots, cinematic trailers (often several are released revealing different aspects of the film) and trailers for different audience groups. In addition, these trailers tend to generate response videos, analysis and lots of discussion, further spreading information about the Marvel product.

New media: new producers and methods of distribution and circulation

The traditional media producers that are doing well in the new digital culture are the ones adapting to new technologies best. Digital and new media is creating an environment in which what we mean by 'media institution' or 'media industry' is changing. Digital media is reshaping the relationship between producer and audience, and the way that media products are produced, distributed and circulated continues to evolve. Some platforms for distribution and circulation are now producing media products – Netflix and Amazon are high-profile producers whose business models are challenging traditional film and TV industries. Platforms such as Facebook, Twitter and Google do not produce original content but they do act to distribute and circulate media products. This is having an impact on the news industry.

Social media news distributors

EXAMPLE: The news and social media

Traditionally people got news and information about current affairs from news organisations that distributed the news in print, on television or on the radio. The supply of news to the public was managed by large news organisations such as (in the UK):

- **Broadcast organisations** such as: BBC News, ITN and Sky News.
  - These organisations now create news broadcasts for television and radio as well as video packages for websites and other online platforms.

- **Print organisations** such as: News International, the Mirror Group and the Mail Group.
  - These organisations have all diversified into the production of online news sites.

Information on the events of the day was traditionally gathered and selected by editors for broadcast or publication. The information itself tended to come from:

- **news agencies**
- journalists and **correspondents** employed by the news organisation
- public records (e.g. the agenda for the day in parliament, a court record, a politician's official diary)
- PR (public relations) sources.

News organisations are bound by professional codes of conduct (see Chapter 6 of the Year 1 book) and are regulated by **IPSO** (print news) and **Ofcom** (broadcast news). Some methods of sourcing news and information can slip into unethical behaviour. For example, chequebook journalism (the practice of paying sources for stories); door-stepping (waiting outside people's homes to catch them for comment as they arrive or leave); and, as highlighted in the **Leveson report**, phone hacking.

For more on professional codes of conduct see pages 128–129 of the Year 1 book.

For more on the Leveson report see page 121 of the Year 1 book.

These sourcing practices are often associated with **tabloid newspapers**, but the competition between news organisations for readers/viewers means that all news organisations are under pressure to gather and present information that will attract as many readers/viewers as possible.

The rise of **satellite/cable channels** and the introduction of dedicated **24-hour rolling news** channels created pressures on traditional broadcast news organisations. The development of multi-channel TV bought competition to the established broadcasters from international news sources such as *Al Jazeera* and *Russia Today*. Both companies are global institutions and offer UK audiences 24-hour English-language news, giving a non-British perspective on stories and events. Critics of the channels see them as propaganda arms for the Qatari and Russian governments respectively, while others see them as welcome alternatives that present news without being tied politically to the British government or Western commercial interests.

The introduction of 24-hour rolling news channels has offered immediate and continuous access to news stories for audiences but has also created some issues in the way events are sourced and reported. Rolling news is uniquely placed to present ongoing developments in breaking news stories and can respond quickly as events unfold. Traditional news broadcasts – usually scheduled in the morning, in the middle of the day, around 6.00pm and finally about 10.00pm – are summaries of events that had already happened. Rolling news created a convention and perhaps an expectation that audiences should be informed as things occur rather than afterwards. However, news broadcasters often don't have much to say – especially as an event is taking place. This has led to the news often being filled with speculation, assumptions and guesses rather than concrete facts and information. One major news event to demonstrate this was on September 11, 2001. The attacks, initially on the Twin Towers in New York, unfolded during the day, with images of events being broadcast live. The moment the second plane flew into the World Trade Center, just after 9.00am, was broadcast live. The commentary from the news anchors demonstrated their horror, fear and lack of clear understanding as to what was happening. News broadcasters were still trying to understand what had happened to the first tower when the second tower was hit and images of the event began to circulate.

In 2017, broadcast news organisations were also criticised on their reporting of the Westminster and Manchester terrorist attacks, for their intrusive interviewing

24-HOUR NEWS CYCLE

of witnesses and, at times, victims or family members of victims of the attacks. Interviews with 'experts' are often offered as ways to develop the story and there have been occasions when the reporters have offered their viewers incorrect information, inaccurate analysis and misunderstandings rather than verified facts in the rush to report on a story.

In addition, the competition for viewers often leads news broadcasters to dramatise their reporting style. This is often criticised for turning news into entertainment. Simon Jenkins (a former editor of *The Times*) also warned that '*sensationalising and dramatising a crime*' makes the media '*a megaphone for the act*' (2017). He suggested that the blanket coverage given to events such as the Westminster attack, could be an 'inspiration' for similar acts. Professor Roy Greenslade (former editor of the *Daily Mirror*) called the amount of coverage of the event '*disproportionate*' (2017). The nature of news events is that understanding of them increases as time passes. An inherent problem with 24-hour rolling news is that it reports moment-to-moment updating and correcting as it goes. There are, of course, no guarantees that audiences will receive accurate information from this type of news source. It all depends on when they watch. This style of immediacy in reporting is also found in online news. Newspapers run 'as it happens' blogs, with summaries presented to round up the developments, which also correct and clarify earlier reports.

The main digital challenge to the dominance of the traditional news organisation, however, is not rolling news but online news. Online news offers written stories, video reports and podcasts – everything that used to be accessed via broadcast or print media. In addition, the majority of online news is free. Some news sources do require a subscription to access their content. *The Times*, for example, is behind a paywall and charges from £6.00 to £9.00 per week to subscribe (with introductory prices and a free Nespresso machine used to tempt audiences in). Audiences can read online editions of traditional newspapers such as the *Telegraph* or the *Guardian* for free, although both sites offer paid membership/support benefits as well as subscription to access digital services such as the news apps for phones and tablets. Audiences can access the BBC, ITN and Sky News websites, which provide news stories illustrated with images, reports and animations. They can also watch news broadcasts from around the world on YouTube or Vimeo. In addition, the internet offers a host of non-traditional sources for news.

For example: **news aggregators** such as *HuffPost*, *The Drudge Report* and *The Daily Beast* use **algorithms** to scour the internet for news stories on a specific topic, which are then repackaged and presented on their website. This enables each site to present stories that best support their own **editorial positions** – *HuffPost* collates stories that support a **politically liberal** set of values while *The Drudge Report* offers **politically conservative** viewpoints.

YouTube offers many videos that are part of the communication of news events. Opinion-based **talking heads** commentators offer political opinions and interpretations of current news and events. Alex Jones is an American at the extreme right of US politics, who presents videos of his radio show on YouTube. *The Young Turks*, again American, offers analysis and opinions from a liberal-left perspective, often quoting from US cable news organisations such as CNN and Fox News. Immediately after the election of Donald Trump as the American president, US TV comedians whose work is largely based on political commentary found their viewing figures rising on TV and online. Samantha Bee's political programme *Full Frontal* and John Oliver's *Last Week Tonight* are watched by a global audience online and their videos regularly attract millions of views. *Vice News* reports on issues and events that are often overlooked by traditional news sources and, in the UK, Russell Brand's YouTube channel, *The Trews*, offers comments and analysis of current affairs as does, with the opposite political perspective, the *Guido Fawkes* website.

The rise in alternative and independent news sources does offer a range of different perspectives and this means that audiences can get their news from multiple and non-traditional sources. Research undertaken by Fenton in 2009, however, found that, despite the potential for a 'diversity of voices in an on-line context' audiences are not necessarily getting a broad range of ideas and opinions when they access the news. Fenton found that:

- *Many of the same **gatekeepers** are in charge and our horizons may be narrowing not expanding.*
- *Most people, most of the time, get most of their information from mainstream news sources, whether that's on-line or not.*
- *There is an immense global archive of information (on the web) but people go to tried and tested sources – people go to mainstream news.*
- *There are more links to other types of material and there's more comment coming through but it's comment on what has already been set by the mainstream **news agenda**, the agendas themselves are not shifting.* (Fenton, 2009)

Most aggregate news sources summarise, reproduce or comment on stories that have been generated by traditional news organisations, but the rise in online news has challenged the economic dominance of these traditional news organisations. To remain competitive, they have had to engage with the changing news environment. In addition to the traditional sources of information, news organisations have looked to use resources found online to help them create interesting and engaging news reports.

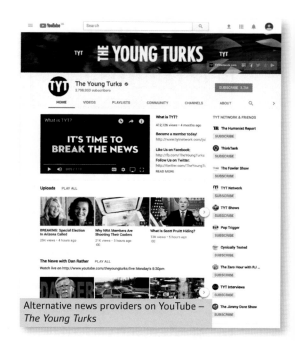

Alternative news providers on YouTube – *The Young Turks*

Social media and the news

A 2017 research project reported that social media had been identified as being the main source of news for young people (Digital News Report, 2018). Of the people who use the internet, 51% use social media to access their news. Twitter and Facebook, therefore, can be seen to be highly influential on what audiences see and, increasingly, the content of the news itself.

Twitter

Twitter offers a source of **citizen journalism** – that is news and information generated by the public. People who witness an event Tweet information, photographs and videos that are used as material for reports in professionally produced news stories and news broadcasts. This is a cheap way for news institutions to gather news and information, and it means that information is available much more quickly than in the past. There are issues regarding **copyright** of Tweets and the images and videos they contain. As they are in the **public domain**, the information can be re-presented in a news article if the source of the information is credited. Some news agencies will contact the producers of Tweets that become popular to offer payment for the use. After a helicopter crash in 2013 in central London, which was illustrated by images taken by a bystander at the scene, a picture editor of the *Evening Standard* said that the paper does not seek out the people whose Tweets they use but they would pay for their use if they were contacted for a payment. Twitter is also used as source of news itself. It is an immediate source of comments and opinions that can be used by journalists. Comments made by politicians and other public figures are used to show the impact of a news story and the opinions of selected members of the public are used to exemplify public opinion. Analysing the content of Twitter conversations on any given topic allows news institutions to evaluate the responses and gives a snapshot of public opinion; maybe helping them decide on their editorial approach. For example, the *Daily Mail* had been consistent in its negative responses to the immigration crisis unfolding in 2015.

The *Daily Mail*, 28 August 2015

The *Daily Mail*, 3 September 2015

Just six days after the *Daily Mail* published the headline on the left, a citizen journalist's photograph was released showing a Turkish policeman carrying the body of a toddler who had died as his refugee family attempted to make their way to Greece. The dominant response on social media had been one of shock and outrage at the tragic loss of a young life. Sensing the public mood, the *Daily Mail* created a front page that seemed to temper its earlier approaches to stories about migration (as shown below left).

Increasingly, Twitter itself becomes a news story. Newspapers often report on **Twitter-spats** between public figures and topics that are **trending** on Twitter are taken up by the traditional news media, so **viral** conversations and events become items on news broadcasts and stories in newspapers thus giving the traditional media cheap and easy ways to appear relevant.

Facebook

Facebook users have always had the ability to post links to news stories in their timeline. Facebook users can follow other users and create their own subject-based filters and their past activities feed into an algorithm that is used to present them with news and information based on Facebook's interpretation of users' interests and political preferences. Facebook offers links to news stories from a range of different sources and, on the surface, this looks like **pluralism** in action. However, there are issues in the way news and information are personalised and delivered to users' Facebook accounts.

Clickbait and fake news

As clicks on a link or a visit to a page is now a commodified event, attracting readers to a story on a website can be financially very lucrative. Traditional news sites often use **clickbait** – headlines and stories selected or constructed specifically to make audiences want to read more. The technique is also used by organisations that create attention-grabbing headlines that lead to websites that are full of adverts. The headlines lead to stories that are very often fictions but look like news stories, and many people remain under the illusion that they are true – especially as many **fake news** sites look very similar to real news websites such as the BBC, Al Jazeera and CNN. The most successful types of clickbait are headlines stories that generate emotion in the reader. Shocking, horrifying and outrageous headlines generate clicks and, even better, are likely to be shared between users, generating even more clicks. **Sensationalism** prioritises tabloid approaches to reporting and **hard news** stories are often reduced to their **soft news** elements to attract readers.

Sensationalism drives users to websites and this increases the advertising value of the site, which has led to the rise of fake news sites. These sites generate sensational stories to attract readers but the content of the stories is completely fabricated. The website can then sell data about the visitors to the site to advertisers making them a valuable commodity.

Echo-chambers

As Facebook analyses a user's interests and behaviours to provide targeted information, the information received by a user tends to reflect their existing world view. A conservative thinker who reads conservative newspapers and websites and clicks on stories with conservative viewpoints will be offered more and more information that reflects conservative values. It is likely that their social network will be made up of other conservative thinkers who will be sharing more conservative news and opinions. This creates a digital **echo-chamber** where people experience their own views being reflected back by a range of sources. This can create a **false consciousness** of consensus (Engels, cited in Eagleton, 1992) where ideas go through a process of **naturalisation** as they are repeated (Barthes, 2009) cultivating (Gerbner) specific ideas and values. This can lead to the unquestioning acceptance of information that confirms the reader's views – particularly problematic given the amount of fake news being generated.

The creation of fake news can be motivated simply by the money it generates but during election campaigns, some fake news stories could have had an effect on people's voting intentions. There are suspicions that during the 2016 US election campaign a fake news strategy was implemented to influence the results of the election. In 2017, the US Director of National Intelligence accused Russia of interfering with the election using, among other things, the dissemination of fake news. The echo-chamber effect means that fake news can often be circulated to a wide audience and be very influential. People, including traditional news institutions, have been caught out and become part of the passing on of fake stories. The realisation that fake news exists and can be difficult to identify means that trust in the media is shaken. The term 'fake news' is itself often used inaccurately to create further distrust in the news media. Critical arguments, awkward questions, alternative viewpoints or questions that challenge misinformation are not examples of 'fake news', but the term is increasingly being used by people whose perspective is challenged in order to undermine news reporting that does not support their point of view.

The spread of fake news has been enabled by changes in the way Facebook generates information that finds its way into users' newsfeeds. In 2012 Facebook allowed advertising in newsfeeds via sponsored stories – that is, stories that pay to be placed on selected newsfeeds. The audience for the sponsored story will be carefully selected by Facebook's algorithm so there is a high chance the reader will interact with the story in some way. Sponsored stories look almost identical to non-sponsored stories but contain advertising content or content designed to generate clicks. Their appearance in a user's timeline will have been paid for. The company will pay Facebook to ensure that its message reaches audiences most likely to respond and Facebook use the data they have gathered on users to provide this service. This allows marketers to create very specific marketing campaigns for very specific types of users and this is used by political parties during elections. Facebook has been criticised for having an undue influence on democracy in the way it creates echo-chambers, allows for niche marketing and both allows and benefits from the spread of fake news.

Until 2016, Facebook took no responsibility for the accuracy of the information that was shared on its platform. With over two billion users its newsfeed is viewed by more people than any other news provider. In November 2016, responding to criticisms that the social media site had influenced the outcome of the US election, Facebook's CEO Mark Zuckerberg denied it was a media company:

> *Facebook is mostly about helping people stay connected with friends and family. News and media are not the primary things people do on Facebook, so I find it odd when people insist we call ourselves a news or media company in order to acknowledge its importance.*

In a later interview that year (Constine, 2016) he went on to say:

> *Facebook is a new kind of platform. It's not a traditional technology company. It's not a traditional media company. You know, we build technology and we feel responsible for how it's used. We don't write the news that people read on the platform. But at the same time we also know that we do a lot more than just distribute news, and we're an important part of the public discourse.*

Facebook's desire to distance itself from being defined as a media company is largely driven by the fact that media companies have to take responsibility for the content they publish, whereas technology platforms do not. techcrunch.com compares Facebook to a newsroom:

APPLY IT

Access the *Independent* online edition.

What features are offered on the website that you think show the influence of online news providers such as Buzzfeed and social media such as Facebook and Twitter?

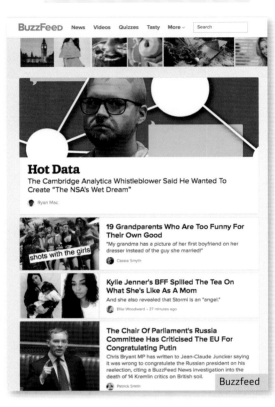

Buzzfeed

You could see [Facebook] users as the reporters creating the stories, while the News Feed algorithm acts as the editor, deciding which stories to run and how prominently. Meanwhile, Facebook's leaders who write the community standards and content policies also act as editors, vetoing or allowing controversial content like reports of police shootings or nude historical photographs.

Facebook writes the code that applies these algorithms and policies like a technology company, but it also makes editorial decisions about what to prioritize and permit, like the editor of a media company.

Facebook has since begun to work with genuine news organisations to help identify when a news story is fake and also to allow users to report fake news. It also intends to scan its webpages to see if sites that are being landed on from Facebook links are ad-based sites, and this data can be used to down-rank some sources of information.

In 2018 Zuckerberg had to respond to revelations about the way Cambridge Analytica used Facebook data to target voters in both the EU referendum and Trump's presidential campaign. Vast amounts of data about Facebook users were analysed in an attempt to send targeted political messages to potential voters in an attempt to influence their voting intentions. Zuckerberg's previous position that sought to distance Facebook from responsibility for the way the platform could be politicised had to be amended and he apologised for his company's inability to protect its customers' data.

KEY TERMS

24-hour rolling news	digital TV channels that show only news and that broadcast 24 hours a day
algorithms	computer technology that gathers and analyses user data
business model	the methods used by an organisation to generate an income and maximise its profits
citizen journalism	the contributions to news reports made by members of the public
clickbait	stories and headlines that are constructed to encourage audiences to click through to access more information. Clickbait usually attempts to create an emotional response
consensus	a state of agreement
copyright	the legal ownership of the content of media products
correspondents	journalists who have a specialisation (e.g. war correspondent) or who serve a specific location (e.g. a Westminster correspondent)
echo-chamber	the phenomenon caused by audiences limiting their media experiences to products and locations that reinforce their existing beliefs and values

editorial position	the political values that influence the way a media product is constructed
fake news	fictional or misleading stories that are presented as news
false consciousness	the belief in ideas that are not based in fact
gatekeepers	individuals and groups who have the ability to select (and reject) the content of media products
hard news	news that is related to politics, economics, science, war, terrorism, etc.
IPSO	the Independent Press Standards Organisation
Leveson report	the report on press behaviour and practices published after the Leveson Inquiry, which was set up after accusations that some newspapers were using illegal methods to gather information for stories
mass consumption	the use of a media product by many people, usually within a restricted timeframe
naturalisation	the belief that an idea is a natural state rather than a human construction
news agencies	organisations that receive and distribute news
news agenda	the prioritising of selected events when planning the news

news aggregators	refers to (usually) online news sources that use software to gather news from other online sources
Ofcom	the governmental Office of Communications standards
pluralism	the idea that the media offers a range of perspectives, so audiences can choose and select to engage with the ideas they wish to
politically conservative	can be interpreted in different ways but generally refers to a belief system based on the prioritisation of individual social and economic responsibility. Social change is often resisted
politically liberal	can be interpreted in different ways but generally refers to a belief system based on the prioritisation of social and economic responsibility. Social change is seen to be both positive and, often, essential

public domain	relates to media products/ideas that are outside the restrictions of copyright law and are freely available to the public
satellite/cable channels	television channels that required audiences to buy specialised technologies in order to access them. The term was relevant as a differentiator between 'terrestrial TV' and 'satellite' TV (BBC1 and 2, ITV, Channel 4 and Channel 5). Since the digital switchover in 2007, 'terrestrial TV has been accessible with other 'satellite' channels on services such as Freebox
sensationalism	a reporting style that seeks to create an emotional response in its readers
soft news	news that is related to celebrities, entertainment, sport, gossip, scandal and human interest stories

tabloid newspapers	a genre of newspaper that favours entertainment, gossip and human-interest stories. Tabloids tends to use a sensationalist style of reporting. The term is often used when the values of tabloid newspapers are replicated in other media products or forms, e.g. the concept of tabloid TV, tabloid magazines, etc.
talking heads	the use of a mid-shot of someone speaking, usually with limited mise-en-scène
trending	the most popular topics of the day as identified by social media activity
Twitter-spats	arguments conducted using Twitter
viral	the electronic passing of images, information, etc. between users. Before digital and social media, the term was used to describe the spreading of information by word of mouth

4.3 The rise of 'digital' producers and distributors

Recent technological changes have offered production opportunities to people from outside the media industries who have developed their own methods of production, distribution and circulation, which rival and sometimes outperform the traditional media industries.

The ability to access production technology that is both cheap and easy to use has radically changed our ways of thinking about who gets to create media products. As identified in this chapter's Introduction, anyone with a digital camera can create an Instagram or YouTube account. Almost everyone has access to the tools that could allow them to become a media producer. Software allows self-taught and self-financed amateurs the ability to record and produce their own music, create 'TV shows', documentaries or fiction films that can be uploaded to YouTube, or create online lifestyle 'magazines' on Tumblr or Instagram. The rise of affordable and easy to access digital production technologies has removed the initial barrier to production that allowed media industries to maintain their powerful position in the past.

Internet-based distribution platforms are also widely available to amateur producers. Creating an Instagram, Soundcloud or YouTube account takes very little specialist technical knowledge and once the accounts are populated with images, sound files or videos the content has a potentially global reach. The internet has made the distribution of media products easier today than it has ever been and, in theory, amateur productions that are hosted online have the same **potential reach** as those hosted by the traditional media industries. These platforms are largely free for the user, as social media platforms rely on the data they receive about users and visitors to the site to create an income. Turow observes that users '*are being quietly peeked at, poked, analysed and tagged as they move through the online world*' (Turow cited in Hesmondhalgh, 2012, page 334). This data is sold to advertisers who wish to create specific targeted advertising – as Turow goes on to say; the '*goal is to find out how to activate individuals' buying impulses so they can sell us stuff more efficiently than ever before*'.

Distribution today is the easiest part of the process. Circulation is, however, much harder – especially for amateur producers. Traditional institutions have the benefit of being known by audiences and so are often online destinations for media audiences. This is certainly true of news organisations that are still the main source of news for most people. The challenge for non-traditional media producers is how to attract audiences to their products. As we saw with Arctic Monkeys in 2006, modern content providers often need 'old media' to help them find wider and broader audiences.

EXAMPLE: *Lights Out*

The Swedish filmmaker David F. Sandberg created a short horror film in 2013 called *Lights Out* and uploaded it to Vimeo and YouTube. The film was made with a very low budget and it starred his wife. The film was spotted and people began to discuss it on social media sites such as Reddit. This created wider interest and the film was seen by a Hollywood producer, Lawrence Grey. Grey contacted Sandberg and bought the rights to the film. Grey was able to attract James Wan (the creator of *Saw* and *The Conjuring*) as a producer for the project and this, plus the viral success of the short film, helped attract studio funding for production, marketing and distribution. Sandberg directed a full-length version of the film that was released in 2016. The film cost $5 million to make and generated an income of $22 million in its opening weekend – a clear financial success.

Of course, this is an exception. A search on YouTube for a 'short horror film' brings up nearly eight million videos. The problem for independent producers is not making their products available to audiences but in making audiences aware of their products. For every Sandberg there are thousands of filmmakers posting online that do not get a job offer from Hollywood.

The rise and influence of social media

Successful YouTubers include Zoella, who is one of a stable of YouTubers managed by Gleam Productions. Having professional management and being part of an organisation that specialises in promoting vloggers helps to maximise the potential for success. Gleam Productions represents vloggers who offer a diverse range of content. In some cases the content is the same as what would traditionally have been found on television, but often Gleam Productions' clients present video formats that are specific to social media. Beauty bloggers such as Caroline Hirons, 'PixiWoo' and 'A Model Recommends' offer beauty tips and consumer advice that may have been part of daytime TV magazine shows in the past, but their style of presentation is very specific to YouTube beauty vloggers. Cookery has always been a popular topic for TV programmes, and Katie Pix and 'Haste's Kitchen' offer recipes and 'how to' guides, while Carly Rowena and 'The Lean Machines' combine healthy eating and fitness on their channels. Joe Suggs' channel contains a range of content from day-to-day vlogs to prank and challenge videos that offer comedic content influenced by TV programmes such as *Beadle's About* or *Jackass*. 'The Saccone Joly's' and 'Mother Pukka' are family-based lifestyle vlogs, which are similar to **fly-on-the-wall documentaries** in the way they present the subjects getting on with their daily lives. The portable nature of video cameras and the ease of access to editing software have made these formats something that people can do for themselves.

Some YouTube videos look very much like conventional television programmes: 'Haste's Kitchen' shows the presenter in mid-shot talking to the camera and intercuts this with close-ups of the food as it is being prepared.

The presenter addresses the camera in mid-shot.

Close-up on food

However, the distinct types of content offered by YouTube has led to the development of specific visual codes. Documenting day-to-day events is often done using a hand-held camera that **pans** quickly between subjects and is often on the move. Presenters often look directly into the hand-held camera and the 'walk and talk' selfie shot is common in this type of video as are selfie shots taken in bed or from the dashboard of a car.

The hand-held selfie shot

Vlogging while driving

The end of the day – the in-bed selfie shot

YouTubers have built their audiences over time, and benefit from the viral nature of the spread of information online. Everyone who watches a video on YouTube is part of a social (media or non-media) network. Media producers want to make products that are not only appealing to the individual audience member but also encourage that audience member to share information about the product with their friends. If one viewer has a network of ten people and each of those people has a network of ten people, then one viewer quickly has the potential to link to 100 more and this can soon expand into thousands and millions of views. This can only work if the people watching feel compelled to share with their network though, so YouTube and other social media sites offer detailed analytics that identify who is watching each video and how they arrived on the channel.

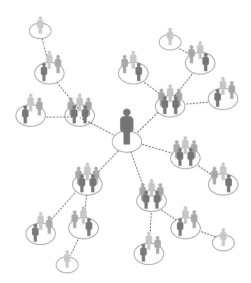

People who have large followings on social media are called influencers. Sometimes known as opinion leaders (Katz & Lazarsfeld, 2005), they have access to a large number of people who follow their recommendations and who are able to create trends. Influencers are valuable to advertisers as they can be used to help promote consumer products and events, and many social media 'stars' generate income by providing promotional space, becoming brand ambassadors and often marketing their own brand of lifestyle related products (what Hearn calls 'the branded self' (Hearn cited in Hesmondhalgh, 2012, page 380)). Influencers are able to promote other media products, whether this is by reviewing games and recording play-throughs (e.g. 'Yogscast' with over seven million subscribers), providing film reviews (e.g. Chris Stuckmann with over one million subscribers) or music reviews (e.g. 'the needledrop' with over one million subscribers).

With over 400 million users, Instagram has become an important social media site. Existing stars such as Beyoncé and Christiano Ronaldo use Instagram, posting images that are both professional and, in some cases, personal. Some accounts are conventional (Jennifer Lopez) and others very idiosyncratic (Miley Cyrus). Dwayne Johnson hosts lots of selfies with his fans, while Nikki Minaj posts lots of inspirational quotes. At time of writing, Selina Gomez has over 135 million followers. As a point of comparison, Katy Perry has the most Twitter followers with over 100 million. Instagram, Twitter and other social media sites are used by celebrities to create and enhance their **personal brand** and create more interest in the products they are selling. As they attract such a large number of followers, their access to audiences makes them extremely powerful. It is reported that Kendall Jenner, Gigi Hadid and Cara Delavigne can charge up to £250,000 to feature a product in their social media posts. A more common cost for an influencer such as Karlie Kloss would be between £20,000 and £40,000 per post. This massive reach gives these celebrities lots of influence and makes them an ideal platform for marketers who wish to circulate their message to as many people as possible.

APPLY IT

Search on the internet to find out whose Instagram and/or Twitter accounts have the most followers.

Access these accounts and analyse the posts.

- How is the celebrity using social media to create a personal brand?
- Is there evidence of the social media account being used to market:
  - products endorsed by the celebrity?
  - other consumer products?

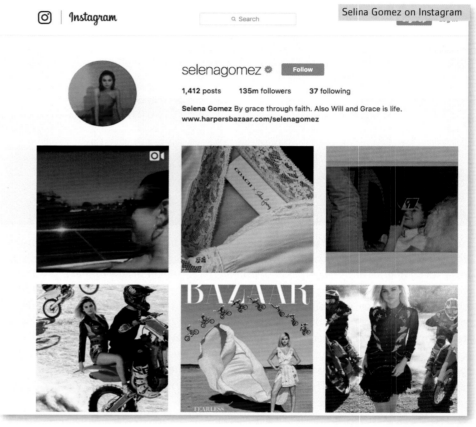

Selina Gomez on Instagram

Instagram has also created non-traditional celebrities who become **instafamous** by attracting followers to their accounts. They may be unsigned models, health and fitness trainers or lifestyle bloggers who attract large numbers of followers and whose followers actively engage with the social media posts. Social media is often a form of advertising, with bloggers, vloggers and Instagramers promoting products both directly and indirectly. Influencers on social media are able to make money from advertising, while traditional media has found this source of income decreasing dramatically.

APPLY IT

Consider the ideas raised in this chapter so far. How has social media and the ease of access to production and distribution technologies impacted on one of the following media industries:

- the music industry?
- the gaming industry?
- the film industry?
- the magazine industry?

KEY TERMS

brand ambassadors	celebrities who are paid to represent a specific consumer product or service and its brand values	instafamous	refers to people who have generated lots of followers on Instagram but who may not be visible on other social media or via traditional media	'walk and talk' selfie shot	the shot used in many lifestyle social media videos, where the subject speaks into a camera held at arm's length. The camera is usually positioned at a slightly elevated angle
fly-on-the-wall documentaries	documentaries that follow subjects, usually with hand-held cameras, to construct a realistic view of the context of someone's lived experience	opinion leaders	people who have the ability to communicate their opinions to others and may influence opinions		
Influencers	people who have the power to lead others and sway their opinions and actions. It is now a marketing term that describes individuals who have large numbers of followers on social media, have gained a level of authority and are trusted by their followers. Influencers can communicate with large numbers of people and this means they are able to spread ideas and promote products	personal brand	the constructed image created by an individual in order to create an identifiable and specific 'personality' with a view to help promote the individual		
		play-through	a video of gameplay often with live commentary from the player(s)		
		potential reach	the possible extent of the circulation of a media product		

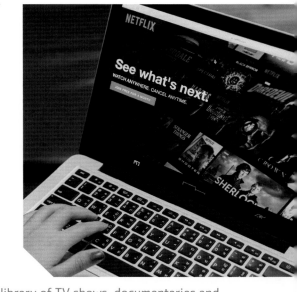

EXAMPLE: Netflix

Netflix is an American company that was founded in 1998 as a DVD rental service. Its initial unique selling point was that rental DVDs were delivered and returned in the post. In 1999, the company moved from charging a fee per DVD rented to a monthly subscription model where customers could rent as many DVDs as they wanted. By 2005 Netflix was mailing a million DVDs every day. The company moved into online streaming of video-on-demand (**SVoD**) in 2007. DVD sales were in decline and Netflix was able to use the developments in broadband and internet infrastructure that made video streaming possible. Netflix stands at the forefront of convergence, as it can be accessed on televisions, phones, tablets and computers, with access being available using online software, apps, internet TV systems and games consoles.

Netflix was launched as an online streaming service in the UK in 2012. It has increased its customer numbers and in 2017 announced that they had reached 100 million global customers (Sweney, 2017).

Netflix is funded by the monthly fee paid by subscribers. The service provides a range of benefits to the customer including:

- instant availability of content
- portable availability of content (either when online or when downloaded to phones, tablets or laptops)
- no advertising
- no additional costs – one fee gives access to all content
- access to products from a range of producers both domestic and foreign, in English and other languages
- access to 'old' products that would no longer be shown by broadcasters
- access to complete box sets of TV programmes
- an increasing library of TV shows, documentaries and feature films
- access (often exclusively) to an increasing library of original programming and films
- home screens that are personalised with recommended content based on previous viewing history
- a search facility as well as grouping by conventional and innovative genre categories – the latter often based on the customer's viewing history.

In the UK, audiences were already using SVoD services including iPlayer (released 2007), The ITV Hub (released 2008) and 4OD (launched in 2006 and now called All4).

These on-demand services provided access to content bought or created by the broadcasting institution. The services were branded as 'catch up' services and were seen to be a secondary distribution channel where live broadcast was presumed to be the primary way an audience would access the content. SVoD was promoted as a way to watch what may have been missed at the time of broadcast.

Netflix programming is not broadcast live,, so streaming video online is used to circulate the material. Hesmondhalgh (2012), page 347 calls this **post-network television**.

UK on-demand services are being influenced by the way audiences increasingly see VoD as a primary service. All4 offers lots of box sets. These are complete series of programmes that are free to watch but viewers have to watch adverts during each episode. All episodes of the second series of *Peter Kay's Car Share* were simultaneously released on iPlayer in 2017 before being broadcast on BBC1. BBC3 is now an online-only service that provides comedy, drama and documentaries which are not available via a broadcast channel.

The monthly cost of a Netflix subscription in 2017 ranged from £5.99 to £8.99, with the increasing cost offering the ability to watch content on multiple screens at the same time and access to **ultra HD** quality images. Its income is generated by subscribers, so its business model is unlike other **commercial television** content providers who look to advertising to generate an income. Netflix seeks to attract and maintain audiences to its service rather than to specific programmes. Of course, the content offered by Netflix will motivate audiences to subscribe, but 'success' on Netflix may not be defined by viewing figures for individual programmes in the same way as it is for traditional broadcasters.

Commercial television companies need to sell advertising spots before, after and within their programming. Commercial broadcasters effectively sell the audience to advertisers. Put simply, the bigger the audience for a programme, the more a commercial broadcaster can charge for the advertising space. Similarly, if a programme attracts a specific marketing group in good numbers, advertisers of products for this group will be attracted to buying advertising time. However, as general viewing figures have declined so too has the cost of advertising space, reducing the income for broadcasters but also reducing advertisers' ability to reach their market.

Product placement in *House of Cards*

Netflix avoids these economic problems as its primary income is direct from subscribers; however, it does attract advertising money in the product placement that can be seen in many of its shows. Apple products are often featured on screen in Netflix's big hit *House of Cards* and actors in US programmes call for 'an Uber' rather than a taxi. The placement of these products and brand names will not be accidental. A company may provide free products that are to be featured in productions or the company may pay to have their brand shown or mentioned on screen. This is a long-established income generator for media producers.

Key to Netflix's success is the diversity of products it offers. This has the potential to meet the needs of a wide audience range. Programmes cover a host of interests and some programmes are targeting specific audience groups. This can be evidenced in some of the Netflix original programming that ranges from documentary series (*The Chef's Table*), irreverent animated comedy (*F is for Family*), serious drama (*House of Cards*), horror (*Hemlock Grove*), teen drama (*Riverdale*) and sitcom (*The Unbreakable Kimmy Schmidt*). Netflix can also ensure that different audiences are catered for in the programmes they buy from broadcasters such as the BBC (*Peaky Blinders* and *Taboo* are available as are *Fleabag* and *Sherlock*). This business model allows it to offer programming that may be for a **niche audience**. Someone who is part of the mainstream audience for *Sherlock* will be paying the same subscription as someone who may have chosen to access Netflix because is hosts full seasons of cult sci-fi programmes such as *Star Trek*. As long as the audience member continues to pay for their subscription they are valuable to Netflix regardless of what and how much they watch.

Netflix keeps detailed data on the activities of its audience and uses this information to help it make decisions on the programming it will buy and commission for production. It spends around $15 billion per year on programming, which includes about $6 billion (2017 figures) on commissioning its own shows (Castillo, 2017). Its first original programme, *House of Cards*, was commissioned based on the analysis of what viewers watched and how they used the service. This led to all episodes of the first series of the programme, based on an existing intellectual property (a series of books and the 1990s BBC series of the same name), featuring a big Hollywood star (Kevin Spacey) and producer/director (David Fincher) being made available at the same time. Netflix had identified that the type of people who would be attracted to this type of TV series would also be likely to want to **binge-watch** multiple episodes rather than watch one episode per week.

According to David Carr in the *New York Times* (2013):

> *Netflix looks at 30 million 'plays' a day, including when you pause, rewind and fast forward, four million ratings by Netflix subscribers, three million searches as well as the time of day when shows are watched and on what devices.*

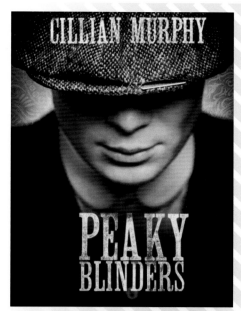

In a report for the *Guardian*, Mark Sweney (2014) reports that Netflix can see everything their subscribers are watching. The head of original content at Netflix says:

> *We can identify subscriber populations that gravitate around genre areas, such as horror, thriller and supernatural. That allows us to project a threshold audience size to see if it makes for a viable project for us.*

This ability to use detailed data to make these decisions takes away some of the risk experienced by traditional broadcasters who invest in productions that may or may not find an audience. No method is guaranteed to create popular television programmes. Some Netflix programmes have received negative reviews. Stuart Heritage in the *Guardian* (2017) writes:

> Friends from College*, which exists exclusively as a warning never to trust* **Big Data***. Individually, all of* Friends from College's *pieces are top-notch – it's a comedy created by Forgetting Sarah Marshall's Nicholas Stoller and starring the likes of Keegan-Michael Key, Cobie Smulders and Kate McKinnon – but the end result is a sludgy, unfunny, tonally uneven mess that's destined to prematurely drown in Netflix's soup of submenus.*

He argues that:

> *This [...] might be down to Big Data. After all, the only thing an algorithm can tell you is what people already like, which encourages repetition.*
> (Heritage, 2017)

Netflix's purchases and commissioning choices show that it thinks about its audience very differently from other television companies. Most TV companies think primarily about creating programmes that will please their local audiences. Much of the programming on Channel 4, BBC and ITV is created specifically to tap into British tastes. Some programmes have success overseas, with ITV's *Downton Abbey* being a notable example and evidence of the increasingly globalised nature of media distribution and circulation. It was broadcast in the US on PBS and Season 5 was watched by 25.5 million viewers, including more than 12 million views via a streaming service. Other shows such as the BBC's *Dr Who* and *Sherlock* have found fans in America via the BBC America channel. Often, UK programmes

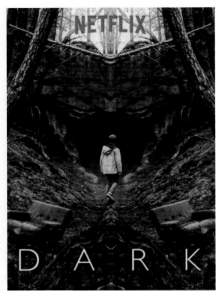
German language drama, *Dark*

are remade for US audiences. *The Office* (US) ran for nine seasons producing a total of 201 episodes. The show was based on a UK series that produced only 12 episodes and two specials. *Shameless* (US) is another highly successful remake of a UK show. Netflix is clearly considering different regions in their programming but this then provides a much more globalised service. Some shows appear very British, for example *The Crown*, but the romanticised retelling of the history of the current British Royal family has a global appeal. Since Princess Diana, the younger generation of royals have been treated like celebrities across the world, so the show has a broad appeal in many different countries. *Sense 8* identified itself as a global product in its settings (including the US, the UK, Mexico, Italy, India and Kenya) and in its diverse cast representing a wide range of races and sexual identities. Programmes from Australia (e.g. *Miss Fisher Murder Mysteries*) and Canada (e.g. *Continuum*) can be found on Netflix. Netflix also works with producers from around the world (e.g. *Lillyhammer* – a co-production with NRK/Norway) and purchases and makes non-English-language programmes (e.g. *3%*, *My Only Love Song* and *Marseille*).

All this makes Netflix attractive to a broad and wide range of audiences, as the service provides lots of choice beyond the selections available from mainstream broadcasters. However, the success of Netflix has raised several issues.

Broadcasting/narrowcasting

Traditionally, TV has been a **broadcast** medium. This term refers to the idea that a TV programme or radio show is 'cast out' in all directions at one time. That is to say, a broadcast television programme would be transmitted by a TV station at a given time and audience members in a single territory (e.g. the UK) all accessed it at the same time regardless of where they were. As previously identified, ever since the rise of the video recorder, there have been challenges to the true broadcast nature of television programming, but in the last ten years or so the idea of 'broadcasting' has become less and less valid. Video-on-demand and streaming services mean that TV shows are becoming more accurately **narrowcast** because of the choices that people have when they access the video content and that more often than not the programmes are created to meet very specific niche audience needs. This makes Netflix more like a library rather than a TV station or channel. Audiences are able to select from a wide range of products that are not geographically or historically limited. The freedom to create their own viewing patterns gives each audience member individual power but can impact negatively on some of the potential gratifications TV shows can provide. The highly personal choices made by people in the way they access media products effectively removes them from general conversation. If a show such as *Orange is the New Black* is released as a whole season on a given day, audience members may make one of the following choices:

- To binge-watch all episodes immediately.
- To quickly watch the whole series over a number of days.
- To watch the whole series but saving some episodes for the weekend.
- To watch the series one episode every now and then.
- To bookmark the series and come back to it at a later date.
- New audiences may find and watch the series several years after its initial release.

Before streaming services, there was the concept of 'watercooler' TV. This referred to the type of shows you could assume most of your friends, school, college or workmates would be sure to watch. Sitcoms such as *Friends*, soap operas such as *Eastenders* and entertainment shows such as *Gladiators* had mass market appeal and, as they were broadcast programmes, would be watched by millions of people at the same time. These and **event television** such as season finales, sports events and royal weddings could safely be the topic of conversation on buses and at office watercoolers. Statistically, most people you encounter would have watched these programmes and those who had not had lost the opportunity to do so. There was no such thing as a **spoiler** at that time.

Blumer and Katz suggest that one potential gratification provided by media products is that of 'social interaction' (cited in Sullivan, 2012). The narrowcasting nature of TV today means that people are not always connected to others in their immediate social and professional networks by the shared cultural experience of watching a TV show. Social interaction is more likely to be found via the gathering of audience groups online, so the interaction is between strangers who share cultural knowledge. Twitter and other social media platforms provide the social interaction gratification as it is impossible to discuss media experiences with others who have chosen to watch programmes later – or who may not watch the show in question at all.

Gladiators

Competition to other broadcasters

One important content producer is currently notable by their absence from the Netflix listings. HBO has made some of the most critically acclaimed TV of the past 20 years, including *The Wire*, *Boardwalk Empire* and *Game of Thrones*. HBO has a similar business model in the US to Netflix, where it is a subscription-only cable TV channel or streaming service (HBO Go). HBO often sells its shows to global broadcasters which use a subscription service too, such as the UK's Sky Atlantic. This is to ensure that HBO properties are treated like premium products that have to be bought by the audience. Those that do not buy pay-to-view channel subscriptions are given an opportunity to buy their own copies of the show after broadcast as DVD box sets or digital downloads.

Netflix is a transnational media organisation. It offers its services to global audiences. In 2017, the only countries it is not available in are China, Syria and North Korea (although Netflix programming is **licensed for broadcast** in China). US law means that it could not operate in the Ukrainian region of Crimea. As a technology business, it is based in California and has registered offices in Brazil, Japan, South Korea and Holland. For UK viewers this means that content is delivered from outside of the UK and this has an impact on the way the service is regulated.

Ofcom is responsible for the regulation of the UK-based delivery of video-on-demand. The way the companies are organised means that Amazon comes under Ofcom's regulations but Netflix does not. Netflix raises a number of issues around the idea of **media regulation** in the digital era. Traditional ideas about regulation are difficult to apply in the digital and globalised context and it is difficult for local regulators such as Ofcom to enforce its rules. Traditional TV broadcasters can be forced to take responsibility for the way content is accessed. For example, the **watershed** controlled the type of content that could be accessed before 9.00pm. As material was being broadcast into homes, the broadcasters had to take some responsibility for the content of programmes that could be seen by children; 9.00pm became a time whereby it was assumed most children would be in bed and the responsibility for controlling their access to adult content was in the hands of the child's guardian. VOD services have removed the relevance of scheduling, as all material is available at any time, so broadcasters cease to have responsibility for keeping children away from adult programming. This is now solely down to the subscriber. Netflix has a responsibility to provide information on programmes to allow choices to be made and to provide ways to lock children out of certain types of material. Netflix accounts offer parental control and can be locked with PINS or profiles can be set up where 'allowed' shows and movies are filtered by predefined maturity levels such as 'little kids only' and 'teens and below'.

The idea of regulation of the media can be very problematic. There are differing opinions on what should be regulated, how and for what purpose. People who see the media as a marketplace and have a commitment to '**free markets**, *individual rights, personal choice* [and] *small government*' tend to favour '*limited regulation*' (Freedman cited in Lunt & Livingstone, 2012, page 115), although there may be a need to regulate the media industries to control monopolies, generate tax income and to moderate '*anti-competitive behaviour between firms*' (Baldwin & Cave cited in Lunt & Livingstone, 2012, page 21). Others see the media as both part of and a potential threat to 'civil society' (Habermas cited in Lunt & Livingstone, 2012, page 9) and so see the need to ensure the media industries are regulated in order that their need to generate profit does not over-ride their responsibilities to the society they serve.

Regulation makes media industries accountable to the wider society for the choices they make. Without it, they would only be accountable to their shareholders. Historically, regulation has begun with nation states. The history of a state will inform its attitude and approach to regulation, and the rules it imposes on media industries reflect the culture's dominant values. For example, the history of UK media is in public service broadcasting, so the regulation of the media in ways that support British values and to strengthen ideas of national identity and cultural heritage is longstanding. In the US, the idea of the media as a marketplace has been historically established, so US regulatory bodies tend to refer to business practices where UK regulations often focus on the content of media products. All media has '*become ever more professionalised and market-oriented*' (Habermas cited in Lunt & Livingstone, 2012, page 8) and globalisation is said to be '*undermining state control*' (Lunt & Livingstone, 2012, page 2). McCheney (cited in Lunt & Livingstone, 2012, page 2) noted that the power increasingly lies with '*global media corporations operating across national border and pushing for open markets*'. Netflix can be seen to be a prime example of this type of corporation. In 2007 it provided streaming services to the US market. In 2012 it expanded to Europe and by 2017, by innovating in its use of technology and in its approach to content creation, Netflix had grown, attracting over 100 million subscribers across five continents. This global reach not only makes the company immensely powerful but also makes it very difficult to regulate.

NETFLIX EXAMPLE: *13 Reasons Why*

13 Reasons Why is a Netflix original programme produced by US company Paramount Television in collaboration with three production companies: July Moon Productions, Anonymous Content and Kicked to the Curb Productions.

13 Reasons Why

- Anonymous Content is a US production company involved in film (including Oscar winner, *Spotlight* (2015)) and television (including critical successes *True Detective* (2014) and *Mr Robot* (2015)).
- July Moon Productions was formed by Selina Gomez, who was an executive producer of the show.
- Paramount Television is one of the Paramount stable of production companies owned by the media conglomerate, Viacom.

The show was based on an existing intellectual property – a YA (young adult) novel of the same name. The show is set largely in an American high school and deals with the social interactions of a group of teens and some of their adult relatives, specifically as they deal with the impact of the death by suicide of Hannah, a member of their social group. All 13 episodes of Season 1 were released simultaneously in March 2017.

13 Reasons Why is both a mystery drama and a teen soap. As such it is a hybrid genre product that offers a range of different gratifications. The mystery elements of the narrative are structured around characters (and the audience) gradually finding out what led the protagonist to kill herself. There are influences in the show from previous teen mysteries such as *Riverdale* (2017), *Pretty Little Liars* (2010–2017), as well as earlier shows such as *Veronica Mars* (2004–2007) and even (although very different in tone) *Buffy the Vampire Slayer* (1997–2003).

In many other ways, the programme follows the conventions expected in a teen soap. Locations such as school sports events and the prom are used. Teens are arranged into social groups and this is evidenced in the seating arrangements shown in the school canteen. Much of the drama of the series takes place at a party and the motivating storylines are based on romantic relationships, parental misunderstanding, sexual identity and high school politics. The show can therefore easily be interpreted as a programme about teenagers, for teenagers.

However, the show subverts many teen-drama codes and conventions. Teen dramas can appeal to a broad age range from adults who enjoy the genre – perhaps experiencing some nostalgia for the teen life represented – and the teens who can identify with the situations presented, to younger teens, who see the lives on screen as aspirational. Teen dramas conventionally offer safe narratives for all these audiences. Traditionally, the genre offers comfort in the resolution of stories where bullies are punished, the virtuous are rewarded and conformity allows individuals to be accepted within the community.

13 Reasons Why was innovative in that it attempted to be more realistic, avoiding romanticising the harsh realities of high school life. Characters swear, drink, have sex and take drugs. Some characters are the victims of cyber-bullying, domestic abuse, violent attacks and rape. The general tone and content of the show created controversy, as many commentators thought it was inappropriate for a show aimed at teenagers. However, other commentators saw the show as gritty and honest, and praised the fact that it addressed issues in teens' lives that are often ignored by mainstream broadcasters. The criticisms of the show do not come from the content itself – some Netflix shows are much more challenging in terms of the topics being discussed and levels of sex and violence than mainstream programming. The criticisms have been aimed at Netflix because, it is claimed, the show was aimed at a teenage audience.

13 Reasons Why is rated differently in different geographical locations:

- MPAA (US): R (restricted – has adult content)
- IMDb informal age rating: 15–17+
- Australia: 15+
- Netherlands: 16
- Singapore: 18
- South Korea: 18
- BBFC (UK): different episodes receive different ratings – some are 15, others 18
- Commonsensemedia.com gave the programme an age rating of 16+.

KEY TERMS

Big Data	the information gathered by digital companies on audience behaviour
binge-watch	an audience activity of watching multiple episodes of a television programme in one sitting
broadcast	to transmit information to a mass audience, usually using radio or television technology
commercial television	television companies whose primary income source is from advertising
event television	television shows that attract large audiences and are reported on extensively. They may be one-off events (e.g. a royal wedding), a regularly scheduled event (e.g. the Olympics) or a specific episode of a popular programme
free markets	trading based on unrestricted competition between private companies
intellectual property	the ownership of ideas, creative productions, artistic works, etc.
licensed for broadcast	the selling of a programme to be broadcast by another organisation or in another country
media regulation	laws and rules that govern the production, distribution and circulation of media products
narrowcast	to transmit information to a localised, niche or specialised audience and to offer choices regarding the timing of access to this information
niche audience	an audience that has a shared any specialist interest
post-network television	the culture of television viewing that no longer relies on traditional broadcast methods

The ratings suggest that, in most locations, *13 Reasons Why* is largely thought appropriate only for adults and older teens. The YA genre in literature is usually thought to be aimed at readers between 15 and 20, so the source material implies a teen audience for the show. The show was extensively marketed using social media, and images used to promote the show focus on the young actors and the high school setting – again implying a predominantly teen audience. Selena Gomez's involvement in the show was also foregrounded during the show's promotion and she too appeals largely to teenagers.

The biggest issue raised about the show was in its depiction of Hannah's suicide. In the *Guardian*, Zoe Williams (2017) claims that '*If there was a list of ways not to portray suicide, [13 Reasons Why] would tick every box.*' It has been accused of trivialising and glamorising suicide, presenting it as a revenge response and the depiction of Hannah's suicide was criticised for being too graphic.

In the *Guardian*, a mental health campaigner claimed that that:

> 13 Reasons Why's *creators claimed they were hoping to 'help' people struggling with the issues shown in the show, but it's a storyline that is about revenge suicide, demonises counsellors and includes none of the characters reaching out for help and receiving it, it's not clear exactly what they think 'helping' is.* (Williams, 2017)

Criticisms began to build after the show was released and Netflix responded by strengthening the wording in the warning cards shown before episodes but they also denied that the show was ever intended for teenage audiences. Netflix made the following statement:

> *Currently the episodes that carry graphic content are identified as such and the series overall carries a* **TV-MA** *rating. Moving forward, we will add an additional viewer warning card before the first episode as an extra precaution for those about to start the series and have also strengthened the messaging and resource language in the existing cards for episodes that contain graphic subject matter.* (Loughrey, 2017)

The show has raised issues as to institutional responsibility in terms of the content provided and the marketing of shows. The Netflix office in London is stated to be for marketing only and, as content decisions are made outside of the UK, Ofcom regulations do not apply. If Netflix were subject to the VoD regulations put forward by Ofcom, Netflix would have to ensure that their service protected the under-18s – specifically:

> *material which might seriously impair the physical, mental or moral development of under-18s, is made available in a way which secures that under-18s will not normally see or hear it.* (Ofcom, 2017)

Ofcom VoD rules must be adhered to by Amazon, the BBC, ITV and Channel 4. Netflix is, however, bound by EU regulations that seek to include social media and other streaming video-on-demand services and to regulate at the point of access rather than the current approach which regulates at the point of origin. This aims to deal with 'problems relating to cross-border services, for instance those arising from providers established in one country but targeting an audience in another' (Advanced Television, 2017). Any EU regulations, of course, may not apply in the UK after Brexit.

spoiler	articles and discussions that give away plot developments
SVoD	streaming video-on-demand
TV-MA	programmes produced for adult audiences

ultra HD	high-quality digital images
watershed	an agreed time (9.00pm in the UK) that restricts when adult content is broadcast

CHAPTER SUMMARY

- Central to the study of media industries is the consideration of production practices and the way media products are distributed and circulated.

- The way that new technologies are impacting on these aspects on industry practice should be considered and examples have been provided of the way technology has influenced the development of a range of media forms.

- Media industries are adapting to try to accommodate changes in audience behaviours and expectations. Digital convergence is seen to be a way to enable traditional media industries to remain competitive in a rapidly changing media environment.

- Production, distribution and circulation can now be undertaken by independent companies and individuals in ways that offer competition to the dominance of traditional media industries.

- The globalised nature of contemporary media is also impacting on the way media products are produced, regulated and consumed.

- The impact of changes in technology and audience behaviour should be considered within specific industrial contexts. Examples have been provided here using examples on film, television and news institutions.

FURTHER READING AND REFERENCES

Advanced Television (2017, 24 May) 'EU Sets 30% Content Quota for European SVoD', http://advanced-television.com/2017/05/24/eu-sets-30-content-quota-for-european-svod/.

Cbronline.com (2018, 26 September) 'Smartphone Penetration Now More than 80% in UK', www.cbronline.com/verticals/etail/smartphone-uk/.

Clarisse Loughrey (2017, 2 May) 'Netflix Adds Warnings to 13 Reasons Why After Backlash', *The Independent*, www.independent.co.uk/arts-entertainment/tv/news/13-reasons-why-netflix-warnings-criticism-backlash-portrayal-of-suicide-parental-controls-a7712696.html.

D. Carr (2013, 25 January) 'Giving Viewers What They Want', www.nytimes.com/2013/02/25/business/media/for-house-of-cards-using-big-data-to-guarantee-its-popularity.html.

D. Hesmondhalgh (2012) *The Cultural Industries*.

Digital News Report (2018) 'Overview', www.digitalnewsreport.org/.

Elihu Katz & Paul F. Lazarsfeld (2005) *Personal Influence: The Part Played by People in the Flow of Mass Communications*.

Guy Fenton (2009, 28 October) *The Media Show*, BBC Radio 4.

J. Sullivan (2012) *Media Audiences*.

John Constine (2016, 21 December) 'Zuckerberg Implies Facebook is a Media Company, Just "Not a Traditional Media Company"', techcrunch, https://techcrunch.com/2016/12/21/fbonc/.

Karl Marx (1867) *Das Kapital, Vol. 1, Section 1*.

Mark Sweney (2014, 23 February) 'Netflix Gathers Detailed Viewer Data to Guide its Search for the Next Hit', *Guardian* www.theguardian.com/media/2014/feb/23/netflix-viewer-data-house-of-cards.

Mark Sweney (2017, 18 July) 'Netflix Tops 100m Subscribers as it Draws Worldwide Audience', *Guardian*, www.theguardian.com/media/2017/jul/18/netflix-tops-100m-subscribers-international-customers-sign-up.

Mark Zuckerberg (2016, 13 November) www.facebook.com/zuck/posts/10103253901916271.

Michelle Castillo (2017, 31 May) 'Netflix is Spending $6 Billion on Content this Year and "a Lot More" in Future, CEO Says', www.cnbc.com/2017/05/31/netflix-spending-6-billion-on-content-in-2017-ceo-reed-hastings.html.

Ofcom (2017, 3 April) 'Section One: Protecting the Under-Eighteens', www.ofcom.org.uk/tv-radio-and-on-demand/broadcast-codes/broadcast-code/section-one-protecting-under-eighteens.

Office for National Statistics (2017) 'Internet Users in the UK: 2017', www.ons.gov.uk/businessindustryandtrade/itandinternetindustry/bulletins/internetusers/2017.

P. Lunt & S. Livingstone (2012) *Media Regulation: Governance and the Interests of Citizens and Consumers*.

Roland Barthes (2009) *Mythologies*.

Roy Greenslade (2017, 24 March) 'Am I Alone in Viewing Media Coverage of Westminster Murderer as Disproportionate?', twitter.com/GreensladeR/status/845213916254887937?tfw_creator=NBCNews&tfw_site=NBCNews&ref_src=twsrc%5Etfw&ref_url=https%3A%2F%2Fwww.nbcnews.com%2Fstoryline%2Flondon-parliament-attack%2Flondon-parliament-attack-media-coverage-triggers-criticism-britain-n738091.

Simon Jenkins (2017, 24 March) 'Media Hype About the Westminster Attack Will Only Encourage Others', *Guardian*, www.theguardian.com/commentisfree/2017/mar/24/coverage-westminster-attack-media-politicians.

Stuart Heritage (2017, 14 July) 'What Happened, Netflix? You Were King of the Hill – Now You're Circling the Drain', *Guardian*, www.theguardian.com/tv-and-radio/2017/jul/14/what-happened-netflix-you-were-king-of-the-hill-now-youre-circling-the-drain.

Terry Eagleton (1991) *Ideology: An Introduction*.

USA Today (2014, 5 February) 'Top 10 Internet-Censored Countries', www.usatoday.com/story/news/world/2014/02/05/top-ten-internet-censors/5222385/.

Zoe Williams (2017, 26 April) 'Netflix's 13 Reasons Why and the Trouble with Dramatising Suicide', *Guardian*, www.theguardian.com/tv-and-radio/2017/apr/26/netflix-13-reasons-why-suicide.

Chapter 5 — Applying the framework: CSPs

5.1 Introduction

The A level examinations asks you to show your knowledge and understanding of the theoretical framework. Questions can ask you to focus on one or more of the close study products set by the exam board to demonstrate that knowledge by providing examples of the application of ideas.

The CSPs are taken from each of the nine media forms and they are divided into two types:

- **in-depth CSPs**, which you should study using all aspects of the theoretical framework

- **targeted CSPs**, which should be approached using two of the four areas of the framework.

> The AS CSPs are also A level CSPs although their status as 'in-depth' or 'targeted' CSPs may not be the same.
>
> The Year 1 book offers case studies on CSPs that are also required for the A level examination.

CSP case studies in AS & Year 1 book	Media form	CSP status for AS examination	CSP status for A level examination
Men's Health	Magazine	Targeted (media language and representation)	In depth – assessed in Media Two
The Missing	One of the options for television	Targeted (audience and industry)	In depth – assessed in Media Two
teenvogue.com	Online, social and participatory media	In depth	In depth – assessed in Media Two

> Each of these case studies provides a starting point for the study of these products applying some of the areas of the theoretical framework.

The A level CSPs are assessed across the two examination papers, with targeted CSPs being assessed in Media One and the in-depth CSPs in Media Two.

The A level CSPs are organised as follows:

Targeted CSPs (media language and representation)	Targeted CSPs (audience and industries)	In-depth CSPs
• Music video • Advertising and marketing	• Radio • Newspapers • Film (industries only)	• Television • Magazines • Online, social and participatory media • Video games

The exam board publishes the names and details of the media products selected as CSPs. It is possible that some changes may be made to the published CSPs, so you should check with the most up-to-date exam board guidance to make sure you are studying the correct products.

Chapter 6 of this book offers two further CSP case studies for products that are identified as being created for alternative audiences. Chapter 6 offers an in-depth study of *Oh Comely*, one of the magazine CSPs that will be assessed in Media Two and *The Killing*, one of the options for television, again, to be assessed in Media Two.

For more about *Oh Comely* and *The Killing* see Chapter 6.

The CSPs in this chapter have been chosen from the list published by AQA and cover the following media forms:

Targeted CSPs

- **Case study 1: Newspapers** (audience and industries): the *Daily Mail*
- **Case study 2: Music video** (media language and representation): Common's 'Letter to the Free'

In-depth CSP

- **Case study 3: Video games:** Tomb Raider: Anniversary (2007)

5.2 Case study one – targeted close study product case study: the *Daily Mail*

Platform: print (and online)

Form: newspaper

Product: your own selected examples from the print version of the newspaper

Targeted elements of the theoretical framework: audience and industry

Assessment information: your knowledge of the *Daily Mail* will be assessed in Media One. You may be asked to compare the *Daily Mail* with an unseen media product. Your knowledge and understanding of this media product will be assessed through your application of ideas and theories of **audience and industry**

Newspapers are identified by AQA as a media form that should be studied in light of aspects of the audience and industry elements of the theoretical framework. It is suggested that you should be familiar with one whole edition of the two named printed newspapers as well as some of the content of the papers' websites (e.g. the homepage and at least one other page).

This case study focuses on the *Daily Mail* but it also offers ideas and approaches

For further information on the audience and industry ideas see Chapters 5 and 6 in the Year 1 book and Chapters 3 and 4 of this book.

that can be used when studying the second newspaper CSP – the *Independent*. You may find that different issues are raised by the specific editions of the newspapers you study and you should attempt to apply ideas from the framework yourself.

Introduction to the form: newspapers

Newspapers are the oldest of all media forms and the idea of passing on information about politics and current affairs goes back many centuries. Publications that we would recognise as newspapers were first published in Britain in the 1660s. The rise of the printing press provided the technology that made mass publication and distribution possible and the bi-weekly *London Gazette* of 1789 can be seen to have set many of the **codes and conventions** of this media form both in terms of design and content.

Contemporary newspapers can be published daily or weekly and some cover local and regional news while others cover national and international news events. They cover a range of stories that are assumed to be of interest to their readers and these are usually divided into:

- **Hard news**: reporting on current affairs, politics. economics, politics, wars and other 'serious' events.
- **Soft news**: reporting on stories related to entertainment, sport, celebrities, gossip, scandals and other human interest events.

In addition, many newspapers run stories on the arts, science and technology, and lifestyle topics such as food, fashion and home decor. Newspapers offer opinion-based features too. Book, cinema, restaurant, art and TV reviews are simply the opinions of the critic. Editorials are based on the writer's opinions and interpretations of events, and each newspaper will offer the official point of view of its editorial team through editorial columns. Most newspapers offer some entertainment content, for example crosswords and Sudoku puzzles, cartoons and comic strips, quizzes, horoscopes and problem pages.

Traditionally, newspapers source their news content in the following ways:

- Newspapers employ **journalists** who report on events as well as investigate and find stories to report on.
- Newspapers receive information on news and events from **news agencies**, for example Reuters or Associated Press. News agencies employ journalists and accept submissions from freelance journalists around the world. This information and written reports are sold to newspaper editors. Associated Press is jointly owned by news organisations, whereas Reuters is a private limited company run on behalf of shareholders. There are many news agencies around the world and their ability to collate information and make it available quickly is vital if newspapers are going to be able to ensure they publish the most up-to-date news possible.

In recent years the sourcing of news has developed. Digital and social media have seen the rise in citizen journalism and crowdsourcing of information. Twitter has become an easy to access and free source of news, information and opinion, and the past few years have seen social media increasingly becoming an important news source for modern newspapers.

The term 'the press' refers to the fact that newspapers traditionally appear as 'hard copy' and the information they communicate is printed on paper. This is still the case but all British newspapers now have an online presence. This case study will focus on examples from the printed version of the *Daily Mail* but will also consider its online edition and the impact that digital media is having on the form.

Media industries – the contemporary British national press

Newspaper companies are businesses and their primary motivation within a **free market** is to make money. Traditionally, profits were generated in two ways: by the sales of the newspaper each day and by the sale of space within the newspaper to advertisers. The monetary value of the space in the newspaper has always been directly related to the number of papers that could be expected to be sold. An advertiser is interested in two things: how many people will see the advert and whether or not the right people will see the advertiser's message. Newspapers have always been able to offer useful profiles of their audience, as they have clearly defined their target audience in a number of ways.

Newspapers have always been thought to target specific social classes. While there may be economic factors that lead a person to buy a specific newspaper, they are more likely to have bought a specific newspaper because of its politics, its ideological perspective and the type of content it offers. This type of detailed knowledge about the target audience is crucial for advertisers who need to know that the people who see their adverts are likely to have a positive response to the product being sold. Advertisers of products that have a broad appeal are able to use this knowledge about audiences to create adverts that target the group quite specifically and attempt to ellicit a positive response by providing advertising that will appeal to the readership of the newspaper.

Many newspapers are experiencing financial difficulties as digital media has had a negative impact on both of the traditional income sources. Newspaper sales have reduced dramatically, as many people now get their news from online sources that are free at source. Since 2000, sales of newspapers have dropped dramatically and the amount of advertising money spent in print news has also decreased.

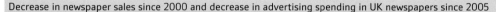

Decrease in newspaper sales since 2000 and decrease in advertising spending in UK newspapers since 2005

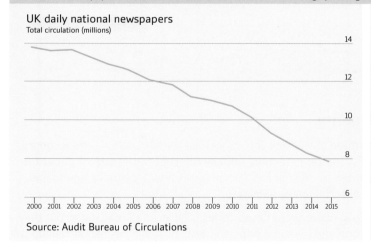

UK daily national newspapers
Total circulation (millions)

Source: Audit Bureau of Circulations

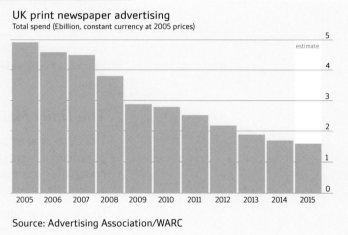

UK print newspaper advertising
Total spend (£billion, constant currency at 2005 prices)

Source: Advertising Association/WARC

Newspaper companies have responded to these financial difficulties in different ways. Some have closed the print versions of their brand. The *Independent* closed its printed paper in March 2016 and now only exists online. Many press companies have announced cost-cutting plans that largely rely on reducing staffing. Costs can also be cut if press companies buy other newspaper titles. In the *Financial Times*, market analyst Douglas McCabe says in an interview with Robert Cookson that '*If you're running printing presses, it can be incredibly cost effective to exploit those assets as best you can, and buying another newspaper is a good way to do that.*' Being a large publisher also makes you '*more attractive to advertisers who want their ads to reach a big nationwide audience*' (Cookson, 2016).

To access the *Financial Times* article quoted above, the reader can either subscribe to the news site or provide information about their shopping preferences. Data about shopping can be used to increase the information available to advertisers about the people who read the *Financial Times*. This increases the value of the website for some advertisers. The page also contains two other examples of the paper attempting to sell its content: the reader is offered a trial of the online newspaper by having stories emailed to them and there is also an advert for a special offer subscription price. The *Financial Times* is keen to encourage the reader to pay for the information provided by the online newspaper.

Generating an income via online advertising is not easy for online newspapers. Google and Facebook take most of the money spent on online advertising. The analyst Jon Herrman (2016) says that Google and Facebook attract 85% of all new advertising spending online, which means the newspapers and all other online content providers that rely on advertising revenue are competing for the remaining 15%.

The *Daily Mail*: genre

The *Daily Mail* is identified as a 'black top' or middle-market tabloid – a sub-genre of tabloid newspapers. The term 'tabloid' initially referred to the size of paper the newspaper was presented on (432mm x 279mm) but is now a genre of newspaper where soft news and entertainment dominate.

Middle-market tabloids do cover hard news stories (similar to a broadsheet) but they tend to focus on the local and personal effects of a story. A middle-market tabloid will also cover a lot of celebrity, entertainment, scandal and **human interest** stories (similar to a **tabloid**). The one other UK mid-market tabloid is the *Daily Express*.

The industrial context of the *Daily Mail*

The *Daily Mail* is owned by the Daily Mail and General Trust (DMGT) and its chairman is Jonathan Harmsworth, 4th Viscount Rothermere, whose great-grandfather was a co-founder of the newspaper. Since 1992, its editor has been Paul Dacre and the newspaper is socially, economically and politically conservative. The paper tends to back the Conservative party but is more than happy to criticise them if the party's values do not match the newspaper's editorial stance. The paper is actively against the Labour party regardless of who leads it and has shown some sympathy for some of UKIP's ideas. The paper has taken negative stances against immigration and what it calls 'benefits culture'. The *Daily Mail* denies all accusations of bias but it remains a confrontational newspaper that can be seen to focus its reporting style on seeking to create an emotional response in its audience. It has a history of campaigning on social and political issues. In June 2018, Dacre announced that he would be retiring in November that year. Geordie Greig, who was the editor of the Mail on Sunday, was announced his replacement.

DMGT also has financial interests in property and business services. The *Daily Mail* has an online edition (MailOnline), which has become one of the most successful online news providers. The *Press Gazette* reported that it had a record number of unique users in August 2016, outperforming other UK online newspapers.

There is a Sunday edition of the newspaper (the *Mail on Sunday*) and the parent company (DMGT Media) owns other newspaper titles including *Ireland on Sunday*, *Mail Today* (published in India) and the *Metro* – a national newspaper that is distributed free largely on the UK rail network. The *Daily Mail*, like other printed titles, has suffered a slump in sales over the years, increasing the importance of **convergence** to reach audiences and to enable the company to succeed in an increasingly competitive market.

UK newspaper website ABC figures for August 2016

	16 Sept	Month on month %	Year on year %	Multiple sales
Sun	1,696,685	–1.48	–5.75	96,274
Daily Mail	1,520,200	–1.2	–5.52	76,0035
Sun on Sunday	1,457,999	–1.24	–2.85	99,122
Metro (free)	1,341,536	1.56	–0.45	
Mail on Sunday	1,328,581	–1.1	–7.42	68,524
London Evening Standard (free)	890,823	3.76	2.3	
Sunday Times	772,614	0.73	–0.11	74,146
Daily Mirror	767,738	–0.59	–10.28	45,000
Sunday Mirror	692,131	–0.15	–14.59	45,000
Daily Star	475,899	–3.61	17.98	488
Daily Telegraph	458,272	–1	–4.7	20,992
The Times	440,048	–0		

Source: ABC

UK national newspaper print circulations for September 2016

Title	Avg. daily browsers	Month on month % change	Year on year % change
MailOnline	15,228,325	2.35	11.13
theguardian.com	8,352,910	–12.84	11.05
Mirror Group Nationals	5,262,564	–0.23	11.05
Telegraph	4,769,878	–8.15	8.04
Independent	3,655,785	8.15	8.04
Sun	2,950,649	14.18	128.75
express.co.uk	1,650,539	–6.34	36.02
Metro	1,251,374	–13.75	–10.62
dailystar.co.uk	964,366	2.92	9.83
Manchester Evening News	833,172	1.28	31.1
Evening Standard	672,455	10.82	58.47

Source: ABC

As the figures above indicate, MailOnline is very popular. The paper's website offers hard news stories with a clear and identifiable political stance. The website publishes opinion columns which often create controversy as the writers often express opinions that generate emotional responses in the readers. For example, Katie Hopkins was employed by MailOnline from 2015 to 2017 as a columnist. In that time she published many sensational columns that generated responses from readers and that sometimes became news stories in themselves, for example when she had to apologise to a teacher she had falsely claimed had taken school children to an anti-Donald Trump protest.

MailOnline offers human interest stories as well as extensive coverage of soft news including celebrity gossip and it makes use of both promotional images (for example, images from Instagram feeds, red carpet photographs) and paparazzi shots of celebrities in informal moments. Access to these soft news stories drives readers to the website with controversial headlines and opinions encouraging online comments and social media debates. It's possible to see some stories being published specifically for this purpose creating click-bait to lure audiences in. Twitter and Facebook posts about online stories act as marketing and the more a story is shared, the more publicity the news site receives.

Each story on MailOnline is organised in a way to encourage the reader to stay on the page and on the site. A typical MailOnline story will offer multiple pictures and videos as well as an outline of the story itself. The story will often be punctuated with other people's comments from social media sources and will often end with a promotional feature that is in some way related to the story. This content takes time to read and look at and as the reader scrolls down they are shown headlines and thumbnail images to many more soft news/celebrity stories. The hope is that these stories will draw the reader in and keep them on the site for longer. As more people stay longer on the website the value of advertising on the website increases.

The print version of the *Daily Mail* is the second most widely circulated British newspaper after the *Sun*. However, like other newspapers its sales are in decline. It was at its most successful in the early 2000s when its circulation was over two million per day but, like most other British newspapers, has found its sales have steadily declined since then. Its sales were never as high as red-top tabloids such as the *Sun* or the *Daily Mirror*, so the downwards trend does not seem as dramatic as some of its competitor papers, but the decline in sales of the newspaper has reduced its income from the sale of the paper itself and has reduced the amount it can charge advertisers.

British newspaper circulation 1950–2015

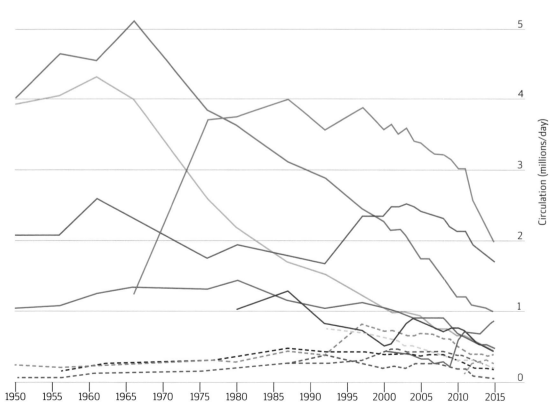

Source: Wikipedia using figures from the Audit Bureau of Circulation

The rise of free, online news was the first blow to traditional newspaper producers but as mobile technology has improved and other sources of news have become more easily accessible, traditional news sources have had competition from news streaming sites, news content on YouTube and the way that news is circulated via social media sites such as Twitter and Facebook. Online news sources can offer the audience a range of different experiences that newspapers cannot. Online news sources can provide information in many ways from the written word and still images like a newspaper to video and audio presentations, as well as offering much more volume of content, access to archived information and the ability to observe or engage in audience participation and interaction.

Another major benefit of online news is its **immediacy**. A newspaper is usually printed overnight for distribution early in the morning. This means it summarises the previous day's events but it cannot respond to any breaking news. Online news providers seek to provide information on news stories as quickly as possible and audiences use social media to ensure they are as up to date as possible. The *Daily Mail* uses social media to attempt to drive audiences to the website. This reinforces the branding of the *Daily Mail* as being a primary news provider. Unfortunately, the rush to put news online can lead to errors and inaccurate information being circulated. On 24 November 2017, a rumour began to circulate on social media that there had been a terrorist attack in London. The *Daily Mail* was criticised for circulating a Tweet that said a lorry had injured people on Oxford Street in London. This Tweet was originally sent ten days earlier and neither the lorry nor the scare on the day was related to terrorism. The *Daily Mail* deleted the Tweet when it was discovered to be inaccurate, but newspapers need to be first with the news and this can lead to inaccurate information being passed to its readership. Newsrooms are under pressure but the economic downturn they have experienced has also led to staff-cuts that adds to the difficulty in making sure all stories are checked for accuracy.

Despite the audience's identifiable move to online sources of news and information, newspapers still have a status that means they still have power. Newspapers influence the news agenda of radio and television news programmes, so the front page of the *Daily Mail* may only reach 1.5 million people through the sale of the newspaper but its headline and its stance on a story may reach many more as it is discussed on *Newsnight* (BBC2), used as a talking point on the *Today Programme* (BBC Radio 4) and is written about in other news outlets such as *HuffPost* or the *Guardian*.

HuffPost reporting on the *Daily Mail*'s reporting

Newsnight reporting on the Paperchase/*Daily Mail* controversy.

The *Daily Mail*'s views sometimes make it the subject of a news story. The pressure group Stop Funding Hate defines some of the editorial attitudes of the *Daily Mail* as being divisive and fuelling hate. The group lobbied the retailer Paperchase to stop paying for advertising space in the *Daily Mail*. In November 2017, Paperchase cancelled its advertising with the newspaper and apologised to its customers for providing it with financial support.

Regulation

The *Daily Mail* is regulated by IPSO. IPSO is a self-regulator, which means that people from within the news industry work for the organisation, investigating and ruling on complaints.

IPSO was formed after the Leveson Inquiry, which had been set up to investigate press standards after the revelations that several newspapers hacked phones and email accounts to access private information. IPSO, however, was not seen as responding fully to the findings of the Leveson Inquiry, so another regulator (IMPRESS) was also set up. IMPRESS is the only press regulator that is recognised by the Press Recognition Panel set up by the government to grant Royal Charter recognition to regulators. Recognition indicates that they are working within the guidelines identified in the Leveson report. IMPRESS was initially funded by individuals and organisations whose complaints about press intrusion had been part of the Leveson Inquiry. IPSO's funding comes from its members and some argue that this undermines its ability to be truly independent.

IPSO publishes an editors' code of practice that British newspapers and magazines agree to abide by. The code covers a range of regulations that define what is seen to be appropriate and inappropriate behaviour by the press. The code covers a range of different areas such as accuracy, reporting crime, and dealing with sources. It also covers the impact of press reporting with codes covering harassment and the potential invasion of privacy. Complaints can be made to IPSO when it is thought that the newspaper is in breach of one of the codes. Complaints will be investigated and newspaper editors should respond to their rulings. For example, in February 2017 the *Mail on Sunday* published a story about global warming science. IPSO ruled that this story breached the rules regarding accuracy, as several claims within the headline and the article itself were incorrect. IPSO stated that:

> *Following an article published on 5 February 2017 in the* Mail on Sunday, *headlined 'EXPOSED How World Leaders Were Duped Over Global Warming', Bob Ward complained to the Independent Press Standards Organisation that the newspaper had breached Clause 1 (Accuracy) of the Editors' Code of Practice. IPSO upheld the complaint and required the* Mail on Sunday *to publish this decision as a remedy to the breach.* (adapted from IPSO, 2017)

The *Mail on Sunday*'s response to the IPSO ruling was as follows:

> *The article reported on claims made by Dr John Bates, a climate scientist formerly employed at the US National Oceanic and Atmospheric Administration (NOAA), about a paper published in the journal Science that suggested that there had been no 'pause' in global warming in the 2000s. Dr Bates had published a blog criticising the way the data used for the paper had been analysed and archived. The article detailed at length the complainant's concerns with the data; it then characterised them as demonstrating 'irrefutable evidence' that the paper had been based upon 'misleading, unverified data'.*

The article was illustrated with a graph. It plotted a red line, described as 'the "adjusted" and unreliable sea data cited in the flawed "Pausebuster" paper', and a blue line, described as the 'UK Met Office's independently verified record', which it said 'showed lower monthly readings and a shallower recent warming trend'. A note at the base of the graph stated that '0 represents 14°C'. (Rose, 2017)

The highly politicised positions often taken by the *Daily Mail* have led to it being accused of inaccurate or extremely biased reporting. In February 2017 the *Daily Mail* was identified as 'generally unreliable' by Wikipedia editors, to discourage it being used as a source of information for entries into the online encyclopaedia. The *Daily Mail* responded that it had only been adjudicated 'inaccurate' twice by IPSO.

Audience

Demographics are the statistical data on a particular group of people identifying their age, income, social status, etc. This information is used to help identify who the audience for media products is, so they can be addressed appropriately, and that the media product can shape its content to meet their needs and desires.

The *Daily Mail*'s readership has an average age of 58. With the *Telegraph*, the *Daily Mail* has the largest proportion of over 65s in its readership (45%) and the lowest proportion (14%) of under 34-year-olds. The percentage of female readers (52.5%) of the *Daily Mail* is slightly larger than male readers (47.5%) but the paper has the largest female readership when compared with other papers and is the only paper with more female readers than male.

National newspaper audience age split

	Guardian	FT	Sun	The Times	Mirror	Daily Mail	Telegraph
65+	21	21	22	30	34	45	46
55–64	17	20	14	18	17	18	17
45–54	17	21	19	19	15	14	13
35–44	17	18	17	14	11	9	10
25–34	14	15	17	9	14	8	8
15–24	14	5	12	9	9	6	7

■ 15–24   ■ 25–34   ■ 35–44   ■ 45–54   ■ 55–64   ■ 65+

Source: Advertising packs

Look at this section of IPSO's Editors' Code on privacy.

Privacy

i) Everyone is entitled to respect for his or her private and family life, home, health and correspondence, including digital communications.

ii) Editors will be expected to justify intrusions into any individual's private life without consent. Account will be taken of the complainant's own public disclosures of information.

iii) It is unacceptable to photograph individuals, without their consent, in public or private places where there is a reasonable expectation of privacy. (IPSO, 2016)

Consider the details of the code.

- Do you think the code threatens the freedom of the press?

- Do you think the code goes far enough to control the actions of journalists and photographers?

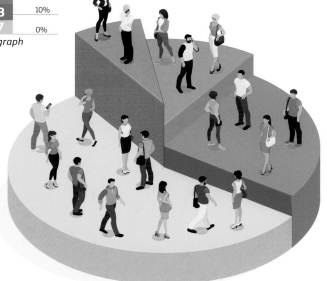

Two-thirds of the audience of the *Daily Mail* are defined by the National Readership Survey (NRS) social grades A, B and C1. These categories relate to the social-economic position as indicated by occupation. Grade A is identified as being higher managerial or professional, while C1 is supervisory level or junior management and administration.

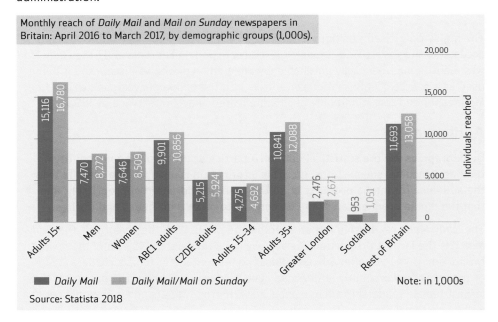

Monthly reach of *Daily Mail* and *Mail on Sunday* newspapers in Britain: April 2016 to March 2017, by demographic groups (1,000s).

Source: Statista 2018

These methods of identifying who the audience are can be very useful. This information can help a newspaper sell advertising space, as advertisers need to know that they will be seen by people who may be responsive to their messages. This knowledge about the audience is also useful when deciding which stories to publish and what editorial stance to follow.

Demographics, however, only offer a partial view on the audience, as not all over 58-year-olds or C1s are the same. With more data, a more detailed picture of the *Daily Mail* reader can be identified.

The YouGov profiles app (https://yougov.co.uk/profileslite#/) allows customers to view more detailed information about the typical reader's personality and lifestyle choices. Here is an overview of the *Daily Mail*'s 'typical' reader.

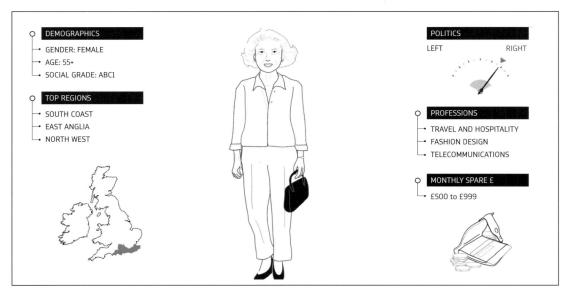

This chart indicates that she has right-wing political views and the charts below offer more about her hobbies and interests.

Readers of the *Daily Mail*

Thinking about the audience in terms of their personal interests is called **psychographics**. This is often a much more useful method than demographics as it allows media producers to target their content more directly to the interests and values of the target audience. This helps the media producers retain their audience and generate brand loyalty. The *Daily Mail* will address its audience as like-minded people, positioning them by reinforcing their conservative, traditional and right-wing values. As many of the *Daily Mail*'s readers share these values, they will find their own values repeated by the newspaper, reinforcing their attitudes and values as being natural or normal. They are more likely to return to a paper that makes them feel included, as most people dislike having their values challenged or contradicted. Loyalty to a specific newspaper often generates an identity for the audience member who adopts the values of the newspaper brand and so the idea of being 'a *Daily Mail* reader' becomes an important part of who they are. Within a peer group of other *Daily Mail* readers, this can create a sense of belonging to a community with a shared viewpoint. Being a member of this group can also offer status as, within the group, being 'a *Daily Mail* reader' holds a level of cultural capital.

Of course, media producers cannot control the way audiences respond to their products. Visitors to the MailOnline could have been drawn to the website for very negative reasons if they have been angered or offended by a headline or the focus of a story, for example. Audiences may visit the website specifically to make oppositional readings. These readers often see being 'against' the *Daily Mail* as part of their own identity and their **cultural capital** can be gained when criticising the publication's perspective or reporting style. Print newspapers, however, are much more likely to be bought by people who identify with paper's values making them the core readership. This is the group that the *Daily Mail* will try to please in the way it reports the news as they are the people who offer continued support to the paper.

On the surface, newspapers are simply a method to communicate facts and information on the day's events to an audience. Newspapers recognise this informative function and, to attract audiences, they try to offer entertainment as well as facts. The brand values of each newspaper offer audience member

APPLY IT

There are several different approaches to psychographics and audience categorisation.

Search online for the following to see how they could be applied when considering the audience of the *Daily Mail*:

- values and lifestyle (VALs) categories (www.strategicbusinessinsights.com/vals/ustypes.shtml)
- MOSAIC categories (www.experian.co.uk/marketing-services/knowledge/videos/mosaic-videos.html)
- Young and Rubicam's cross-cultural consumer categorisation
- the Class Calculator (BBC) (www.bbc.co.uk/news/magazine-22000973).

For more on cultural capital see Chapter 3.

something to identify with (or rail against) and this may become part of the audience member's social interaction, either in their day-to-day lives by giving them access to cultural conversations, or via the online community that exists on newspaper websites and social media platforms. Beyond this though, British newspapers are political and they promote specific ideas and values in the way they tell their stories. The values they promote can often be seen to reflect the interests of the owners of the newspaper rather than, necessarily, the interests of the reader.

Product analysis: the *Daily Mail*: Tuesday 22 November 2016

Media language – content and layout

The print edition of the *Daily Mail* published on 22 November 2016 follows the **codes and conventions** of the mid-range tabloid in its layout and design. It consists of 82 pages that contain the following types of content:

- general news – approximately 11 pages
- 'Battle for Brexit' feature – two pages
- human interest news – approximately nine pages including a two-page 'Life' feature
- editorial and comment – approximately six pages
- celebrity/fashion – two pages

- health – approximately 15 pages including an 11-page 'Good health' section
- recipes, puzzles, games, etc. – approximately five pages
- readers' letters – half-page
- TV guide – four pages
- city and finance – five pages
- sport – 13 pages.

There are 11 full pages taken up by advertising and approximately another ten pages of smaller-sized adverts. Major advertisers include Sky TV, Marks and Spencer, Morrisons and Renault. Smaller companies advertise health-related products in the 'good health' section, including several stair-lift retailers.

Readers are offered money-off vouchers for the Body Shop and WH Smith, offers for Christmas gifts and 'Mail Travel' holidays to Norway and trips that take in Iceland, Niagra Falls and New York.

Most of the pages follow a simple five-column layout, although some work on six columns and others four. Images are used to illustrate the story on each page and, where there are multiple stories on a page, placement of the story and the size of font used in the headline indicate the relative importance of the story. The use of images is largely to illustrate the stories and are mainly representations of people in the stories being reported. Some images illustrate objects being discussed in the stories, for example a map and a picture of a Russian missile carrier are used to illustrate a story about the deployment of arms in Russia (page 10) and an 'artist's impression' of cryogenic technology is used to illustrate a story based on speculations about future scientific developments (page 11).

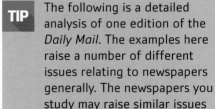

TIP

The following is a detailed analysis of one edition of the *Daily Mail*. The examples here raise a number of different issues relating to newspapers generally. The newspapers you study may raise similar issues but you should also look out for any additional ways you can apply your knowledge of the form and ideas from the theoretical framework.

While you should study the newspaper from an audience and industry perspective, you should always try to offer examples from the newspaper to demonstrate and support your points. This means you will need to study the way the newspapers use media language and construct representations.

Media language, narrative and representations

The **front page** of the paper can be divided into three horizontal sections. At the top is the masthead that provides the name of the paper, the date of publication and the statement that this is the 'DAILY NEWSPAPER OF THE YEAR'. The masthead also shows the purchase price and the paper's web address.

The second horizontal section is dedicated to promoting a special section of the day's paper – 'Good Health'. This offers a reason for people to buy the paper (and this top third of the page is what is likely to be seen first by potential buyers in newsagents and supermarkets). The paper makes an extravagant claim that the cure for the common cold has been found. Curious readers will need to purchase the paper to find out more. Below this are two news stories – the lead (hard news) story and a celebrity story that is illustrated with a 'red carpet' photograph. Both stories begin on the front page but continue inside the newspaper.

The lead story takes up two-thirds of the height of the page and three-quarters of the width. There is no image attached to this story but its importance is indicated by the size of the headline. The eight words of the headline take up three times more space than the information provided on the story itself. The **serif font** used for the headline **connotes** formality and authority and the use of capital letters gives a sense of urgency to the alarmist, declarative headline. The headline infers an absolute, in that people *will* have to show their passports to get National Health Service (NHS) treatment but the subheading above, smaller and in less formal **sans-serif font**, uses the word 'proposal', which underplays the certainty of the headline.

Found! A cure for the common cold

Health mandarin's proposal for ALL patients

SHOW YOUR PASSPORT IF YOU WANT HOSPITAL TREATMENT

PASSPORT checks to curb health tourism may have to be extended to every hospital, it emerged yesterday.

By **Daniel Martin**
Chief Political Correspondent

The top civil servant at the Department of Health said the idea would be controversial but had proved a success in trials.

Chris Wormald's officials are examining whether the checks – used in areas of high immigration – should become national policy. British citizens would need to prove their identity to confirm their eligibility for free treatment. Non-urgent hospital treatment and maternity services would be targeted initially, rather than casualty and GP services.

Under current rules EU governments should be billed for the treatment their citizens receive. Non-EU citizens should pay themselves or use insurance. However many of the charges are not collected because staff fail to carry out checks.

Britain paid out £674million to other European countries for the treatment of Britons abroad in 2014/15 – but received only £49million in return for NHS treatment of Europeans.

Charlie Elphicke, Tory MP for Dover, said hospitals failed to charge health tourists because of political correctness. In a fraught session of the Commons public accounts committee

Turn to Page 4

Marion & Brad's touching display
SEE PAGE THREE

The final column on the right (where the page will be turned) is dominated by a full-length picture of Marion Cotillard photographed on the 'red carpet' attending the premier of her film *Allied*, which also stars Brad Pitt. The image is overlaid with a caption 'Marion & Brad's touching display'. No further information is given and the reader is directed to page 3.

The whole of the front page can be seen as a marketing tool for the paper. It foregrounds hard news (the NHS), soft news (a film premiere) and a human interest story (health), so offers something for a wide range of audience members.

Each story on the front page develops existing narratives. Scientists have been searching for a cure for the common cold for many years and so the health story appears to offer a narrative resolution to this health problem. The NHS story is linked to the ongoing debates around immigration and 'health tourism' and Marion Cotillard had previously been drawn into the ongoing narrative surrounding Brad Pitt and Angelina Jolie's divorce. This front page offers a continuation of stories that many readers will be familiar with. It provides an introduction to each of the stories but detailed information is only available for those who purchase the paper or those who go online to read the stories on the website.

Page 4

Daily Mail, Tuesday, November 22, 2016

Doctors 'too scared to save lives in case they are hauled to court'

Top NHS adviser's warning after surgeon cleared

By **James Slack**
Political Editor

PATIENTS will be denied life-saving operations if the police and prosecutors continue to hound doctors doing their best, the NHS's most senior clinical adviser warns today.

Professor Sir Norman Williams said prosecutors were now being more 'energetic' in trying to secure convictions against surgeons whose patients suffer harm.

And he warned that, as a result, the fear of police knocking on a doctor's door was having a chilling effect on patient care.

In the worst case scenario, people may not be given a pioneering treatment because the doctor does not believe it is worth the risk of being thrown behind bars. It follows the case of David Sellu, a surgeon, who at the age of 66 was locked up in a top security prison after a patient died under his care.

In an exclusive Daily Mail article, Sir Norman, senior clinical adviser to Health Secretary Jeremy Hunt, writes: 'Every day doctors and nurses have to make decisions, often in an atmosphere of high intensity and under considerable pressure. If they get these wrong they have the propensity to harm patients.

'Such decisions can always be criticised and at times acts of omission or commission might constitute negligence, which is normally resolved by civil proceedings. Until recently it was unusual for a criminal case to be brought before a court of law and it was even rarer for a prosecution to be successful. Such cases are now being pursued more commonly and the bar for conviction may have been lowered.'

In what will be considered a controversial intervention, Sir Norman adds: 'We all want to see a safer system but is the energetic pursuit of criminal prosecution the right way to proceed?'

The ex-president of the Royal College of Surgeons said that, while blatant criminal activity by doctors should be punished, such cases were 'rare'. There have been only 12 successful convictions in the past 15 years.

He adds: 'For every charge of gross negligence manslaughter brought against clinicians there will be a significant number that are investigated.

'One can only imagine the anguish that the individual innocent practitioner and his or her family will endure whilst undergoing such an investigation not to mention the inevitable professional damage.

'This will not produce a change in culture. On the contrary, it is likely to result in a climate of fear encouraging defensive medicine and a reluctance to take on high risk cases which might benefit from medical intervention.'

His intervention comes after a surgeon had a manslaughter conviction quashed by the Court of Appeal last week.

Mr Sellu, who is 70 today, served 15 months of a two-and-a-half-year prison term for manslaughter by gross negligence – some of it spent inside high-security HMP Belmarsh in south-east London alongside Islamist terrorists.

James Hughes, 66, was under Mr Sellu's care when he died at the Clementine Churchill Hospital in Harrow, north-west London, in 2010. The Court of Appeal ruled that his November 2013 conviction over the patient's death was not safe.

The original case against Mr Sellu, of Hillingdon, west London, was based on the standard of his care. Mr Hughes became ill after a routine knee replacement carried out by another surgeon.

Mr Sellu later carried out surgery to repair a perforated bowel, but there had been delays in performing that operation. Mr Hughes died two days later.

The surgeon said he knew Mr Hughes needed an urgent operation but an anaesthetist was not available for several hours and it was not safe to move the patient to the nearby hospital.

The Crown Prosecution Service said it would not appeal against the Court of Appeal ruling.

Exonerated: Surgeon David Sellu with his wife Catherine

by **Professor Sir Norman Williams**
SENIOR CLINICAL ADVISER TO HEALTH SECRETARY

Climate of fear doesn't help NHS or patients

ON November 5, 2013 Mr David Sellu, a 66-year-old consultant surgeon, with a previously unblemished record, was found guilty of gross negligence manslaughter for failing to provide the care expected of a clinician of his standing. He was sentenced to two and half years in jail.

The case was complex but pivoted around Mr Sellu's 28-hour delay in operating on a patient who was found to have peritonitis as a result of a perforated bowel following routine knee surgery and who sadly subsequently died.

I was President of the Royal College of Surgeons at the time and had mixed emotions. I felt huge compassion for the patient and his family. Seeing a loved one who appeared relatively healthy pass away as result of a perceived serious error must have been unbearable.

Nevertheless the verdict and sentence made me uneasy. I received countless communications from surgeons around the country expressing the same sentiment: 'There but for the grace of God go I.'

We all knew that no doctor is above the law but believed that a miscarriage of justice may have occurred in the case of Mr Sellu, who had given excellent and unstinted surgical care to his local community.

A dedicated group of clinicians and lawyers, therefore, supported him in his appeal against the judgement and last week three Appeal Court judges quashed the conviction. Although there is a degree of relief in the clinical community, there remains significant concern about the prevailing atmosphere of blame and retribution around healthcare errors.

Every day doctors and nurses have to make decisions, often in an atmosphere of high intensity and under considerable pressure. If they get these wrong they have the propensity to harm patients.

Such decisions can always be criticised and, at times, acts of omission or commission might constitute negligence, which is normally resolved by civil proceedings. Until recently it was unusual for a criminal case to be brought before a court of law and it was even rarer for a prosecution to be successful. Such cases are now being pursued more commonly and the bar for conviction may have been lowered.

It is estimated that 3.6 per cent of all deaths in the NHS ie 9,000 annually are avoidable. We all want to see a safer system but is the energetic pursuit of criminal prosecution the right way to proceed?

Of course, blatant criminal activity by healthcare workers should be pursued and punished accordingly but such behaviour is rare. Gross negligence manslaughter and other serious incidents are very unlikely to be the result of one individual's poor performance. Many factors may come into play which are outside the influence of the clinician.

For every charge of gross negligence manslaughter brought against clinicians there will be a significant number that are investigated. One can only imagine the anguish that the individual innocent practitioner will endure whilst undergoing such an investigation.

This will not produce a change in culture. On the contrary, it is likely to result in a climate of fear encouraging defensive medicine and a reluctance to take on high risk cases which might otherwise benefit from medical intervention.

Health Secretary Jeremy Hunt wishes to develop a learning as opposed to a blame culture. Only by providing a 'safe space' environment akin to that which exists for investigations by the Air Accident Investigation Branch will staff feel uninhibited in admitting mistakes so lessons can be learnt.

This environment was created around air disasters and, importantly, safety has been transformed. In healthcare this will not be achieved by the overzealous pursuit of individuals through the criminal courts.

Continued from Page One

yesterday, Mr Wormald admitted he could not guarantee an official target to claw back £200million a year from Europe would be met.

The permanent secretary at the DoH said: 'On the general question of "Are we looking at whether trusts should proactively ask people to prove their identity?" – yes we are looking at that.

'Individual trusts like Peterborough are doing that and it is making a big difference – they are saying "Please come with two forms of identity, your passport and your address", and they use that to check whether people are eligible.

'It is quite a controversial thing to do to say to the entire population you've got to prove your identity.'

Peterborough and Stamford Hospitals trust covers an area with a high number of Eastern European immigrants.

Mr Wormald added: 'Some trusts are looking at the moment to see whether they need to require people to prove their identity by bringing in a passport or some other form of ID – which is not the culture of the Health Service up to now.

'We are looking at whether more trusts should go down that route, as had been done in London and elsewhere on people having to prove their identity.

'And we are looking at whether that is proportionate – whether in just some places or whether you want to apply it to the whole country.'

Earlier this year it emerged that women would be asked to show passports if they wanted to give birth at St George's in Tooting, south London. They have to provide papers showing they are eligible for free care when they arrive for scans.

Those unable to do so will be referred to the Home Office and could face deportation. Managers at the hospital said they were facing a growing problem of women flying in from Nigeria solely to have babies.

'Trusts are asking for two forms of identity'

But Mr Wormald's comments show that such an approach is being considered even more widely – not just for maternity care.

He said: 'We are not here to criticise NHS frontline staff, but what we want is a culture of everybody who works in it to understand financial rigour. We need a culture where we are more careful with the tax pound.'

Bob Alexander, deputy chief executive of NHS Improvement, told the committee that trusts needed to raise their game by making sure all staff understood the importance of cost awareness.

He added that it was extremely difficult in busy clinical areas to identify every health tourist.

Caroline Flint, Labour former health minister, said the failure to claw back money undermined confidence in the NHS.

In 2014/15, Britain received £1.5million from the Polish government to pay for its citizens' healthcare – but paid out £4.3million in return, despite hundreds of thousands of Poles being in Britain.

Mr Elphicke, who sits on the accounts committee, said: 'The taxpayer is being taken for a ride not just by NHS tourists but by the incompetence and political correctness of the NHS bureaucracy.

'It's unbelievable Poland has been claiming more money from the UK than we've been charging Poland. Hundreds of millions of pounds is at stake. If we collected this money, we could provide so much more healthcare for needy Brits.'

IS suicide bomb kills 27 Afghans

A SUICIDE bomb killed at least 27 people and wounded 64 as worshippers gathered at a mosque in Afghanistan yesterday.

The attacker was mingling with worshippers inside the Shiite mosque in Kabul when he detonated the bomb.

The blast left a large crater inside the two-storey building and bodies covered in blood could be seen on the ground among shattered glass.

Worshipper Ali Jan said: 'I was in the mosque, the people were offering prayers. Suddenly I heard a bang and windows broke. I had no idea what had happened. I rushed out screaming.' Women and children were among those injured.

The Islamic State group has claimed responsibility for the attack.

President Ashraf Ghani said in a statement he strongly condemned the 'barbaric' attack, which the UN called an 'atrocity'.

The continuation of the lead story can be found in the fifth column of page 4. This page offers a second NHS story and one small story about Islamic State (IS) suicide bombers. The page offers a negative outlook on the NHS with one story reinforcing the other. The second story is based on the results of a case taken against a doctor. The fact of the case is that a surgeon was cleared of negligent manslaughter after the death of a patient. The bulk of the story at the top of the page is, however, based on an assertion by the writer of the opinion piece at the bottom of the page rather than a factual report on the court case and its outcome. The *Daily Mail* acknowledges that the point raised in the headline 'Doctors "too scared to treat patients" is a 'worst case scenario'. The headline and the opinion-article both focus on speculation rather than fact. This combined with the lead story about passports act together to 'confirm' that the NHS is an institution beset with many problems – 'health tourism' and too many legal actions taken against doctors.

The primary headline at the top of the page makes an assertion of fact (although placed in quote marks and identified as a warning).

The second headline dominates the page as, although lower down the page, it has more weight and the white text on a black background stands out from the rest of the page. The headline suggests that a 'climate of fear' is not helpful, but the two stories use language, design and speculation to create fear about the accessibility of NHS treatment. The final story on the page appears unrelated as it is a short report on the death of nearly 30 people during an IS-attributed suicide bomb attack in Kabul. The story appears unrelated but as the lead story is reporting on issues caused by non-UK citizens using health services, the inclusion about foreign terrorism is clearly intended to reinforce fear of 'others' in the shape of foreign visitors and immigration. All three stories act to create fear but the fact that they are presented together shows that the editorial team is aware of the way close proximity on a page can lead to associations being constructed even when the connections between the stories are not made explicitly clear. The anchorage of the two stories may help reinforce a number of negative **stereotypes** about immigrants, Muslims and Islamic terrorists.

The paper does not say the three groups are connected but the placement of these stories allows the audience to make the connections for themselves directly. Bringing these stories together could also create a subconscious connection between the groups. Placing two negative NHS stories close together is an example of **selective representation**. The ideas about the NHS being created are negative and there are no stories presented that show a more positive side to the NHS. With a focus on bad news, the newspaper is **positioning the audience** to expect stories about failures in the health service. **Selective representation** ignores stories and events that could undermine the general messages being communicated and is an important technique that enables newspapers to reinforce ideas and values. The repetition of ideas such as implied links between immigrants, Muslims and terrorists can help to **normalise** attitudes to other groups based on fear. These representations reinforce prejudices and can contribute to the idea that the world is a dangerous and scary place.

The soft news story featuring Marion Cotillard from the front page is continued on page 3. The story is illustrated by three images – two taken at the film premiere for *Allied* and a third taken from the film itself. The images have been chosen to imply a connection between Cotillard and Pitt. This is achieved through the **anchorage** created by the combination of images and commentary in this article. The two actors were linked during Twitter and other social media responses to the announcement of Pitt and Jolie's separation in September 2016. Pitt and Cotillard were known to be starring in a film together and, as Pitt and Jolie met on a film set while Pitt was married to Jennifer Anniston, commentators speculated that history had repeated itself.

All the actors involved denied that Pitt and Cotillard had any type of relationship – a point noted in the final line of the story. However, the story uses language that allows the reader to maintain the idea that there is 'something going on' between the co-stars. The story begins by acknowledging the 'flurry of rumours' that have surrounded the stars but described them as 'playing it cool' and 'avoiding eye contact' – actions often associated with lovers who are attempting to hide their relationship from onlookers. The photograph of the moment the two actors met on the red carpet has no inherent connection to a potential relationship that is anything other than professional, but this meaning is suggested by the use of an image of the two actors greeting one another and kissing. At no point does the article claim they are in a relationship but neither does it challenge the rumours that had been circulating on social media.

Daily Mail, Tuesday, November 22, 2016 — Page 3

Awkward: Their embrace contrasted with the film's steamy scenes, right

Brad plays it cool with his steamy co-star...

By **Kate Pickles**

THEIR sizzling chemistry during filming was enough to spark a flurry of rumours.

But Brad Pitt and Marion Cotillard were playing it cool last night as they crossed paths on the red carpet last night.

Seemingly avoiding eye contact, the actor, 52, attempted a limp high-five with his co-star, 41, as they met in Leicester Square for the premiere of their film, World War II blockbuster Allied.

The pair also went for a rather awkward embrace in the cold night air – in stark contrast to their steamy scenes in the film, in which they play married freedom fighters. Both were dressed to impress last night,

with the Oscar-winning actress in an elegant black gown, and Pitt in a smart suit beneath a winter coat and scarf.

Yesterday's meeting was only the second time they have appeared together in public since Pitt announced his split from wife Angelina Jolie in September – amid rumours that Miss Cotillard may have played a role in the break-up.

However the actress, who is pregnant with her second child by long-term partner Guillaume Canet, has strongly denied any romance has ever taken place.

At arm's length: Brad Pitt and Marion Cotillard on the red carpet in London last night

The article has, however, connected itself to the social media conversations about the stars and this is what has made the story front page news. Its **news value** is because it features members of the celebrity **A-list** and they are of interest to many readers. The story is also 'the next instalment' in the real-life celebrity soap opera narrative based on the lives of Pitt and Jolie. Both stars generated media interest before they became a couple, so this story has been running for over 20 years in one way or another.

Celebrity lives are presented to audiences as ongoing narratives where conflicts and resolutions to conflict drive the story forward. Pitt and Jolie were discussed when they had relationships with other actors before they met and started a family together. Their relationship has developed its own narrative trajectory with Angelina initially being pitted against Jennifer Anniston, as the former was presented as having 'stolen' the latter's husband. At this point of the narrative Jolie was the villain and Aniston the victim. Pitt and Jolie became 'Brad and Ang' or 'Brangelina' and their narrative became focused on their growing family and humanitarian work as much as for their films. Jolie's role as 'homewrecker' changed as she became the maternal head of a large family and her health scares and charity work rebranded her as a nurturing and caring mother and campaigner.

This latest instalment to the story refocuses on the personal lives of Pitt and Jolie and the news story on 22 November is part of this latest development in the 'Brad and Ang' story. A disruption to the story has been reintroduced now they are separated.

These ongoing stories are good for newspapers as audiences are familiar with the 'characters' and 'past events', so even stories based on very little happening can still be appealing to the audience. As with any narrative, the audience is keen to see what happens next, and this encourages stories like this to be shared and discussed further on social media. So, in addition to hoping the inclusion of the story on the front page will encourage people to buy the *Daily Mail* when they are choosing their morning paper, there is also the hope that this kind of story will be shared on social media and drive more visitors to its website.

Page 3 of the *Daily Mail* is laid out in two sections on the horizontal, with the Cotillard/Pitt story taking approximately two-thirds of the space at the top of the page. This story is dominated by images, with only two short columns being used to tell the story in seven sentences.

The second story fills the bottom third of the page and has a mid-sized headline (serif font in upper and lower case) and a smaller subheading (sans serif font in upper and lower case). The story is presented in five columns and is accompanied by a small humorous cartoon. The readability of the story is enhanced by the use of a pull quote half-way through the story, where the key emotional message is identified. This is a story about a 'more enjoyable environment' in supermarkets. The story is a human interest story about the suggestion that supermarkets could provide slow-lanes for shoppers who want a chat or who take their time at the checkout. The first paragraph addresses the reader as someone who may want to take their time. The story begins: 'If you fear the wrath of customers queuing behind you' and it goes on to cite the findings of a study that could make supermarkets better for older customers. The article is based on research findings, and social care of the elderly, health services, shops and politicians are all identified as institutions that could make use of the findings, but the article is presenting the information in a semi-serious way turning it into a human interest story. The use of the phrase 'a tax-payer funded report' in a light-hearted article may act to undermine the importance of social research funded in this way. The *Daily Mail* is known to be critical of government funded institutions

A light-hearted article

(especially the BBC) and regular readers may read 'tax-payer' funded as implying a waste of money. Placing this story beneath the celebrity gossip story on the page **consolidates** the idea that the research is of little importance.

Page 9 of the newspaper contains three stories – one a soft news story about a *Great British Bake Off* winner and the second a hard news story about the banning of a speaker at a school. The third story is related to the ongoing story of the governmental enquiry into historic sex-abuse.

The story at the bottom of the page is presented in five columns and the inquiry story is in column five at the top right-hand side of the page (although the upper story uses an uneven four-column design). The story at the top left of the page is separated by overlaying the story on a photograph and placing the text on a white background so it can be seen. This story is also enclosed in a box to separate it from the other stories on the page. The colourful picture and the large serif font give the story dominance on the page, although the larger, darker capitalised text headlining the story below ensures that both stories are visible but are clearly two different stories.

The Great British Bake Off story continues the narrative of the TV show as it features the most recent year's winner (at time of writing) Candice Brown and informs the audience of what she is up to now the show is over. The story details her 'agonising' decision to leave teaching to pursue a media career. The photograph has been provided by the *Radio Times* and it is more than likely to be an article written from a **press release** rather than an interview with Brown herself. The article presents *The Great British Bake Off* winner in a positive light and puts a positive spin on her leaving teaching. She is cited as saying she was encouraged to inspire her pupils to 'follow their dreams', reinforcing positive **stereotypes** about teachers acting in the best interests of their students. The article has provided positive **PR** for Brown but ends the article by claiming that 'some' people seemed to imply that her trademark lipstick wasn't suitable for *The Great British Bake Off* tent. However, there is no source for this claim nor any explanation as to why the lipstick was deemed unsuitable. The final sentence adds a small criticism that is not present in the rest of the article.

There is a slight connection between the two main stories on the page as they both deal with schools and decisions made by teaching staff and head-teachers. The second story is based on the fact that a far-right-leaning commentator with links to the controversial news website Breitbart News has been stopped from speaking to students at a British grammar school. Milo Yiannopoulos has connections to the US alt-right movement that supported Donald Trump's presidential candidacy and is known for having his Twitter account shut down after he was implicated in an online bullying campaign that was racially motivated. His proposed appearance at a school led to complaints being raised from the local community. Staff and students from the school were in favour of him attending. Yiannopoulos has claimed he is being punished for having the 'wrong opinions'. The school's decision was based on their own interpretation of governmental guidelines about guarding against supporting and encouraging extremist views within schools.

The bottom story links to *The Great British Bake Off* story at the top, with its focus on British schools.

The story is largely sympathetic towards Yiannopoulos and the one-word declarative headline makes the newspaper's position clear. This is reinforced by the pull quote that identifies the key message of the story (placed in inverted commas to distance this from the paper's own opinion) 'Attack on free speech'. The sub-heading is less clear on the facts as it implied that the headmaster had little choice and that the 'officials' were forcing his hand. This is not supported by the facts of the story itself. The *Daily Mail* often criticises 'political correctness' and Yiannopoulos is called 'a scourge of political correctness'. Breitbart News is identified as being connected with both Donald Trump in the US and UKIP in the UK. The *Daily Mail* supported the Leave campaign in the 2106 EU Referendum so has some political similarities to UKIP and, by association, Breitbart News. Yianopoulos seemed surprised to learn that the UK government act tries to discourage radicalisation and extremism in schools but the article does not correct Yiannopoulos' assumptions about its role in schools and leaves his misunderstanding unchallenged in the story.

The third story is also linked to ideas of 'freedom to speech'. The article takes a critical approach to the fact that lawyers who have resigned from a sexual abuse inquiry have not passed on information revealed to them by their clients and the headline uses a quote claiming the inquiry is 'gagging' the lawyers. This quote is not repeated in the story and nor does it say who made this claim. The story itself does not repeat this claim but does say that the inquiry refused to 'waive legal privilege'. When someone speaks to their lawyer, everything they say is 'privileged' — that is, it is against the law for lawyers to pass on what has been said, thus lawyers, rather than being gagged, are abiding by the rules of their profession and obeying the law. The story intends to create a sense of outrage about the 'gagging' of lawyers, especially as this relates to an emotive story and an inquiry that has been beset with many problems. Its close proximity to the story headlined 'Censored!' uses **anchorage** to create the general message that any form of censure or censorship is a bad thing. This may seem like a common-sense viewpoint but it is worth considering the way the press has sometimes been criticised for the lengths it goes to in order to get a story or some of the tabloid's personal attacks on people. For example, the *Daily Mail* was heavily criticised for its response on 4 November (see left) to the High Court ruling made the previous day that the mechanism for leaving the EU could only legally be triggered by an act of parliament rather than the outcome of the referendum.

The *Daily Mail* reported this story inaccurately and in its reporting made personal attacks on the judges who made the ruling. When newspapers are criticised they often use arguments about the need for a free press with the rights to free speech as an important principal. It serves the newspapers' interests to reinforce these values and to make the idea of free speech seem simple and incontrovertible rather than the complex and nuanced concept it is.

Free GIANT map of Britain inside tomorrow

Daily Mail

FRIDAY, NOVEMBER 4, 2016   www.dailymail.co.uk   DAILY NEWSPAPER OF THE YEAR   65p

The fencer: Sir Terence Etherton   Worked with Tony Blair: Lord Justice Sales   The Europhile: Lord Chief Justice Thomas

Fury over 'out of touch' judges who defied 17.4m
Brexit voters and could trigger constitutional crisis

ENEMIES OF THE PEOPLE

MPS last night tore into an une-lected panel of 'out of touch' judges for ruling that embittered Remain supporters in Parliament should be allowed to frustrate the overwhelming verdict of the British public.
The Lord Chief Justice and two senior col-

By **James Slack** Political Editor

leagues were accused of putting Britain on course for a full-blown 'constitutional crisis' by saying Brexit could not be triggered without a Westminster vote.
The judgment by Lord Thomas – a founding member of the European Law Institute, a club of lawyers and academics aiming to 'improve' EU law – throws

into chaos Mrs May's timetable for invoking article 50 in March next year.
Senior MPs – led by an ex-justice minister – said it was an outrage that an 'unholy alliance' of judges and embittered Remain backers could thwart the wishes of 17.4million Leave voters. They warned that Mrs May could be forced to hold an election early next year if the courts did not back down. Leave **Turn to Page 2**

Turn to Page 2

KEY TERMS

broadsheet	a term used for certain British newspapers that used to refer to the size of paper they were printed on but now refers to the content and approach taken in the selection and reporting of stories. Broadsheet newspapers are characterised by a focus on hard news, offering more in-depth analysis and a more global perspective than tabloid newspapers. Broadsheets do cover soft news stories but tend to analyse the issues raised rather than simply offer gossip and scandal. *The Times* and the *Guardian* are broadsheet newspapers
crowdsourcing	obtaining information from a large number of people
editorial stance	the political and/or ideological position of a newspaper that influences the way stories are reported

headline	the heading given to a news story, presented in a larger font
lead story	the main story presented on the first page of a newspaper
masthead	the title of a newspaper, presented at the top of the first page
middle-market tabloid	British newspapers that offer hard news and soft news. They offer more sensation and gossip than broadsheets and more hard news than tabloids. The *Daily Mail* and the *Express* are middle-market tabloids
PR	stands for public relations – this is the professional management of a public image. PR professionals work for companies, public organisations, brands and individuals and work to control the way their clients are reported on and, therefore, perceived

press release	a summary of information or an official statement given to journalists
tabloid newspaper	a term used for certain British newspapers that used to refer to the size of paper they were printed on but now refers to the content and approach taken in the selection and reporting of stories. Tabloid newspapers are characterised by their reliance on soft news and entertainment over hard news. Tabloid newspapers often use a sensationalist style when reporting and focus on human interest stories, scandal and gossip. The *Sun* and the *Daily Mirror* are tabloid newspapers
unique users	the separate and individual visitors to a website

5.3 Case study two – targeted close study product case study: 'Letter to the Free'

Platform: Broadcast

Form: Music video

Music video is identified as a targeted media form, so the music video products should be analysed using ideas from two areas of the theoretical framework: media language and representation.

Assessment information: your knowledge of 'Letter to the Free' will be assessed in Media One. You may be asked to compare 'Letter to the Free' to an unseen media product. Your knowledge and understanding of this media product will be assessed through your application of ideas and theories of **media language and representation**.

This music video can be watched online by searching for 'Common – Letter to the Free'.

Introduction

'Letter to the Free' by Common was released in 2016 and was taken from the album *Black America Again*. The album was released on the imprint record label ARTium, which is owned by Universal Music. The album was distributed by Def Jam – another subsidiary of the same parent company. *Black America Again* was Common's 11th album and it marks almost 25 years of success in the music business. The album was deliberately released just before the US general election in 2016. Common identifies the political element of some R&B and hip-hop saying in an interview with Trevor Smith (2016):

> I think hip-hop truly has been the voice of this time-period in speaking of the times, speaking up. You're just starting to see hip-hop artists really participate in the political campaigns and using their voices to say, Get out and vote.

A poster for the Netflix-produced documentary *13th*

'Letter to the Free' was used on the **soundtrack** to the documentary *13th* (2016, dir. A. DuVernay) The documentary argues that the modern US prison system perpetuates the practices of slavery, ostensibly outlawed in the 13th amendment of the US constitution. The documentary was nominated for an Oscar and Common won the Emmy for Original Music and Lyrics for 'Letter to the Free' in 2017. Common's first performance of the song was during a concert performed at the White House during the final year of Barack Obama's presidency.

The video for 'Letter to the Free' was directed by Bradford Young who had worked on the award-winning *Selma* (2014) – a film about the American civil rights movement of the 1960s. Common collaborated with John Legend on the song 'Glory' for the *Selma* soundtrack. The song won the Oscar for Best Original Song in 2015.

Common is an established and award-winning hip-hop artist and actor. He has had a successful recording career since the early 1990s, receiving critical and commercial success. He co-starred as an actor in *Selma* and has acted in many films ranging from action films such as *John Wick 2* and *Terminator Salvation*, dramas such as *American Gangster* and comedies such as *Date Night*. In addition, Common has written poetry, published his memoirs and modelled for Gap and Diesel.

Common is also well known for his activism, having spoken out on a number of social and political issues. He supported Barack Obama, speaks on animal rights issues and started a charitable foundation. He has actively supported black rights issues as an activist and within his music.

Media language and representation

Music videos have three elements: the music, the lyrics and the visual images. In this case, the lyrics are an integral part of the meaning created by the video. The lyrics are used to make direct statements, to create poetic imagery and make political and historical references. The choice of musical styles in the arrangement and production of the song also relate to the message of the song and these two elements combine with the video's visuals to create **anchorage** that helps construct the meaning of the song.

The music

Common is identified as a hip-hop/rap artist. 'Letter to the Free' is, however, an unconventional hip-hop track. Hip-hop usually mixes rap and singing and Common raps the verses of the song while Bilal (who is given a 'featuring' credit) sings the main refrain. However, the song's musical style has strong references to jazz and blues. It features non-traditional instruments for a hip-hop song, with flute, jazz piano and trumpet dominating the arrangement. The track is slow-paced and features a marching percussion beat that is unchanging throughout. The march is common in Gospel music and New Orleans jazz funerals, but it also references the chain-gang and prison work songs where the slow steady drum beat replicates the sound of the hammers and picks used by black slaves and prisoners undertaking forced labour. Chain-gang songs are mournful dirges that grieve over the enslavement of a race of people while wistfully dreaming of experiencing freedom in the future. This freedom is linked to Christian belief systems, so is often presented as coming after death.

Image taken from the video for 'Berta Berta' – an example of a chain-gang song.

Common is an established hip-hop artist and has often created tracks that are a **bricolage** of musical styles. The choice of Gospel, jazz and blues references within this track refer to the roots of modern popular music. Gospel, jazz and blues were musical forms that gave a voice to black American culture in times when systemic racism meant that African-Americans had little or no power within the social structures of the time. The style of music is directly related to the subject matter of the song itself as it focuses on giving a voice to disempowered African-Americans in the context of the modern US prison system.

The lyrics

The lyrics of 'Letter to the Free' make references to the history of racism in the US as well as contemporary racial issues. The song's intended message is to critique the current US prison system, and it uses cultural and historical references, word play, metaphors and direct commentary to do so.

Annotated lyrics of 'Letter to the Free'

Southern leaves, southern trees we hung from,[1]
Barren souls, heroic songs unsung,
Forgive them father they know this knot[2] *is undone,*
Tied with the rope that my grandmother died.

Pride of the pilgrims[3] *affect lives of millions,*
Since slave days separating, fathers from children,
Institution ain't just a building
But a method, of having black and brown bodies fill them.[4]

We ain't seen as human beings with feelings[5]
Will the U.S. Ever be us?[6] *Lord willing!*
For now we know, the new Jim Crow[7]
They stop, search and arrest our souls.

Police and policies patrol philosophies of control[8]
A cruel hand taking hold
We let go to free them so we can free us
America's moment to come to Jesus.

Freedom (freedom)
Freedom come (freedom come)
Hold on (hold on)
Won't be long (won't be long)
Freedom (freedom)
Freedom come (freedom come)
Hold on (hold on)
Won't be long (won't be long)

The caged birds sings[9] *for freedom to bring*
Black bodies being lost in the American dream[10]
Blood of black being, a pastoral scene
Slavery's still alive, check amendment 13[11]

Not whips and chains,[12] *all subliminal*[13]
Instead of 'nigga' they use the word 'criminal'[14]
Sweet land of liberty, incarcerated country
Shot me with your ray-gun[15]
And now you want to trump[16] *me.*

Prison is a business, America's the company
Investing[17] *in injustice, fear and long suffering.*
We staring in the face of hate again,
The same hate they say will make America great again.[18]
No consolation prize for the dehumanized.
For America to rise it's a matter of black lives,[19]
And we gonna free them, so we can free us,
America's moment to come to Jesus.

Freedom (freedom)
Freedom come (freedom come)
Hold on (hold on)
Won't be long (won't be long)
Freedom (freedom)
Freedom come (freedom come)
Hold on (hold on)
Won't be long (won't be long)

[1] Refers to the song 'Strange Fruit', the words of which can be found online, that deals with the lynching of black people in America. The song was written by Abel Meeropol in 1937.

[2] Word play – not/knot – referring to the ropes used in lynching and Jesus Christ's final words when being crucified.

[3] White European settlers.

[4] Referring to the idea that the US prison system has created a modern-day slave culture populated largely by non-whites.

[5] Dehumanisation is a technique that is often used to help naturalise/justify discriminatory behaviour.

[6] Word play identifying the separation of the power structures of the US and 'out groups'.

[7] Jim Crow laws enforced the segregation of people by race. In many US states, these laws included defining where people could sit in public places and in some cases where they were educated – all based on their race. These laws were largely overturned by the Civil Rights Act passed in 1964.

[8] Reference to racism identified in elements of hard and soft power in the US – constructed by ideologies and reinforced by law enforcement.

[9] A reference to *I Know Why the Caged Bird Sings* – a book by Maya Angelou that reflects on her childhood in the 1930s – and to a poem called *Sympathy* written by a black poet called Paul Laurence Dunbar in 1899.

[10] 'The American Dream' is a concept that there is equality of opportunity in the US for anyone with a strong work ethic.

[11] The 13th Amendment to the US Constitution abolished slavery and an involuntary servitude unless this was in punishment for a crime.

[12] Identifying that the methods of modern slavery are different from those used in the past.

[13] Identifying the use of ideologies and politics to create oppression.

[14] Identifying a change in discourse where language changes but has a similar oppressive effect.

[15] Reference to Ronald Reagan, the US president between 1981 and 1989, who used 'the war on drugs' to start the process of mass incarceration and to focus its application on urban (largely non-white) communities.

[16] Donald Trump was the President-elect at the time the song was released.

[17] Use of language referring to the corporate nature of the US prison system that exists to create profit and so benefits from the rise in numbers of people incarcerated.

[18] Referring to Donald Trump's campaign slogan 'Make America Great Again'.

[19] Word play on 'Black Lives Matter'.

APPLY IT

If you can, watch the Netflix documentary *13th* to learn more about the political and historical references made within the lyrics of 'Letter to the Free'.

The song offers an element of hope in the repeated refrain of 'freedom come; hold on, won't be long' but in the context of its relationship to the history of the chain-gang song this hope feels restrained rather than celebratory. The song has a religious message with the repeated line that this is 'America's time to come to Jesus'. This reflects Common's Christian faith and the tradition in African-American culture of Christianity offering comfort to an oppressed race. The violent history of racism in America is referred to directly as well as in cross-textual references to music and literature. The lyrics also make comments on historical and contemporary political contexts that relate to the current situation where the US incarcerated a largest percentage of its population than any other country in the world and where most inmates of the US prison system are from non-white racial backgrounds

The visuals

The video for 'Letter to the Free' is presented in **black and white**. Black and white film stock holds a number of connotations:

- **History**: black and white footage connotes ideas of history, as early photographs were black and white and older media products were filmed in black and white.
- **Realism**: early photography was thought to be a representation of reality and newsreel was originally filmed in black and white, hence black and white often being used to create the idea of realism in modern media. Newspaper photographs were traditionally printed in black and white, which also feeds into the **symbolism** of this **aesthetic choice**.
- **Seriousness**: black and white footage looks stark and offers clean lines and contrast rather than the **visual spectacle** of colour images. This can bring a serious tone to the work. These **connotations** also come from the associations made between black and white news footage/photography.

These **connotations** all combine to set the tone of the music video. The idea that the song is rooted in history, reflects an **authentic reality** and deals with serious subject matter is reinforced with other media language choices throughout the video.

The opening shot of the video is a slow forwards **tracking shot** through a corridor. The corridor is largely unlit so much of the **mise-en-scène** is hidden. A beam of light is shown coming through a window, revealing that the corridor is in an institution of some sort. The décor is minimal and we are shown doors at the end of the corridor that look like the doors within a prison. As we follow the camera down the corridor we are taken towards and then through the doors, taking us inside the building. A second shot turns us to the left and it is clear this is a prison as there is enough light to show cells on either side of the corridor. The camera moves slowly and smoothly and **straight cuts** take us further into this environment during the opening moments of the video. The song begins with a drone that creates an ominous tone and as a drum beat begins to build we see someone sitting at a drum kit in an enclosed prison exercise yard. This **exposition** sets the tone and identifies the main location for the video. There is an **ironic juxtaposition**, as the exercise yard location for part of the video includes a sign banning 'excessive noise' identifying the location to be repressive, but the drummer ignores the sign, challenging its ability to constrain behaviour.

As the lyrics of the song begin, the images **intercut** between musicians performing the song in a variety of locations within the prison, including a gym, an exercise yard and a cell. The camera continues with its slow movement into the locations and it tracks around the musicians providing the audience with multiple **viewpoints**. Often the camera track takes the audience from a dark location to a lighter one which could, at first, appear to create a **narrative** of hope. Each location is, however, lit using **low-key lighting**, creating dark and light areas within the frame. Conventionally, the brightly lit areas of the frame would be used to show, while darkness and shadow would be used to hide. In this video, however, the brightly lit areas highlight aspects of the mise-en-scène but do not offer what the audience might expect: a clear look at the performers. The mise-en-scène and the lighting locate the narrative problem within the prison system. In this video, however, media language choices obscure rather than reveal the performers, so, while they act to communicate the message, they do not offer a solution to the problem.

The performer **in mid-shot** with his face in shadow and light reflecting off the keyboard.

Performers are in **long-shot** and are, therefore, too small to make out in detail. Bright light enters through the open roof of the exercise yard but its structure casts shadows across the location.

The performer is in **mid-shot** but lighting from above obscures all but his profile.

The room is well lit but positioning the performers in front of the window places them in silhouette.

A single light source places the performer in the **spotlight** and the rest of the **mise-en-scène** is in full darkness. However, the performer is facing away from the camera and is in **long shot** so the lighting does not show him to the audience.

The performers are in **long-shot** and the **overhead lighting** is reflected off the walls rather illuminating the performers.

APPLY IT

'Letter to the Free' and 'Earth Song' by Michael Jackson are both performance-based videos that deal with a political issue. Compare the representation of the performers in the two videos.

Michael Jackson: a Christ-like pose from the video for 'Earth Song'.

These lighting choices act to create a **coherent visual style** for the video. Despite the changes in location, each shot clearly belongs within this video. These visual connections are crucial in the creation of meaning within the video despite the fact that it is made up from a series of images in **montage** rather than creating a **linear narrative**. The **cumulative** effect of the combination of these images acts to communicate meaning for the audience. These images of a largely dark prison environment, where light is fleeting and does not act to fully illuminate, reinforces the mournful message of the chain-gang song. The anonymous nature of the performers means that they cannot be identified as '**heroes**' within this story. They are present but do not offer solutions. Although Common can be identified, he is one of several performers rather than the focus of the audience's attention.

The images in the video are linked to the lyrics both directly and indirectly. The setting is the prison, which is referred to as a 'business' in the lyrics. It stands as a **symbol** for the racist past and a literal representation of the racist present being discussed in the song. The 'whips and chains' of slavery and the lynchings of the past have been replaced by the forced labour of prison and the ruined lives that become shaped and defined by the experience of incarceration.

The final shot of the video takes the audience outside the prison environment into a rural location described in the lyrics as 'a pastoral scene'. This location comes as a shock after the claustrophobic confines of the prison. It offers a wide-open sky and grassland. In the **mid-ground**, one house is clearly visible and others can just be made out on the horizon. The shot appears as the song finishes and is accompanied by the sound of birdsong. The **sound effect** creates an idea of a rural idyll. This could be interpreted in a number of ways – it could be seen as a depiction of the 'freedom' still to come but the lyrics link the pastoral scene to the blood of black bodies – perhaps identifying that the image of the American Dream is built on systemic racism as 'slavery's still alive, check amendment 13'. The sky appears dark and the scene is presented using a ground-level point of view that undermines a fully utopian reading of the image.

One of the final images of the video for 'Letter to the Free'

Another aspect of the video that is open to interpretation is the inclusion of a floating black/mirrored square. It is shown in various locations within the prison, first appearing in the exercise yard/gym where it reflects the windows in the roof. As the camera **tracks** in towards the mirrored square the reflection creates a cross shape that could refer to the Christian symbol.

Symbolism in the video for 'Letter to the Free'

As a mirror, the square shows the viewer what is not shown in the shot itself – it extends the viewer's **point of view**. However, in other shots, the square is also depicted as being solid black and so obscures rather than reveals. Here the square acts in a similar way to the black bars used to anonymise people in photographs and video images (also see image on the right).

The square in the cell blocks the view, shields the viewer from reality and hides the truth. Its intense blackness creates an empty space and could **symbolise** a lack of knowledge and understanding about the way US prisons are used.

Abstract imagery in the video for 'Letter to the Free'

Of course, this is speculation, as the geometric shape holds no inherent meaning in itself. Meaning is created by the viewers and this will be influenced by their knowledge of the issues raised in the video and their own personal perspectives.

 APPLY IT **Look at the examples of the use of the black square in the music video. What meanings do you think are created by its use?**

Genre: the video

The video for 'Letter to the Free' reflects the song's musical style in its visuals. The use of black and white and the **slow camera movements** subvert expectations for rap and hip-hop videos but is more conventional for jazz and blues music. This **bricolage** of styles offers the audience familiarity while also offering them something new. Musically it is a **hybrid** of several styles and visually it refers to these styles. The piano player's T-shirt lists the names of genres associated with music of black origin (R&B, hip-hop, funk, soul, among others), Common wears a simple black outfit reminiscent of a style worn by jazz musicians, while the barefoot drummer and the headwear of one the female singers hold connotations of African culture.

The video is based on the **performances** of the musicians but the performances are low-key, so this **positions** the audience to focus more on the mise-en-scène and the messages within the video rather than on the **star persona** of Common and the other musicians. His performance is central but the video presents a collection of performers rather than an individualised star. The **narrative** is constructed through the representation of place. The prison is empty (apart from the performers) and the internal doors are largely open. The camera allows the audience to 'wander' through the prison and its stark emptiness **juxtaposes** with the issue being highlighted – that of mass incarceration. Although the audience can move freely within the prison, until the final shot, there is no escape and the **low-key lighting** creates an oppressive atmosphere. A very similar visual style is used in the video for 'Black America Again' (the title track of the album), which also uses stark black and white imagery (although it is intercut with some full colour images).

A still from *Black America Again*

This visual style can be seen to be part of the **construction** of a **brand image** for Common, whose music often combines social and political messages that are reflected in his music videos.

Representation and cultural context

The song's political viewpoint is made clear in the lyrics and is reinforced by knowledge the audience may have about the film *13th* or other examples of Common's work, including the album *Black America Again*. The song is commenting on the disproportionally large numbers of African-Americans who are incarcerated in the US prison system.

Common includes **historical references** in his lyrics to show how the contemporary experience of black Americans, especially black American males, is shaped by racial politics and ideas about racial identity. 'Letter to the Free' identifies a direct link between the way that African Americans had been mistreated in the past to contemporary racial issues. The song points out how racism is not just a personal belief system but how it can be part of the systemic organisation of a culture. This last idea is **reinforced** by the setting of the video within a prison environment.

The **representation** of black culture in the video is not through the **direct representation** of the issues being discussed; rather, the video encourages the audience to make connections between the setting of the video and the experiences of many members of the African-American community. This reflects a **double consciousness** (Gilroy) as members of this culture are both part of the African **diaspora** but they also identify as Americans. The lyrics of 'Letter to the Free' show that African-Americans are still treated as outsiders to the **dominant culture** and laws have allowed segregation and separation of races to continue even when this was largely assumed to have been legislated against.

Western culture, including the media industries, is still dominated by white culture. Non-white culture is, therefore, often depicted as '**other**' or different in some way. African-Americans can still be depicted as a single **homogenised** group and they are represented in ways that **reflect the values** of the dominant white culture. Debates about whitewashing and cultural appropriation have highlighted the way that white culture can adopt and subsume ideas from other cultures. This has the effect of maintaining white culture's dominance, as black culture is often depicted from a white point of view, what Hall calls '**the white eye**'.

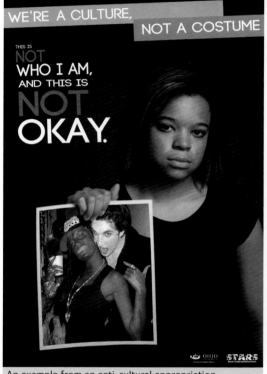

An example from an anti-cultural appropriation campaign

'Letter to the Free' depicts African-American culture from the point of view of an African-American person, so it has more authenticity in its message about the African-American experience than if the representations were created by a non-African-American. The song uses the musical traditions of African-American culture and communicates ideas that come from being part of these traditions both musically and culturally.

The video offers an alternative discourse on incarceration to the one usually presented by the dominant mainstream culture. Much of American politics is dominated by law and order debates, and these debates are often characterised as presenting incarceration as punishment rather than as an opportunity for rehabilitation. There is evidence that many people in the US feel that retribution is a form of justice. For example, the 'three strikes' law that exists in many US states, means that someone who has committed three serious offences will receive a mandatory life imprisonment sentence. This law is seen by some as being effective and it has been credited with reducing crime, although other studies have shown it has not had a significant effect on deterring criminal behaviour. Some argue that the inevitability of a life sentence for repeat offenders has led some criminals who would be facing a life sentence to feel they have nothing to lose. This may (in part) account for an increase in the fatal shootings of police officers.

At the time the song was released America had seen a rise in racial violence. The activist group Black Lives Matter (BLM) was formed in 2013 via social media after the trial of George Zimmerman, who shot and killed a black teenager, Trayvon Martin. Zimmerman was acquitted for the murder of the teenager and this was interpreted as a reflection of the lack of value placed on the lives of young black men. The Black Lives Matter hashtag became an activist movement after African-Americans were killed by white police officers in Fergusson. Since 2013 there have been many examples of police brutality against people from the black community that have been highlighted via social media, so the group became an international movement that protests and comments on acts of racism, particularly police brutality.

The politics of Black Lives Matter have proven to be unpopular with the politically conservative. BLM has been accused of being anti-police and being divisive – a common conservative counter to BLM is that 'all lives matter', demonstrating a lack

Images from a protest referenced in an advert for Pepsi.

It could be argued that the Pepsi advert is an example of whitewashing, cultural appropriation and an attempt to reframe the discourse of racial politics, police brutality and freedom of speech. Pepsi apologised for any offence its advert may have caused.

of awareness about differences in the way black people are treated. The alt-right movement in the USA has been highly critical of BLM, as have the Republican party.

BLM offers an **alternative narrative** about the black cultural experience. Contemporary media often shows the black community as being lawless and violent. Black culture has been offered as a contemporary 'folk devil' (Cohen, 1972) without acknowledging that many black people lead lives far removed from the criminal gang stereotype so often depicted in the media. BLM focuses on the violent extremes of the racism that black people encounter on a regular basis and, in doing so, highlights the racial tensions that still exist in US culture.

'Letter to the Free' offers an alternative to the mainstream version of black racial identity:

- Where black culture is **simplistically** and under-represented, the video refers to its complex history.
- Where black culture is regularly linked to criminality and violence, the video's message identifies the structural inequalities in the US that are disproportionally negatively impacting on black culture.
- Common creates a positive representation of a black man who is intelligent, thoughtful, and both historically and politically aware. This acts as a **counter-type** to the negative images of black men that are common in the media.
- Common's brand persona also offers an alternative to the more positive but still stereotypical ideas about black men that are reduced to assumptions about sporting prowess and/or physical strength.

Common works within media industries that are often run by black entrepreneurs and he has some control over the way he is represented and how he represents himself as he has creative and economic power. His work reflects the complex issues of racial identity in contemporary US culture from an African-American perspective.

APPLY IT

Test yourself on the theoretical framework:
- In what ways is 'Letter to the Free' a typical music video?
- How does 'Letter to the Free' use and/or subvert the conventions of an R&B music video?
- How is media language used to:
  - create tone/atmosphere?
  - reinforce Common's brand image?
  - create a point of view for the audience?
- How do these uses of media language combine to create an overall story/message within the video?
- How has the social and/or cultural context influenced the construction of the music video?
- How might the video be seen to offer representations of groups that are often under-represented or misrepresented?
- Why might different audience members interpret the messages in the video differently?

5.4 Case study three – in-depth close study product case study – Tomb Raider: Anniversary (2007)

- **Platform**: e-Media
- **Form**: Gaming
- **Product**: the game; the game cover
- **Gaming is identified as an in-depth media form, so the products should be analysed using ideas from all four areas of the theoretical framework**: media language, representation, audience and industry
- **Assessment information**: your knowledge of Tomb Raider will be assessed in Media Two. You could be asked to discuss it in light of ideas from any area of the theoretical framework. As Media Two has a synoptic element, it is possible that you may be asked to discuss Tomb Raider using more than one area of the theoretical framework

Introduction

Games are identified by AQA as a media form that should be studied in light of all aspects of the theoretical framework. For the purposes of the examination, gaming is grouped with online, social and participatory media. There are several products within this group and any of them could come up in the examination. As far as Tomb Raider is concerned, it is suggested that you should be familiar with the game itself and the printed cover for the game box. It is not expected that you will necessarily have played the game but you should have analysed examples of gameplay in some way. One way that this can be done is by watching videos of gameplay online. The exam board suggest two YouTube videos that can be used to analyse the media language and representations in the game itself:

- 'Tomb Raider Anniversary HD Walkthrough – Peru Tomb of Qualopec pt 1'
- 'Tomb Raider Anniversary HD Walkthrough – Peru – The Lost Valley pt 1'.

These videos and the game cover will be referred to in this case study but if you have a broader knowledge of the game you can use any examples to support the points you would like to raise about it.

A detailed five-hour, walkthrough of the game can also be found on YouTube:

- 'Tomb Raider Anniversary Full GAME Walkthrough No Commentary Gameplay'.

Industrial context

Tomb Raider: Anniversary is a video game that was released in 2007. It was the 11th version of the Tomb Raider game, which is a media **franchise** giving its name to many media products including films and other forms of merchandise. As the name suggests, Tomb Raider: Anniversary was launched to mark the ten-year anniversary of the release of the original game.

The original Tomb Raider was released in 1996 and was created by an **independent** British games company called Core Design. This company has since been bought by Eidos Interactive, publishers of the original game, which in turn were bought by Square Enix, who are the current publishers for the franchise. Square Enix is a **transnational** publisher based in Japan. Square Enix is involved in the publishing of video games and online games as well as developing games and game engines. It develops and publishes games across multiple platforms including Facebook games, console games and online massively multiplayer online role-play games (MMORPGs). The company is also involved in the production of films (*Kinsgalive: Final Fantasy XV*) and an anime series distributed on YouTube (*Brotherhood: Final Fantasy XV*).

Tomb Raider: Anniversary was developed by Crystal Dynamics and Buzz Monkey. Both are American games development companies. Crystal Dynamics is owned by the publisher, Eidos Interactive, and the parent company Square Enix.

Tomb Raider: Anniversary's industrial background demonstrates the way many large media **conglomerates** are made up from a range of different media companies covering all areas of **production**, **distribution** and **circulation**. Developers such as Core Design and Crystal Dynamics are the technical and creative specialists who make the game. All games need a games engine – put simply, a software infrastructure that the game is built on – and the parent company Square Enix can provide this. Eidos Interactive is the publisher, which means it is involved in the distribution of the game and will create a budget for **marketing** activities that will help increase the sales and circulation of the product. Square Enix creates and sells **merchandise** for its gaming and manga titles on its website and has **subsidiaries** across the world that can offer a range of supporting services for the circulation of games and related media products.

This industrial structure demonstrates the way that large companies can control all aspects of production. Having this level of control allows companies to reduce the costs when everything is done 'in-house'. The costs associated with all aspects of the production, distribution and circulation of media products stop individuals and small companies from being able to engage in these activities and even mid- and large-sized companies can find it difficult to compete with the larger media conglomerates.

Production
- Games design companies owned by Square Enix
- Games engine development in-house by Square Enix

Distribution
- Publishing company owned by Square Enix
- Square Enix has media businesses based around the world

Circulation

Square Enix involved in:
- Merchandise
- Movie production
- Gaming arcades
- Manga/animation production
- Comic books/magazines
- Online gaming

Angelina Jolie as Lara Croft in the *Tomb Raider* films.

Tomb Raider: Anniversary is a remake of the original Tomb Raider game. In 2007, when Tomb Raider: Anniversary was released, the Tomb Raider franchise had previously released ten games. The original game was released exclusively for the Sony PlayStation but subsequent games have been released for all major consoles and now is available on multiple platforms (online, console and mobile); the franchise is successful across all platforms. Since 2007, there have been further titles released in the game series and more releases are planned. Tomb Raider spin-offs include a mobile puzzle game (Lara Croft Go) and a subseries of games under the title Lara Croft have also been released. Lara Croft has been featured in comics and novels, there was a short-lived *Tomb Raider* animated TV series and a host of Tomb Raider merchandise has been sold since the franchise began. In addition, there have been two *Tomb Raider* feature films (*Lara Croft: Tomb Raider* (2001) and *The Cradle of Life* (2003)) and, at the time of writing, a third film is in production and is due for release in 2018.

In its earlier releases, the Tomb Raider brand was linked to a range of **advertising campaigns** for a wide variety of products from cars to soft drinks. Synergy between the brands was created, as consumer product companies wanted to tap into the popularity of Lara Croft by associating themselves with the Tomb Raider brand. In return, the Tomb Raider's **brand imagery** was repeated across multiple media forms, and both the brand and the character became a household name, creating more **brand awareness** for Tomb Raider itself.

Lara Croft was featured on the cover of *The Face* magazine. Here a fictional animated character was depicted by a model and presented to the audience as if she were a 'real' celebrity. The **representation** had become its own reality and the gaming character became a **simulacrum** of celebrity. Models were employed to 'be' Lara Croft at live events and across all manner of media, so the animated character also became part of the real world.

The extensive marketing campaigns created a brand identity for Tomb Raider that has been built on by subsequent releases in the franchise. In terms of sales and critical approval, the first game has been the most successful, but Tomb Raider remains one of the most recognisable game brands. In 2015, Square Enix announced that the Tomb Raider gaming franchise had **global sales** of $58 million. Tomb Raider is an example of the successful **commodification** of an idea that has been reworked and sold on in multiple formats and versions.

Lara selling Lucozade

Lara on the cover of *The Face*

Games regulation

Games publishers need to ensure that games abide by the publishing laws in the countries they wish to trade in. PEGI (Pan European Gaming Information) is an organisation that publishes information about games for customers to help them make informed purchasing decisions. It offers a certificate that clarifies the levels of violence, sexual imagery, swearing, etc. within a game and offers recommendations as to the age appropriate nature of individual games.

PEGI does not have the power to 'ban' a game but it has published a **code of conduct** that games publishers sign up to if they want to receive PEGI ratings. PEGI uses five age groups with colour-coded icons. It also offers icons to give an indication of the content of the game. Information could be provided on content that may be seen to be problematic from the level of horror to the inclusion of gambling elements within the game. The PEGI code of conduct also includes the marketing and packaging of games.

PEGI has no legal control over the content of games but games with a PEGI rating identify the game as being produced within a professional framework and will help generate consumer confidence. PEGI is an example of a **self-regulatory framework**.

APPLY IT

Find out what the PEGI rating for games within the Tomb Raider franchise are.

What does this tell you about the type of content a buyer may expect within the game and who the target audiences for the game are?

Tomb Raider: Anniversary (2007) – the game

Tomb Raider: Anniversary is a remake of the original 1996 game. It was released for multiple consoles, PC and Mac. The Nintendo Wii version had special features related to the active gameplay offered by this console and Tomb Raider: Anniversary was also the first full game that was available to **download** on Xbox Live Marketplace, where practice levels were offered as free downloads and the game itself was split into chapters for sale.

Tomb Raider: Anniversary is based on the original game but includes updated graphics and gameplay. The game included many of the improvements that had been made to gameplay in the ten years since the original release, with Lara Croft being more agile, more realistic visuals and faster gameplay. As such it provides a **nostalgic** reference back to the origins of the game but, also, an updated graphical experience for gamers.

Its sales, however, did not match the success of other games in the franchise. Tomb Raider: Anniversary sold 1.3 million copies, which was much lower than other titles in the series.

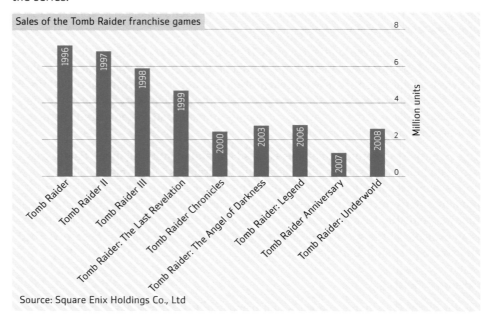

Sales of the Tomb Raider franchise games

Source: Square Enix Holdings Co., Ltd

Media language and genre

Tomb Raider: Anniversary itself is a remake of the original Tomb Raider game from 1996. It is an action-adventure game that replicates many of the visual and narrative codes from the action-adventure genre.

> ### Action adventure
>
> The action adventure genre is based around a quest narrative where the protagonist has to face a number of challenges as they seek to reach their goal. The genre focuses on physical action and is often characterised by set pieces that involve perilous journeys, fights and chases. The modern action adventure often uses high-budget special effects to create a visual spectacle and to create excitement and tension for the audience. The protagonist will need to deal with a number of dangers as they seek their goal, and they will use their physical strength and ingenuity to help them get out of dangerous situations. The peril/villain in the action adventure genre can sometimes have a fantastical or supernatural element and the settings used are often exotic. This separates the genre from the action genre, where action is based in an exaggerated reality rather than given a mystical framework. In film, the *Indiana Jones* series of films epitomises a modern interpretation of the genre.

The protagonist in the Tomb Raider franchise is Lara Croft. She is also the **avatar** for the gamer. Lara Croft is an English archaeologist who embarks on global adventures seeking treasure and historical artefacts. The original game set the conventions of the franchise, taking Croft to many different exotic locations as she hunts for the pieces of an ancient artefact. On her **quest**, she meets many dangers and has to complete physical challenges to allow her to proceed further. During her travels, she learns more about the history and mythologies surrounding the artefact. She progresses through a number of challenges until the **climax** of the **narrative** where Lara confronts the main **antagonist** for the final time. Tomb Raider: Anniversary uses the same basic **plot** as this first Tomb Raider game.

Narrative, gameplay and audience gratifications

The action adventure plot sees Lara Croft **dispatched** (Propp) on a quest, and during the game she must overcome obstacles and solve puzzles to get closer to achieving her **goal**. She will pass through dangerous situations and have to use her physical skills and intellectual capabilities to survive so that she can complete the quest. The narrative is driven by **enigma** and **action codes** (Barthes) as the player seeks to solve the mysteries within the quest and needs to master the physical challenges presented along the way.

Although this basic **narrative structure** is the same as other action adventure stories from film or television, rather than **passively watching** a character who makes decisions and engages with the challenges, a gamer is **actively** involved in 'creating' the story. Their skill as a player will determine how successful Lara is and decisions made in the act of playing will help shape the story and control its pace. A film audience is a relatively passive recipient of a story that has been created and shaped by a team of people but, while games developers make many decisions that shape the gaming experience, the game player experiences a more direct relationship with the story. They play the game and so, in some ways, 'become' Lara Croft. This level of **identification** with the character and the situation creates **visceral gratifications** and offers a more intense and personalised experience.

Lara herself is a **lone-wolf hero** who works alone to solve the problems in her path. She may receive information from others that helps her but she represents a self-motivated and self-reliant individual in the story. This reflects the **dominant ideologies** of the producing culture where individualism is valued. In this way, Tomb Raider: Anniversary can be seen to be part of the **genre of order** (Schatz). Croft works alone to restore order that has been **disrupted**. This disruption is seen at the start of the game, within the prologue set in New Mexico after a nuclear explosion frees a pterodactyl-like creature. Croft is **dispatched** to recover part of an ancient artefact called 'the Scion of Atlantis'. This is the **goal she works towards** throughout the game. Working alone reflects the individualised experience of the gamer and so helps to create a close identification with the character. Having a female avatar means that male players will need to **identify** with the female experience and be **performing** aspects of femininity (Butler) in some areas of the game, for example, when Lara Croft has to deal with the sexism of male characters she encounters.

Audience – gratifications

Scott Rigby, in his book *Glued to Games* (2011), argues that there are three main gratifications offered by gaming:

- **competence** – the development of skills
- **autonomy** – the feeling of being in control
- **relatedness** – the way the game brings players and fans together.

The gratification of **competence** can be achieved through the development of skills within the gameplay. Tomb Raider: Anniversary offers a number of different types of gameplay. Each offers a different type of experience and potential gratification.

Gameplay	Gratifications
Exploration	The game provides complex and detailed locations that can be explored. Locations offer a range of hidden or secret areas and through exploration the player gains a sense of the world they are inhabiting during the game.
Overcoming physical obstacles	Much of the pleasure of Tomb Raider: Anniversary comes from the challenges posed by the location itself. Lara Croft has to cross ravines, climb cliff walls and swim across rivers. Lara Croft interacts with her environment using ledges, ladders and ropes that she finds to help her on her way, and the environment is always a threat. She needs to progress through the environment using movements that allow her to overcome obstacles. Audience gratifications come from meeting the challenges that the environment offers. Players need to develop their **competence** and gain mastery in the skills that enable them to collect items and progress through the game. This can cause frustration at first as the player needs to work out which movements or techniques will move Lara closer to her goals. This may not always be simple, so players will need to practise and develop their knowledge and skills as they play. The player will feel a sense of achievement when they work out how to move Lara successfully through an environment.
Puzzles	Puzzles provide an intellectual experience that creates a cerebral pleasure. Players get a sense of achievement when they are able to solve puzzles and progress through the game.
Fighting	Lara has to engage in face-to-face combat with some of her adversaries and players can use Lara's strength and agility to beat her opponents. Players need to practise the skills required to control Lara's movements. The fights generate an excitement for the player and they gain a sense of achievement when they manage to beat the opponent.
Gunplay	Some parts of the game require Lara to shoot at monsters, wild animals or villains. Gunplay is often combined with physical challenges, so Lara needs to combine these skills. These exchanges are exciting and offer visceral pleasures. Lara also uses her guns as a tool to help her progress. For example, she may have to shoot at some ropes that will free a ladder she can use.

APPLY IT

Research the game The Stanley Parable (2013). This game appears to give the player freedom to choose how the game develops but in fact it shows how options are limited and game outcomes are controlled by the game's programming.

The interactive nature of the gameplay places the player in the centre of the action and they can, to some extent, control the way the game is played, which can create a sense of **autonomy**. This control is, however, limited, as the way the game progresses is controlled by the **game design**. A player can choose to make Lara run around in never-ending circles if they wish but they cannot progress through the game unless they manage to make their way through the environments using the correct gaming moves. The ability to jump across a broken platform or climb up a cliff face is essential. Without this ability, the gamer will get stuck on a level or Lara will die.

Tomb Raider: Anniversary offers the usual pleasures of a quest narrative because the player feels a sense of satisfaction as Lara progresses towards her goal. It is satisfying to see enemies defeated and challenges met. The gameplay represents the problems and complications that Lara must travel through in order to restore **equilibrium**. The personal interaction with this and the fact that the narrative is extended over potentially many hours of play, makes the payoff of the resolution even more rewarding for the player.

While the game itself is a single-player game, fans of Tomb Raider can use the game to create a sense of shared identity. This **relatedness** can occur via social media as well as in the real world, through fan conventions. In the game's heyday, Lara Croft was a common choice for **cos-play** and being part of the Tomb Raider community can offer a sense of collective identity (Gauntlett) that unites fans in their shared interests. Getting involved with **fan culture** is one way that audiences can engage with Tomb Raider beyond the game itself and the fictional world feeds into the audience's real-world experiences.

Audience – demographics

The target audience for video games is often assumed to be young males. This demographic can be identified as a central audience group and the YouGov infographic below identifies the typical Tomb Raider: Anniversary audience member as being male and aged between 18 and 24.

APPLY IT

Most people have played games of some sort. From your own experience of gaming, identify the way different games provide different gratifications.

What types of games appeal to you the most? What does this say about the way you use and select media products?

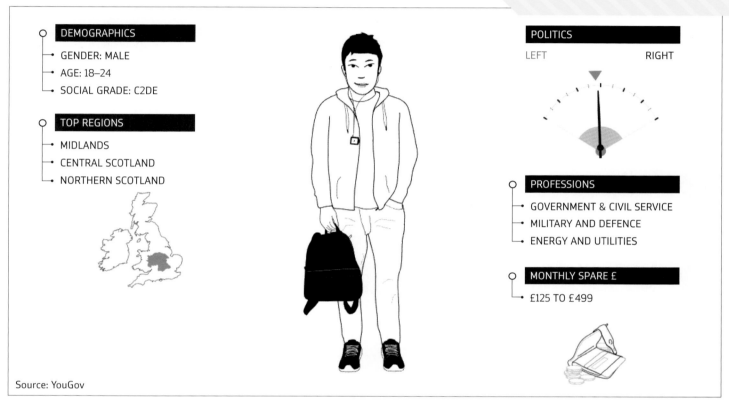

DEMOGRAPHICS
- GENDER: MALE
- AGE: 18–24
- SOCIAL GRADE: C2DE

TOP REGIONS
- MIDLANDS
- CENTRAL SCOTLAND
- NORTHERN SCOTLAND

POLITICS
LEFT   RIGHT

PROFESSIONS
- GOVERNMENT & CIVIL SERVICE
- MILITARY AND DEFENCE
- ENERGY AND UTILITIES

MONTHLY SPARE £
- £125 TO £499

Source: YouGov

When looking more closely at the audience by age, the largest groups of players are in fact in the older age groups. As Tomb Raider: Anniversary is a re-make of an older game, it will have offered a nostalgic appeal for older gamers who remembered the original version.

AGE: FULL DATA Sort by...	SAMPLE %	ALL %
18–24	25.7	16.7
25–39	34.9	28.7
40–54	23.3	28.1
55+	16.1	26.5

Source: YouGov

Although a smaller group, the percentage of females in Tomb Raider: Anniversary's audience demonstrates that females are an important market for games manufacturers and this challenges the idea that gaming is exclusively for males.

GENDER: FULL DATA		
Sort by...	SAMPLE %	ALL %
Female	39.6	37.5
Male	60.4	62.5

Source: YouGov

The game cover

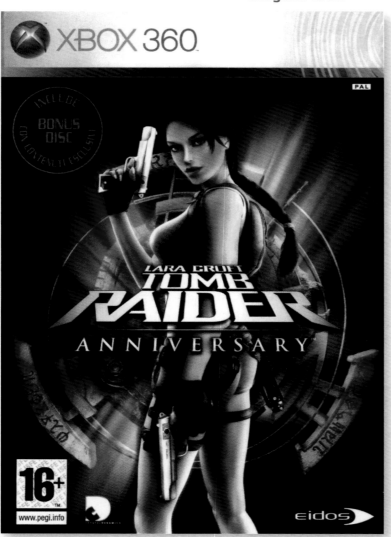

The cover of the game box contains information for the audience:
• the PEGI rating
• the publisher's logo
• console and regional compatibility information.

It uses a logo for the Tomb Raider franchise based on the design used for Lara Croft Tomb Raider in 2001, which helps with brand recognition. The franchise has redesigned its logo several times, so the most recognisable aspect of the game's cover is the image of Lara Croft. She has appeared on the cover of all the games over the years and she has become a recognisable **symbol** for the brand.

Lara Croft is posed on the front cover, wearing the outfit created for the original game that is now the one most associated with her character and has become **iconic** for the franchise. She is wearing shorts, black fingerless gloves and a green vest. Her hair is in a plait, she carries a backpack and is wearing a gun belt on her thighs.

The Tomb Raider: Anniversary cover uses **lighting effects** to highlight parts of Lara Croft's body, specifically her breast, shoulder and legs. This could be interpreted as a sexualised image, as her body parts are emphasised but the image does not reduce her to a simple, passive sexual object. Lara Croft is shown in an **active pose** and returns the audience's gaze by making eye contact with the camera. The game cover provides genre and narrative information by placing Lara Croft in front of the Scion artefacts that are the heart of her quest. The artefacts are engraved with runes, which **symbolise** ancient history as well as magic. The earth tones of the cover create anchorage with the other elements and together they connote archaeological exploration. This replicates the codes and conventions of the action adventure genre as shown in the *Indiana Jones and The Crystal Skull* cover below right.

The primary function of any game cover is to create an image that will be recognisable in the context of a retail environment. This cover offers the **familiarity** of the **brand** for audiences who are already aware of the game, thus creating audience expectations and, hopefully, a desire to buy. The game's genre is clearly communicated and the active representation of Lara posing with her gun highlighted offers information about the gameplay and the experience the game will offer.

The game

The game is presented via a third-person perspective. While the player controls Lara's actions they observe the action from a distance. The player has control over the placement of the 'camera' in the game and can view the action from a slight distance, which offers a full-length view of Lara Croft and provides detailed information on the environment she finds herself in.

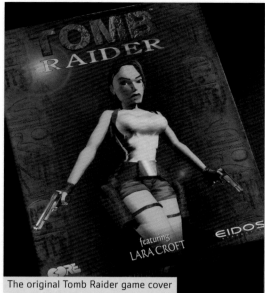

The original Tomb Raider game cover

The player can move the camera to look at specific aspects of the location when required and can **zoom in** to create **close-ups**. During gunplay the camera provides a point of view that is close to Lara Croft's to help build excitement and drama. At times these shots come close to a **first-person perspective** but the player is always kept just outside Lara Croft's point of view. These shots position the player above the action and reinforce a sense of control over the actions of the character.

An example of the action-adventure genre in film

However, in some of the action scenes, the camera provides **reaction shots** of Lara as she battles for her survival or celebrates a victory. These shots help to create empathy with her as a character and help to position her as a **hero**.

The games are set in **locations** that **represent ideas** about ancient civilisations. Most gaming levels are set in ancient ruins or isolated rural locations. The **mise-en-scène** itself provides many of the physical challenges that Lara needs to deal with, from cliff faces and rope bridges to rivers and ravines. The locations offer dangers that the player has to learn to avoid or overcome. **Low-key** lighting, music and **sound effects** help to enhance the suspense and anticipation generated by the game.

Lara swings across a ruined walkway.

Representations

Tomb Raider provides a strong and active female **protagonist**. This subverted the convention, as games protagonists, particularly in 1996, tended to be male, and females were often used in passive, *supporting roles* such as the '**princess**' or the '**damsel in distress**'. Alternatively, they were portrayed as sexualised characters whose role in the narrative of the game was secondary.

However, Tomb Raider also raised some controversy over the physical representation of Lara Croft. In the construction of the character, her body was created in a way that emphasised her breasts and her bottom. Her proportions are an exaggerated version of reality and, as such, this representation can be seen as hyperreal (Baudrillard). In the documentary *Lara Croft: Lethal and Loaded* (2001), Toby Gard states that this depiction depiction of Croft was intended to 'exaggerate feminine characteristics'. The elements of this exaggeration are those aspects of the female body that are assumed to appeal most to a heterosexual, male audience, so Lara Croft can be shown to be presented for the **male gaze** (Mulvey). As well as her physical form, the player views Croft via a **third-person** view that provides a full body view, where her bottom is usually placed in the centre of the screen. In an analysis of women in video games on her YouTube channel, *Feminist Frequency*, Anita Sarkeesian, in her video 'Body Language & the Male Gaze – Tropes vs Women in Video Games', notes that this is a common point of view presented when protagonists are female whereas males are often shown from the waist upwards or from above. She also argues that this type of gaze tends to objectify the female characters, which makes identification with them more difficult for the player.

This **sexualisation** of Lara Croft was evident in the 1990s when patches could be downloaded that allowed gamers to control a naked Lara Croft and this supported the claims that Croft was not an embodiment of a feminist role model but was more likely to be seen as a sexual fantasy figure. In 1999 one of the models hired to 'be' Lara Croft posed in role for *Playboy* magazine. She was sacked shortly afterwards by the games company but the idea of Lara Croft being a sex object was consolidated by this representation.

This analysis supports the idea that, in the early days of Tomb Raider, the audience for the game was largely thought to be male, although the complexity of the representation meant that female gamers could create a negotiated reading, rejecting the sexualisation and focusing on the fact that Croft was a skilled, intelligent, autonomous and independent female. This is the idea of Lara Croft that her creator says was his original intention. Gard, resigned from Core Design in 1997, saying he felt uncomfortable with the way that Lara Croft was being represented in increasingly sexualised ways. He also felt uncomfortable about her use as a **marketing device** and that the character was being developed in ways that were not true to his original ideas. His stated intent was to make her an active character that subverted the expectations of women in these kinds of narratives.

Gender discourse in 1990s media

Lara Croft is one example of the way gender discourse was changing in the late 1990s. Representations of female characters were reflecting the way women's roles in society had changed since the feminist movements of the 1960s and 1970s.

Buffy Summers was the **hero** of *Buffy the Vampire Slayer*. Her creator, Joss Whedon, said he was deliberately trying to **subvert the role** of the blonde female in the horror genre. Traditionally, the blonde female would be the victim in horror but Buffy fought and defeated monsters. The character first appeared in a film in 1992 and was made into a successful TV show that ran from 1997 to 2002. Her **active role** was often interpreted as having a feminist sub-text that offered a positive and non-conventional role model.

However, an alternative interpretation was also made of the character. She was created by a man and, in the fictional world, is frequently controlled by the males in her life. She is often defined through her relationships with male characters and, in early seasons, was often depicted wearing short skirts and low-cut tops that could be seen to be presenting her for using the **male gaze**.

Representations of women in this period reflected the way that women's roles in society had changed and the tensions that these changes created. During the 1970s, when women were more restricted by social structures as well as social expectations, it was clear that media representations of women often worked to reinforce **patriarchal** values. Mulvey's theory of the **male gaze** was written in 1975 in response to decades of male dominance in the **construction of representations**. Both *Buffy the Vampire Slayer* and *Tomb Raider* reflect a time when gender roles were less clearly defined and social expectations of both men and women were changing. Feminist theories were reassessed from a post-feminist perspective which acknowledged that these types of representations were not simply positive or negative. A sexualised female could still be presented for using the male gaze while having power and agency. Both Lara and Buffy **challenge the binary** nature of gender by exhibiting traditionally 'masculine' traits without losing their femininity and their femininity was not identified as being a weakness.

Buffy the Vampire Slayer

The sexualisation of Lara Croft was reinforced by some of the marketing activities that accompanied the release of subsequent games but as the series developed there have been moves to attempt to ensure that Lara Croft is presented less as a sexual object. Her body has been redesigned and modern versions of Lara Croft, while still thin and buxom, have more realistic proportions. The development of the representation of Lara Croft can be seen to be in a mid-point in 2007 for the anniversary release. Her body is less exaggerated than in earlier versions but she has still not become as anatomically 'realistic' as she becomes in more recent representations. In addition, as the Tomb Raider series progressed, Lara was given a personality and a back story making her a more realistic character.

The evolution of Lara

Contemporary issues: gender and gaming

The physical changes to Lara Croft over the years show a development in gaming regarding the representation of females which is, in part, responding to criticisms and changing cultural attitudes. Since the release of the original Tomb Raider game in the 1990s, there has been a growing awareness that games are not simply 'boys' toys'. Females make up almost half of the potential gaming market and female participation in gaming increases in older age groups. The gaming industry does not wish to exclude this potential market, so it makes good business sense to create visual representations that appeal to both male and female gamers.

However, there have been some high-profile stories regarding the sexism and, at times, misogyny that can be experienced within gaming culture. Women who play online games report experiencing bullying and harassment when their biological sex is identified in the gaming environment. In discussing her experiences, games developer and gamer Leena Van Deventer says that, to avoid having to deal with abusive behaviour, she 'will play incognito' and this allows other players to assume she's male (O'Halloran, 2017).

In 2014, Anita Sarkeesian was harassed online for seeking investment for a video series that intended to analyse the representations of women in video games. She received death and rape threats and had to cancel an appearance at a university in Utah as she had received an email claiming that her presence would lead to a shooting massacre.

Brianna Wu, a games developer, received death and rape threats, and had her home address and personal information hacked and published online because she had publicly mocked what was called the Gamergate movement. This term was used to define a collection of attacks on women connected to gaming culture in some way. Men who spoke out against Gamergate were not routinely attacked in the same way that women were and this lead many commentators to note that the attacks were largely motivated by sexism.

The status of women within gaming culture is still not as established as men's but games such as Tomb Raider acknowledge the fact that games can appeal to both sexes and can be seen to be part of a changing culture.

From the complex breakdown of the binary nature of gender in the 1990s, some of the gendered responses within gaming culture today can appear to be reflecting a much more simplistic response to gender roles. The conflicts in Gamergate can be interpreted as coming from an attitude where males and females are perceived to have separate and clearly defined roles. This is a return to binary ways of thinking about gender and Gamergate demonstrates that challenges to this are often responded to aggressively.

It is important to point out that not all gamers (male or female) hold these attitudes. The amplification effect of online communications can magnify certain ideas and beliefs making them seem more widespread than they actually are. However, the amplification of sexist attitudes and their repetition can also act to normalise these attitudes within the gaming community. Women's presence in the gaming community as games developers, journalists, critics and players is growing as is their influence in the way games are developing and in the **discourse** of gaming culture.

APPLY IT

Test yourself on the theoretical framework:

- What are the audience expectations of games within the Tomb Raider franchise?
- In what ways does Tomb Raider: Anniversary conform to the codes and conventions of the action adventure genre?
- How does Tomb Raider: Anniversary provide gratifications for its audience?
- How does the game maintain the interest of the player?
- How might the player's gender alter their experience of the game?
- How do you feel about the representation of women in Tomb Raider: Anniversary via the character of Lara Croft?

FURTHER READING AND REFERENCES

D. Rose (2017, 4 February) 'IPSO Adjudication Upheld against MoS Climate Article', *Daily Mail*, www.dailymail.co.uk/sciencetech/article-4192182/World-leaders-duped-manipulated-global-warming-data.html.

IPSO (2016) *Editors' Code of Practice*, www.ipso.co.uk/editors-code-of-practice/#Privacy.

IPSO (2017) 01032-17 Ward v The Mail on Sunday, www.ipso.co.uk/rulings-and-resolution-statements/ruling/?id=01032-17.

John Herrman (2016, 17 April) 'Media Websites Battle Faltering Ad Revenue and Traffic', *The New York Times*, www.nytimes.com/2016/04/18/business/media-websites-battle-falteringad-revenue-and-traffic.html.

Kate O'Halloran (2017, 23 October) '"Hey Dude, Do This": The Last Resort for Female Gamers Escaping Online Abuse', *Guardian*, www.theguardian.com/culture/2017/oct/24/hey-dude-do-this-the-last-resort-for-female-gamers-escaping-online-abuse.

R. Cookson (2016, 10 April) 'UK Publishers Look to Consolidate in Print Battle', *Financial Times*, www.ft.com/content/2f0fa2ec-fc9e-11e5-b5f5-070dca6d0a0d.

Scott Rigby (2011) *Glued to Games: How Video Games Draw Us In and Hold Us Spellbound*.

T. Smith (2016, 6 November) 'Common Explains Decision to Release "Black American Again" Right before Election Day', hnnh, www.hotnewhiphop.com/common-explains-his-decision-to-release-black-america-again-before-election-day-news.25254.html.

Chapter 6

Media for non-mainstream audiences

What you will learn in this chapter

- This chapter offers detailed analysis of two CSPs as examples of media produced outside the commercial mainstream. The analyses demonstrate how the theoretical framework can be applied to media products that are produced independently, that target non-mainstream audiences and are presented in a language other than English

- Apply It activities will help you practice the application of ideas from the theoretical framework and help you develop your own ideas about the CSPs. You can apply the approaches to the CSPs here to other media products

6.1 Introduction

It is a requirement of A level Media Studies that you are able to demonstrate your knowledge of media products produced outside the mainstream. This includes media products targeting or produced by a minority group and those produced for non-English-speaking audiences. CSPs have been chosen by the exam board to make sure you cover these requirements. As with all CSPs, you need to study them by applying the theoretical framework.

The non-mainstream CSPs selected for this chapter are both **in-depth** CSPs, which means they need to be studied using all areas of the theoretical framework – media language, representation, audience and industry. It's important to consider each CSP in light of the historical, social, cultural and economic context of its production. Your knowledge of these CSPs will be assessed in Media Two.

The CSPs in this chapter have been chosen from the list published by AQA in 2017. They contribute to the study of two of the media forms, magazines and television. The chosen CSPs are:

- *The Killing* (2007) – a Danish television series produced for a non-English-speaking audience.
- *Oh Comely* – an independently published magazine targeting a non-mainstream audience.

The full list of the current CSPs is published each year by the awarding body. Do check the most up-to-date list in case any changes have been made to the named CSPs.

6.2 Media products produced for non-English-speaking audiences

At one point, an audience's access to media products was determined by their location. Audiences could only watch television programmes broadcast by their own national broadcasters. British broadcasting institutions selected programmes for British audiences based on assumptions about what their audiences would want to watch. This meant that the vast majority of television programmes made available to British audiences were those in the English language and represented British or American culture.

Pre-digital national broadcasting technologies meant that British audiences did not have easy access to media products from mainland Europe, Asia, South America or other non-English-speaking cultures. Occasionally, non-English-language programming was shown on UK television but was presented in a way that focused on cultural differences and presented non-English-language television as 'odd' and 'strange'. Programmes such as *Clive James on Television* (1982–1997) and *Tarrant on TV* (1990–2006) presented clips from foreign television shows and advertising as a comedic view of 'foreign' cultures. While some non-English-language programmes were broadcast, they tended to target niche groups (the children's programmes *Monkey*, *White Horses* and *The Singing Ringing Tree*, for example) or were broadcast on the more specialised broadcast channels such as BBC2, BBC4 or Channel 4.

The Singing Ringing Tree from East Germany

In his discussion about attitudes towards foreign-language films, Huw Jones (2014) identifies some reasons why UK audiences may resist watching them. These ideas can also be applied to other non-English-language products.

The reasons offered are:

- **Subtitles**: there can be physical issues with reading on a screen and keeping up with the action while reading subtitles can sometimes be difficult. Translation limitations may also impact on the enjoyment audiences get from non-English-language products.

- **Perception**: UK audiences were found to assume that non-English-language products would have a lower production value (especially when compared with Hollywood productions).

- **Ghettoisation**: non-English programmes are often perceived as 'artsy' and 'intellectual', so are assumed to be less entertaining. This explains why non-English-language programming tends to be on Channel 4 or BBC4 in the UK.

- **Cultural prejudice**: British culture has been identified as having insular qualities – perhaps caused by the dominance of English as an international language and this could make them less open to non-English-language programming. According to a British Council survey, two-thirds of British people do not speak a foreign language, although the number of languages spoken in the UK has increased as the British population has become more culturally diverse.

- **Distribution**: non-English-language products tend to have limited distribution

Monkey from Japan

Changes in technology have expanded distribution methods and have made access to global media easier for audiences. In the 1980s and 1990s, the rise of video and then DVD access to media products meant that audiences had more power to select what they wanted to watch. Truly international viewing of films and television programming was limited, though, as viewing technologies were not compatible across the world. Video came in two formats (PAL and NTSC) and not all video players could play both formats. PAL was accessible in Europe while NTSC was the format that could be viewed in the US. Similarly, DVDs were coded for specific regions. Region 1 DVDs could be played in the US and region 2 in the UK and Europe. A total of six different region

Key	
Region code	**Area**
1	Canada, the USA, Puerto Rico
2	Europe (per 2020, also including Belarus, Ukraine, Moldova and the 3 Caucasus countries), Egypt Iraq, West Asia, Japan, South Africa, Greenland, French Guiana
3	Southeast Asia, South Korea, Taiwan, Hong Kong, Macau
4	Latin America (the Americas except Canada, French Guiana, Puerto Rico, the USA) and Oceania
5	Africa (except Egypt and South Africa), Russia, Central Asia, South Asia, Mongolia, North Korea
6	Mainland China

For more on Netflix as a global provider see Chapter 4.

Black Panther offers familiar locations for a globalised audience, with scenes filmed in the USA, South America, Africa and Asia.

codes made the global movement of one nation's DVDs releases to another difficult. However, DVDs did allow for multiple subtitle options to be included on each disc, so the production language was not a barrier for audiences who could play the DVD.

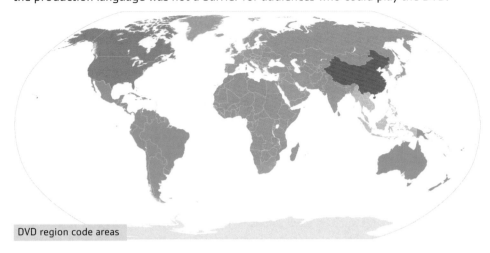

DVD region code areas

Online and digital culture is increasingly more globalised and video platforms such as YouTube, for example, allow free and easy access to media products made around the world. Many non-English television series have been broadcast on BBC4 and Channel 4. Channel 4 also offers many non-English programmes via its streaming service All4. Netflix is a global provider of streaming content and offers its audiences programmes and films from around the world. The audience members' location no longer limits their access to media products made by other cultures in other languages.

Accessing products made in other countries can give an insight into the cultures of others. Attitudes and values vary across the world and watching entertainment programming can offer UK viewers different perspectives and will represent different social norms. International products may also act to highlight the similarities between people regardless of where they come from. Television shows around the world tend to focus on similar stories within familiar genres. Different cultures may offer alternative approaches to the way these stories are told and may utilise genre codes and conventions in ways that are specific to their country. Despite the differences, many international programmes show that humans share many attitudes and experiences, fears and concerns. Whether it is the quest for justice or for romance, fighting crime or dealing with personal tragedies, non-English-language programmes can offer UK audiences stories and characters they can recognise and identify with.

In this way, the ability to access media products from all around the world could be seen to be contributing to what Marshall McLuhan called the 'global village', where technologies act to create a global community linked via our shared cultural experiences. Others, however, worry about the way globalisation can cause identity confusion and the West's dominance in cultural terms is resisted by some cultures. Jameson, for example, is concerned about: '*the standardisation of world culture, with local popular or traditional forms driven out or dumbed down to make way for American television, American music, food, clothes and films*' (McLuhan, 1964). While other cultures produce media products, American products still dominate modern popular culture.

Marianne Gilchrist discussed 'The Sad Disappearance of Foreign TV' in an article in the *Guardian* in 2010. Just six years later, in the same newspaper, Gabriel Tate (2016) wrote, '*since BBC4's Danish import The Killing arrived on British screens four years ago, viewers have embraced a steady stream of foreign language dramas*'. The globalised nature of modern media has provided many more opportunities for British audiences to engage with media products from around the world.

6.3 Case study: *The Killing*

Platform: Broadcast

Form: Television

Product: *The Killing* (2007) with a focus on Series 1, Episode 1

In your work on television products you need to study two named close study media products. If you are studying *The Killing*, you also need to study Episode 1, Season 1 of Channel 4's *No Offence*.

- **Television is identified as an in-depth media form, so the products should be analysed using ideas from all four areas of the theoretical framework:** media language, representation, audience and industry.

- **Assessment information:** your knowledge of *The Killing* will be assessed in Media Two. You could be asked to discuss this product in light of ideas from any area of the theoretical framework. As Media Two has a synoptic element, it is possible that you may be asked to discuss *The Killing* using more than one area of the theoretical framework.

Introduction

The Killing is a Danish crime drama initially broadcast in Denmark in 2007 under the title *Forbrydelsen* (meaning 'The Crime' in Danish). Series 1 follows the investigation into the murder of a teenage girl and focuses on the lead detective in the case, Sarah Lund. The series is a long-form drama and the investigation provides the main narrative arc. *The Killing* is an example of the Nordic-noir or Scandi-noir genre.

The first season of *The Killing* was broadcast in the UK in 2011 on BBC4. It was deemed a success for the niche channel as it attracted around 500,000 viewers for each episode. The programme was also a critical success and generated a keen and active fan culture. The viewing numbers almost doubled when Series 2 was broadcast on the same channel later in 2011 and the programme maintained this audience for Season 3, broadcast in November 2012.

The Killing won many international awards including a BAFTA for best international TV programme and an International Emmy for 'best drama series' and 'best performance by an actress' in 2008 after its initial broadcast run. *The Killing* became a global success and was shown in over 100 countries. The programme was remade in America by Fox Television and was broadcast by AMC and, later, by Netflix. The American version of *The Killing* (2011–2013) relocated the story to Seattle but retained the basic story of the Danish version, including the lead character, renamed as Sarah Lindel.

Industrial context

The Killing was made in Denmark and its production was jointly financed by DR and ZDF Enterprises.

Production

DR (the Danish Broadcasting Corporation) is a public service broadcaster that is owned by and financed through the Danish government. Its funding model is similar to the BBC in that the Danish public pay a licence fee if they have access to television programmes, whether that is via television sets or digital devices. DR is then broadcast and is free at the point of access. DR produces radio and television programmes and can supplement its licence fee income by selling DVDs and electronic downloads, merchandise and through the international sale of its programming.

DR provides a number of channels targeting different audience groups. Its channel profiles are similar to the BBC's: DR1 is its primary, mainstream channel, DR2 targets a more specialised audience, DR3 broadcasts its youth programming and DRK specialises in the arts, documentaries and global programming. DR also has two specialised children's channels. It also provides an online streaming service where programmes can be watched live or on demand.

As DR is funded with a licence fee its broadcasts do not carry advertising. DR operates under a public service contract. This means that, among other things, DR is required to provide programming that reflect and caters for the various groups within the wider society. It is required to reflect diversity and variety as well as make its output accessible for everyone. It is obliged to promote Danish cultural output and provide educational material.

The Killing was broadcast on DR1 in 2007 and its production was funded by DR in collaboration with ZDF Enterprises. ZDF (Zweites Deutsches Fernsehen (Second German Television)) is a German public service broadcaster. It too is funded by television licence fees but it also generates an income by running advertising on its channels.

Distribution

The British broadcaster for *The Killing* was BBC4. BBC4 is one of the **niche** audience channels run by the BBC. It offers a different type of programming to the more mainstream BBC1 and 2 channels and caters to different audience interests. BBC4 is characterised by programming that covers the arts and culture. It produces and broadcasts many documentaries that cover a broad range of subject areas from music to mathematics. In this way, BBC4 helps the BBC fulfil its remit to provide programming that '*promotes education and learning*'. BBC4 also has a history of broadcasting global media, so is active in '*bringing ... the world to the UK*'. Its focus on programming that is less conventional could also be argued to contribute to the '*stimulation of creativity and cultural excellence*', making BBC4 an important part of the BBC's output.

Following is an extract from the BBC Charter – the document that defines the BBC's public service roles:

> **Public purposes and purpose remits**
> *The Charter defines the main objective of the BBC as the promotion of six public purposes. These are:*
> * *Sustaining citizenship and civil society*
> * *Promoting education and learning*
> * *Stimulating creativity and cultural excellence*
> * *Representing the UK, its nations, regions and communities*
> * *Bringing the UK to the world and the world to the UK*
> * *In promoting its other purposes, helping to deliver to the public the benefit of emerging communications technologies and services and, in addition, taking a leading role in the switchover to digital television.*
> (BBC Trust, 2018)

BBC4 is a digital channel that is free to access. Viewers are expected to have paid the UK licence fee, which allows them free access to all BBC output. It was initially conceived as an alternative to the mainstream BBC channels and offered a wide variety of programming but with a clear focus on the arts and documentaries. It has a production budget and makes its own shows, including documentary series, comedies and dramas. It also buys in programming from around the world, often focusing on programming that is critically lauded and that is seen to have a high cultural value.

> **Cultural capital/high art**
>
> Cultural capital is a term used by Bourdieu to describe the idea that certain things (knowledge, objects, appearance, behaviours) give a person status and power within social groups. Art has a high cultural value and those who know about it, understand it and are able to discuss it, often being seen as having a high status. High art (fine art, opera, ballet, classical music, etc.) is perceived as having more cultural value than low art (cartoons, pop music, street dance, etc.). High art is usually seen as having some form of higher purpose (artistic expression) and needs specialist knowledge to understand it properly. High art has intrinsic meaning. Low art is seen as motivated by money and is easy to access by anyone but is ultimately meaningless. Television is usually considered low art, so has a low cultural value.

The BBC4 remit states:

> **BBC Four**
>
> *BBC4's primary role is to reflect a range of UK and international arts, music and culture.*
>
> *It should provide an ambitious range of innovative, high quality programming that is intellectually and culturally enriching, taking an expert and in-depth approach to a wide range of subjects.* (BBC Trust, 2016)

BBC4's own programming often receives high praise but is unlikely to attract the higher viewing figures of BBC1 and BBC2. For example, *Detectorists* attracted approximately 1.5 million viewers for an episode broadcast in December 2017. This is compared to the 4.96 million that watched the more mainstream comedy panel show *Have I Got News for You* or the variety game show *Michael McIntyre's Big Show* both broadcast on BBC1 the same week. *Detectorists* is, however, seen by many critics as a 'quality' comedy show that has an elite value. A review in the *Guardian* called it 'beautifully written and performed – sparse, droll, understated and believable' (Wollaston, 2017). Michael McIntyre was described by the same critic as someone who 'squawks out his standup routine. You know, family-friendly, safe, observational, have-you-noticed stuff'.

Primary to its role as a broadcaster is the remit to provide an international perspective. BBC4 has a history of broadcasting non-English-language programming. Many of the non-English-language television shows broadcast on the channel are European long-form crime dramas. BBC4 is the British broadcaster for critically acclaimed programmes such as France's *Spiral*, the Belgian programme *Salamander* and *Inspector Montalbano* from Italy. It purchased the rights to the Swedish production *Wallander* (also remade in English and broadcast on BBC1 between 2008 and 2016) and this became a forerunner for other Nordic-noir programmes broadcast on the channel, including *The Killing*. A later Nordic-noir programme, *The Bridge*, is one of the most watched shows on the channel, attracting 1.8 million viewers in 2015.

The nature of the success of *The Killing* was unexpected. Not only has this encouraged BBC4 to purchase several other non-English-language programmes but Channel 4 has done the same. Channel 4 offers a range of international TV series as online on-demand box sets under the banner 'Walter Presents'. Many of the programmes available here are European crime dramas but it also offers programmes from South America and Israel and in other genres such as spy thrillers, romances, and historical and prison dramas.

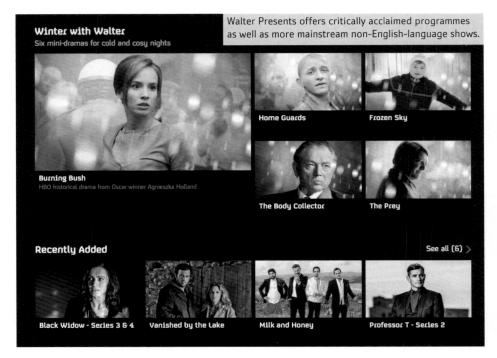

The global nature of Netflix as a content provider also allows audiences to access an increasing number of international titles. Netflix offers television programming (and films) from around the world. Some are dubbed into English and others offered with subtitles. Many are examples of mainstream programming. In 2007 it was unusual to have access to a non-English-language television programme but the global nature of media industries is making it easier to access and watch shows from all around the world.

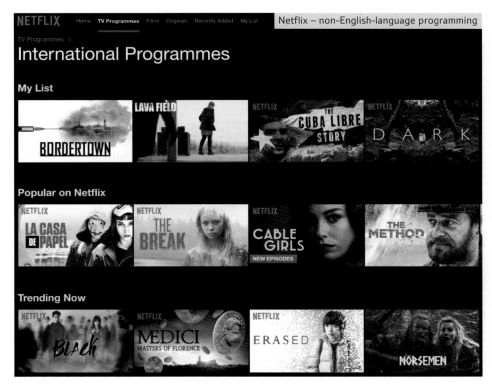

Audience

The audience for BBC4 is a specialised and niche audience. The programming offered on the channel does not necessarily have appeal to a broad audience but it would be incorrect to assume that the BBC4 audience fits into a specific demographic.

YouGov offers the following statistical information about a 'typical' BBC4 audience member.

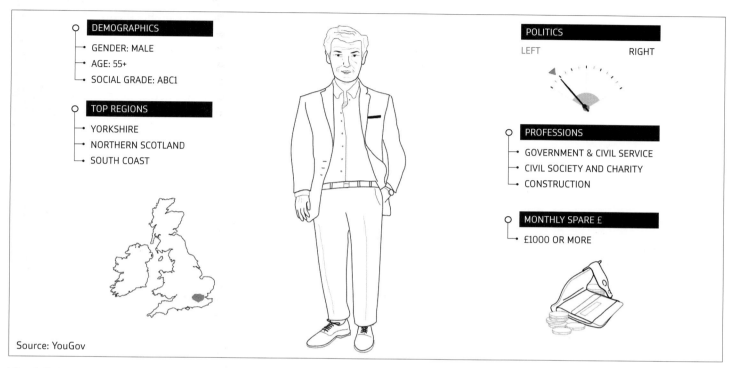

Source: YouGov

The full data show that women are, however, a significant group in BBC4's audience.

GENDER: FULL DATA			
Sort by...	SAMPLE % BBC FOUR	ALL %	CORRELATION Z SCORE
Male	58.0	48.0	+15.4
Female	42.0	52.0	-15.4

Source: YouGov

The full data confirm the fact that older viewers are the largest group in BBC4's audience with 77% being over 40 years old.

AGE: FULL DATA		
Sort by...	SAMPLE % BBC FOUR	ALL %
55+	45.9	32.2
40–54	31.5	27.8
25–39	18.4	27.4
18–24	4.2	12.6

Source: YouGov

Making the assumption that the channel is for 'men' or 'old people' is clearly not fully accurate. A better way to think about the audience for BBC4 programmes would be by considering the way people access television programmes, the types of programming available on the channel and the way audience members use the media.

Before the advent of multi-channel, digital television, people often gravitated to one or two channels and watched the programming at a time determined by the broadcasting schedule. Technological developments have changed audience behaviours and programmes can now be accessed on multiple platforms at any time. This means that a broadcast channel such as BBC4 will often pick up audience members who see its programmes on lists on iPlayer or who are driven to the programmes by social media discussions within special interest groups. BBC4 only broadcasts in the evening but its output is available on iPlayer at any time. The audience for a documentary about musical theatre needs to be interested in musical theatre. The documentary series *Shock and Awe: The Life of Electricity* will appeal to people who are interested in physics and the history of scientific developments. BBC4's programming offers content that may not be widely available on other channels. These programmes offer specific types of gratifications, so, the audience of BBC4 will be those who seek these types of programmes and who have an interest in the type of content the channel offers. BBC4 is a niche channel that offers programmes to special interest audiences, but it is the content of each programme that will attract an audience rather than the channel itself. Of course, some people may self-identify as a BBC4 audience member as they enjoy the diverse range of programming offered by the channel.

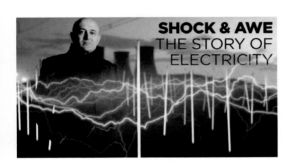

A mainstream programme is one that seeks to include all potential groups and provide content that is likely to appeal to large numbers of people. Mainstream programming will be accessible to everyone regardless of their age, gender, race or prior knowledge or experience. However, mainstream programming does not necessarily appeal to everyone. Variety shows such as *Strictly Come Dancing*, *The X Factor* and *Michael McIntyre's Big Show* appeal to huge numbers of people, but if you have no interest in dancing, talent shows or comedic quiz shows, you will not want to watch these programmes. The actual audiences of these programmes could be young or old, male or female and are likely to be diverse in their ethnic backgrounds and in their life experiences. However, this type of programming can be rejected by people both young and old, male and female and from diverse backgrounds.

As BBC4 largely offers arts, culture and documentary content, it would be safe to say that the audience for this channel are those who largely prioritise information and education and who experience this type of content as entertainment. Some audiences seek out cerebral pleasures that are generated by learning something new and/or having ideas and expectations challenged. Uses and gratification theory notes that audiences are 'goal oriented', so the audience for BBC4 will actively seek information and knowledge from the programmes they choose to watch – or at least that is what they are prioritising at the time of choosing to watch a BBC4 programme. They may prioritise more mainstream entertainment pleasures at another time.

Documentaries offer information and that is an intellectual gratification. Fictional programmes can also encourage intellectual engagement. For example, BBC4's *Detectorists* is an unconventional example of the sitcom. Traditional sitcoms are often shot in studios using a multi-camera set-up, while *Detectorists* is largely shot on location using a single-camera technique. Its humour is low key and based on character rather than being broad and based on events. Its visual presentation, the setting and the characters are very different to those found in conventional sit-coms. BBC4 audiences may enjoy the challenge of engaging with less conventional products and this could be seen as another type of cerebral pleasure.

The Killing offers a range of different gratifications. Some of which can be linked to its visual presentation, its position within the crime drama genre, the way it uses narrative devices and creates representations. The fact that *The Killing* was broadcast on BBC4 creates a set of expectations based on an understanding of the channel's brand. The audience would be justified in expecting *The Killing* to offer something new or an unconventional approach to the genre and/or the story. The audience may expect to have to be active and work with the programme to gain the gratifications on offer, so the complexity of the story and the storytelling techniques and the fact that the show is subtitled and needs to be read while being watched will be part of the appeal for audiences who enjoy an active, intellectual engagement with fictional stories. BBC4 scheduled two episodes of *The Killing* back to back each week during its initial broadcast and this demonstrates that the broadcaster is assuming the audience will enjoy engaging with the drama over an extended period of time. Given the other types of programming broadcast on BBC4, *The Killing* was likely to find a receptive fan-base within the channel's audience.

Among many other things, the audience for *The Killing* could be:

- curious BBC4 viewers
- fans of crime drama as a genre
- fans of Nordic-noir specifically
- people who are curious about Danish culture
- those who seek cultural capital by accessing a critically lauded, subtitled TV series
- people who seek a new and unusual television experience
- Danish speakers.

Each group would access the programme and gain very personalised gratifications as well as the gratifications offered by the aesthetics, the genre, the narrative devices and the representations.

Audience engagement (and circulation)

The interactive nature of e-media may have helped spread the word about *The Killing*. The *Guardian* ran a week by week episode summary while the programme was being broadcast on BBC4. The episode summaries were open for comments, so audience members could gather to discuss the most recent episode, and share theories and ideas about the case and its potential resolution. A community of fans was soon established with a shared discourse of 'in-jokes', shared grumbles and comments on topics as diverse as Scandinavian décor and Sarah Lund's jumpers.

The *Guardian*'s audience are likely to overlap significantly with that of BBC4 and, therefore, *The Killing*. The weekly discussion online and the fact that the show was available on iPlayer for audiences who missed the scheduled broadcasts, meant that it was able to build its audience before the end of the run. Each week, hundreds of comments were left below the line on the episode recaps and this culminated in nearly 1,000 comments as the series concluded.

26 March 2011

The Killing: episodes 19 and 20

Vicky Frost's series blog: Finally the case is explained. So were your theories correct? And what did you make of the finale?

THE KILLING

© 11:03 PM 949

Episode recaps published by the *Guardian*.

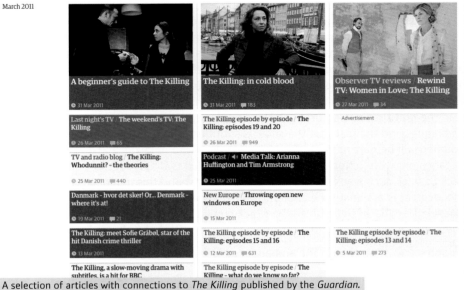

March 2011

A beginner's guide to The Killing
31 Mar 2011

The Killing: in cold blood
31 Mar 2011 183

Observer TV reviews / Rewind TV: Women in Love; The Killing
27 Mar 2011 34

Last night's TV / The weekend's TV: The Killing
26 Mar 2011 65

The Killing episode by episode / The Killing: episodes 19 and 20
26 Mar 2011 949

Advertisement

TV and radio blog / The Killing: Whodunnit? - the theories
25 Mar 2011 440

Podcast / Media Talk: Arianna Huffington and Tim Armstrong
25 Mar 2011

Danmark - hvor det sker! Or... Denmark - where it's at!
19 Mar 2011 21

New Europe / Throwing open new windows on Europe
15 Mar 2011

The Killing: meet Sofie Gråbøl, star of the hit Danish crime thriller
13 Mar 2011

The Killing episode by episode / The Killing: episodes 15 and 16
12 Mar 2011 631

The Killing episode by episode / The Killing: episodes 13 and 14
5 Mar 2011 273

The Killing, a slow-moving drama with subtitles, is a hit for BBC

The Killing episode by episode / The Killing - what do we know so far?

A selection of articles with connections to *The Killing* published by the *Guardian*.

TIP Take care not to make lots of generalisations and assumptions about audiences. It may feel logical to assume that BBC4's audience are 'clever' or 'well educated' or even that they are all from a particular socio-economic background. This would be to ignore the fact that people from different educational and economic backgrounds have broad and diverse interests and use television as a source of information, education and intellectual stimulation.

The *Guardian* maximised on this interest publishing lots of related articles, interviews and analyses. This activity was good for the programme, providing free publicity on a regular basis, targeting people who are likely to be interested in the show. This was also good for the *Guardian*. Not only did it provide entertaining, interactive articles that created a positive response from audiences, its fan-community would have encouraged readers to the news site. This audience engagement generated wider activity on the news website. In addition, both the show and the newspaper gain from the **cultural capital** generated by the other.

Analysis: *The Killing* (2007)

Media Language

Genre

The Killing is an example of a crime drama. Crime drama is one of the most popular and widespread genres in television fiction products. It is a genre based on the type of story being told – where the plot centres around a crime of some sort and, often, the investigation that follows. As the shared characteristic that makes a television show a crime drama is this one element of plot, crime drama can be divided into many different sub-genres – each with a different approach in the way the plot is presented.

For example:

- Some crime dramas are **hybrids** where the crime plot is presented within the codes and conventions of another genre. Crime dramas can be westerns, science fictions and even comedies. *The Expanse* is a crime drama that is set in a future society where space travel is a day-to-day reality. *Riverdale* is a crime drama that is also a typical US teen drama.
- **Police procedurals** are crime dramas that focus on the investigation into the crime. Police procedurals often focus on an investigative team within a specific area of the police force. They are sometimes called cop shows. *CSI* was one of the most successful police procedurals of all time. The original series (*CSI: Las Vegas*) led to three spin-offs (*CSI: Miami, CSI: New York* and, more recently, *CSI: Cyber*). *CSI* was the most watched TV show for several years during the 2000s.

- **Single detective crime dramas** focus on one detective (sometimes a member of the police force, but not always) who has a personality quirk that makes him/her able to solve the mysteries of a crime. In *Sherlock*, Holmes is represented as a genius whose personality issues (he is an addict and describes himself as a 'high-functioning sociopath') allow him to see the world in a way that others cannot, thus helping him to find the truth when investigating cases. Not all 'detectives' are detectives. They can be lawyers, authors, journalists or, in the case of *Miss Marple*, observant elderly ladies.

- **Heists**, unlike most other crime dramas, usually provide the audience with the criminal's point of view. Heists tell the story of a theft of some sort and they often involve a criminal gang. The gang are usually presented sympathetically. *Hustle* is an example of this sub-genre, where the protagonists are con artists.

Crime fiction is a long-established and popular literary genre. Many television crime dramas are based on characters and situations taken from successful books. Some of the most successful crime dramas in the UK have been based on literary detective stories. Television programmes featuring popular detectives such as Poirot, Sherlock Holmes, Miss Marple and Father Brown are based on 19th- and 20th-century crime novels. Crime fictions were popular in silent films at the start of the 20th century and later became a mainstay of television programming.

The Lodger – directed by Alfred Hitchcock in 1927.

Dixon of Dock Green – popular in the UK from 1955 to 1976

The longevity of the genre shows that it has great audience appeal and the genre's fundamental simplicity means that it can be presented to audiences in lots of different settings. The genre can be reinvented in many ways and, as long as a crime story is still central, it is possible to give the audience what they expect from the genre while also providing the audience with new and different experiences.

Noir

One sub-genre of crime drama is noir.

Noir began as a film genre. Film-noir (black film) was the term used by Nino Frank to identify a genre of American crime films that were being made in the 1940s dealing with dark themes and using a dark visual style. This style was seen to be reflecting the dark aspects of American post-war society and the genre often told stories about crime gangs, hard-bitten private investigators or lone-wolf policemen. The stories were often violent. Antagonists were usually arrested or killed but the protagonists often ended the story alone and isolated making the genre part of what Schatz (1981) calls the 'genre of order'. While many examples of film-noir were set in the crime world of urban environments, the content and settings are not what defines it. Film-noir is a genre that is defined more by its feeling and tone and the style of its story. Noir is a genre that deals with power and sexuality and often engages with taboo topics. It is a genre that aims to attract an adult audience.

Visually, noir was influenced by German expressionism, a style of filmmaking that made use of the high contrast between dark and light, shadows and brightness. Two highly influential German expressionist films are *Nosferatu* (Murnau, 1922) and *The Cabinet of Dr Caligari* (Wiene, 1920). These were horror films that aimed to create feelings of suspense and uncertainty for the audience. They used surreal imagery and high-contrast (low-key) lighting to tell their dark stories of murder and madness influencing the style and content of film-noir.

A still from *The Third Man* (Reed, 1949) – a classic Hollywood film-noir

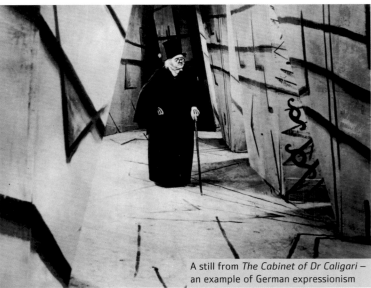
A still from *The Cabinet of Dr Caligari* – an example of German expressionism

In cinemas, the rise of the use of colour meant that noir style was edged out of cinemas but it could be used in the presentation of television dramas, as television programmes were commonly made in black and white through the 1950s and 1960s. Police procedurals, murder mysteries and detective shows were very popular in that period and their popularity has been maintained.

APPLY IT Search YouTube for clips from old TV crime dramas. There are many examples you could look at but some popular programmes from the past include:

- *Dixon of Dock Green* (1955–1976)
- *Z Cars* (1962–1978)
- *The Sweeney* (1975–1978)
- *Juliet Bravo* (1980–1985)
- *Bergerac* (1981–1991)
- *The Bill* (1984–2010)
- *Miss Marple* (1984–1992)
- *Sherlock Holmes* (1984–1994)
- *Inspector Morse* (1987–2000)
- *Agatha Christie's Poirot* (1989–2013).

In what ways is *The Killing* a typical crime drama?
How has the crime drama changed over the years?

Neo-noir

This is a term used to define modern films that use many of the conventions of the style and tone of classic noir but in the context of contemporary filmmaking – specifically, using colour rather than black and white. Films such as *Seven* (Fincher, 1996), set in the contemporary world, *Blade Runner* (Scott, 1982), set in a dystopian future and *The Dark Knight* (Nolan, 2008), a superhero story, are examples of neo-noir. Each of these films uses stylistic conventions of noir: crime-ridden urban contexts, low-key lighting, troubled protagonists, etc. but the style is updated to meet modern audience expectations. *True Detective* and *Jessica Jones* are examples of neo-noir in television.

Nordic-noir/Scandi-noir

The terms Scandi-noir and Nordic-noir were first used to define a specific style of crime fiction that was being written in the Scandinavian countries such as Denmark, Iceland, Finland and Sweden. As in other cultures, Scandinavian countries have a long history of crime fiction and many of these Scandinavian writers were translated into English and found an audience in the English-speaking world. Many of these stories were adapted for film and television in Scandinavia and their success has led to English language versions also being made. Detectives such as Beck and Wallander have proved to have a global appeal as did the character Lisbeth Salander, who appeared in the books/films *The Girl with the Dragon Tattoo* (Fincher, 2011), *The Girl who Played with Fire* (Alfredson, 2010) and *The Girl who Kicked the Hornet's Nest* (Alfredson, 2010). *The Killing* itself was written for television but it has also inspired a series of novels, taking the genre back to its literary roots.

Nordic-noir has shared characteristics with film-noir and neo-noir. The stories deal with the darker side of modern life, focusing on violence, crime and their impact. The settings can be both urban and rural but the genre often focuses on the desolate nature of these locations, using isolated areas of the countryside or run-down parts of cities and towns to create a dystopian landscape. The locations and the crimes act as symbols for the wider culture where the external appearance of families and social institutions hide dark, violent and corrupt behaviour. Scandinavian countries are known for their cold winters with short, dark days and the climate is often used to influence the presentation of the story. Historically, Scandinavian countries are associated with strong welfare state systems and low levels of wealth inequality. The region is thought to be socially liberal with progressive attitudes to gender and sexuality. Nordic-noir often engages with this idealisation of these countries and uses the crime drama to explore and, at times, critique these ideas of national identity. Protagonists in nordic-noir are usually flawed in some way – they may struggle with human interaction or relationships and they often find themselves in conflict with authority figures. The stories often have female protagonists and deal with taboo subjects.

Narrative

The Killing is a long-form serial drama. Series 1 consists of 20 hour-long episodes that focus on one case – the murder of Nanna Birk Larsen. The series begins with the discovery of the teenager's body and then progresses through a number of mysteries: Who is she? How and why did she die? Who killed her? Each episode represents one day of the investigation. The lead protagonist is a female detective (Sarah Lund) who investigates the crime with her partner (Jan Meyers).

The series has a number of storylines that run parallel through the series:

- **The investigation**: following the police's progress in trying to solve the crime.
- **The family**: following the emotional impact of the murder on the victim's family and their attempt to understand what has happened.
- **Local politics**: following a politician (Troels Hartmann) who is campaigning to be Mayor of Copenhagen.
- **The detective's personal life**: following the impact the investigation is having on Lund's family and relationships.

The connection between the political storyline and the murder develop over the course of the series. The investigation takes the detectives into different locations that represent different areas of Danish society; for example, the school and social lives of teenagers. Later in the series racism and attitudes towards sexual behaviour are dealt with.

Episode 1 offers exposition for the audience and creates the equilibrium for each of the storylines. The story begins in media res (in the middle of the action) and the audience are shown a young woman running through a forest, clearly in fear for her life. She is shown to be terrified and bloody, and, with the anchorage created by the programme's title and the intercutting of the action with the title sequence, it is clear that the first scene is the main disruption to the narrative. Offering the disruption at the start of the narrative in this way creates immediate enigma. Who is she? What's happening to her? Why is she running? Who or what is she frightened of? As *The Killing* tells its story slowly, it is important to engage the audience immediately, so they will be prepared to take some time to get to know the other characters in the story. This cold opening gives the audience a reason to stay with the episode as it starts to reveal the main characters in the story.

Nina's parents

Much of the first episode is spent creating character and location exposition. As the whole series deals with one case, *The Killing* develops its story slowly, unlike an episodic crime drama where the culprit needs to be revealed within one hour of television. This makes for a slower, more detailed story where characters can be established and then developed. For example, in Episode 1 Nanna's mother Pernille calls her husband, Theis, home to help her deal with a flood in their kitchen. This mundane, domestic scene shows their relationship in a positive way. Pernille teases Theis and they are shown to be comfortable and playful with each other. At this point, the audience know that their happy life is about to be disrupted and seeing them happy creates pathos, heightening the audience's identification with the characters when they receive the news about their daughter. This scene also contrasts with the way their relationship is impacted on as they try to deal with loss of their daughter. Events cause the characters to change and this makes them more complex and realistic.

In the first episode, we learn that Sarah Lund is about to leave Denmark to marry her boyfriend and make a new life in Sweden with him and her son. We are shown that she is a popular and well-respected detective. We are also introduced to Troells, his campaign team and his political opponent as well as Nanna's best friend at school. The characters are part of separate narrative strands that are drawn together via Nanna's murder.

The whole of Episode 1 is a slow disruption of the equilibria of the various narrative strands within the story. The normal lives of all the characters we are introduced to begin to disintegrate as the episode progresses. This shows the audience that the diverse characters and situations are in some way connected. There is an early connection between the murder of Nanna and the political campaign as the politicians have to cancel a debate because of the investigation – held at Nanna's school. Nanna's best friend is also drawn into the story, as is the young man who is assumed to be Nanna's boyfriend. Pernille and Theis' domestic life is about to change forever and Sarah's domestic plans are postponed as the investigation begins. The episode ends with the identification of Nanna's body, confirming the audience's assumptions about who the victim is and finalising the various disruptions. The end of the episode reinforces a state of disequilibrium in all the storylines. The episode ends with multiple open narrative strands. Enigma is maintained as the narrative is restricted, so the audience knows little more than the characters. The montage at the end of the episode acts as a summary for the various narrative threads within the story. In order to find out the answers to the questions the audience will need to watch the next episode and, ultimately, the whole series.

Media language

Nordic-noir has a distinct aesthetic style. The colour tone used is muted and dominated by cool colours such as greys, blues and greens. The colours represent the wintry, often rainy settings of the stories and the limited use of bright and primary tones reinforces the darkness of the genre's tone and content. This limited palette creates an effect similar to the black and white of classic-noir and, by using these earthy, natural tones, the shots can be lit using low-key lighting to create the effect of light and shadows. Many of the scenes are set at night, which also offers the same scope for high-contrast lighting. Diegetic lighting can be used from sources such as torches and streetlights. By hiding some of the content of the frame, an idea of mystery is maintained as the audience is unable to get a clear image of what is happening. There is very little light in the opening scene of Episode 1. Nanna is shown largely by hazy moonlight, although we are shown that there is someone else in the woods who is carrying a powerful torch. As Nanna runs we are shown glimpses of her, so the final shot of the opening sequence creates a shock for the audience. In this shot Nanna is lit by the lights of a plane as it passes above her. This light acts as a spotlight and reveals the character as well as her emotional and physical state. The shot only lasts a very short time though, so the audience is not able to dwell on this but they are given an opportunity to engage with the character's terror.

Nanna revealed

APPLY IT

What questions do you have at the end of Episode 1:
- about the crime?
- about Sarah?
- about Sarah's family?
- about Jan?
- about Nanna's family?
- about Nanna's friends?
- about the politicians and the political campaign?

Diegetic lighting is also used in interior shots to break up the light and create shadow, reflection and silhouette. In this way the light is used to hide as well as reveal. The shot of Lund in her office (below left) in the police station shows her in partial shadow and silhouette. The light source is the natural daylight coming in through the window and the reflection of an overhead strip-light. As viewers to this scene, we are positioned outside the office, looking in through the blinds and our view is obscured by the reflections – the police officers on the left and the strip lights are not in the office with Lund but are reflections from the room behind the camera.

- Did Mark lend a hand?
- He went off to school.

Sarah in her office

The cut to mid-shot (above right) allows us to see more of Lund's face but the audience is still looking at her from outside the office through the blinds. The camera has pulled in close but the audience is still being kept at a distance. The bright morning light behind Sarah puts her in silhouette and the blinds create shadow.

The Killing is set in early November. The exterior scenes use the diffuse nature of winter light to create tone and atmosphere. Here the crane shot (below) emphasises the vast and bleak landscape as the police begin their search. The damp ground, the grey sky and the blue tone are evocative and communicate the cold and damp nature of the setting of the story. There is no life in this landscape, which reflects the genre's theme of death and decay.

A long-shot of the desolate landscape

As each episode represents one day, the lighting changes as time passes. Nanna's body is found as the sun goes down and the change in tone as the light fades reinforces the desolate nature of the landscape. As night falls, the scenes are lit with police lights, floodlights, torches and headlights. This takes the audience back to the lighting used in the first scene of the episode: Nanna's terror as she tried to escape her attacker has been replaced by her mother and father's grief when her body is discovered.

The lighting quality of dusk, enhanced to add atmosphere.

Stark low-key lighting in a night-time scene

Fast-cut editing is used in the opening scene of the programme. The titles are intercut between the images of Nanna running. The speed of the editing makes it difficult to make out detail but it communicates the panic and fear being felt by the character. However, the programme is characterised by a slower editing style in the main. The camera is often static or moves slowly in a pan or a tracking movement to create a sense of space or scale.

Towards the end of the episode, when Sarah joins the search for Nanna, she is presented in ways that encourage the audience to identify with her and her point of view.

The audience is shown what Sarah is looking at. Close-ups and shallow focus shots invite us to identify with her further.

I'd prefer to have her sleep there rather than on the sofa...

I'd prefer to have her sleep there rather than on the sofa...

Camera work and shallow focus encourage the audience to empathise with Sarah.

The slow editing and camera movements reflect the slow pace of the storytelling within the genre. The soundtrack to the episode works in the same way, with music being used to lead emotional responses.

When Sarah is looking for Nanna the music is quite sparse and consists of some piano notes, some ambient chords and extended gaps where low-level background noise replaces the soundtrack. The music is used to reinforce the desolate atmosphere created by the mise-en-scène as well as the action at that moment in the narrative – the search for the missing girl. As the police get closer to and finally discover Nanna's body, the music becomes more ominous and when Theis is told they have found his daughter, the tension breaks with a mournful theme.

The music that accompanies the montage at the end of the episode communicates tension and a sense of urgency. Rhythmically it is reminiscent of a heart beat. Close-ups are used to create an emotional focus which is reinforced by the music.

APPLY IT

Watch Episode 1 of Season 1 of *The Killing*.

Identify specific media language choices made in the production of Episode 1. Why have these choices been made? What effect do they have?

	Media language observation – where and how?	Reason the choice was made?	Effect of the choice?
Camera			
Editing			
Lighting			
Mise-en-scène			
Special effects			
Sound			

Audience appeal

Crime dramas work on the gratifications created by the enigma of the narrative. Mysteries offer a cerebral appeal for audiences who want to engage with the mysteries in the story. For some audience members this will mean trying to work out the answers to the mystery as the story develops, while others will enjoy the act of watching the investigation unfold. Long-form crime dramas will often offer narrative surprises with twists to the plot and in the actions of characters. These surprises can often include the presentation of false heroes. Red-herrings (false clues) can divert the viewer and they may be encouraged to see a character as being suspicious only to have their innocence revealed later. The use of restricted narrative creates mystery and suspense, and the ability to surprise the audience when events occur or when information is revealed.

As crime dramas deal in dark and often taboo content, there is an element of voyeurism (Borstin) in the audience experience. The audience are shown events that they are not usually able or allowed to see. These events may be things that people would actively avoid in their real-world experiences. Episode 1 offers Nanna's fear and terror, Pernille and Theis's grief and anguish, as well as Sarah and Jan's horror and dismay when Nanna's body is discovered. The characters' emotional journeys provide a vicarious gratification for the audience.

The violence of the crime drama is sometimes thought to be potentially problematic. Direct audience theories, though, which suggest that seeing violence can make someone behave violently have been largely discredited. But, the popularity of the crime drama genre means that audiences are shown many versions of a dark and dangerous world full of violence. This could create a view that the world is more dangerous than it actually is (Gerbner's mean world syndrome). Statistically, very few people are impacted on personally by the type of crimes depicted in this type of programming but serial killers, child abductions and other types of violent crime are often shown in TV and film fictions. In addition, the news and documentaries often focus on these types of crime, so audiences may assume they happen more often than they do.

It is also suggested that the repeated viewing of violent imagery could desensitise the audience to the real-world consequences of violence. Some crime dramas may do this by dehumanising the victims of crime or by glamourising violence and violent characters. Other crime dramas try to avoid this by humanising victims so audiences feel the loss of a character, or by dealing with the outcome of the violence in the way it affects family members, the investigators or the local community. The initial focus on Nanna's emotional state and then on her family encourage the audience to engage with the terror and grief caused by violent acts rather than just enjoy them.

There are gratifications offered by the genre and its approach to narrative but *The Killing* offers some gratifications that are specific to the programme itself. The slow development of the story provides more in-depth studies of place, character and motivation that some audiences may appreciate rather than the fast-paced storytelling offered in episodic programmes such as *Criminal Minds*. Long-form drama has become more popular since the rise of box sets and streaming gave audiences alternative ways to watch serial dramas. This type of storytelling requires a commitment of time by the audience but they can choose to watch one episode a week or binge-watch multiple episodes at a time. Long-form drama can tell more complex stories that require audience engagement, which in turn offer gratifications in the rewards provided by the story. Complex narratives and characters require the audience to engage, so the pleasures offered by the form are often intellectual ones. Long-form dramas can also provide excitement by having fast-paced elements within the story. *The Killing* combines both elements. The need for exposition in the first episode means it takes its time to introduce the characters and the problems within the narrative. Later episodes include dramatic scenes that keep the audience engaged with the twists and turns of the narrative as it develops.

The Killing provides the audience with realistic characters from Sarah Lund who is, like all people, a little flawed, to Pernille and Theis, who are loving parents who make mistakes and react badly when under pressure. These realistic characters encourage the audience to identify with them and their situations, which heightens the emotional connection the audience has with the programme. This type of engagement encourages audience loyalty, helping to retain viewers and encouraging audience interaction through social media, etc.

British audiences may be attracted to a drama set in Denmark that offers them an insight into Danish culture as well as showing the landscapes and interiors of a society that is both similar and different from our own. The climate reflects the damp, grey winters of the UK and its landscapes look similar at times but also offer differences. While the language and some aspects of Danish culture may feel exotic to the British viewer, *The Killing* also offers a story set in a northern European culture that feels very familiar, and this may be part of its appeal in this country. Scandinavian style has been used to sell products for many years and British audiences are familiar with IKEA and, more recently, the concept of Hygge (a focus on wellbeing through simple pleasures, encapsulating ideas of cosy, snug, warm and comforting). Sarah Lund's jumper became iconic, representing the idea of Hygge as well as being a no-nonsense, practical article of clothing. People sought to buy a 'Sarah Lund' jumper and it even has its own website (www.sarahlundsweater.com/) giving a short history of the jumper, telling people where they can buy it and offering knitting patterns for people who want to make their own.

1   Media products that offer violence to entertain audiences can be very popular.

There are many reasons why audiences are drawn to these products. Do you think *The Killing* offers any of the following? If so, where and how?

- The excitement of an adrenaline rush.
- The ability to see taboo images/engage with taboo ideas.
- The experience of things that are not part of our everyday lives.
- The experience of anxiety or fear (while being in a safe environment).
- The ability to use our emotional imaginations.
- The ability to experience chaos (while being in total control of our environment).

2   Dyer says that we use media products to provide solutions to things that we lack in our own lives. What solutions might *The Killing* offer for the audience?

Sarah Lund jumpers

Sarah Lund

Representations and contextual issues

The representation of women in *The Killing* offers several characters who have different roles in the story and the narrative:

- **Sarah Lund**: mother, working mother, detective, fiancé, protagonist
- **Pernille Birk Larsen**: mother, wife, sister
- **Nanna Birk Larsen**: daughter, friend, teenager, victim
- **Rie Skovgard**: politician, lover.

Sarah is represented as a woman who has to deal with both the professional and the domestic spheres of her life. Pernille and Rie are in some ways more conventional. Pernille is the mother and wife, who begins by being depicted firmly located in the domestic. She is defined through her relationship with her children and her husband. Rie is shown at first purely in a professional role. She is a political advisor and it is only later in the episode that it is revealed she is also Troels' lover. The introduction to Sarah shows her in the process of leaving the Copenhagen police force to move to Sweden to marry her Swedish fiancé. She has a teenage son, although little is revealed about her previous relationship. She is pranked by her colleagues as a way to mark her leaving and it is clear she has a status within this professional environment as well as the respect of her colleagues.

There appears to be a male-dominated culture in her team (Sarah is given a sex doll as a joke present) but both she and her colleagues are comfortable with Sarah's place within the group. We are told that she will be working with the Swedish police once she has moved but it is clear that relocating will cause her to lose some of her professional standing. At first she appears to have made choices where her domestic role will be more dominant but when she begins her investigation she begins to make choices that show her prioritising her professional role over her domestic one. In this way, Sarah reflects the conflicts experienced by many women who have to balance domestic roles with their professional ones. The police station is male dominated and this heightens the fact that Sarah's experiences are different from those of her male colleagues.

When Sarah is preparing to leave for Sweden she looks relaxed and feminine. She is shown with her hair loose, wearing jeans and a T-shirt. When she leaves to begin the investigation, she ties her hair back and, for the rest of the episode, is shown wearing a Fair Isle jumper and an overcoat. Her clothes and the fact that Sarah wears very little make-up allow her to avoid a sexualised gaze. She is an attractive woman but this is not presented as an important part of her character. The camera presents Sarah in ways that communicate where she is, what she's doing and her thought processes. The audience is encouraged to see her as a skilled professional rather than judge her on the way she looks. Sarah experiences conflict in her professional role (the investigation) and in her domestic life (she prioritises her professional role over her domestic commitments) and this latter issue is something that is related to her gender.

The representation of Sarah Lund, however, avoids creating a gender-based conflict between her and the men she works with. The gender issues Sarah is dealing with are based in the realistic tensions created by the needs of both parts of her life. Even in the first episode it appears as if Sarah is more successful in what might traditionally be seen to be the more masculine aspects of her life. She has a tense relationship with her son and is distracted by her work when speaking to her fiancé.

APPLY IT

There are many ways to approach representations in *The Killing*. It would be interesting to engage with representations of:

- the police
- families
- teachers
- race
- politics/politicians
- Denmark
- other ideas.

In what ways do the representations in *The Killing* relate to different contextual issues?

Context – gender and the crime drama

There have been criticisms of crime dramas and other media products that use violence against women as a narrative device in that they may:

- naturalise the idea of violence against women
- repeat the idea that women are weak and vulnerable
- reinforce the idea that women are victims
- deflect attention away from the violence experienced by males
- offer prurient pleasures showing battered women's bodies and the brutalisation of women.

There are concerns voiced about the way so many crime dramas are based on the victimisation of women and that the way this violence is represented belittles women. Female victims are often used as devices to allow the story to focus on its main subjects: the detective and the criminal – often male characters. US series such as *True Detective* and *Hannibal* used images of anonymous dead women as aesthetic displays. These disposable victims reinforce ideas that women have less value than men – other than to be used and/or looked at. Women's bodies are often on display in the genre, either as murder victims on mortuary tables or where the camera focuses on a woman's injuries. The way the camera often lingers on dead or injured women could be interpreted as being misogynistic – revelling in and fetishising their injured bodies. It is the repetition of these types of images that are argued to desensitise the audience to the violence used to create them.

Jessica Jones

However, a counter-argument could be that the use of female victims in these narratives reflects the fact that women are statistically more likely to be the victims of violence. Some crime dramas attempt to sensitise the audience to the violence to draw attention to the horrifying nature of these acts. Some crime dramas create more audience identification with the victims so they do not act as anonymous cyphers but are realistic characters. Violence against realistic characters is more likely to shock the audience and create an emotional response that is empathetic with the victim. We are asked to experience the terror of Nanna's final moments alive in the opening sequence of *The Killing*. Although Nanna as a character does not appear again in the main storyline, the audience are encouraged to see her as a real person through the slow reveal of her back story as the series progresses. The audience is also positioned to see the impact of the murder on her friends and family showing the broader consequences of the violent act. Similarly, female detectives can offer an alternative to the 'woman as victim' narrative. Women like Sarah Lund are active and powerful. Although she is a flawed character, she shows that women can act to protect themselves and others around them. Sarah Lund's gender becomes irrelevant as she is a detective first and foremost. The conflict between her professional and personal lives shows that women often have to make choices and sacrifices but they are not always victims.

The Bridge

Happy Valley

Broadchurch

The Fall

Female detectives

The issue of the media's representation of violence against women is complex. Real-world violence affects many women as victims of crime and domestic violence. Media products that engage with this are reflective of a reality where violence against women can come from many different sources. Some real-world violence against women is intertwined within cultural norms and some is becoming more prevalent through the use of social media.

Revelations about sexual abuse in show-business and politics started the #MeToo movement in 2017, which highlighted the extent of a range of different types of sexually aggressive behaviours experienced by women. *The Killing* offers a representation of a female victim who is terrorised, abused and discarded. However, it also offers a range of other women who, in their own ways, show strength and reject the idea of being victims to violence or sexual objectification. Women in *The Killing* are shown as strong within the home and the workplace, and their feminine characteristics are shown positively rather than being a problem to be overcome, but the programme also acknowledges that violence is also a reality for some women.

6.4 Independence and the mass media

In the Year 1 book, you briefly looked at the distinction between the terms 'independent' and 'alternative' as applied to the mass media. It was made clear that while most 'alternative media' can also be defined as independent, not all independent media is necessarily alternative. This does mean that we have to use some caution when using the terms, and also that we need to be aware that even academics cannot agree entirely on what alternative media actually is in today's climate. As Media Studies students, you can focus on identifying aspects of alternative practices and forms, while recognising that often there may be mainstream influences or complex commercial relationships behind apparently independent or alternative products which can undermine their credentials. You will also be considering how apparently alternative media products can actually contribute to cultural hegemony. It's also vital that you are sure of exactly what is meant when you talk about the mainstream media.

The mainstream media is usually thought of as having several qualities that help us to think about by contrast what is meant by alternative or independent media.

Mainstream media products are:

- Often produced in ways that follow industrial production practices established over a long period of time. Mainstream media working practices have often been gradually built up over many decades and will tend to share a great deal in common with other media organisations in the ways in which they produce and distribute their products.

- Widely distributed, easy to access and extensively consumed by audiences – most people will not deliberately seek out alternatives to the generally available product that can be accessed and consumed with ease because of its commercial availability. Because of the high level of investment in commercial mainstream media, many audience members will associate them with high production values, quality and choice, have brand loyalty to their products, or otherwise consider access to certain premium packages and so own a status symbol.

- Owned by large companies which may in turn form part of huge media conglomerates that have a global reach. These kinds of business models do not often provide an environment where it makes sense to take risks with products. Market forces often drive the production of genre products, for example, where formulas have been tried and tested and likely to continue to sell.

 Read about #MeToo on page 50.

APPLY IT

The theoretical framework – test yourself

1 In what ways is *The Killing* a typical crime drama?

2 How does *The Killing* use and/or subvert the conventions of the crime drama?

3 How is media language used to:
   a create tone/ atmosphere?
   b communicate character information?

4 What gratifications does *The Killing* offer?

5 How does Episode 1 engage the audience and maintain their interest?

6 What do you think about the representation of women and violence in *The Killing*?

7 Why do you think *The Killing* achieved international success?

- Carry mainstream values which are broadly supportive of the dominant ideologies in a particular culture and therefore contribute to cultural hegemony. It simply doesn't make sense to produce products that don't conform to the majority of the population's tastes.

- Exist in most cases for commercial purposes and are therefore at the heart of capitalist societies – it is not necessarily in their interests to challenge the status quo. There is often a complex relationship between business and politics, which means that the two are closely linked. States often issue broadcasting licences and govern regulatory bodies, making challenges to dominant ideologies from these organisations and their media products even less likely.

- Often less participatory – they are run by professional staff and gatekeepers who tightly control the content.

'Independent' usually refers to a mode of media production and/or distribution outside the mainstream, commercial media. It may also have political nuances when applied to some media, as it is by definition free from government influences.

Independent media organisations may or may not have alternative values. It's important not to confuse independence with alternative media because:

- their independence from the mainstream may be due to entrepreneurship rather than philanthropic reasons

- they may just seek to capitalise for commercial purposes on an untapped sector, targeting a niche audience that is not already catered for by the mainstream media

- they may be independent but specialise in producing content that is nonetheless commercial in nature and conforms to mainstream ideologies.

6.5 What do we usually mean by alternative media?

Alternative media is any media product that is produced outside the commercial mainstream. It is still, however, subject to the usual regulations, rules and laws of a country. Organisations that are based on the web primarily may do so in order to circumvent some of these rules if it suits their agenda. Alternative media organisations tend to produce content that is not already available through commercial mainstream media. It may have a political or campaigning function to it, but this is not always the case. Some of the possible features of alternative media products are given below, although it should be remembered that each alternative media arises in its own unique way. If you're finding your own examples, you will need to think carefully about whether these factors apply in your case.

- Its products arise from a perception that there is a deficiency or lack in mainstream media, or that it is not catering for the tastes of a sector of the audience. It may be non-commercial in nature.

- It caters for a niche audience.

- It employs alternative methods of distribution or production, or harnesses digital technologies to their full potential. May be citizen-produced and more likely to be non-hierarchical in its approach.

- It may have a global reach or be local. It may challenge transnational media corporations on a domestic scale or may have a global reach itself.

- It may be short lived, or it may have longevity.

- It may pass from alternative into the mainstream.

Today's alternative media producers have very little problem in gaining access to the technologies of media production, since these technologies have become so cheap and widely available. Print production can easily be organised by anyone with access to a home computer, photo-editing and design software, and a desktop publishing package. Video productions can be recorded on relatively low-cost digital camera technologies and simply edited at home using digital editing software. Podcasts and radio recordings can easily be made using a computer, a USB microphone and some audio-editing software. Because of this, digital media production outside of the mainstream has become so commonplace that it's hard to imagine what the world was like without it.

6.6 Case study: *Oh Comely* magazine

Platform: Print

Form: Magazine

Product: *Oh Comely* magazine, front cover and two specified articles.

In your work on magazines, you will study *Oh Comely* and compare this with *Men's Health*.

- **Magazines are identified as an in-depth media form, so the products should be analysed using ideas from all four areas of the theoretical framework:** media language, representation, audience and industry.
- Your knowledge of *Oh Comely* will be assessed in Media Two. You could be asked to discuss this product in light of ideas from any area of the theoretical framework. As Media Two has a synoptic element, it is possible that you may be asked to discuss *Oh Comely* using more than one area of the theoretical framework.

Introduction

Oh Comely publishes bi-monthly and is a London-based British indie magazine. The word comely means attractive, pleasing or fine. Older definitions confined the word's usage to describing an attractive woman, but it now has a broader meaning that can be used to describe anything which has fine qualities. The choice of name sounds admiring, nostalgic and quirky. It makes the reader feel personally addressed and flattered, but also connotes refinement, and the beautiful things and ideas inside. The extracts set as your CSP are taken from Issue 35, which has as its theme 'Strength'. The website for the magazine introduces it as follows:

> Oh Comely *is a curious, honest and playful independent magazine. It's a place to meet strangers, hear their stories and look at life a little differently – where our readers are our writers and our models, too.*
>
> *Each issue we pick a theme and see where it takes us. We try something old, something new and something that scares us a bit. Then we present our findings in a beautiful, artbook style, putting new writing, photography and illustration talent at the heart of it.*
>
> *We believe good things come in threes. We began as the bedroom project of three pals at university and we're now produced by a small publishing house started by another set of three friends.*
>
> *You can find us all over the world in small newsagents, indie mag shops and cafes. Or hop over to our shop, where you can get hold of the latest editions, 'surprise me!' packages and never-miss-an-issue subscriptions.*

The genre of the magazine as a lifestyle magazine is signified by its website strapline 'stories/culture/curiosities/makers/ideas', making it stand out significantly from its contemporaries on the mainstream women's magazine circuit with their blend of celebrity, fashion, body image and beauty. The crossover in terms of content with the mainstream is in its coverage of lifestyle and fashion, both of which are included in the contents – although the take on fashion and lifestyle is distinctly alternative when compared with mainstream magazines.

Industrial context

Oh Comely magazine is an independently produced magazine, launched in 2010 by three university friends. The magazine preserves its sense of difference and arguably exclusivity by being distributed through means that are likely to appeal to the target audience – subscription or '*small newsagents, Indie mag shops and cafes*'. Initially, it was launched in WHSmiths as well, but the most mainstream stockist listed on the website in 2018 was the supermarket Waitrose – many other locations that stock the magazine are artistic venues such as galleries and other cultural spaces such as art-house cinemas.

The magazine makes a conscious virtue of being print media, a real, physical object in the world of its digital native readership. This physical presence of the magazine was emphasised for a period in its publication by the addition of gift box subscriptions, which contained artefacts such as illustrations and small craft items to add to its value.

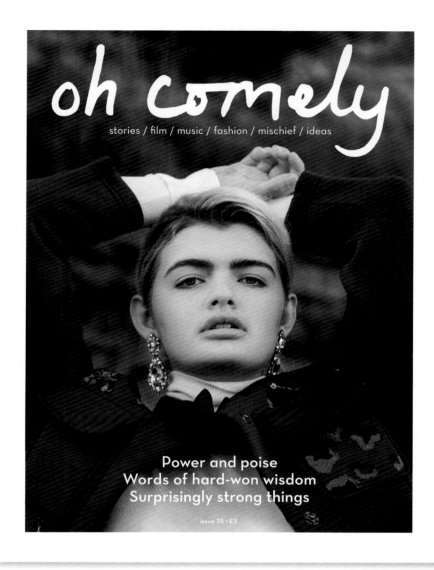

The website for *Oh Comely* is an important part of the strategy of a brand that is heavily integrated with social media plugins, appealing to a generation of Instagram lovers and inviting contributions from its audience. Everything about the site encourages a sense of inclusion. Its personal mode of address reduces the sense of distance between the magazine's audience and its readership, and increases their sense of participation in the culture it both constructs and reflects. It is worth, as part of your close study, exploring the website and considering how it works alongside the main print product.

Its publisher, Iceberg Press, has close links with the founders of the magazine. Their business model is exclusively based on the publication of *Oh Comely* and *The Simple Things.* They also have another project in development, but the small scale of the operation clearly gives it independent status compared with the dozens of titles published monthly and weekly by international giants such as Condé Nast. Iceberg emphasises the nature of this relationship in its mission statement on the website:

Iceberg exists to do things differently. To usher in a new age for magazines and media brands.

We are proudly independent and put the reader at the heart of everything we do. The world of magazines has never been more vibrant and innovative, but you wouldn't know it from the average newsstand today. We aim to bridge that gap. To bring the best of the spirit of the independent publishing scene to a wider audience using the skills and knowledge we gained working for some of the world's biggest publishing companies.
(www.icebergpress.co.uk/who-are-we/)

This statement signifies a number of significant points about independent magazine publishing. Firstly, alternative credentials as a media producer are implied by the idea that they '*do things differently*'. This is closely followed by the phrase '*proudly independent*'. Its suggestion that the reader is '*at the heart*' of its publications is borne out by the publications, which consciously construct the sense that the target audience are included. It contrasts its own offerings with the mainstream. The binary opposition of the '*vibrant and innovative*' products it aligns itself with versus the '*average newsstand*' is essential to its status as an accessible alternative. Like the editors of *Oh Comely* itself, it is careful to insist that this kind of publishing is for anyone, referring to a '*spirit*' that can be brought to a '*wider audience*'. This '*spirit*' is the values and ideologies of the magazine and its alternative offering to the mainstream.

More about the implication of this in terms of the media audience and identities is discussed in the section on audiences. We should remember that whatever the purported intentions of the magazine's producers, *Oh Comely* remains a product that will exclude some sections of the female audience who lack the cultural capital to access some of its content and familiarity with the world it represents in its pages.

In this online article from 2012, *Oh Comely* Editor, Liz Bennett, discusses entering the independent magazine sector:

> **L:** *There are pros and cons to being an independent magazine. I think they're having a moment at the moment. People are really interested in things that are authentic and genuine and have a sense of community and personal passion … There's so much more potential to self-publish these days. On the other hand, I think stuff like distribution is still really difficult for independent magazines, they face big barriers.*
>
> **How long did it take you to get such wide distribution?**
>
> **L:** *We were in Smiths from the beginning … They liked the idea, they agreed to take it before they'd even seen it, which was really, really good and I don't think we could have gone to print without that happening.*

Elsewhere in the interview, the editors discuss their intentions for the magazine. They state that they didn't wish to be seen as exclusive, but to offer something different for a female readership to connect with who don't feel well-served by the mainstream women's magazines. Whether they have succeeded in this is debateable, and something you can consider as a class. How the target audience access the text – and who might feel alienated by it and why – are discussed in more detail in the section on audiences.

The '*authentic and genuine*' credentials seem to refer to a counter-narrative against the shallowness and narcissism of a world lived through the digital media experience. Ironically, this is where many of the participants in this kind of sub-culture may exist and connect at least some of the time. At the same time, the credibility of independent publishers in general has gained from a culture of the prosumer. Audiences no longer have an expectation that a product coming from

For more on this issue, see 'We the media' and discussion of the changing relationship between the audience and industry.

the traditional media outlets and distribution chains is in any way 'better' than one which is self-published.

Oh Comely's advertisers are comparatively few for a 130-page magazine. All the companies who advertise in the magazine are small, independent from mainstream brands, and/or offering an alternative. The comparatively high cover price of five pounds, coupled with the decreased reliance on advertisers for income, means they can afford to work with advertisers whose brand images are commensurate with the ideologies and values of the magazine.

This subverts the traditional industrial relationship that was established early on by the US market, and subsequently adopted by the UK, which places the commercial imperative to make profit from advertisers at the top of the business agenda. Filling the pages in between with content that encourages commercialism and consumption among the readership has long been the norm, and mainstream audiences are used to seeing pages and pages of advertisements in fashion, beauty and lifestyle magazines. The target market for *Oh Comely* could reasonably be assumed to be suspicious of consumer culture and critical of any incursion into its pages of off-message advertisers.

Dash fashion brand (page 77) – this online retailer stocks smaller independent fashion chains, available mainly though mail order or online. It is an alternative to fashion on the high street.

London Loop knitting and crochet suppliers (page 9) – emphasises that the magazine's readership may be as interested in making their own clothes and accessories as buying them. It provides an alternative to the mainstream adverts in fashion magazines for perfumes, jewellery and high-end clothing brands.

Heavenly Recordings indie record label (page 12) – offers an alternative to the mainstream artists promoted by big record labels. Indie labels give a sense that they are offering a connection between genuine and original artists and the audience, running counter to the manufactured and homogenous pop product.

Tick Tock Redbush Tea (page 80) – made from the rooibos bush, is a caffeine-free alternative to tea that has had a following among health shop customers and people who are nutrition conscious for many years.

In-house advertising is also present, including a feature on a photographer and creative agency, a double-page subscription advert and an *Oh Comely* Playlist which co-promotes relevant bands and adds to the cross-media presence of the magazine.

APPLY IT

Visit the website for *The Simple Things*, the other magazine published by Iceberg Press (www.thesimplethings.com).

- What impression do you gain of the magazine? Does it share any similarities with *Oh Comely*?
- Where does its subject matter or audience diverge?

Media language

Since Issue 38, the magazine has ceased using cover stars and chosen instead to use illustrations, further signifying its departure from the mainstream and more firmly reinforcing its art and design aesthetic.

Your own close study involves three sections from the magazine: the front cover and two articles. The first article, 'Speaking Out', introduces five women notable for their strength and positive contribution to feminist issues. The second, 'More than Gender', explores through interview the relationship between two siblings: one born female and the other born male who has transitioned to female and now does not identify strongly as either. The analysis that follows picks out some of the ways in which you might use closer evidence from the text to support the bigger ideas about cultural meanings, identity and representations that are so central to discussion of this text. There will be other points you could add for yourselves to the analysis.

The front cover

At face value, the front cover of Issue 35 of *Oh Comely* magazine looks rather sparse. This minimalist look is common to high-end print publications and is aesthetically distinctive. It tells us that the cover's job is to promote a lifestyle in a tasteful way. The lower-case lettering of the masthead and the forward slashes separating elements of the strapline connote digital communication, but the typographical code mixes a feeling of being handwritten and personal, with a cleaner look to the strapline, emphasised by the choice of white.

The strapline itself is more developed than for many magazines, and deals with more abstract content such as 'ideas' and 'mischief' in the lexical coding, as well as more familiar content of 'stories/film/music/fashion'. This serves to orient a curious reader new to the magazine who may find the cover otherwise tells them little about the specific articles inside. The use of coverlines is distinctive and more enigmatic than a mainstream audience would be used to encountering. Although the magazine uses a familiar repertoire of elements – masthead, strapline, cover-girl and coverlines – it does so in a way that clearly contributes something new to the corpus of women's lifestyle magazines.

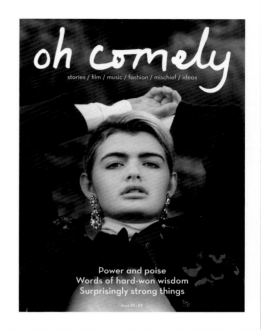

Today, many mainstream women's magazines perpetuate the cult of celebrity by featuring recognisable faces from the entertainments industries rather than the anonymous but perfect cover-girl. It's worth remembering this and comparing it with what the cover doesn't do rather than what it does, since the glaring neons and busy multiple coverlines, packed-out sweet spots, puffs and secondary images are all conspicuously absent. This paves the way to a structuralist reading of the text as a cultural product positioned among many. It also allows us to understand the ways in which texts can signify meaning by subverting our generic expectations when compared with more typical examples. Rather than relying on repetition and sameness, here we have a clear example of variation and change.

The magazine features model 'Deeann'. The use of a cover model in head and shoulders shot on a women's magazine is not unusual. Her position and the low angle of the shot, however, are. They strongly signify the theme of the issue, which is 'strength'. This is corroborated by her non-verbal codes, which function on a semantic level, such as her determined expression in direct mode of address as she meets the gaze of the reader through the lens. A feminine slight parting of the lips makes her appear more open and communicative. Her hands are raised and crossed above her head – a powerful pose.

The model has been dressed well, covered up in an eclectic mix of vintage and customised clothing with power costume jewellery. The overall look, despite the highlights of sequins, is rather dark. It is a world away from the high-key lighting, canted poses, exposure of skin, complex styling of hair and heavy make-up of a conventional studio shot of a cover-girl. Her make-up is soft and natural rather than a highly polished look, and her hair drawn back in a simple style that almost looks like a short crop. Although the model is conventionally attractive, everything else about the cover image as a sign promotes distinctiveness from the mainstream.

This sets up clear binary oppositions, almost signified more by what the magazine does not do rather than what it does. From this we can see that the magazine rejects the hard promotion of content on the cover in favour of developing a more subtle and sophisticated aesthetic. The coverlines function as hermeneutic codes but work powerfully to critically engage our understanding of cultural myth, realigning strength – a masculine quality – with femininity. 'Power and poise' anchors the image placed centrally above. The second coverline uses lexical coding that signifies traditionally strong qualities which are more feminine such as 'words of hard-won wisdom'. This speaks directly to the reader's knowledge of cultural codes and the figure of the wise woman in myth and legend. 'Surprisingly strong things' connotes that women can be strong as well as men, a key idea in both first and second wave feminism.

Speaking out

This article celebrates the positive contribution being made by five women to the lives of women in the UK today. It features a FGM campaigner, a poet and youth campaigner, a body positivity blogger, a former child detainee and activist, and the CEO of a company that encourages girls to engage with computing.

The overall layout is clean, and makes a lot of use of white space against which the portrait shots stand out. A simple design flow is used which is comprised of the same elements of design from page to page, meaning there is no real hierarchy to the way the women are represented and that all their roles in society should be valued equally. Each portrait shot is centred on the page, and the look of the page has symmetry with image and text taking up similar space. This results in a tasteful and uncluttered layout in keeping with the design aesthetic of the magazine. The centred text that accompanies each article gives the feel of a card placed under an exhibit – a sense that each has been 'curated' for the readership. Other information kept consistent from page to page is a quote from each woman, her name and role, and their Twitter handle, which appears at the end of each article and encourages a sense of community.

The women selected for interview are all featured in head and shoulders shots with the exception of the body image campaigner, who is photographed in three-quarters body shot. The portraits all aim to signify something about the character of the subject or their individual 'strengths':

"People go to extraordinary lengths to control the humble vagina"

Fahma Mohamed, FGM Campaigner

At 14, Fahma Mohamed discovered that female genital mutilation was rife within her own Somali community in Bristol, and was shocked into action. Since then, she has juggled her high school studies with a fierce campaign to emphasise the needless, illegal damage that is occurring behind closed doors. That campaign has translated into solid legislation, and at just 14 she has persuaded key government players to commit to ending FGM by 2030. Because of Fahma and her team, public sector workers are now helping teachers, doctors and social workers to identify and assist girls at risk. She has already been awarded an honorary PhD in law in recognition of her hard campaign work, and is due to begin her undergraduate degree in Biomedicine. An unstoppable force, and a Sister of whom we can collectively be proud.

@FahmaEndFGM

"Possess an opinion / Get noticed through it"

Deanna Rodger, Poet

At 16, Deanna Rodger become the youngest British Poetry Slam Champion ever to be crowned. Since then, she has written commissions for and performed at the 2012 Olympics, at Buckingham Palace and at Downing Street—bringing life and urgency to the issues that affect the most disenfranchised members of society. Whether speaking on behalf of London's homeless, addressing the housing crisis, or rapping about the conflicts of her identity as a Jamaican-Scottish Brit, her goal is always to the same: to empower young people to "see themselves as protagonists in their lives, and as creative entrepreneurs within their territories". Arming the unconfident and unsure with prose and power they need to become activists, she is also a fearless facilitator and mentor, working with a number of youth engagement programmes and universities internationally.

@DeannaRodger

"My beauty ripples. My thighs make waves"

Megan Jayne Crabbe, Body Positivity Blogger

Standing up for unapologetic self-love in a self-loathing world, Megan lights up our lives and Instagram feeds with her airy commentary and joyful #donthatethenshake jiggle-dance routines. A recovered anorexic, she has paved her own way to freedom, and reminds us every day that pretty is not the rest you pay to exist in the world. We love a woman who has this to say about cellulite: "I know that I'm supposed to hate it, but I don't. The canvas of my body is made up of so many textures... I place my fingers in those tiny crevices and trace them lovingly while I sit. I see magical constellations sprawling across my skin." She's a warrior in a mermaid costume, bravely treading where most will not – posting candid photos, fiercely holding the diet industry to account, and maintaining authenticity and honesty in a space so frequently filled with nothing but highlight reels.

@bodyposipanda

"I'm sure every woman can build their life again if they are just given that chance"

Meltem Avcil, Former Child Detainee, Activist

Aged 13, Meltem was woken at 6am by the sound of eight immigration officers breaking down her front door, their heavy footsteps filling every room of the house. From there, Meltem and her Mother were thrown into a caged van and driven to Yarl's Wood detention centre. Robbed of all autonomy and deprived of her basic rights, Meltem gathered signatures and support from behind bars and spearheaded the 2010 campaign that ended the detention of children seeking asylum in the UK. Now, she is hell-bent on achieving the same for all refugee women. She is currently writing a film script, in which she aims to provide different portraits of the lives of refugees, and is particularly keen to spread her campaign throughout schools and universities.

@MeltemAvcil

- **Fahma Mohamed** has a youthful dress code in keeping with her young age. The yellow hijab signifies fun and extroversion paired with the simple T-shirt and denim jacket, as well as signifying an aspect of her cultural identity. The background of the shot features bright tiled artwork which has an urban vibe. Her expression is warm and direct and her look very natural.

- **Deanna Rodger**'s portrait signifies that performing poetry live is a key part of her work. Her dress code, hair and make-up are feminine and fit her role as a performer. This is also signified by the passionate expression on her face, expressive body language and the microphone, which all centre us on the idea of her as a charismatic and powerful person who can also be glamorous.

- **Megan Jane Crabbe** flaunts her body image in a playful but demure pose that emphasises her confidence. Her smile is broad and open, her dress code connoting femininity expressed in alternative ways. Flowery lingerie is paired with vividly dyed colourful hair.

- **Melton Avcil** is simply photographed against a pale background which almost feels like a passport photograph. Her expression again has warmth in it, and she looks away from the camera in a self-effacing way. Her look is simple, bold and urban – long feminine hair in a relaxed and unselfconscious style but paired with immaculate make-up, a bold flash of lipstick and dark clothing.

- **Amali De Alwis** appears in an office setting. Her serious look marks her out from the other subjects of the portraits – her hands are clasped together in a way that makes her look thoughtful but also authoritative. Her glasses further signify her seriousness, but rather than adhering to the smart business dress codes we might expect, her look is more entrepreneurial with the bright scarf connoting freshness to her ideas.

More than gender

This article is simply laid out in familiar column format. Rather than a Q&A, the piece is set out as a conversation between the two siblings: Andrea and Ash Allan, about Ash's shifting gender identity. The slug on the first page anchors the overall theme of the conversation – that going for drives and walks together in their local area was a backdrop for more profound discussions about what each experienced.

Some shots of the road and a wooded landscape in the pair's locality are included. These may signify the journey the siblings have been on – and the preferred reading that for Ash, his shifting gender state is natural. The article features three selected shots from the siblings' history, each marking a different period in Ash's expression of gender identity. In two of the selected images, the siblings appear together – in Andrew's childhood as a boy, and in a strip of passport booth shots as Andrea's sister Ash. Coupled with the first-person mode of the article without apparent focusing from an interviewer, these lend a sense of intimacy and personal histories shared directly with the reader. It makes their story feel very natural and unmediated. The two separate shots where Andrea appears alone, with Ash presenting as non-binary, perhaps signify the differences they have had to overcome and the separateness of their experience of gender. Each, however, is still positioned with their left and right should facing, as though they continue to stand side by side.

"Why aren't there more women in tech? It shouldn't just be a boy's club"

Amali De Alwis, CEO of Code First: Girls

More than gender

Siblings Andrea and Ash Allan talk about their experience with shifting identity, and share the local landscapes that freed them up to talk things through

words and photos: andrea allan

APPLY IT Take some short sections of the copy for each article. How does it help to anchor the images that have been used on the same page? Give specific examples of lexical choices, mode of address and verbal coding that support the preferred reading.

Audiences

The average age of the readership is 27, young women who are probably graduates, ethically aware, diverse and with a reasonable level of disposable income to spend on cultural artefacts to feed their sense of identity. They value creativity and individual expression highly. Their politics are likely to be left-leaning and libertarian rather than authoritarian. It is also quite likely they are at the age where they are still living a single, urban-based lifestyle. They are less likely to have children, may still be living in rented accommodation or house and flat-shares, and will still be living a lifestyle that allows a high degree of personal autonomy and self-direction. They will probably identify as feminists, and this issue, which focuses on female strength and empowerment, signifies this particularly strongly. Other editions have taken as their themes topics such as sisters, adventure, magic and letters – although since the changing of branding in Issue 38 a theme is no longer promoted.

Applying audience theory to *Oh Comely*

The preferred reading and therefore the intended 'effect' of *Oh Comely* on its audience is to make them feel part of a sub-culture that values authenticity and experience over mass consumerism. The negotiated reading could manifest in a range of ways, but we could question how many of the readership would part with the cover price for a magazine they were not going to enjoy. It is possible that some members of the target audience, such as feminists, might feel that the positive and upbeat nature of the magazine and its interleaving of entertainment with some of the bigger issues trivialises them. It arguably still reduces women to being free to explore a dilettante, 'comely' existence but only until long-term relationships and child-rearing replace autonomy. Likewise, some may find the magazine's emphasis on the aesthetic in some articles and its fashion shoots too similar to the mainstream content it purports to offer an alternative to.

Pick and mix theory as proposed by Gauntlett works well with mainstream magazines, and was certainly relevant to the study of *Men's Health*, which was Gauntlett's original example in *Media, Gender and Identity* (2008). However, it is less relevant to the readership of *Oh Comely*. An oppositional reading of the magazine would be likely from anyone with conservative values, who would find the issues contained in its the left-leaning articles irrelevant or counter to their world view. They would probably find the rejection of mainstream consumerist values pretentious. For many women in lower socio-economic classes, whose existence may be dominated by childcare, running a home on a low income, or those who are concerned with maintaining image and outward appearance, there would probably be little of interest in its pages.

In terms of a cultivation effect, the target audience are consciously seeking an antidote to the effects of mean world syndrome. They are resisting enculturation and looking for alternative viewpoints and perspectives on their society to the messages contained in the dominant ideologies that saturate the mass media. They are looking to realign their outlook with a more upbeat and positive world view.

Many of the readers will be millennials in creative professions or finding their feet through internships.

The uses and gratifications model also works well in understanding the appeal of this product to the audience. It is clearly diverting, offering a temporary escape from some of the realities faced by millennials such as low-paid internships or problems accessing home ownership. It also offers a pleasurable vacation from fears experienced by everyone who has access to the mainstream media, such as the narrative of fear we experience in news coverage of terrorism, or stories of abuses of human rights worldwide. The comparatively privileged nature of the target audience compared with, for example, the precariat allows this form of diversion to be particularly appealing.

Social, cultural and economic capital

In Chapter 3, Media audiences, you considered the role of cultural capital in the lives of consumers and its connections with social class. You also looked at participation identified by Fiske in a 'shadow' cultural economy. The consumption of *Oh Comely* magazine falls between the two – it is not mass culture, but its small circulation and independent production methods as well as its alternative ideologies when compared with mainstream women's publishing make it more typical of a product in the 'shadow' cultural economy, albeit one that exists to make a profit by exploiting a niche audience.

In 2013, the BBC published a survey of its audience with the intention of identifying the structure of social class in modern Britain. The outcome used Bourdieu's ideas (see Chapter 3) and expanded on these to redefine the shape of British social class in a way which is much more complex than the traditional divisions of working, middle and upper social classes. The seven categories that emerged were interesting and highly relevant to our study of *Oh Comely*. They are also articulated using the ideas of social, economic and cultural capital.

The readership of *Oh Comely* are most likely to be in the classes of new affluent workers and the established middle class. Their cultural capital will be high, especially their participation in middle-class preoccupations such as art, music, literature, theatre and art house cinema. The emphasis on creativity in the magazine supports this. Participation in sub-cultures high has long been associated with middle-class youth, having the economic capital required to explore alternatives to the mainstream behind them even when they are not necessarily cash-rich on a day-to-day basis.

Most interesting to us in exploring the audience for *Oh Comely* is social capital – connections and networks. Who you know is essential to the values of the *Oh Comely* readership and promoted explicitly through the website and magazine, which consistently reinforces participation by the audience in the making of the product as writers, models and photographers. It is also emphasised in the narrative of three friends from university running their own business. Entrepreneurship is not seen as a counter-value to the left-leaning ideologies of the audience, as long as it is transparent, and the spirit of collaboration in business rather than competition is appealing to a female audience.

Identity

More about how the representation of femininity is constructed in the magazine is discussed in the section on representations, but it is important to reflect explicitly on how the magazine engages so powerfully with its niche audience's sense of identity.

In terms of fluidity of identity, there is a clear sense of a rejection of more mainstream feminine identities present in *Oh Comely*. Cultural identity is seen very much as secondary to personal identity – although gender is strongly signified, gender is seen as being expressed in ways not associated with traditional femininity, which promotes passivity and compliance as desirable female qualities. This is particularly important in the article about different ways in which women are 'speaking out' and also in the article about Andrea and Ash Allan. This explicitly references 'shifting identity' in the slug as a concept the audience is expected to be familiar with.

In a sense, by reading *Oh Comely*, the audience are using the text in part to construct their identity and frame it in an alternative way to mainstream ideals. They use the magazine to reinforce their difference from mainstream identities and see the women featured in the magazine and even its editors as role models. They are

negotiating their identity in relation to different ideals about what it means to be female in 2017. The fashion shoot, for example, names vintage clothing stores and mixes one-off pieces from retro designer brands mixed with cheap high street gear and customised pieces with sequins and embroidery to model a 'look' that cannot be bought off the shelf and encourages readers to explore their own individuality and uniqueness through fashion. Also, in feeling that they belong to a small readership with shared ideals and outlook, they gain a sense of collective identity – that they are not alone in rejecting some of the more mainstream identities on offer in conventional women's magazines.

Representations and contexts

In exploring *Oh Comely*, most of the aspects of representational study are focused around two issues – femininity and an urbanised, cultured 'alternative' lifestyle. In exploring audiences, you have already considered to some extent how some women may feel included or excluded by the subject matter and mode of address of the magazine.

You applied Hall's concept of different readings of the text, which is also a theory of representation since it considers the meanings audiences decode from the text and their polysemic nature. The preferred reading is likely to be accepted by the majority of the readership of all three sections you are required to study, and is strongly encoded with a very specific niche audience in mind. The cover would be decoded as tasteful, understated and deliberately opposing the comparatively brash covers of many other women's magazines. The women, selected for their power as role models, would be approved of as having more validity than the shallow world of celebrity, and the readership gains an illusion of social capital from 'knowing' who they are.

The conversational article based on the personal histories of Andrea and Ash Allan offers insight into the experience of shifting gender identity in a way that makes it feel like a natural and accessible idea to the readership. It can be argued that the articles and cover would simply fail to engage a mainstream audience who might experience some oppositional readings.

This issue also contributes to your understanding of media identities, and you reflected on some of the ideas discussed by Gauntlett defining different aspects of identity study – the notion that identities may be fluid, constructed and collective, or a combination of these in any one reader of the magazine. All of these issues are as important to the study of representations as audiences, and form a bridge between the two dimensions of our study of this text, with audiences buying into this idealised view of an independent, creative and powerful femininity they identify with to varying degrees.

One of the articles explicitly explores the whole concept of gender identity being something that can shift, and Judith Butler's ideas are interesting to apply to the experience of both siblings in this article as they negotiate their own experiences of Ash's shifting identity and the family's experience of it too. The article actively constructs an insight into how culturally entrenched both our own and society's understanding of gender as a set of biologically predetermined binary qualities can be, and resolves these as restrictive.

There is no doubt that *Oh Comely* can be considered a feminist magazine. Men are largely absent from it; in many women's magazines, even where men are not physically present, they are referred to in their roles as potential partners of relationship goals. In *Oh Comely*, the emphasis is almost entirely on women and what they can accomplish in a world that usually favours men to succeed in many of the roles they appear in here.

APPLY IT

Choose a range of media products online, in print and on television, which you think might be consumed by this target audience. How might these also contribute to their sense of negotiated and collective identity?

bell hooks' ideas about intersectionality are very interesting when used to explore *Oh Comely*. The magazine itself is produced in London, and much of its lifestyle content is of most relevance to women living in urban areas that are more multicultural. The women we see in the 'Speaking Out' article are quantitively representative of London's women as ethnically diverse. The magazine focuses a great deal on women who are successful, but different feminist approaches for different women could result in negotiated readings of the magazine's content. For example, hooks might suggest that the mainly middle-class educated audience who have the privilege of engaging with the pursuits or ideals of the magazine are not those who would benefit the most from its depiction of inspirational female role models. She would probably also feel that the uniformly positive depiction of successful women from ethnic minorities does not reflect the everyday battles faced by many of these women, which are largely ignored in favour of representing them simply as 'women', oversimplifying the issue.

A critical reading of the magazine might find that it constructs a representation of femininity that is actually rather narrow and idealised despite attempting to do quite the opposite. Its message of acceptance of difference and female empowerment does not always sit comfortably with its commodification of a lifestyle that is supposedly anti-materialist. The pressures that many women feel in the real world, where many feminist thinkers would argue that barriers established by patriarchy still persist, are largely ignored by the magazine. Diverting though it is, the construction of femininity in the magazine as empowered and successful is still little more than coffee-break wish fulfilment for aspirers to the creative, energetic lifestyle and culture it represents.

CHAPTER SUMMARY

- There are some aspects of the theoretical framework that become more relevant when you study texts which are produced for non-English-speaking audiences and outside of the mainstream.

- British cultural attitudes towards mainstream products have been historically quite insular.

- Globalisation and changes in distribution technologies have increased audience access to and familiarity with texts from other non-English-speaking cultures.

- Independently produced media texts are not necessarily alternative in their values.

- Alternative media often caters for a niche audience, may be non-commercial in nature, and may use alternative methods of production and distribution when compared with mainstream media products.

FURTHER READING AND REFERENCES

BBC Trust (2016) BBC Four, www.bbc.co.uk/bbctrust/our_work/services/television/service_licences/bbc_four.html.

BBC Trust (2018) Public Purposes and Purpose Remits, www.bbc.co.uk/bbctrust/governance/tools_we_use/public_purposes.html.

David Gauntlett (2008) *Media, Gender and Identity*.

Gabriel Tate (2016, 2 January) 'How Foreign TV Drama Became de Rigueur with UK Reviewers', *Guardian*, www.theguardian.com/tv-and-radio/2016/jan/02/foreign-tv-drama-bbc-channel4-netflix.

H.D. Jones (2014, 12 November) 'The Circulation and Reception of Foreign-Language European Films in the UK', paper presented at the TFTV Departmental Research Seminar, University of York, http://mecetes.

co.uk/wp-content/uploads/2015/06/Jones-Circulation-and-Reception-of-NNE-films-in-UK.pdf.

Marianne M. Gilchrist (2010, 1 September) 'The Sad Disappearance of Foreign TV', *Guardian*, www.theguardian.com/commentisfree/2010/sep/01/sad-disappearance-foreign-tv.

Marshall McLuhan (1964) *Understanding Media*.

Sam Wollaston (2017, 9 November) 'Detectorists Review: More Tender Comedy About Men, Middle Age and Metal-Detecting', *Guardian*, www.theguardian.com/tv-and-radio/2017/nov/09/detectorists-review-third-series-tender-comedy-men-middle-age-metal-detecting.

Thoas Schatz (1981) *Hollywood Genres: Formulas, Filmmaking and the Studio System*.

APPLY IT

The theoretical framework – test yourself

1 How does *Oh Comely* expand the definition of lifestyle content beyond the mainstream to engage a niche audience?

2 How well does the magazine conform to you understanding of what is meant by independent and/or alternative media?

3 How can structuralist and post-structuralist theories, especially of narrative, be used to understand how the magazine addresses its audience?

4 How is media language used to:

   a distinguish the magazine from conventional women's magazines?

   b promote aspects of alternative female identities?

5 How can cultivation theory help us to understand why the audience might read *Oh Comely*?

6 How does the front cover promote the contents of the magazine?

7 How can some of the theories of gender and the mass media you have encountered on the course be applied successfully to this magazine?

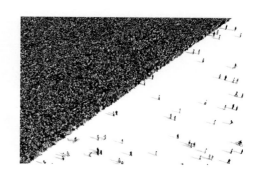

Chapter 7 Making media

What you will learn in this chapter

- An introduction to the practicalities of production by offering some general information regarding the basic principles of producing work in print, e-media, audio, and moving and still images

- This information will support your practical production and should be supported by your research and planning

- You will be offered ideas to help you create production work that is both effective and accurate. If you are confident in your understanding of codes and conventions and how technology can be used to help replicate them, you will have more time to create visually appealing and engaging products that succeed in communicating ideas to their audience and creating a product that meets the aims given in the Statement of Intent

7.1 Print production

Desktop publishing (DTP) software

When you are creating print production work you need to use software that gives you as much control over the different elements of a page as possible.

You need to be able to control:

- your font: its style, size and positioning
- your page size: different publications use different page sizes
- the presentation of your text: most print production has a lot of text and uses **columns** in the page design
- the presentation of your images and illustrations: you need to be able to position images accurately and resize them to fit with your page design.

Although you may take some time to work on your print production, something that should be considered as soon as you begin is printing. Most of your production decisions will be made while you are looking at your work on screen. What works on screen may not necessarily work on paper, so you should make test prints as often as you can to check how your work looks on paper. You will need to use a printer that allows you to print the correct size and weight of paper, and some productions need a printer that will print to the very edge of the page rather than leaving a margin.

Basic principles of page layout and design

Regardless of the format of your print production work, there are some basic principles of layout and design you will need to consider as you begin.

Page size and proportion

Before you start creating your layout and design, you will need to set up your paper size. Most desktop publishing programs allow you to do this in centimetres, so this is a very easy job. You should base your page size on the conventions of the form you are making.

So, to ensure your finished work is accurate, you will need to find out what the correct size and **page proportions** are for your publication. You may be able to search for this information online but you can measure the media product that you are going to emulate so you know that your page size and proportion will be precise. Most printers use A4 paper and some A3, but not all print products match these sizes. Where your media product is too large to be printed at the correct size, you will need to set up your page for your product proportionally.

For example, a large **billboard** advertising poster measures 304.8cm high x 1219.2cm wide. This means that a billboard poster needs to be (roughly) four times wider than it is high. You clearly can't create a life-sized billboard poster but you could use a template on a landscape A4 page that measures 10cm high x 30cm wide and your poster would have roughly the correct proportions.

Newspapers tend to come in two standard sizes:

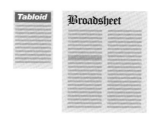

- tabloid 28cm x 43cm
- broadsheet 60cm x 75cm.

Magazines can vary in size. Smaller magazines called 'digest size', such as *Glamour*, have much smaller pages than a 'standard-sized magazine'. *Glamour*'s pages measure approximately 14cm x 21cm, whereas a standard-sized magazine measures 27.5cm x 21cm. Most magazines are taller than they are wide (*Elle* measures 28.5cm x 22cm) but others may be wider than they are tall.

If you are attempting to emulate a specific title for your production work you will need to measure the page size to be sure your finished work is accurate. If your pages are not the right size you are likely to get the proportions of the **design elements** incorrect and this will limit the effectiveness of your production. If you are creating your own newspaper or magazine title, you should check which page sizes are most often used in the form and genre you are working in.

Magazine and newspaper **adverts** are sized by the percentage of the page covered – so an advert's size is determined by the host publication's size. A half-page advert in the *Sun* would be larger than a half-page advert in *Glamour*. By identifying where your advert would be published you can demonstrate your understand that different publications are different sizes. You can also show you understand the relationship between your product and the target audience by placing your advert in a publication that shares your target audience.

You may be asked to create standalone advertising materials such as flyers or posters. The brief may be specific, detailing what type of advertising product or products you must create or it may allow you to make decisions on what advertising products are suitable for the given task. In either case, an understanding of your target audience should help you decide what forms of advertising product would be the most appropriate to get your message to the right people. As advertising products come in all shapes and sizes, you should decide on the placement of your advert and/or the distribution method so you can set up your **DTP** page accurately before production begins.

You should use existing media products to investigate the different approaches to print advertising used today. To get the full effect of your magazine or newspaper advertising, and to show your understanding of advertising and marketing, you might want to consider presenting your work within the page or pages of the publication it would be found. For standalone advertising, you could show it in its final location.

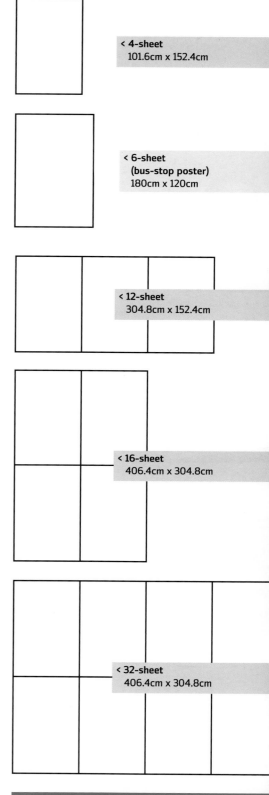

< **4-sheet**
101.6cm x 152.4cm

< **6-sheet**
(bus-stop poster)
180cm x 120cm

< **12-sheet**
304.8cm x 152.4cm

< **16-sheet**
406.4cm x 304.8cm

< **32-sheet**
406.4cm x 304.8cm

Billboards can come in a variety of shapes and sizes

However you approach your production, make sure that you set up your page correctly in your desktop publishing software and, once your page size is set up, you should then start to consider your main design elements.

Proportion in design

You will have a number of design elements you will want to place on your print production page, including images and text and, depending on the form you are creating, you may have design conventions that you need to follow.

As we discovered earlier, a billboard poster is up to four times wider than it is high. If the billboard poster is to be used to sell a consumer product, for example a perfume, your poster would need to include:

- the perfume's name/brand name
- an image of an aspirational model
- a background
- an image of the product itself
- a tag line (perhaps)
- a web address and/or hashtag (perhaps).

Before you start taking photographs or laying out your page you should create a flatplan to help you work out what you want your finished product to look like. When creating a flatplan you could consider how you would combine the poster elements on your page. You would need to consider where each element should be placed and also how large or small each element needs to be.

Looking at the real billboards on the left, it is clear that the names of the perfume, the perfume bottles and the images of Hollywood actors are the most dominant elements. If you look closely, each poster can be divided into three sections vertically and horizontally. The J'adore Dior and Chanel No 5 posters have one of the elements above in each section of the poster : the name/logo – then the bottle – then Charlize Theron; Brad Pitt – then the product – then the product name/ logo. The Miss Dior poster uses the Hollywood star Natalie Portman across the whole length of the poster, so her face and the bottle are together in the right-hand section of the poster and this is balanced with the name of the perfume being placed in the top-left corner.

The conventional design elements of a poster are present in all these examples but the elements are used differently in each. The three posters all use images and text that are sized appropriately given the size of the poster. The information is clearly visible from a distance, faces are recognisable and the branding is clear. The posters work because all the elements are in proportion to the size and shape of a billboard poster. They look appealing because they are using the space in a way that feels balanced and logical.

> **APPLY IT**
>
> **List the design elements needed on one of the following print products:**
>
> - a cover for a PC game
> - the front page of a women's fashion magazine
> - the back page of a tabloid newspaper
> - a flyer promoting a club night.

Print layout and design

Whatever size or shape you choose for your page, you should try to apply the following design principles as you lay out your page.

Columns

As identified on the billboard posters, print pages are designed using a grid with each page being divided into vertical and horizontal sections. In text-based print publications, these vertical sections are used to divide text into **columns**. Magazines tend to use a three- or five-column layout depending on the size of the publication. Tabloid newspapers use a five-column layout and broadsheets often use six columns per page. Double-page spreads are often treated as a single page with column design, considering the look of both pages when seen side by side.

Page designers use columns to help them create pages that use pictures, text, adverts and headings in the most appealing way for the audience.

Columns make it easier for audiences to read text, thus making the content easier to follow. Long lines of text are hard to read and make it difficult to find the next line when returning to the left-hand side. Columns are used to ensure lines of text are neither too long nor too short for the reader.

Columns help designers create pages that are visually balanced and logical for the reader to access. When designing a page it is important that the reader knows which column follows on from the last.

Compositional balance

Compositional balance is created when the weight of the page is balanced top to bottom and left to right. The placement of your design elements will impact on the balance of the page. Large bold and black text is 'heavy', as are dense images. Small or thin fonts, black and white sketches and white space are 'light'. A balanced page has similar weight in the top-left and bottom-right sides of the page. This creates the feel of stability on the page and is pleasing to the eye. A well-balanced page guides the reader and makes it clear which images belong to which blocks of text.

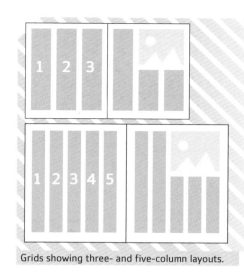

Grids showing three- and five-column layouts.

Heavy image

Light image

Heavy Text   Light Text

Light pages

Heavy pages

Well-balanced pages

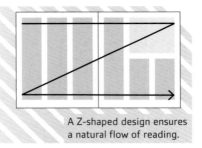

A Z-shaped design ensures a natural flow of reading.

Columns also help guide the way the eye travels across the page from left to right and ensures that images don't interrupt the natural flow of reading. Most readers don't take in the fine detail of the page at first. Readers tend to scan the page in a Z-shaped eye movement. This Z-shape eye movement is used across double-page spreads too.

Column design is one of the first steps in making sure pages look balanced, coherent, aesthetically pleasing and are legible.

As well as columns, page design considers the balance of the page on the horizontal. The page is usually divided into three and designers use these three spaces in addition to the columns to create **compositional balance** on the page.

Font style

Fonts are split into three basic types:

1 **Serif**: font styles that have small tails at the ends of the letters:
   - for example, Times New Roman or Georgia.
2 **Sans serif**: font styles that use simple forms for the letters:
   - for example, Arial and Gill Sans.
3 **Decorative** or **novelty** fonts: stylised fonts that can create a very specific look or feel:
   - for example, Papyrus or *Snell roundhand* (the fonts that look similar to handwriting are sometimes called script fonts).

Serif and sans serif fonts are both very easy to read, whereas decorative ones can be more difficult for the reader and should never be used in large blocks of text.

When choosing font styles for your work, unless you have a specific reason for doing otherwise, consider choosing one font for your body text and a second for headings. It is possible to use the same font for both. Tabloid newspapers tend to use a sans serif font for headlines and a serif font for body text. Use decorative fonts sparingly and if you do use them ensure they are large enough so they can be read easily. A page that uses too many different fonts or that over-uses decorative fonts can look chaotic and unappealing to the reader.

Different styles of font have the potential to add meaning to your publication. Fonts create connotations, so make sure you choose fonts that create the tone and atmosphere that suits your publication, your message and your audience. Serif fonts are sometimes thought to look more formal and authoritative, whereas a sans serif font feels more friendly and accessible. Experiment with different fonts and see what kind of tone or feel they create. Consider the tone you wish to create and use fonts to help.

You may wish to create a publication that:

- is traditional (Bookman Old Style)
- is modern (Futura)
- is friendly (Comic Sans)
- is quirky (Bauhaus 93)
- looks typed (Courier)
- evokes the 'wild west' (Blackoak)
- is a little bit 1920s (Braggadocio)
- looks handwritten (Mistral)
- is formal (Times New Roman)
- is casual (Chalkduster).

Font size

Don't forget to use a font size that is appropriate to your publication. Posters tend to use small amounts of text and need to use large-sized fonts for visibility. Newspapers and magazines use large-sized fonts in headlines but smaller-sized fonts in the body text. Headlines can be as large as 72pt (pt = points – the numerical measurement of font size) in some newspapers, whereas the body type can be as small as 8 or 9pt. A typical font size for a magazine article is 9pt. Font size choices should also ensure that the content of the product is legible for the intended audience.

---

1 This sentence may be difficult to read because the font is too small.

2 This sentence will look clumsy on the page because the font is too big.

3 This sentence should look just right as the size of the font has been considered very carefully in relationship to the size and general design of the pages in this book.

If you are creating your own original print publication rather than emulating an existing product, you can select your own page size and proportions as well as the general composition of your pages. You should use existing media products as guides, but have readability at the heart of all your design choices. If you are attempting to recreate an existing publication, these decisions have already been made. You should closely analyse the products to see how they use columns and fonts, so you can emulate their house style and the way they use design elements.

Approaches to different forms (magazine, newspaper)

In addition to general layout principles, for all print products different forms and genres use different codes and have their own conventions. You need to consider the theme and topics offered in the NEA brief but there is no constraint as to what type of product you make, so try to be creative as you make your production decisions. For example:

- You may choose to create a broadsheet- or tabloid-sized newspaper – you could show you understand the codes and conventions of the form and your chosen genre by replicating them, but you could subvert those codes in terms of the content you create.

- If you create your own magazine title you won't be tied to a specific page size. Once you've chosen the page size you wish to create, do some research to see how real magazines design content for their pages and then you can mix and match some of the best ideas you find.

- Advertising gives a lot of scope for creativity. You could create a range of flyers with similar design elements but content that targets a specific audience sub-group. You could come away from box-shaped designs and present your information in a much more appealing and interesting way. Perhaps you could be innovative in making booklets or flyers with unusual approaches to the presentation of the information?

Before you can be accurate and creative in your production work, you need to know what the conventions are.

Newspapers

Genre: tabloid

Each UK tabloid newspaper has developed its own house style based on page design choices in the fonts and page layout conventions used. While the house styles of the *Sun* and the *Daily Mirror* (red-top tabloids) or the *Daily Mail* and the *Daily Express* (middle-market newspapers) make each newspaper recognisable, they share presentation codes and conventions that mean they can all be identified as tabloid newspapers. Tabloid newspapers are not all the same size but they are significantly smaller than broadsheets. Tabloids tend to be printed on paper sized around 56cm x 43cm and this creates four pages of the newspaper (43cm x 27.9cm each).

Grid showing a typical double-page spread layout.

The sheet of paper is printed front and back and then folded. The page has a print margin of approximately 1–2cm on all edges of the paper.

The horizontal top-third of the paper will contain the paper's masthead and a teaser for further content to be found inside the newspaper. The teaser will usually fill the full width of the page. The furthest top-right corner may advertise a special feature, a competition or perhaps a special offer. Promotions information will often be placed under the masthead. Traditionally, newspapers were displayed in newsagents folded so that only the top third of the page was visible. Sometimes they were kept in a large pile on or close to the ground. This makes the top third the most important part of the page when it comes to selling the newspaper. This section of the page is what was most likely to be seen by potential readers.

Front pages of tabloids tend to use a five-column vertical layout. The **headline** for the lead story often uses the first three columns from left to right and most of the lower two-thirds of the page. A standfirst often appears just beneath the headline, providing additional information or a very brief summary of the story. Standfirsts are usually presented in a contrasting font to the headline. The headline and/or an image will usually take up the majority of the space on the page leaving two or three short columns at the foot of the page for the first few paragraphs of the lead story. There may be subheadings within the article. The news story will continue inside the newspaper, as image and headline rather than text dominate the layout of a tabloid front page.

Unless the news story is particularly important there is usually a secondary story on the front page. This will often be a celebrity or human interest story and a photograph is likely to take up most of the remaining space on the page. A small headline covering the two-column width may be provided but, again, the detail on the story will be provided inside the picture itself.

Inside the newspaper, some pages are designed individually as single pages while some are double-page spreads. It is common for two pages to be split into five columns with one headline across both pages at the top. Where the copy for the article is quite long, the body text may be designed with pull quotes to help break up the text and two full columns may be followed by text only towards the bottom of the page with subheadings, images and captions filling the top two-thirds of the page. These illustrations may go onto the second page and the main article could end with a supplementary article containing additional or explanatory material in a sidebar, usually on the right-hand side of the page.

Not all feature articles take up the full double-page spread. Where this happens a different story will be positioned below, to the left or to the right of the feature, and will have its own headline, pull quotes and illustrations. The pages will be designed using different-coloured backgrounds, dividing lines and/or boxes to ensure the readers recognise that there are two different stories on the page.

Magazines

Genre: gossip

Gossip magazines are traditionally published weekly and are printed on relatively thin, coloured paper. The content of this type of magazine is primarily celebrity-based stories but they also contain beauty, travel, fashion and other lifestyle content for their predominantly female target audience.

Gossip magazines generally use close to standard magazine-sized paper. The front cover will feature the title of the magazine at the top of page and where the name is short enough (heat, Now!, OK!, etc.) it will be positioned on the left.

All gossip magazines will have their own brand and house style that differentiates them from one another, but there are conventions that are used across the genre. The gossip magazine cover tends to use a basic three horizontal x five vertical grid and there will be at least one celebrity on the front cover, normally in the middle section of the page positioned towards the right. The celebrity will usually be presented in mid- or medium-long-shot in this genre. Their eyes will be looking into the camera and they will generally be positioned towards the centre or centre top of the page. There will be small blocks of text in a large-sized font towards the left-hand side and the bottom of the page. The **coverlines** offer information to the audience on the content of the stories being published and they implicitly offer more detail inside the magazine itself.

Gossip magazines use bold, bright colours to get themselves noticed. Red, orange, bright pink and yellow are commonly used colours in this genre. The front cover will be **busy** with lots of text and maybe some smaller images that tease the reader by alluding to the stories that are expanded on inside the magazine.

There are many different types of layout used inside gossip magazines, as they contain lots of different types of feature, including beauty, fashion, cookery and celebrity lifestyles. Some pages are designed individually and, as with newspapers, some are treated as double-page layouts. It is not unusual to have a full-page image in a double-page layout with the story itself told in the bottom two-thirds of one page and the text being split between three or four columns. A large headline and sometimes a smaller subheading will fill the top third of the page and the two pages will feel **coherent**, as a limited colour palette will be used. Gossip magazines also often use geometric shapes and/or fancy fonts to add visual interest to a page. These shapes and fonts will often pick out a colour from the pages' palette.

3 x 5 grid

APPLY IT

Create a written description of the layout of a front cover and selected inside pages of these other genres of magazine:

- men's lifestyle magazine
- home décor magazine
- cookery magazine
- TV listings magazine.

In your own print production, you should be accurate in your recreation of the codes and conventions used by the form and genre you are working in. Your work will be effective if it appeals to your target audience, so you should consider the content and imagery you choose so that they combine to create the message you wish to communicate in a way that meets your audience's expectations. You will need to use technology to reproduce the codes and conventions accurately but you can approach using these conventions creatively and with flair. Reproducing codes is not just about copying what has already been done but you should put your own spin on the way the conventions are used.

KEY TERMS

balance (page)	a balanced page has been designed to ensure that the heavy objects and lighter ones are positioned to create a harmonious feel
billboard	a large outdoor location for advertising. Traditionally a board for the placement of print adverts but electronic billboards can be found in some locations. Electronic billboards can present all types of video material but they are often used to broadcast adverts
busy	the effect of pages that are created with many design elements, font styles, etc. Busy pages are sometimes difficult for the reader to access and can be confusing and visually offputting

columns	a way to organise text and images on the page by dividing the page vertically
design elements	the individual parts that combine together to construct a page
DTP	a commonly used abbreviation for desktop publishing that refers to software specifically designed to support the design and publication of print and, in some cases, e-media production
font	the design of the letters used within a specific typeface. Fonts have pre-defined proportions, weight and style. All letters and numbers within a font will be designed to harmonise
page proportions	the size of the page and the relationship between its height and length

subheading	a heading for a subsection of an article
teaser (newspapers/ magazines)	a brief indication of the content within the publication. Used to encourage the reader to purchase the publication to be able to read further
weight (visual)	a term used to refer to the effect of the depth, darkness and/or intensity of a design element. Large, dark, textured and warm-coloured elements tend to appear 'heavier' – they have more visual weight. Elements in the foreground or higher on the page tend to appear heavy on the page as do regular shapes and vertical (rather than horizontal) objects. Images of things that are actually heavy also have weight on the page

7.2 Producing and working with still images

Photography is an important part of media production. Photographs will be needed to illustrate print and e-media productions, and they can be used to demonstrate your knowledge of codes and conventions as well as creativity and technical skills.

The style and content of the photographs you need for your production will depend on what you are making, who your product is for and what your product needs to achieve. The best way to find inspiration for your photos is to look at the way photography is used in existing media products.

If you are making a newspaper product you will note that tabloids and broadsheets tend to use photographs that give information on the story being reported. Photographs are often simple illustrations of the 'who?', 'what?' and 'where?' of the story being reported. News photographs are often sourced from **photojournalists** or **paparazzi** and can often look simple and denotative, as they are taken on the spot, giving the impression of immediacy.

News photos are selected to help reinforce the specific message a newspaper wishes to communicate and are carefully constructed and/or edited to create a specific effect.

Construction includes the positioning on the page, the size of the image, the way the image has been **cropped** and the anchorage that is added to the page. The presentation choices are made in an attempt to lead the reader towards a preferred reading of the events being reported. Newspapers also use maps, diagrams and graphs where these help communicate information to the reader. Broadsheet newspapers will sometimes use more metaphoric or symbolic images to illustrate a story, while tabloids prefer images that are directly connected to details within the story. Newspaper feature articles use posed portraits taken from photoshoots and they too are selected, cropped and possibly edited to reinforce the tone and values within the article itself.

You should take inspiration from products that are similar to the one you are making and/or that are trying to appeal to the same target audience when you start to think about how you will use images in your own production.

- Does your production need to communicate **genre** through images? How does this work in real media products?
- Will images be part of your creation of **audience** appeal? How does this work in real media products?
- Does your production need to use images to create **representations** that communicate values and **ideologies**? How does this work in real media products?
- Do you need to construct **narrative** information in your images? How is this done in real media products?

Once you have ideas about what you want to achieve with your photographs you should start to plan your photoshoot. In your planning, consider how you intend to use media language to construct the messages you wish to communicate.

Again, you should analyse the way the photographs in real media products are constructed. Breaking down the media language choices that are used helps you to create images that are effective and creative.

Your planning should include how you intend to create your mise-en-scène and should include ideas about:

- **Location** – what background to you want to use? Should your images be interior or exterior shots? Do you want to create a specific atmosphere or tone using the location or should your image be set in a certain place? You may wish to check out potential locations, even taking a few snapshots to see how the locations look on camera.
- **Make-up** – do your models need make-up and, if so, what effect are you aiming for? Are you intending to create character with make-up or use it to recreate a specific genre convention? You may wish to design the make-up you want in the planning stage. It's also a good idea to practise it before the photoshoot, again taking some snapshots to see how it looks.
- **Wardrobe** – what should your models wear in your photographs? If you have any specific costume needs you may have to source items before your photoshoot.
- **Props** – what objects do you need in the shots? Should your models be holding items? Do you need a specific type of chair for your models to sit on? Are there items that you want to include in the mise-en-scène that you will have to source?
- **Lighting** – will you use natural light or do you want to have other light sources? Will you use the flash on your camera or an external flash? Do you want to try and control the colour, position or strength of the lighting? Perhaps you can use domestic lamps in interior shots? Can you access professional lights to help create tone and shadow in your photographs?

Does your model need make-up and is special lighting required?

APPLY
IT

What connotations about characters or situations might you make based on these mise-en-scène choices?

Style of décor	Connotation	Genre
Clean, modern décor with minimalist, modern art objects and functional furniture.		
A mix and match décor with a collection of retro objects in many different styles and colours.		
While clean and tidy the décor is shabby and in a state of disrepair.		

Mise-en-scène can be used to create a shorthand that communicates ideas and information quickly and efficiently. It can offer the audience clues to a character's background and personality, the historical or geographical setting, the economic status of characters and what they do.

For example, the following **props** give character information:

- a briefcase on the table can indicate that at least one of the characters is a professional
- ensuring that a character's wedding ring is in shot can indicate they are (or have been) married
- lots of pizza boxes lying around can indicate that a character is lazy.

Certain **settings** are common in specific genres:

- a cabin in the woods usually means something horrific will be on its way
- a British suburban kitchen will often be the location for family dramas or sitcom misunderstandings
- a steel and glass skyscraper will often be the setting for a corporate thriller.

Costumes can be used to indicate a character's personality, class position or profession and many genres have costume conventions.

You should also consider the **framing** and **composition** of your shots in your planning to ensure you have the content you want. You should consider how you need to position the people and objects in the frame. Do you want to create close-ups, mid-shots, and/or long-shots on your shoot?

Note: you can plan for framing and composition but it is always a good idea to take a variety of shots from different positions, angles and heights so you can select the ones that work best within your production.

Although this will be dealt with later, you should also consider what post-production effects you may want to create after the shoot. You should make sure you plan to take photographs that allow you to achieve what you need. For example, if you plan to insert one of your models into a stock background image you must take photographs of your model in front of a white or at least plain background. If you don't do this, you may find you cannot cleanly extract the image of the model from the original photograph when you are using photo-editing software.

There are no rules as to how you should approach planning your photoshoot but you may find using a **storyboard** template, similar to one you would use for moving images, helpful. You can sketch the images you want to create and make notes about specific effects you wish to create while taking your photos.

Downton Abbey and *People Just do Nothing*: costume, performance, props and setting communicating ideas of class, historical period and genre.

Basic principles of photography

Photography has two stages: in-camera and **post-production**. Most digital photography offers a range of in-camera options, and lenses are usually automatically set up to take the best image possible given the conditions present at the time. This means that, today, many in-camera decisions are, in fact, made in post-production.

To save you time later in the process, you may try to ensure that the image taken is as close as possible to the one you need for your production. However, as you will see, many issues or problems can be sorted out later in image manipulation software.

Decisions about mise-en-scène and lighting should have been made before you take your pictures. During your photoshoot, but before setting up your shot, you should consider the following:

- **Focus** – relates to the sharpness of the image. What element of your photograph should be clearly in focus? Do you want any elements within your photograph to be out of focus? Mobile phones, tablets and most digital cameras will make focus decisions as the photograph is being taken. You can alter focus in post-production software but bear in mind it is easier to blur some aspects of the image than sharpen them. Try to make sure that the most important element in the shot is in focus when you take it.

Good photo

- **Exposure** – relates to the amount of light that enters the camera when the shot is taken; an under-exposed image is too dark and an over-exposed image is too light. Digital cameras tend to use an automatic exposure calculated on the amount of light that is available at the time the picture is taken. Post-production software can create exposure effects.

- **Framing** – refers to the positioning of elements in the image. If you have a main subject for your image, do you want it to be the only image in the shot? Do you want it to be a small image to the edge of the frame? Do you want it to share the frame with other objects? When you look through the viewfinder you will create a frame for your image – your subject will be 'framed' by the edges of the lens – so you should make sure you have positioned your subject where you want it before you take your photograph.

Bad photo

- **Composition** – also refers to the positioning of elements in the image but in this case it is the way elements are positioned in relation to each other. A well composed shot has a clear **focal point**, considers the whole frame (often using the rule of thirds) and is well balanced.

As you will be able to crop your image during post-production, you may think that you can create the framing and composition you need after the photoshoot. To an extent this could be true but some framing and composition errors are very difficult to correct. For example, it is difficult to correct an image where the subject does not stand out because the background in the composition creates a complex and muddled view. Similarly, if the head of your subject is outside the frame, this cannot be corrected in post-production.

Getting creative (on a shoestring budget)

Not all Media Studies students have access to professional cameras or equipment. The digital camera on your phone or tablet can create images that are perfectly suitable for a Media Studies production. You may have access to a digital stills camera. This will be fine too and may give you more control over exposure and focus.

You may be able to use the software provided with your camera, phone or tablet to create effects as you take your photographs. Internal software can alter the colour tone of the images you take and the aspect ratio of the image. You may prefer to take all your images using a standard setting and then make changes in post-

An extreme close-up

A low-angle shot

production. There may be limitations to the in-camera effects that can be created with these types of camera but there are ways to take creative photographs using a bit of imagination.

The easiest and cheapest way to create effects when taking photographs is to consider and vary camera distances and angles when creating your shots.

Try taking the same shot from a number of different **distances**:

- Put your subject in context with **long-shots** that include aspects of mise-en-scène that provide information to the viewer.
- Use **mid-shots** to show some aspects of the location but that allow your audience to focus more on your subject. This is a good position to use to communicate character through non-verbal communication codes. Head and shoulders shots can be used to exclude most elements of mise-en-scène.
- Use **close-ups** to show detail. Take care with focus – make sure that the focal point of the image is in sharp focus.
- Use extreme close-ups to exclude all information apart from one small detail.

Try taking the same shot from a number of **angles**:

- Use **low-angle shots** where you shoot your subject from below. This makes your subject loom large in the frame.
- Use **high-angle shots** where you shoot from above to minimise the subject or perhaps create the idea that they are being spied on.

  Unless you have the hardware, it can be difficult to get high-angle shots by hand. Take great care if you decide to climb up to create the shot. You may find it easier to use a selfie-stick to safely elevate your phone. Do test it first to make sure the selfie-stick will hold your phone securely.

You could get even more creative by mixing your distances and angles or by experimenting with lighting effects during your photoshoots by:

- using torches or domestic lamps to create spotlights or low-key lighting effects
- creating reflectors made of card and tin-foil to create soft light fills or high-key lighting effects
- using objects to create shaped shadows in your image
- using natural light in a number of different ways, for example shoot with the light behind you, shoot with the light to the side or shoot with the light behind your subject. Each position will create a different effect.

During your photoshoot take lots of images using different types of shot and play with light effects, framing and composition as much as you can. Ask your models to try different poses, change the way you use props and alter make-up and costumes during the shoot. You can decide which images work best during post-production. It is always better to have too many photographs than too few.

Still-image editing and post-production

The work you undertake in post-production is where you get another opportunity to demonstrate your creative and technical skills. You can use standalone software to edit your photographs or you could use one of the many free editing packages available online, or an app for your phone or tablet.

Most post-production software offers similar functions. These are some of the post-production effects you may consider using to enhance your photos:

- **Cropping and slicing** – post-production software allows you to re-shape and re-size your photographs. You can remove parts of the image that you do not want

What effects do you think would be created by the following camera shots:

- low-angle mid-shots?
- high-angle long-shots?
- eye-level close-ups?
- low-angle close-ups?

APPLY IT

to use by selecting an area of the photo to keep. Cropping usually allows you to keep a rectangular section of the image but some software allows other shapes to be selected. Cropping also allows you to improve the framing of your shot and, to a certain extent, its composition. Some software packages allow you to select and extract specific elements from the photograph, and add in elements from other photographs. Slicing allows you to select an area of the original image by dividing the image into sections and deleting the parts you don't need.

- **Colour/light editing** – post-production software allows you to alter the overall look of the photo by changing its colour. For example, colour images can be turned into black and white or can be 'aged' by colouring them in a sepia tone. The 'exposure' of the image can be changed as can the contrast between the dark and light tones. Shadows can be added and specific areas of the image can be brightened.

The ability to edit the colour of photographs also allows them to be 'retouched'. Small areas of the photograph can be changed. This is a technique that is sometimes used to 'perfect' the look of models and celebrities. Skin blemishes can be removed and a common technique used to 'brighten' the face is to lift the corners of the mouth and the eyes, and raise the arch of the eyebrows. Female models are often 'reduced' by erasing the edges of their body to produce a slimmer profile. This technique is often referred to by the name of one of the most well-known photo-editing software packages, Photoshop, and is known as 'photoshopping'. You don't need access to Photoshop to edit your images.

- **Effects filters** – post-production software offers a range of different finishes and textures that can be applied to photographs. Photos can be filtered to look like paintings and drawings; colour filters can create retro effects and leak or enhance the colours; some filters allow you to alter the depth of field while others can create grainy, glass or crackle effects.

KEY TERMS

colour tone	the properties of colour – its shade, hue, warmth, brightness, saturation, etc.	mise-en-scène (m-e-s)	everything that can be seen within the scene – set design, props, performance, lighting, costume and make-up, location and lighting
head and shoulders shot	a shot where the camera is positioned close to a human subject so that the frame excludes all of the body, apart from the head and shoulders	non-verbal communication	methods of communication that do not include words. Body language and modes of dress are both examples
high-key lighting	the use of light fills to create a low-contrast lighting effect	paparazzi	a professional photographer who seeks to capture informal images of celebrities or other people identified as being newsworthy
in-camera	decisions made to influence the look of images while shooting with the camera. This includes using camera settings as well as using external sources such as music, props and lighting to create specific effects	photojournalist	professional photographer who uses images to tell a story
		post-production	decisions made to influence the look of images after the footage or images have been captured. This is usually done using post-production software
light fills	a light used to reduce the contrast between light and shadow within the frame		
low-key lighting	a style of lighting used to create shadow and areas of bright light within the frame		

APPLY IT

- Go online and search for 'image manipulation effects'.

- Scroll through some images to get an idea of the types of effect that are possible.

- Go online and search for 'free online image manipulation'.

- Access one of the websites and use one of your own photographs to explore the effects that you can create.

7.3 Moving image production

Creating a moving image production is an excellent way of demonstrating your knowledge of media concepts, your understanding of audience and institution, and your creativity and technical ability.

Whichever form you are creating you will need to think very carefully about the way you use technology and how you will present your work using **camera**, **sound**, **lighting** and **mise-en-scène**. You will **edit** the different shots you have taken and may also choose to enhance your work by adding special effects during **post-production**.

In order to ensure you get the footage you want and need, planning is key. Like photography, you may create the effects you want in-camera and/or in post-production, but you need to know what footage you will require so you can make sure you have everything needed when you come to edit. Before you begin to film you should research your locations, source your props and costumes, find your actors, and put together a storyboard and script. During your planning process you can consider whether you need to find light sources to help create the effects you want. One of the challenges in creating moving image productions is that you will inevitably need to work with others in some way – even if it's just with your actors – and this means you need to be able to plan carefully and be prepared to organise other people in order to get the footage you need.

There are many things you need to consider before you start shooting and it is easier to work out how to answer these questions while you are planning rather than during your shoot. Moving image productions need to be 'written' before they are filmed. A script is needed to give your actors dialogue, a **shooting script** adds images and direction to the words on the page, **shot lists** and storyboards help provide information on how to set up each shot and may also contain information about editing and other post-production elements. In addition to these production issues, there are decisions that need to be made that are dependent on the form and genre you have chosen to make, who your target audience is and what effect you are trying to create. These decisions should have been made during research so now you can think practically about how to achieve what you want in your production. For example:

- What are the conventions of the form you are creating? Which conventions will you follow? Which (if any) will you subvert?
- What are the genre conventions that you need to use? Do you wish to subvert the genre conventions and audience expectations? How will you do this?
- How will you approach telling the story? What visual devices will you use to create narrative information for your audience?
- What tone or atmosphere do you wish to create? How will you do this?
- What representations do you wish to create? How will you achieve this?
- How will you create audience appeal?

Basic principles of filming

Using the camera

You may have access to professional equipment or you may have to 'make do' with limited resources – either way there is still plenty of scope to make effective moving image production pieces. Mobile phone and tablet cameras can be used to capture your footage but do be aware of the difference between landscape and portrait modes and make sure you have selected the correct one for the form you are making. It is unlikely that you will want to use images recorded in portrait for many media productions unless you wish to replicate the type of user-generated content that is sometimes used in news reporting. News broadcasters, however, repackage this footage by adding visuals to the side of the original video to make it more appealing to viewers.

The size and portability of mobile phone cameras means that they can help create shots from perspectives and angles that may be difficult to achieve with larger cameras. If a tablet or mobile phone is used to create a media product that would usually be made by a professional camera, you may want to think about how you can make your work look as professional as possible. For example, using a tripod would help create steady shots and horizontal pans. Tripods are relatively cheap and they can make a big difference in the quality of your work. *Tangerine* (2015, Baker, S.) was filmed on an iPhone but the film still uses professional framing and filming techniques.

Whatever type of camera you are using, you need to familiarise yourself with it and what it can do. The best way to do this is to experiment and make some short videos using some of the settings and effects that are built in. You should test out the light-settings (if you have them) in different lighting conditions, both inside and outside. You should try some of the effects such as slow motion or time-lapse to see if they are effects you would like to use.

Setting up your shots – framing and composition

As with photography, you need to know how to frame your shots. You may wish to consider the composition of your shots by using a 3 x 3 grid to help you design the positioning of people and objects in it. Some cameras come with a grid visible in the viewfinder and this helps you to create balance in the frame. You should think about the **position** of your subject (or subjects) and the relationship between subjects and the background. How you compose your shots will depend on what you want to include in the frame and the effect you want to achieve. When composing the shot, you should consider the objects in the foreground and background and how they look together. You should also consider the balance between left and right areas of the frame as well as the top and bottom.

There are many things to think about when considering the position of the camera. Following are just some of the questions you should be addressing when you set your shot up:

- How high or low do you want your camera to be? What point-of-view do you wish to create?
  - Do you wish to create a high-angle or low-angle shot?
  - Do you want your camera to look straight ahead at your subject or look from the left or right?
- How far away should your subjects be?
  - Do you wish to create a long-shot, a mid-shot or a close-up?
  - Do you want to change the distance from your subject within the shot? Will you zoom in or out? Will you track in or out?
- Do you want subjects and/or objects to move within the frame? Will you move the camera during the shot?
  - Do you wish to tilt or pan during the shot?
  - Do you want to track the movement of subjects and/or objects in the shot? If so, how will you achieve a smooth camera movement?
  - Have you blocked the actors' movements so that the camera can follow them?

There are some basic rules that can be applied when setting up certain shots. Part of your research may be to look at media products and work out what conventions are often used.

Making a video filmed in portrait mode, suitable for broadcast

A video filmed in landscape mode

Tangerine

For example: filming a conversation

The conventional way to shoot a conversation between two people is to film the conversation three times from three different positions:

1. **The two-shot** – shooting the conversation with two people in the frame together (sometimes different two-shots will be from different positions or angles).

2. **Over the shoulder shots** – filming over the shoulder of one actor to capture the other actor's dialogue and their reactions to the first actor's lines.

3. A repeat of the **over the shoulder shot** from behind the second actor (the combination of these two shots is a **shot-reverse-shot** technique).

The conversation is then put together during editing, with shots being cut and edited together to show the conversation as one continuous event, but presented from a combination of positions and points of view.

APPLY IT

1. **Find one of the following scenes (or similar) in a TV programme:**
   - a family discussion around the dinner table
   - a character walking down a city street
   - a woman getting ready to go out
   - a man meeting his friends at a sporting event.

2. **Select one minute from the scene and make a list of the shots used.**
   - Consider camera angles, distance and movement.
   - How many different shots are used in the extract?
   - How are they edited together?

Lighting

You can use lighting to help with composition by highlighting certain parts of the frame. Lighting is often used to help create tone and atmosphere whether that is the high-key lighting that is used in hyperreal genres such as reality TV or sitcoms, or the low-key lighting that is a convention in horror. Sitcoms use off-screen lighting to create a brightness in the frame, whereas soap operas tend to attempt to create a more naturalistic effect with by using on-screen light sources such as lamps and candles, which can create contrast and shadow. The horror genre often uses low-key lighting to emphasise the contrast between light and dark and to create a mysterious tone. Shadows become as important as light in this genre, as what is hidden is often more frightening for the audience than what is seen.

A **three-point lighting** set up is often used on professional shoots and altering the position, strength and direction of the lighting can dramatically change the feel of the image being shot. The quality of the light (hard, bright or soft, diffuse light), the colour of the light (natural daylight, yellow-tone interior light, red light for effect) and the position of the light (from above, from the side, from below) all act to alter the feel of the image within the frame. The more you use and control light the more you can control the final look of your moving image footage and its impact.

When setting up your shots, consider whether the light you have is creating the effect you want. You may have to shoot outside at a specific time of day to get the shot you need for exterior shots. When shooting inside you may find using lamps, torches or other light sources helps you create the correct tone for your shot. When thinking about light, always bear in mind that shadows can be useful in a shot but can also be a nuisance. Try to avoid unwanted shadows by making sure you are aware of where the light source is in relation to the subject and the camera. Altering

your shooting angle or repositioning the frame can help you avoid unwanted shadows that may distract your audience. Don't forget, if your camera is between a bright light and your subject, you camera operator's shadow may appear in the shot.

Sound

Sound can be recorded in-camera at the same time as the images or can be recorded separately and then added in post-production. The latter technique is most often used where sound effects are needed to add to or replace the natural sound of the footage itself and is called foley. Voice-overs and soundtracks will be recorded separately and added to the footage in post-production but where there is dialogue within a scene, the most common approach is to record at the time of filming. Some cameras will have extremely sensitive microphones and others less so. You should create some test-footage with sound to see how well your microphone picks up conversations and the diegetic sounds you might want to include in your work. You should also see how much your microphone picks up the natural ambient sound within your location.

Unwanted ambient sound can be very irritating and you should try to shoot in a location where you can control noises as far as is possible. External sounds such as traffic, distant conversations, washing machines and telephones should usually be avoided. When shooting outside this can be very difficult and external noises such as the wind can drown out actors' dialogue if care is not taken. Of course, you may wish to use a certain amount of ambient sound in your scene to create a realistic environment. Before shooting, though, you should test the volume of the background noise and ensure that your actors can be heard. In order to control ambient noise some moving image producers record the ambient sound separately and then shoot dialogue in a quiet environment. When you see a club scene in a drama, the extras may be dancing in silence and miming their conversations in the background while the primary action is recorded. The sound of a club is then added in post-production, keeping the actors audible at the top of the sound mix. Not only does this ensure that the background noise does not become a distraction, it also means that the **continuity** issues that would come from cutting and editing a scene with music are avoided.

Controlling sound is often easier inside but it is worth checking the **acoustics** before capturing your footage. Some interiors can cause sound to echo or there may be **dead spots** in certain areas. Where there is dialogue, the most important thing is to ensure the audience can hear everything clearly. Creating test footage is the best way to check if there are likely to be sound issues when recording in-camera.

Getting creative (on a shoestring budget)

While using professional equipment can offer you lots of ways to show your technical skills when producing moving image productions, demonstrating how you have overcome technical and practical limitations to get the effects you want shows great creativity.

Camera

Don't be afraid to experiment and create new and unusual effects. Don't just stick to one type of shot in your moving image production, show creativity and use a carefully selected variety of shots. When conventions are overused they become clichés, so can you tell your story in a more interesting way by varying angles or shot distances? Without lots of equipment it can be very tempting to use a lot of static shots or create movement with hand-held shots. Often this can look unprofessional and a little dull so can you think of new ways to create movement in your camera work, maybe using home-made dollies or by using cheap equipment such as selfie-sticks in a creative and interesting way?

You may want to experiment with framing and composition. The directors of *Mr Robot* (an American drama) have broken lots of conventions in the way they place objects in the frame. This has amplified the unsettling nature of the programme and created an individual media language style. These images show how the programme positions characters and action towards the edge of the frame and the majority of the screen is often out of focus mise-en-scène.

Images from *Mr Robot*

Lighting

Lighting helps you control the tone and feel of your moving image production. You can use it to direct the audience to a specific part of your shot, create emphasis or hide elements of the frame. If you're feeling creative and have access to the equipment, you can use coloured lights or in-camera lighting effects such as strobing. You could use strong lamps to create shadows, halo effects, demonic faces or spotlights. Where professional lighting is not available you can use domestic lamps and torches to create specific lighting effects. Coloured lighting can be created using coloured transparent plastic, and soft lighting can be created with tissue paper placed carefully over a light source (but not touching the bulb itself, of course) or by using the reflection of light on the subject rather than the light source itself.

You could use light to create shadows for atmosphere but you could also create shadows to indicate an off-screen object or even a character. A small cardboard cut-out of a city skyline could be used to create a city-shaped shadow or a monster could appear only as a shadow or in silhouette using a back-light.

Sound/mise-en-scène

If your camera doesn't record sound well you could experiment with creating your production with no recorded dialogue, so all the sound, including voice-over, is sourced and recorded separately. You can then **dub** it in during post-production. When capturing your video footage you should be thinking about how you can tell your story using images rather than sound. Using a visual shorthand reduces the need for dialogue and may help you show how creative you can be with a camera. Early filmmakers told their stories through props, use of camera, setting and performance, and while some of these silent film techniques have become a little clichéd, visual storytelling can be very effective. The passing of time can be shown with a close-up of the hands of a clock moving (either fast or slowly depending on the idea being communicated) or the pages of a calendar peeling away. Narrative information can be provided using newspaper headlines or a montage of social media conversations – newspapers cut up and pinned to a wall can be used to communicate a lot of story information or it could show us the troubled workings of the mind of a serial killer.

Mise-en-scène

Mise-en-scène is a term that refers to everything that can be seen within the frame. It includes the location, set dressing, costumes, props and performance. Lighting is also considered part of the mise-en-scène. Your research should have given you a clear indication of what codes and conventions of mise-en-scène you need to try to emulate for your production. There will inevitably be practical limitations: if you live in a landlocked location, shooting a beach scene may be a little impractical, but you should choose your locations carefully to create the most appropriate backdrop possible for the message you wish to communicate.

A lot of information can be communicated through the mise-en-scène. The location you choose, and the objects you choose as set dressing and for the props can provide lots of narrative information in both denotation and connotation. For example, imagine you are to dress the set of a domestic living room for a broadcast fiction production. The style of décor and the objects in the room will communicate ideas about the characters and their situation to the audience. Perhaps some set dressing choices will also create connotations of a specific genre.

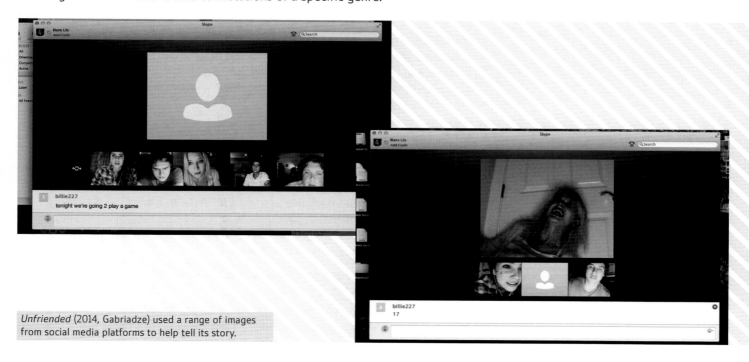

Unfriended (2014, Gabriadze) used a range of images from social media platforms to help tell its story.

Editing and post-production

Post-production in moving image production usually means editing. It can also refer to the addition of visual and audio effects. What effects you are able to achieve will depend on the software you use, but you could consider changing the look of your footage by converting a colour image to black and white or heightening specific colours or textures. You can create titles and add on-screen text or animations to your moving image footage using editing software. Some software allows you to change your footage by adding backgrounds and other objects to your work. You may be able to create special effects such as explosions.

When editing you need to consider the speed and style that will best suit your production.

Speed

- **Fast editing** moves quickly from one shot to the next. An average shot length in a film is approximately eight seconds. In fast editing, each shot is shown briefly before moving to the next. Overly fast editing can be difficult for audiences to engage with, as they may struggle to make sense of the flashes of imagery that are shown. When done well, fast editing creates a dynamic and exciting scene. Fast editing is often used in music videos, action films and fight scenes. *Mad Max: Fury Road* (2015, Miller, G.) averaged 2.1 seconds as the average shot length and *Taken 3* (2015, Megaton, O.) 1.7 seconds.

- **A medium-speed** edit with average shot lengths of between three and six seconds allows the audience to take in more detail from the mise-en-scène and the dialogue. The edit still moves the images along fast enough to be visually engaging. This feels more 'natural'. A human blink averages 4–6 seconds, so moving image editing at this speed emulates the 'editing' of images we do ourselves as we look. Soap operas use a naturalistic style that includes medium-speed editing. They are shot on several cameras, so edits usually move from one angle to another with movements such as pans and zooms being created in-camera.

- **A slow edit** allows shots to remain on screen longer between cuts, so the action of a scene can feel slowed down. Long-shots often include camera movements such as tracking, and hand-held and crane/drone shots. Nordic-noir tends to use a lot of long edits to give a sense of place and atmosphere. *Children of Men* (2006, Cuarón, A.) presents three important action scenes in single shots, creating a sense of urgency in each. The use of hand-held cameras in the final battle scene (a single shot of over seven minutes) brings the audience into the action and the style has connotations of documentary footage or war reportage. This technique was used in *True Detective* (Season 1, Episode 4) when a drugs raid was filmed in a single, six-minute take. Slow editing can be used to create verisimilitude or can simply be used to slow the action down. Michel Gondry is known for his single shot or slow editing techniques in films and music videos.

Style

A **straight cut** is the most commonly used editing style. It mimics the human eye, creating a blink-like transition between shots. It feels like a natural way to move from one image to the next and often goes unnoticed by the viewer, hence it being part of the technique called invisible editing.

There are many ways to move from one shot to the next and different styles have different connotations.

- A **fade to black/fade up** transition seems to offer a firm end to the previous scene and allows the following scene to start a new part of the story, or change location or tone without it jarring the audience.

- A **dissolve** allows the first image to slowly dissipate and the new image to come in gradually. Dissolves can connote movement or the passing of time.

- When one image moves across the screen to make way for the next, this is called a **wipe**. Wipes can be simple – a 'barn door wipe' simply slides one image out of the frame and the second one in. Editing software offers a range of shapes for wipes from the simple iris wipe that uses a circle that grows (or shrinks) in the centre of the frame, to a clock wipe that sweeps across the frame like the hands of a clock, or matrix wipes that use patterned images to change from one shot to the next. Wipes can be obtrusive and tend not to be used very often. *Star Wars* films famously use lots of wipes.

Other uses of editing

Editing is often used to move between two different parts of the story. The edit may allow the audience to follow parallel narratives by swapping between the two storylines. These edits are called **cutaways**.

Edits should usually be subtle and unobtrusive. They should be smooth and show the viewer what they need to see, moving them gently between viewpoints or perspectives. It is best not to edit between long-shots and close-ups as this creates a jump for the viewer. Similarly, moving between shots of the same size (one close-up to a second) can also be jarring. Editing should maintain the continuity of the world being presented to the audience, so subjects should not be shown 'leaping' from one side of the screen to the other or changing in size or proportion. Continuity editing maintains the 'reality' of the world presented within the video production.

When capturing your footage you should plan for editing. When you are out filming you may want to consider filming a few seconds of 'run-in' and 'run-out' footage to give you space for your edit at the start and end of each shot. You should also shoot 'cover shots' – that is, long-shots of the scene you are filming as well as mid-shots and close-ups. Both these techniques give you more flexibility when you edit. You may also want to shoot images that give geographical or atmospheric information that can be added as intercuts.

Sound

You can add sound effects, musical soundtracks and voice-overs into your production work using editing software.

You could create your own foley (sound effects) by recording sounds using objects around you. For example, the sound of horses running is often created using coconut shells and helicopter propeller sounds can be made with plastic coathangers. You can also use post-production software to edit sound levels so that dialogue, music, sound effects and/or ambient sound are balanced correctly for the audience.

You can download copyright-free sound effects to use in your work, so you can create off-screen sounds or enhance and add to the sounds you recorded during filming.

Music is an important part of the creation of moving image productions. Again, you can download copyright-free music online and, if you select the music carefully and edit it into your work effectively, you can communicate your genre and help steer your audience's emotional responses.

Dialogue that has been recorded separately can be dropped in during post-production. This is a common practice in professional moving image production. The dialogue is first recorded in-camera and then the actors record another version in a controlled environment. They will use the moving image footage to ensure the second version is recorded at the same speed as the original and that **lip-sync** is possible. Sometimes sections of in-camera sound are replaced by studio recorded sound – this is not an easy technique as it can be tricky to get a match with the ambient sound and to get the sound to match lip movement. It is often used in professional media to add dialogue to the scene when the actor who is 'speaking' is not facing the camera.

KEY TERMS

acoustics	the sound qualities of a specific environment		invisible editing	an editing style that appears natural to the viewer, usually exemplified by straight cuts
back-light	a light positioned behind the subject		lip-sync (synchronisation)	matching the lip movements of a moving image production to words recorded on a separate sound track – or recording the silent lip movements of an actor replicating pre-recorded dialogue or singing
blocking	the positioning of props and actors for a sequence that allows for specific camera moves and distances to be pre-planned			
continuity/ continuity editing	the creation of logical and/ or visual coherence and consistency		pan	a horizontal camera movement where the camera remains on a fixed point
dead spot	an area created by local acoustics where sound is reduced in volume or flattened in tone		shooting script	the written text of a video/ film product including details of the use of camera in individual scenes
dub	to add sound elements to recorded images		shot list	a descriptive list of the shots required for a moving image production
edit (moving image/audio)	the arranging of images or sound to create a coherent visual or audio sequence			
intercuts	to insert shots from other locations or narrative lines including flashbacks and flashforwards			

7.4 Audio production

Creating an audio production can be done quickly and easily using mobile phone and tablet technology. If you are lucky enough to have access to sound recording equipment you may have a microphone that provides a better sound quality in your recordings but the quality of mobile technology will usually be fine for your NEA production.

You may want to emulate music programming or create a podcast, radio drama or documentary. Your initial research into the form you want to make should help you break down the codes and conventions you want to recreate and inspire you to create interesting and engaging content for your audience.

Like moving image production there are some basic principles that should be considered when recording and editing sound, and there are techniques you may wish to experiment with when constructing your audio product.

Basic principles of recording

Be aware of your environment

Try to record all parts of your production in a similar environment (the same environment if possible) so that any recording done at different times has a similar audio quality. Make a note of the distance between the speaker and the microphone as this will help you set up the environment again should you need to. If you have access to a soundproof environment, that is ideal. If not, try to remove any exterior noise from your environment so that you are recording in as close to silence as possible.

If you are going to record on location, try to avoid loud, intrusive noises, and try to record all you need in one location at the same time so that the ambient noise sounds the same. You may even decide to record ambient noise separately and then add it to your 'studio recorded' voices in post-production.

Check your equipment

When you begin your recording, do some tests so you can check the sound levels and any ambient sounds that your microphone picks up. Here are some pre-production tips:

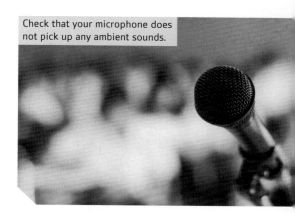

Check that your microphone does not pick up any ambient sounds.

- In a room or studio, record silence and listen to it on full volume. Have other sounds been picked up?
- On location, record the ambient sound and check how intrusive it is. Can you position your microphone closer to your subject to ensure the sounds you want are not being drowned out?
- Check to see if your microphone picks up the page turning of your notes or if your breathing is loud.
- Check the sound of your voice. Do you need to move your microphone a little to avoid it exaggerating your 'p' and 'b' sounds?
- If you are able to adjust your recording levels, experiment with them to see which work best for your environment.

You may have identified a number of elements that need recording or sourcing. This may involve going online to download music and/or sound effects, or you may record your own.

Depending on what you are creating, you may wish to create jingles and idents, intros, outros and even audio adverts. If you are creating audio drama you will need to record several voices and include sound effects to help tell the story. Audio documentaries often use incidental music to create tone or help steer the listener's emotional response. Audio products are rarely just one voice, so there is plenty of scope for you to show your creativity and technical ability in the recording stage of production. You will then need to use software to put all the various elements together for your finished production.

Editing and post-production

Sound editing, like moving image editing, is the bringing together of the different elements of sound that make up the audio production. Sound editing should move the listener from one sound element to another smoothly, so there should be no jarring movements, for example big changes in volume, as the audio production progresses. Sound can move simply from one sound to the next or transition effects such as fade-outs and fade-ins can be used. Transition sounds can be downloaded online and may include 'whooshes', 'swishes' or sound effects such as glass breaking or doors closing. Transitions like these should be used for specific sound effects – and then sparingly – or they can become irritating to the listener.

APPLY IT

Listen to the first couple of minutes of a podcast and write down everything you hear.

- What sounds could you source online?
- Make a list of all the recording you would need to do to recreate the start of the podcast.

It is worth thinking about sound in layers as at any given time there may be several sounds playing at the same time. A presenter could be speaking over a music **sound-bed**. Post-production includes mixing the levels of sound so that some elements (e.g. music) sit below others (e.g. the presenter). In music programming, a DJ names the next track over the introduction and the music may be faded down towards the end as the DJ begins to speak again.

Serial Season 2, Episode 1 begins like this:

1 A 35-second, spoken word advert for 'Rocket Mortgage' is read out. They are the sponsors of the *Serial* podcast.

2 The presenter introduces the story and includes audio taken from the video source (audio from video is dropped below the voice and the presenter's voice dominates). The presenter describes the video and occasionally the audio from the video rises in the mix – sometimes it is the sound of voices and sometimes the sound of a helicopter. At the end of the description the audio abruptly cuts to silence.

3 The theme tune to *Serial* is played and the presenter announces the name of the podcast and she introduces herself. The sound of a military spokesperson, news reporters and politicians, including Donald Trump and his cheering followers calling for military deserters to be shot, can be heard as the music continues to play. The voices create a montage of sounds from various sources that provides a range of opinions on the podcast's subject matter and the opening ends with (what is assumed to be) the voice of the subject Private First Class (PFC) Bowe Bergdahl, a US soldier who had been captured by the Taliban after, according to some people, he had deserted his military post.

4 The presenter proceeds to outline the context of the story, as incidental music plays below the voice track and the voice of the subject of the podcast is heard.

To create this opening, the following sounds have been recorded or sourced from elsewhere:

Recorded	Sourced
The advert	Podcast theme tune
The script read by the presenter	Audio from a video
An interview with the subject	Incidental music

These six elements will have been edited together in post-production and great care will have been taken in the sound balance of the music and the audio from the video – the latter alters as the extract progresses.

KEY TERMS

idents	sounds used to identify the programme, radio station or brand. This could be a jingle or a theme tune
outro	the concluding piece of a recording

sound-bed	sounds, sound effects and/or music that plays below the main content of an audio production. Sound beds can communicate narrative information such as location or they can create a tone or atmosphere for the production

7.5 Approaches to e-media production

E-media production uses elements of all the production areas already outlined in this chapter, and it may:

- need to be designed in the same way as a print page. It will need to consider basic layout and design conventions but also the codes and conventions of the form being constructed
- need to use photographs as illustrations
- include moving image and audio productions as part of its presentation of content.

E-media is often a combination of different presentation forms that provide audiences with various ways to access and engage with the information being communicated. Of course, some e-media forms are simply replications of 'offline' formats. A podcast follows the conventions of radio programming and YouTube videos are very similar to television products that offer similar content. However, as user-generated content has developed, it has adopted some professional techniques while maintaining some of its amateur approaches.

Once you have decided what you are making, as with all the other production areas, you should undertake research of existing products to identify the approaches you could take in your own production. Although you need to show you can use software and equipment when making your productions, Media Studies does not require you to learn coding or other specific programming skills. You may have ideas that you would like to include in your production but lack the specialist technical skills to create them as fully functional elements. In this case you can indicate the feature that would be included in a real product even if it doesn't work fully. However, this is another great opportunity to show your understanding of contemporary media and your creativity using multi-media and audience participation. E-media products are more engaging when they contain movement and sound, so you could include moving image or audio recordings to your e-media work. Even a simple animation can give a visual interest to your e-media work that is not available in print.

E-media allows more audience participation and interactivity than other platforms and it allows audiences to communicate with producers and each other. E-media has changed the way audiences want to be entertained and a crucial part of any media production will be the way it is used to encourage and communicate audience participation. Interactivity can range from asking audiences to click on a simple poll to register their opinion, to providing opportunities for audiences to share ideas and opinions. Audiences could be persuaded to share media such as photos and videos or they could be encouraged to participate through competitions or getting involved in events and experiences in real life. It may be appropriate for your e-media product to include a comments section or be linked to social media. E-media products can offer choices that allow the audience to feel as if they are able to personalise their experience. For example, it is common practice for online adverts to offer the audience a choice of two or three different versions. Audiences can choose the version that looks most interesting or relevant to their needs and advertisers can use different marketing techniques for different parts of the target audience or offer further information, competitions and other ways for the audience to participate. Inspiration for the use of multi-media and encouraging audience participation can be found by researching existing media productions.

Go online to the following websites and detail how the sites use multi-media to present information and how they try to get audiences involved.

Website	Multi-media?	Audience interaction?
www.theguardian.co.uk		
www.bbc.co.uk		
www.mailonline.co.uk		
www.loreal-paris.co.uk		
gillette.co.uk/en-gb		
www.zoella.co.uk		
www.manutd.com		
marvelcinematicuniverse.wikia.com		

Offline e-media production

You can create e-media productions using offline software such as specialised web design or desktop publishing packages. You are not expected to be able to use computer code, so consider using software that allows you to design your e-media production and add in multi-media features. If you use offline e-media production software you will need to ensure that you are able to convert your work to an e-media format that will, in most cases, be accessible via a browser. Some offline software is complex to use and can limit the look and functionality of your finished production, so make sure you choose software that you can use effectively and that can achieve what you want to achieve.

Online production tools (to include websites, social media and video games)

It is very likely that you will want to use an online production tool to create an e-media production. You might use a blog site, a social media platform or an online game creation tool to create materials for your coursework. These tools allow you to use templates and pre-formed pages that make it very easy for you to present your work online. Some production tools require you to make design and layout decisions, and your choices will demonstrate your understanding of the platform, the form and your audience. As you won't be creating everything yourself you should spend time creating content for your online product. This means that you should be using still images, moving images and/or audio within your online production to create audience engagement and appeal and meet the function of your product.

Most of the online tools for e-media creation are intended to be simple to use and allow personalisation. Social media pages are often quite uniform in their layout and design but the choice of images and written content will set your pages apart from others. You will need to be sure about what you want your social media pages to achieve and how to best appeal to your target audience.

If you are creating gaming material using an online tool, you need to make a number of choices. You need to select the style of gameplay that is appropriate for the genre of game you wish to produce. You should also consider your target audience to ensure that you are making a game they will enjoy. You will select the style and design of the game as you choose the visual design of the locations, backgrounds and characters, and you will be able to choose the sounds and the music. You should try to ensure that your gameplay is both suitable and easy for the audience to engage with and that the codes and conventions you use accurately reflect the conventions of the genre and type of game you are replicating.

CHAPTER SUMMARY

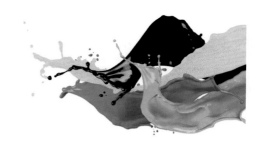

This chapter has dealt with a range of different things you need to consider when embarking on your practical production.

You need to:

- Choose one of the forms offered in the briefs.
- Identify or choose the genre to work on for your production.
- Consider the basics of the way the form is usually constructed by researching existing examples of the form.
- Consider the issues raised by the institutional context presented in the brief.
- Consider how to address the audience identified in the brief.
- Engage with the codes and conventions of the genre by researching existing media products.
- Consider what equipment and software you need to create your productions.
- Plan your productions carefully and taking your approach to the brief into account.

Chapter 8 The NEA

What you will learn in this chapter

- This chapter offers an overview of the A level Non-Exam Assessment (NEA). You will need to complete the NEA to be awarded the A level qualification. The NEA is worth 30% of the A level

This chapter will offer advice on responding to the A level NEA briefs and discuss some of the types of media you may be asked to create and how this work will be assessed. The second half of this chapter will demonstrate approaches to each stage of the production process using a sample production brief.

> **Chapter 8 offers further advice on:**
> - Practical approaches to a range of production tasks covering print, e-media and broadcast productions
> - Advice on layout and design, photography, audio recording and capturing moving images
> - Software and equipment requirements for different types of production tasks
> - Codes and conventions of a range of media forms

8.1 Introduction to the NEA

You will be asked to create two practical pieces that combine to make a cross-media production. You will be able to choose your project from the six briefs provided by AQA. The NEA productions will ask you to make two media productions that will be linked in some way to the media forms studied for the examination.

You could be asked to make products related to:

- television (broadcast: moving image)
- radio (broadcast: audio)
- newspapers (print and/or e-media)
- magazines (print and/or e-media)
- advertising and marketing (broadcast: moving image/audio, print and/or e-media)
- online, social and participatory media (e-media but could include audio/video)
- video games (e-media)
- music video (moving image and/or advertising and marketing).

In addition, each brief will, in some way, be linked to at least one of the CSPs.

You will not be asked to make a film product but it is possible that products related to film promotion could be included in the briefs on offer – for example, film posters, a film website, a magazine article promoting the release of a film, etc.

Six briefs will be published each year and each brief will offer a different combination of media products for you to create. As there will be new briefs each year, check that you are choosing from the correct list before you start your research, planning and production work.

Each brief will ask you to create two of the following:

- a video product
- an audio product
- an e-media product
- a print product.

> **A note about AS briefs**
>
> The briefs for the AS level will be used and added to in the following year's A level briefs. You may find that your teachers use the AS briefs in your first year to help you develop your practical skills and get you used to responding to a brief. This means that some of the A level tasks will be familiar to you but you will have more choice for your second-year project and you will be asked to create two rather than one production piece.

The briefs you should choose from will be published at the end of your first year and the two products in each brief will be connected in some way. The connection provided in the brief is what will make your production a cross-media project. You will be given a clear indication of the minimum requirements for each element of the production including the number of pages required, length of video or audio production, the content of e-media materials, etc.

You should research and plan for your production but do not submit this material at the end of the project. Your final submission will consist of two elements – a 500-word Statement of Intent and the two finished productions. You will be given deadlines for submission by your teacher who will be marking your work.

What will you be assessed on?

Your NEA will be assessed on your ability to

> *create media products for an intended audience, by applying knowledge and understanding of the theoretical framework of media to communicate meaning.*

You will receive a mark for your Statement of Intent and another for your productions.

Statement of Intent

The Statement of Intent is worth a maximum of 10 marks or one-sixth of the NEA marks. There is a specific template provided by AQA that you are able use to present your Statement of Intent. You'll find it in the Student Book for the NEA published by AQA. Write your Statement of Intent before you create your media products and discuss the way you intend to respond to your chosen brief based on the research and planning you have undertaken after selecting your brief. Include in your Statement of Intent ideas and terms from the theoretical framework applied specifically to the project you intend to complete. Make your statement detailed and specific and refer directly to what you will do in your production work.

In your Statement of Intent identify how you will be responding to the specific requirements of the brief you have chosen, especially how you will address your target audience and how your products will fit in with the industrial context provided in the brief. Also show that you have considered the relationship between the products and how they work in light of the digitally convergent nature of modern media.

Productions

The mark you receive will be based on the effectiveness of your application of ideas from the theoretical framework in a practical context.

The marks are allocated between the following areas:

- media language
- representation
- industry and audience.

The evidence you offer for your knowledge and understanding of the theoretical framework will be in the practical work you produce.

The following are some suggestions as to how you can show evidence of your knowledge in your practical work.

Media language

You need to use media language effectively to communicate meaning to the audience identified in the brief. This could include:

- using identifiable denotations and connotations to help create your message
- using techniques such as symbolism and/or anchorage to help create meaning
- creating (or subverting) the genre codes as appropriate
- sonstructing narrative codes and markers to help communicate your ideas
- using postmodern techniques such as bricolage or intertextuality as appropriate.

Representation

You need to use media language effectively to create representations that communicate meaning. This could include:

- using or subverting stereotypes as appropriate
- using representations to reinforce or challenge dominant values
- using representations to construct an idea of identity if appropriate
- using representations to highlight specific gender or race issues if appropriate.

Audience and industry

You need to demonstrate an understanding of who the target audience is and how best to attract them, address them and meet their expectations.

You should consider the industrial context of production. This could include:

- considering the distribution methods used
- seeking to increase circulation
- issues around finances such as funding, commodification, generating an income, etc.
- issues around regulation as appropriate
- issues related to globalisation, diversification, convergence, etc.

Of course, how you approach demonstrating your knowledge and understanding will depend on the requirements on the brief and on the decisions you make in your response to it.

For more on representation see Chapter 4 of the Year 1 book.

8.2 Working on the NEA

Selecting the brief

Your first task is to choose which brief you wish to complete. You may make your decision based on your media interests, so, for example, a brief based on the music industry may interest you more than any other. Being interested in the topic will certainly help you do well as it is so much easier to research into and engage with topics that spark your enthusiasm. Your level of interest will inevitably come across in your work too. Alternatively, you may base your choice on the actual productions you will create. Your choices may be limited by your access to equipment and/or software. However, what you create is more important than how you create it, so you may wish to refer to the AS & Year 1 book for further suggestions as to how to approach using equipment and finding and using production software. Another valid way to help you choose which brief to work on could be the experiences you had when undertaking practical work in Year 1. You may have found you enjoyed some types of practical production over others, so you may decide to pick a brief that helps you play to your strengths.

Based on your studies of the CSPs, give each form a mark out of 10 to indicate which areas of the media you are most interested (10) or least interested in (1).

Media form	Level of interest
TV	
Radio	
Newspapers	
Magazines	
Advertising and marketing	
Online, social and participatory media	
Video games	
Music video	

Give each of the following production areas a mark out of 4 to put them in rank order based on the criteria given.

Production area	Your own experience	Level of expertise	Level of enjoyment
Print			
E-media			
Video			
Audio			

The briefs will cover different media forms and ask for different types of productions each year, but knowing your own interests and strengths will help you decide which brief you should select for your NEA.

Working with the brief

Each brief provides two distinct types of information.

1 **The brief's instructions**

   This is where the specifics of what you must produce are provided. You will be told what you need to produce and who it is for. You will also be given some information about the industrial contexts of the production and/or the convergent nature of the project that you should to keep in mind when making your products.

   The brief will leave you to make some key decisions. You may be told what to make (e.g. adverts as part of an alcohol-aware campaign) but you will need to decide what persuasive techniques to use. All decisions you make should take the information provided in the brief into account. So, if the brief identifies you are targeting your public service advertising campaign towards older adults you should choose persuasive techniques that are likely to be more effective with this age group.

2 **The minimum requirements**

This section of the brief gives you a clear indication of what needs to be included in each of your productions. You will be told how many products, pages and/ or minutes you are to produce. You will be given a clear indication as to what specific features should be included within each production, including the number of original images, how much written content, etc.

It's worth noting that these are the minimum requirements, so you can always do more.

Researching

Once you have chosen which brief to work on, you can begin your research. It's important to undertake different types of research in preparation for your planning and production, as the production decisions you make should be based on your knowledge and understanding of how media products are constructed, how they attempt to appeal to their target audiences and the impact of the industrial context.

- Research **real media products** to find out how media professionals construct media products.
- Research your **target audience**. You can do this through the study of existing media products to find out how media producers attempt to appeal to the target audience. You can look at a range of media products and this will help you work out what media producers assume your audience will respond to.
- Apply ideas from the **theoretical framework** to your product research and this may involve further theoretical research.

For example, if you were going to make a series of public service adverts for magazines and for billboards, you could investigate:

- the codes and conventions of magazine advertising
- the codes and conventions of billboard advertising
- the codes and conventions of public service adverts
- the codes and conventions of the genre of public service adverts you are making
- the codes and conventions of adverts aimed towards your target audience
- the way your target audience is usually addressed
- the needs, desires and interests of your target audience that are assumed in other media products
- the narrative codes that are conventionally used in public service adverts
- the representations that are conventionally used in public service adverts
- the industrial context of advertising and, specifically, public service advertising
- the regulations that should be considered when making public service advertising.

APPLY IT

Using this advert, what can you learn about advertising techniques, public service adverts, the way the audience is addressed and how the adverts have to conform to advertising regulations?

Complete the table below by making observations about the advert and then linking your observations to the media language choices. You can then extend your analysis by considering why these choices have been made.

What does the advert do?	How does it do it?	Why does it do it?
Shows a young woman having fun on a night out		
Attempts to show the negative side of drinking to excess		To help persuade the audience to regulate their alcohol intake

Planning

Once you've some clear ideas as to how real media products work, you can decide what ideas and techniques you will replicate in your own production. You may, of course, decide you want to do something original, so you may decide to subvert some conventions and/or expectations. You should judge which conventions you wish to follow and which you want to ignore. In your planning, always keep your target audience in mind and make sure that you are considering any industrial issues.

Base your planning on the research you have undertaken, which will vary depending on the product you are making.

For example:

Planning for video production	Planning for audio production	Planning for e-media production	Planning for print production
Locations for filming	Locations for recording	Layout and design of pages	
Casting	Casting	Planning for photographic shoots – location, lighting, props, casting, make-up, costume, etc.	
Props, costume, make-up	Script	Written content	
Script	Plans for music, sound effects etc.	Illustrations	
Shooting script	Editing/post-production plan	Plans for post-production image editing	
Sound, music and sound effects plans		Plans for audience interaction	
Plans for lighting		Multi-media content plans: audio and/or video	
Editing/post-production planning		Planning for the integration of social media	

Statement of Intent

It is at this point that you should write your Statement of Intent. Try to have a clear idea as to how you will approach the practical productions and, most importantly, why you will approach the tasks in the way you have selected. The Statement of Intent should be carefully constructed to enable you to outline your plans for both production pieces. Discuss them separately but also make sure that you explain how the two artefacts are linked as a cross-media production. Make it clear how you intend to target your audience, and how you will use media language to create appropriate representations to communicate the intended message. Be clear about the industry context of your production. Also show your knowledge from the theoretical framework and demonstrate your understanding of ideas by using media terminology.

It will be important to show that you have engaged with the brief when you write your Statement of Intent – so make sure you explain what you intend to do in your productions and how your intentions relate back to the brief's instructions.

8.3 A sample brief

The brief	Minimum requirements
Create a front page, a contents page and double-page spread for the print version of a new independent cross-platform youth magazine aimed at young people aged between 15 and 25. The magazine offers some lifestyle content but its main unique selling point is that it offers comments and opinions on current affairs for its youth audience. You should create four pages in total, including at least eight original images. This magazine would be published by an independent publisher.	**Front cover to include:** • Title for a new magazine and masthead • Selling line • Cover price • Dateline • A main cover image (this image should not be used on the other pages created for this brief) • At least five cover lines **Contents page to include:** • Full list of contents for the magazine • Reference to the magazine's website and social media • At least three images related to different articles (these images must not be the same as those used on the front cover or in the double-page spread) **Double-page spread to include:** • Headline, standfirst and subheadings • Original copy for double-page feature (approx. 400 words) that links to one of the cover lines on the front cover • Main image plus at least three smaller images • Representations of a social group, event or place that is relevant to the magazine • Pull quotes and/or sidebar **All pages:** • Clear brand and house style for the magazine, including use of images, colour palette and fonts
Create a new functioning website as an e-media version of the magazine **The website should include:** • a homepage featuring information on the website's sections and content including a link to … • a feature article on a topic appropriate to the magazine/website's brand • a third page based on audience interaction and/or user-generated content The site will incorporate one minute of audio material and you can choose where this should feature on the website Like the magazine, the website is aimed at young people aged between 15 and 35 At least six of the images you use must be original, so your concept should allow you to take appropriate photographs	**The website:** • At least six additional original images across the three pages that communicate the magazine/website's branding message. • Use of appropriate language and register for the target audience **The homepage should include:** • Original title and logo for the website • Clear navigation and working links to the rest of the site • One main image plus at least two other images that are appropriate for the website's brand and style **Pages 2 and 3 should include:** • At least 100 words of copy on each page • One minute of audio including two different voices and other sound sources such as music, sound effects, etc. on at least one of the pages • At least three further original images • Working links to the other pages • The ability for users to interact, e.g. by adding comments or liking other comments on the page, submitting images, video or audio for publication or any other interaction that is appropriate for the website

Research

Having selected the brief, the first part of the process is to undertake some research based on the brief's requirements. There are several 'clues' in the brief itself that indicate the type of knowledge required to complete the brief effectively.

Codes and conventions of the form

The first stage is to be clear about the codes and conventions of the products identified in the brief – in this case magazine front covers, contents pages and feature articles and website homepages, articles and user-generated content/ interaction pages.

Magazines

There are two magazine CSPs and both offer examples of the layout and design of their front covers and contents pages. These magazines have different target audiences and are published by very different institutions; however, the way the front covers, contents pages and feature articles are presented follow similar conventions. By looking at these, and other non-CSP magazines, the general codes and conventions for each part of the magazine can be identified. At this stage, the content of the magazine is not important as the codes and conventions are the shared characteristics of the form, which will then be used in ways that suit individual magazines' content and target audience.

Front covers	Contents pages	Feature articles
Magazine title using recognisable font at the top of the page	Heading used to identify the contents page	One large image and two or three smaller images used to illustrate the story
One main picture of a model or celebrity – sometimes someone featured in the magazine	Contents sometimes broken up into sections	Large, short, punchy headline – often crossing two pages
Limited colour palette used – magazine title's colour sometimes changed to reflect this	Page numbers indicate the location of specific articles	Smaller but longer subheading
Dateline and cover price sometimes included	Titles of articles provided	Text laid out in columns
Cover lines provide information about the magazine's content and often use a punchy phrase followed by brief explanation of content	A brief summary of the contents also provided	Text broken up with short subheadings, pull quotes or other visual devices
A small selection of fonts used to create visual interest (but always legible)	Images used to illustrate the contents of the magazine that are connected to some or all of the articles	Text often broken up with small illustrations
Advertising language used to 'sell' the magazine		Text laid out for easy legibility/ readability
Numbers often used to indicate that there is a lot of information/content in the magazine		Sidebar often used to offer additional, related information
		Pages are often designed using a limited colour palette
		Fonts and other design elements are used to illustrate the page

PHOENIX

Autumn / Winter 17-18
Issue 22
The Space Issue

A season of life and style

Kacy Hill

GQ
AUSTRALIA

THE BUSINESS ISSUE

WHY YOUR JOB IS MAKING YOU FAT!

GENTLEMEN'S QUARTERLY

TONY ABBOTT
GQ GRILLS THE PM'S ARCH-RIVAL

HALLELUJAH!
MEET THE PORN STARS TRADING GANG BANGS FOR GOD
(PAGE 120)

COULD YOU BE A CUDDLE PIMP?
WE REVEAL THE JOBS OF THE FUTURE

STYLE UPGRADE
YOUR 2012 WARDROBE STRATEGY

LEO RISING
DICAPRIO ON MONEY, SUCCESS AND POWER

MEN AND THE BOTOX EPIDEMIC

SHEAR GENIUS

Tailoring makes a welcome return with unexpected cuts and exaggerated proportions

Photographer Leo Hick
Stylist Annie Swain

THE STORIES OF THE YEAR
BY THOSE THAT MADE THEM

Q

Awards Special Edition

ESSENTIAL!

50 ALBUMS OF 2014
Your definitive must-hear list

NEIL YOUNG
EXCLUSIVE! ON FAMILY, CSNY & THE FUTURE

ROYAL BLOOD
ON HOW THEY SAVED ROCK MUSIC

Ed Sheeran

AN EVERYDAY TALE OF ONE MAN, HIS GUITAR AND GLOBAL SUPERSTARDOM...

WILKO JOHNSON
ON THE MIRACLE OF BEATING CANCER

PINK FLOYD
ON THE ENDLESS RIVER & THE END

KASABIAN
ON GLASTONBURY & VINDICATION

CULTURE CLUB
ON REBIRTH & SURVIVAL

PLUS! ST. VINCENT CARIBOU THE WAR ON DRUGS & THE RETURN OF AC/DC...

THE VACCINES

The Final Redemption Of The Vaccines

They became rich and famous quickly and young. Then came the difficult third album, the band implosion, the cheeseburgers. Now rejuvenated and fighting fit, The Vaccines take Andrew Perry for a stroll down memory lane. "I wanna be in my gang again!" proclaims Justin Young.

Photography: Alex Lake

RED EARTH

A gripping outback western set in the 1920s, Warwick Thornton's *Sweet Country* exposes the racism and brutality at the heart of the colonial project, as a posse hunts down a pair of Indigenous Australians accused of murder
By Trevor Johnston

Q Contents

May 2018

This month's highlight: delving deep back into this issue's Maverick, Lawrence from Felt/Denim/Go-Kart Mozart's immortal back catalogue.

FEATURES

THE IRREPRESSIBLE AGNES VARDA

After decades working contentedly in the margins, the artist and filmmaker is finally gaining the wider recognition she deserves. Over the pages that follow, our writers discuss key aspects of her brilliantly idiosyncratic work, outlining her central role in the French New Wave and exploring her rich visual style, deep love of play and sharp sense of place – while Varda herself discusses her career

---

CONTENTS

PAGE 188

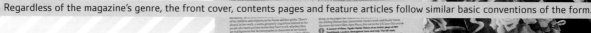

Regardless of the magazine's genre, the front cover, contents pages and feature articles follow similar basic conventions of the form.

- This sample brief requires materials to be made for a lifestyle/current affairs magazine. Look at some examples of these magazine genres to see if they have their own codes and conventions in the way they present front covers, contents pages and feature articles.

- You are asked to produce an independently produced magazine. Look at other independent magazines to find out whether they use codes and conventions in similar or different ways to those magazines produced by large publishers.

- The target audience for your production is young people. Look at other magazines for young people to see what design elements they use and how they address their audience.

What ideas would research into these three types of magazines offer to help you create your own production work?

Once this research has been undertaken and you are familiar with the conventions of the forms you are making, you may want to look a little more closely at three other types of magazines to help you make your own examples:

- magazines from the genre(s) you are working in
- magazines with a similar institutional background
- magazines for your target audience.

The A level NEA will always ask you to make two productions so you should research both productions in terms of codes and conventions, industrial context and the way the audience is appealed to and addressed.

In this sample brief the second production is a website. Website design has changed over the years as it adapts to new digital technologies and audience behaviours. For example, the placement of menus has changed to allow audiences accessing websites on tablets and mobile phones a better visual experience.

Your website research should look at a range of websites to identify their codes and conventions:

- a range of different homepages
- a range of different online articles
- a range of pages featuring user-generated content
- a range of pages that encourage and use audience interaction
- lifestyle magazine sites
- current affairs sites
- sites for young people
- sites for independent magazines.

This level of research will give you the knowledge of contemporary web design and it is from this position that you are able to engage with the requirements of the brief. You can then use this knowledge to create your production plans, your Statement of Intent and, finally, the productions themselves. You should use the knowledge you gain while analysing existing media products to make production decisions. Your production decisions should always be based on creating a recognisable product that will be appealing to your target audience and meet the brief's requirements. You may decide that the best way to achieve all of this is to create a media product that subverts conventions and offers the audience something different. This is a valid choice as long as your approach enhances audience appeal and effectively communicates your messages.

Pop star homepages from the 1990s, 2000s and the present day. Note the menu logo at the top left of Taylor Swift's animated website.

Planning

Once you have researched existing media products you can create your own plans for production. As indicated earlier, the plans you create will depend on what you are making. Planning is an important part of the process. You should consider the layout and design of print and e-media work; you're advised to script audio and video work and consider what arrangements you should make to ensure you have the correct actors, props, lighting and other equipment available. Photography should be carefully planned and not only are you likely to want to find models but you should also make decisions about shooting locations, props, costume and make-up before you start taking photographs. Use plans to explore what equipment, resources and software you will need. If your plans include using a dozen different models on one photoshoot, you should consider if it is possible to get all your models in one place at the same time. It's better to find out what you can and cannot do at this stage so you can alter your plans rather than discover a problem later that means you have to start again. A lot of time can be saved by planning effectively.

The Statement of Intent

Your Statement of Intent is a 500-word written document that outlines how you intend to meet the requirements of the brief. Your teacher will set a deadline for its submission but it should be written after you have completed your research for the productions but before the productions are completed. The Statement of Intent should show the outcome of your research, not by describing what you found, but by discussing how the research has influenced your approach to the production tasks. Try to be explicit in how you are using your knowledge of the theoretical framework in your approach to the tasks set in the brief.

The production

Most students find the production part of the project fun but time-consuming. Your teacher will provide you with a deadline so you should make sure you give the NEA enough time. After the pre-production planning, you will want to shoot footage, record audio and/or take photographs, and you may wish to edit and enhance your work in post-production. You are also advised to give enough time to the design of print and e-media products and the addition of any multi-media elements you require.

You should also give yourself enough time to review your finished productions so you can make improvements to your work. You are being assessed on how your practical work demonstrates your understanding of the theoretical framework, so when reviewing your work you should ask the following questions:

Media language

- Are the media language choices appropriate for the form and genre of the production?
- Are the products recognisable and easy to follow/understand?
- Do the media language choices effectively communicate the intended message?

Representations

Have representations been created in a way that is appropriate to:

- the form?
- the genre?
- the audience?
- the industry?
- the brand image?
- the function of the product?
- the effective communication of the product's messages?

Sample Statement of Intent

Media Studies A level NEA Statement of Intent

Centre Name *Anywhere College*   Centre Number *56789*

Candidate Name *Any Student*   Candidate Number *6789*

This form must be completed and given to your teacher before 1 April 20XX

How will you use media language and media representations in order to create your product, meet the requirements of the brief and the needs of the target audience and reflect the appropriate media industries for your chosen brief? (Maximum 500 words)

Be specific about the ways in which you will use aspects of media language, media representations, target your audience, reflect the appropriate media industries for your chosen brief and exploit opportunities for digital convergence.

I will be creating pages from an independent magazine for young people and the website for this magazine. I will create audience appeal by making a conventional magazine front cover but will try to create an 'unconventional' brand image by using two models on the cover – one male and one female, so my magazine does not appear to be targeting a specific gender. The models will be dressed in a hipster/indie aesthetic to help reinforce a brand image that positions this magazine title outside the mainstream. Filters will be used to create a vintage effect on the cover image and a cool, neutral colour palette will be used throughout the magazine and in the magazine title design. These visual identifiers will be repeated on all pages of the magazine and the website. The magazine's feature article will be an interview with a celebrity who is also a social activist and the contents page will indicate that the magazine offers content on fashion, music and entertainment, as well as issues such as gender and sexuality, the environment, politics and money.

The website's front page will be designed with an image from the same photoshoot as the magazine's main image and the interview with the celebrity activist will be heavily promoted showing convergence. The homepage will also contain links to each of the sections of the website and featured stories will be promoted on the front page using an image and a brief summary of the story. The homepage will be designed on a simple grid and images will dominate over text.

One of the stories identified on the homepage will be produced as a full feature and will demonstrate the lifestyle aspect of the brand. The story will be a fashion feature and models will represent different races and be chosen because they look 'ordinary'. They will model casual, affordable clothes. The audience interaction page will contain Tweets, Instagram posts and texts from readers providing their own fashion tips. Some will be illustrated with images sent by the reader. The readers will be encouraged to send in their own tips, which could then be selected to feature on the site.

The brand image for the magazine and the website is that it is intelligent, knowledgeable, sometimes serious and sometimes fun. The brand is inclusive and it wants to appeal to a broad and diverse audience. The brand will use images of different races and genders but its general aesthetic will reflect a non-mainstream approach. It will use images that reflect the audience's familiarity with social media and will address them using some colloquial language and making pop-culture references. The current affairs topics will always relate to the lives of young people and the lifestyle topics will be approached from a non-mainstream perspective.

(461 words)

Audience

- Have the target audience been identified?
- Is the audience addressed appropriately?
- Does the product create audience appeal?
- Does the product encourage audience interactivity (where appropriate)?

Industry

- Has the product been created in a way that is appropriate for the distribution method?
- Does the product have a recognisable brand image?
- Does the product act to attract its audience?
- Does the product demonstrate an attempt to increase circulation?
- Does the product reflect its industrial context?
- Are the products convergent?
- Does the product meet any regulations that impact on this form?

Finally, check your finished work against the brief and the minimum requirements:

- Have you created work that responds to the tasks set in the brief?
- Does your work contain all the minimum requirements identified in the brief?

Presentation of work

After all your hard work you want to make sure that your work is presented in the best possible way, so it can be seen as you intended. You may have used specific software to make/edit your work but as it could be sent off to the exam board you should make sure it is easily accessible.

> Always check for the current advice about submission of work that will be provided by the exam board.

Audio/video: data files

You should convert any video/audio files to a universally accessible format. MP3s and MP4s are usually playable on a range of devices but .mov, .avi and .mkv are often better quality for video work.

e-media: offline submission

You should send your work in a format that means it can be accessed via a browser and not as the working file you have used in your software package. Convert your finished work to an .html file that can be sent to the exam board on a flash drive or other storage device.

Check your offline e-media work through different browsers to make sure it looks the way you want. It's also a really good idea to send some screen grabs of your e-media work with your folder just in case there are any technical difficulties accessing it.

e-media: created online

Work that is created online and cannot be exported to a flash drive may need to be submitted as a hard copy. You could print your online pages for submission. Alternatively, you could create screengrabs and submit them pasted into word processing or presentation software. If you have added video or audio material to your e-media production, this will need to be submitted as a data file. An alternative way to submit online work would be to record a 'walkthrough' using screen recording software.

Again, always check the most recent submission guidelines from the exam board.

TIP Test your production work before you submit it

- Do test prints of your print and/or online e-media work – first, in black and white so you can check your print margins and the proportions of your pages, then in colour to make sure your images, fonts and text are as you want them.

- Make sure you have tested to see if your audio/video files play properly – including any e-media walkthroughs.

- If you are submitting an off-line e-media production check that all your pages and links work properly. Does everything look the way it should? Do any multi-media elements play correctly? Do links work? It's a good idea to check e-media productions work using several browsers before submission.

Print

You should send print outs to the exam board so they can see your work in the correct format. It is always a good idea to do some test prints of your work, as it can look different on screen than on paper and you may wish to make changes before it is assessed. You should also check your print settings to make sure your work is not cut off by the printer or that the printer's margins don't impact on the way your work looks. It's also a good idea to print your work on paper that is the correct size, weight and finish for the project you are making. If you are creating pages that are an unusual shape (not A4 or A3) then you could print on bigger paper and cut your work out so it is presented at the right size and shape. For bigger pieces, you could reduce the size but keep the correct proportions to make printing easier. Do consider the quality of the print out you submit. It would be a shame if your hard work was hidden by poor quality printing.

GRETA

THE ESSENTIAL STUDENT FASHION GUIDE

SUBSCRIBE TO OUR WEEKLY EDITION STARTING AT 99p

contents

FASHION ON A BUDGET AN EXCLUSIVE WITH OUR VERY OWN KAYLEIGH COOKSON -PAGE 1

MONOCHROME IDEAS TO HAVE YOUR OWN STYLISH 'UNIFORM'-PAGE 3

5 SIMPLE STEPS TO A MINIMALIST WARDROBE -PAGE 5

BERETS ARE BACK AND YOU DON'T HAVE TO SPEND AS MUCH AS YOU THINK-PAGE 7

THE APP YOU NEED TO HAVE TO CREATE NEW COMBOS OUT OF THE CLOTHES YOU ALREADY HAVE.-PAGE 9

TOP TEN TIPS WITH JESS MOND THAT YOU DIDN'T KNOW YOU NEED - PAGE 11

NEW TRACKS FROM 'VINYL MC' THAT ARE PERFECT TO GET READY TO IN THE MORNING-PAGE 13

HOW TO KEEP YOUR SKIN SMOOTH AND CLEAN WITH LUKE DENT-PAGE 15

10 WAYS TO FIND QUALITY JACKETS ON A BUDGET-PAGE 17

FASHION ON A BUDGET

STUDENTS CAN STILL LOOK TRENDY WHEN EARNING MINIMUM WAGE.

One source gives us an insight into where you can find quality clothing without spending as much money as you would with new branded clothing. "People really underestimate what you can find in charity shops. Although its given a bad name you can find quality items for a low price and you're supporting the group you are buying from which helps someone else with little effort from yourself. The red jacket on the cover of this magazine itself was bought in a charity shop for less than £10. This goes to show how little you need to spend to provide benefits all round by saving waste, donating to charity and gaining a fresh 'garm' for yourself!" For example I can guarantee your local town or village has at least three charity shops. So reserve yourself a Saturday morning for some self care.

PAGE 1

Vintage clothing to save money and the planet by giving new life to something else!
(FY4drycleaning [EMAIL?] for more information)

GRETA // PAGE 2

MONOCHROME FASHION:
HOW TO CREATE AN EFFORTLESS WARDROBE

WHEN IT COMES TO CREATING AN EFFORTLESS WARDROBE, SOMETIMES IT'S THE SIMPLEST IDEAS THAT ARE THE BEST. THERE'S A REASON WHY CLASSICS EARN THEIR ENDURING STATUS — AND WITH MONOCHROME, IT'S EASY TO SEE WHY IT ENJOYS SUCH A HIGHLY REGARDED REPUTATION.

TEAMING BLACK AND WHITE IS AN EASY SHORTCUT TO PARED-BACK ELEGANCE. A HIGH-CONTRAST APPROACH TO GETTING DRESSED THAT CAN BE AS FORMAL OR AS LAID-BACK AS YOU LIKE.

THE SIMPLICITY OF MONOCHROME MAKES IT A TIMELESS CLASSIC, AND ONCE AGAIN IT'S SET TO DOMINATE OUR WARDROBES THIS SPRING.

IF YOU'RE WONDERING HOW TO WEAR THIS SEASON'S TREND THEN IT'S ALL HERE IN BLACK AND WHITE. WHETHER IT'S PRINTS, STRIPES OR COLOUR BLOCKING, WORKING THE MONOCHROME LOOK IS SO EASY. THERE'S NONE OF THE WORRY OF WEARING COLOURS THAT DON'T COMPLIMENT EACH OTHER. BLACK AND WHITE MAKE THE PERFECT PARTNERSHIP.

MONOCHROME IS A PERFECT COMPROMISE, OFFERING AS IT DOES THE FRESHNESS OF WHITE WITH THE SAFETY AND SECURITY OF THE INFINITELY MORE FORGIVING BLACK.

"When you photograph people in colour you photograph their clothes, but when you photograph people in black and white you photograph their souls" - Ted Grant

WHEN THE OUTFIT IS SO NICE YOU HAVE TO WEAR IT TWICE THERE'S NO NEED TO WORRY ABOUT LOOKING UNKEMPT WITH A MONOCHROME WARDROBE BY SIMPLY CHANGING ONE ITEM YOU CAN CREATE A WHOLE NEW OUTFIT TO ADD TO YOUR "UNIFORM" SO THERE IS NO NEED TO WORRY ABOUT WHAT TO WEAR THE NEXT DAY. SO YOU CAN HIT SNOOZE CARE FREE KNOWING YOUR OUTFIT IS GOING TO LOOK GOOD.

GRETA // PAGE 3

GRETA // PAGE 5

INTERVIEW:
DEIVIDAS TOLEIKIS

From London, Milan to Paris. UK-based street style photographer Deividas Toleikis has been travelling around the world to capture some of the most stylish people during fashion week. At only 19, Deividas Toleikis has worked with the likes of Vogue Japan, Glamour Russia and Storm Model Management. We at GRETA got a moment to discuss his career.

WHAT WOULD YOU CLASS YOUR TITLE AS A PHOTOGRAPHER CURRENTLY?

A fashion documenter. I'm not only a street style photographer anymore, which is super exciting as I never stop learning. It more of a way of life than a job description as corny as that sounds.

WHEN YOU STARTED DOING STREET STYLE PHOTOGRAPHY, WHAT WAS YOUR PLAN?

I started out around Liverpool just taking in the sights and people I came across. This was just for fun really. My friend was into Design, and I was more into fashion and photography.

We thought it would be great to combine our passions and create a platform where we could share our influences and our work as designer / fashion photographer. We met loads of amazing people so this hobby quickly became a full time job!

WHAT IS THE BEST THING ABOUT STREET STYLE PHOTOGRAPHY?

What I love it is that amazing energy you have from the creative people around you. On the streets in front of fashion shows, you're constantly inspired and always learning from photographer working next to you. The creative vibe is really intense. The challenge here is to be open-minded, and let your work be influenced by what is surrounding you and what you agree to include in your process! The range of amazing people I meet on a day to day basis is unreal. You get people from all walks of life, all fashion eras and all ages contributing to the work we carry out without even realising it.

GRETA // PAGE 7

GRETA // PAGE 8

Thanks to year one Media Studies students, at Runshaw College, for providing some of their in-progress production work.

Final production checklist

What have I created and who is it for?	
What did I need to achieve in terms of the instructions in the brief?	
What is the institutional context of my production?	
How have I made my product appealing for the audience?	
How effectively does the product follow the conventions of the form?	
How successful have I been in replicating or subverting the conventions of the genre I am working in?	
What representations have I created and why?	
Is the content clear?	
Have I created meaning in a clear and understandable way?	
What ideas and values are being created by my production and why?	

Analysing your practical work in this way may give you some ideas as to how to improve your production work before it is submitted and marked.

CHAPTER SUMMARY

The NEA is an important part of the assessment of the A level. You should give enough time to planning and producing your products.

This chapter offers advice and guidance on:

- Selecting your brief and making sure you meet the brief's requirements.
- Researching and planning your practical productions.
- Writing your Statement of Intent.
- Making appropriate choices in the production of your media products.
- Submitting your work for assessment.

Glossary of key terms

24-hour rolling news	digital TV channels that show only news and that broadcast 24 hours a day
acoustics	the sound qualities of a specific environment
agenda setting	theory relating mainly to news media that views the media as actively selecting certain issues and shaping public opinion of these by reporting on them more frequently
algorithms	computer technology that gathers and analyses user data
archetypes	basic, rather simple character types who appear over and over in narratives
back-light	a light positioned behind the subject
balance (page)	a balanced page has been designed to ensure that the heavy objects and lighter ones are positioned to create a harmonious feel
bardic function	the modern role of television in our lives as an aggregator of many different ideas and cultural influences
Big Data	the information gathered by digital companies on audience behaviour
billboard	a large outdoor location for advertising. Traditionally a board for the placement of print adverts but electronic billboards can be found in some locations. Electronic billboards can present all types of video material but they are often used to broadcast adverts
binge-watch	an audience activity of watching multiple episodes of a television programme in one sitting

blocking	the positioning of props and actors for a sequence that allows for specific camera moves and distances to be pre-planned
brand ambassadors	celebrities who are paid to represent a specific consumer product or service and its brand values
bricolage	a product that is made from other media texts, or borrows signs from them
broadcast	to transmit information to a mass audience, usually using radio or television technology
broadsheet	a term used for certain British newspapers that used to refer to the size of paper they were printed on but now refers to the content and approach taken in the selection and reporting of stories. Broadsheet newspapers are characterised by a focus on hard news, offering more in-depth analysis and a more global perspective than tabloid newspapers. Broadsheets do cover soft news stories but tend to analyse the issues raised rather than simply offer gossip and scandal. *The Times* and the *Guardian* are broadsheet newspapers
business model	the methods used by an organisation to generate an income and maximise its profits
busy	the effect of pages that are created with many design elements, font styles, etc. Busy pages are sometimes difficult for the reader to access and can be confusing and visually offputting
causality	the way in which the events, usually driven by the desires and motivations of characters and the events that impact on them, drive the logic of a narrative forwards

circulation	the act of getting media products to an audience
citizen journalism	information, images and videos used in news reporting that have been sourced from members of the public
clawback	the way in which television can give a sense of recognition of the self and cultural identity, our experience of our culture
clickbait	stories and headlines that are constructed to encourage audiences to click through to access more information. Clickbait usually attempts to create an emotional response
cognitive surplus	the way in which people globally now use their free time to develop collaborative online projects
collective identity	sense of ownership of media representations and fandoms or the sense of belonging to a sector of a media audience
colour tone	the properties of colour – its shade, hue, warmth, brightness, saturation, etc.
columns	a way to organise text and images on the page by dividing the page vertically
commercial television	television companies whose primary income source is from advertising
commercialisation	the practice of running an institution or creating media products specifically with an aim to generate financial gain
commodification	to turn something into something that can be sold
conditions of consumption	a wide range of factors that can affect how a media text is interpreted by the audience, both in terms of ideological reception and physical consumption practices
consensus	a state of agreement

constructed identity	the view that the mass media constructs identities in the representations it offers us	
consumer culture	a model of culture where the audience receives texts but does not 'interact' with them	
content providers	individuals, groups or organisation who create the content of media products; they may or may not be media producers	
continuity/ continuity editing	the creation of logical and/or visual coherence and consistency	
convergence	the use of different technologies and/or platforms to produce and distribute media products	
copyright	the legal ownership of the content of media products	
correspondents	journalists who have a specialisation (e.g. war correspondent) or who serve a specific location (e.g. a Westminster correspondent)	
crowdsourcing	obtaining information from a large number of people	
cultivation differential	how much someone's world view and perception of their social reality aligns with television is based on their level of consumption	
cultural absolutism/racial essentialism	the linking of a person's cultural and racial heritage to a place of national or ethnic origin	
cultural capital	the ability to mix in higher levels of society because education has given you qualifications, ownership of cultural products or access to works of culture	
cultural categories	a way of understanding genre labels as products of both industry and audience	
cultural industries	the industries that are involved in the production, distribution and circulation of cultural artefacts, including media products	

cultural poverty	social condition where consumers may have access to material goods and high-status technological gadgetry, but little connection with traditional cultural capital in the way in which these devices are used	
cultural relativism	the idea that we tend to judge other cultures based on the values and ideologies of our own	
cultural syncretism	the blending of different influences to form a new means of expression	
cumulative effects theory	collective term for audience theories that consider longer-term exposure to media texts	
dangling cause	an action, event or motif the inclusion of which remains unclear until later in the narrative	
dead spot	an area created by local acoustics where sound is reduced in volume or flattened in tone	
demotic turn	the appearance by ordinary people in mainstream media	
design elements	the individual parts that combine together to construct a page	
diaspora	a scattering or spread of people	
digital divide	the term used to describe the fact that there are disparities in power between those who have access to digital technologies and those who don't	
digital immigrant	the older generation who have had to acquire the skills to participate in the digital world more consciously	
digital native	community of media users who have grown up with the internet	
discourse	an academic discussion or debate about a subject embodying a range of perspectives around a similar subject	
distortion	the phenomenon by which the way the media usually represents women's lives does not reflect the reality of many real women	

distribution	methods used to make media products available	
diversification	the act of producing different products or targeting different markets	
double consciousness	two aspects of black experience; living within a predominantly white culture and having an aspect of identity rooted somewhere else	
DTP	a commonly used abbreviation for desktop publishing that refers to software specifically designed to support the design and publication of print and, in some cases, e-media production	
dub	to add sound elements to recorded images	
early adopters	individuals who take advantage of technological developments before they become mainstream	
echo-chamber	the phenomenon caused by audiences limiting their media experiences to products and locations that reinforce their existing beliefs and values	
edit (moving image/audio)	the arranging of images or sound to create a coherent visual or audio sequence	
editorial position	the political values that influence the way a media product is constructed	
editorial stance	the political and/or ideological position of a newspaper that influences the way stories are reported	
embodied cultural capital	the acquired knowledge of culture experienced and outwardly presented by a person	
end of audience theory	changes in the way in which we conceptualise audiences and understand how we should even define audience	
enunciative productivity	sharing the meanings and ways of talking about the text – 'fanspeak' and wearing clothing, or styling hair or make-up in a particular way	

event television	television shows that attract large audiences and are reported on extensively. They may be one-off events (e.g. a royal wedding), a regularly scheduled event (e.g. the Olympics) or a specific episode of a popular programme
expository mode	style of documentary featuring heavy use of narration in the form of a voice-over
fake news	fictional or misleading stories that are presented as news
false consciousness	the belief in ideas that are not based in fact
female gaze	the subversion of the male gaze in which men become the subject to be looked at by women
fetishistic scopophilia	an obsessive love of looking at women
fluidity of identity	the concept that people do not have a fixed identity which is wholly and permanently a part of them
fly-on-the-wall documentaries	documentaries that follow subjects, usually with handheld cameras, to construct a realistic view of the context of someone's lived experience
font	the design of the letters used within a specific typeface. Fonts have pre-defined proportions, weight and style. All letters and numbers within a font will be designed to harmonise
framing	a news story's bias and the way in which it is read by the audience according to their own interests and situation
free markets	trading based on unrestricted competition between private companies
gatekeepers	individuals and groups who have the ability to select (and reject) the content of media products
genres of order and integration	systems of genre categorization that foregrounds the social and cultural uses of genre and classes them as essentially male or female

globalisation	the economic and/or technological removal of nation state boundaries
habitus	the way in which a person has been socialised and interacts with the world according to their education, social class, etc.
hard news	news that is related to politics, economics, science, war, terrorism, etc.
head and shoulders shot	a shot where the camera is positioned close to a human subject so that the frame excludes all of the body, apart from the head and shoulders
headline	the heading given to a news story, presented in a larger font
high-key lighting	the use of light fills to create a low-contrast lighting effect
hyperreality	merging of the real and media worlds to the point where it is difficult to distinguish between them
idents	sounds used to identify the programme, radio station or brand. This could be a jingle or a theme tune
ideological reading	a conclusion that aims to expose how power relationships between social groups operate and manifest themselves in cultural production
implosion	the media's constant recycling of itself and its signs
in-camera	decisions made to influence the look of images while shooting with the camera. This includes using camera settings as well as using external sources such as music, props and lighting to create specific effects
Influencers	people who have the power to lead others and sway their opinions and actions. It is now a marketing term that describes individuals who have large numbers of followers on social media, have gained a level of authority and are trusted by their followers. Influencers can communicate with large numbers of people and this means they are able to spread ideas and promote products

instafamous	refers to people who have generated lots of followers on Instagram but who may not be visible on other social media or via traditional media
institutionalised cultural capital	recognised qualifications that symbolise someone's worth in terms of cultural capital
intellectual property	the ownership of ideas, creative productions, artistic works, etc.
intercuts	to insert shots from other locations or narrative lines including flashbacks and flashforwards
interpellation	the normalisation in media texts of certain ways of thinking, attitudes and values so powerfully that they become part of a person's identity
intersectionality	the acknowledgement that issues of power relating to gender, race and social class all intersect
invisible editing	an editing style that appears natural to the viewer, usually exemplified by straight cuts
IPSO	the Independent Press Standards Organisation
lead story	the main story presented on the first page of a newspaper
Leveson report	the report on press behaviour and practices published after the Leveson Inquiry, which was set up after accusations that some newspapers were using illegal methods to gather information for stories
licensed for broadcast	the selling of a programme to be broadcast by another organisation or in another country
light fills	a light used to reduce the contrast between light and shadow within the frame
lipstick feminism	a brand of third wave feminism that allows women to portray themselves as equal to men in terms of their sexuality by expressing it in any way they choose

lip-sync (synchronisation)	matching the lip movements of a moving image production to words recorded on a separate sound track – or recording the silent lip movements of an actor replicating prerecorded dialogue or singing
long tail effect/ theory	in marketing, the idea that increased accessibility to media for a longer duration due to changes in distribution mechanisms means a product can continue to be consumed beyond its previous marketable shelf-life
low-key lighting	a style of lighting used to create shadow and areas of bright light within the frame
male gaze	describes the way we all are conventionally positioned to look at women in film in an inferior, and often sexualised, way
mass amateurisation	state of the media today, where professionally made media that was consumed by audiences in a fairly simple model no longer predominates
mass consumption	the use of a media product by many people, usually within a restricted timeframe
masterplot	an overarching group of bare narrative elements that are meaningful to a particular culture
masthead	the title of a newspaper, presented at the top of the first page
media literacy	the level of awareness of the audience about factors affecting the production of meaning in media texts
media regulation	laws and rules that govern the production, distribution and circulation of media products
middle-market tabloid	British newspapers that offer hard news and soft news. They offer more sensation and gossip than broadsheets and more hard news than tabloids. The *Daily Mail* and the *Express* are middle-market tabloids

mise-en-scène (m-e-s)	everything that can be seen within the scene – set design, props, performance, lighting, costume and make-up, location and lighting
monopoly	when one corporation dominates the provision of a specific product or service so there is no choice for the consumer
mytheme	small unit of myths that Lévi-Strauss identified in the traditional stories of tribes he studied
narrowcast	to transmit information to a localised, niche or specialised audience and to offer choices regarding the timing of access o this information
naturalisation	the belief that an idea is a natural state rather than a human construction
negotiated identity	ways in which we negotiate the various influences on our composite identities – how we perceive ourselves in relation to others
news agencies	organisations that receive and distribute news
news agenda	the prioritising of selected events when planning the news
niche audience	an audience who has a shared any specialist interest
non-verbal communication	methods of communication that do not include words. Body language and modes of dress are both examples
objectified cultural capital	a cultural artefact that confers status on the person who owns it
observational mode	style of documentary where events appear to simply unfold as we watch
opinion leaders	people who have the ability to communicate their opinions to others and may influence opinions
orientalism	prejudiced Western view of other cultures, which defines them as inferior
outro	the concluding piece of a recording
page proportions	the size of the page and the relationship between its height and length

pan	a horizontal camera movement where the camera remains on a fixed point
paparazzi	a professional photographer who seeks to capture informal images of celebrities or other people identified as being newsworthy
parallax design	a graphics technique where separate elements scroll at different rates on the screen, making the resulting text feel as though it has more depth
participatory gap	the effect of economic poverty, in particular, producing a divide in access to digital culture and the information age
participatory media	media that allows not only interaction but also contribution by audience members, blurring the traditional distinction between audience, producer and even 'text'
participatory mode	style of documentary where the filmmaker is a visible part of the narrative and has a role to play within it
pastiche	the making of a new media text from components of another
PBS	public service broadcaster – television companies whose main income stream comes from public money or investments
performative mode	style of documentary similar to participatory but frequently more emotive
personal brand	the constructed image created by an individual in order to create an identifiable and specific 'personality' with a view to help promote the individual
photojournalist	professional photographer who uses images to tell a story
play-through	a video of gameplay often with live commentary from the player(s)
postcolonial theory	the study of the many ways in which the legacy of colonialism affects race representations

post-network television	the culture of television viewing that no longer relies on traditional broadcast methods
post-production	decisions made to influence the look of images after the footage or images have been captured. This is usually done using post-production software
potential reach	the possible extent of the circulation of a media product
PR	stands for public relations – this is the professional management of a public image. PR professionals work for companies, public organisations, brands and individuals and work to control the way their clients are reported on and, therefore, perceived
precession of the simulacra	the series of stages between simulacrum and simulation
press release	a summary of information or an official statement given to journalists
production	the manufacture of media products
prosumer	media producer who spans the categories of both audience and producer of media texts in variable proportions
public domain	relates to media products/ ideas that are outside the restrictions of copyright law and are freely available to the public
queer theory	critical approach that explores LGBT perspectives on culture and the media
raunch culture	specifically associated with music video but with cultural resonance seen elsewhere – the overt sexualisation of female artists
real persona	the star's image outside of role, often also highly managed and constructed
reel persona	the sum of all the 'roles' an audience member has seen a star perform in

regulation	a term used to cover the legal and/or voluntary rules that are used to offer guidance and, in some cases, control the actions and output of media producers
semiotic productivity	the meanings made from the source texts by the fan
shadow cultural economy	the space in which fan culture exists
shareholders	groups or individuals who are part owners of a company, as they have invested money by buying shares
shooting script	the written text of a video/ film product including details of the use of camera in individual scenes
shot list	a descriptive list of the shots required for a moving image production
simulacrum	state of semiotics where a sign no longer refers to any original meaning, but to other signs, like a hall of mirrors
simulation	end product of the precession of the simulacra. In the simulation we no longer perceive any difference between representation and reality
sound-bed	sounds, sound effects and/ or music that plays below the main content of an audio production. Sound beds can communicate narrative information such as location or they can create a tone or atmosphere for the production
spoiler	articles and discussions that give away plot developments
subheading	a heading for a subsection of an article
SVoD	streaming video-on-demand
synergy	the way different media products can act to promote one another

tabloid newspaper	a term used for certain British newspapers that used to refer to the size of paper they were printed on but now refers to the content and approach taken in the selection and reporting of stories. Tabloid newspapers are characterised by their reliance on soft news and entertainment over hard news. Tabloid newspapers often use a sensationalist style when reporting and focus on human interest stories, scandal and gossip. The *Sun* and the *Daily Mirror* are tabloid newspapers
teaser (newspapers/ magazines)	a brief indication of the content within the publication. Used to encourage the reader to purchase the publication to be able to read further
textual poaching	the act of reappropriating a cultural product which may result in new meanings
textual productivity	fan-made texts as sense of ownership of the source text
transnational	working across national borders
transnationality	in the case of text, having a presence or value that crosses cultural and geographical divides
TV-MA	programmes produced for adult audiences
ultra HD	high-quality digital images
unique users	the separate and individual visitors to a website
'walk and talk' selfie shot	the shot used in many lifestyle social media videos, where the subject speaks into a camera held at arm's length. The camera is usually positioned at a slightly elevated angle
watershed	an agreed time (9.00pm in the UK) that restricts when adult content is broadcast

weight (visual)	a term used to refer to the effect of the depth, darkness and/or intensity of a design element. Large, dark, textured and warm-coloured elements tend to appear 'heavier' – they have more visual weight. Elements in the foreground or higher on the page tend to appear heavy on the page as do regular shapes and vertical (rather than horizontal) objects. Images of things that are actually heavy also have weight on the page

Glossary of key thinkers

bell hooks	(1952–) an important contemporary American feminist and social activist, bell hooks has written extensively about issues relating not only to gender representation but also its connections with race and social class, so is considered an important thinker on intersectionality
Clay Shirky	(1964–) Shirky is an influential contemporary thinker who specialises in the field of how digital media and communications may be shaping our society. He has written and lectured extensively about the new dynamic between media producers and audiences
David Gauntlett	(1971–) Gauntlett is a British writer and academic who was well-known for his influential exploration of a range of critical approaches to reading gender and identity in media texts, as well as contributing his own research into the field to test out some established ideas

Edward Said	(1935–2003) Palestinian-American postcolonial theorist whose ideas about how we perceive the Orient in the West transformed cultural studies in the second part of the 20th century
Henry Jenkins	(1958–) Jenkins is a notable contemporary American academic theorist whose work has focused on fandoms and participatory culture, as well as the impact of digital connectivity on society and the cultural artifacts it produces
Jean Baudrillard	(1929–2007) French philosopher who contributed the key ideas of simulacra, simulation and hyperreality often debated in relation to postmodern thinking. Baudrillard is sometimes also regarded as a post-structuralist thinker because of his interest in semiotics and new ways of understanding how signs are interrelated in a complex web of meanings

Judith Butler	(1956–) American feminist and author of Gender Trouble: Feminism and the Subversion of Identity who is well known for her theory of gender and performativity
Liesbet van Zoonen	(1959–) Dutch author of feminist media studies, van Zoonen developed a wide-ranging theory of the importance of looking at all aspects of media production and content in exploring representations of women
Paul Gilroy	(1956–) Gilroy is a contemporary British cultural theorist who writes about race relations in the UK and US

Further reading and references

Advanced Television (2017, 24 May) 'EU Sets 30% Content Quota for European SVoD', http://advanced-television.com/2017/05/24/eu-sets-30-content-quota-for-european-svod/.

Anderson, C. (2004) 'The Long Tail', www.wired.com/2004/10/tail/.

Barthes, R. (2009) *Mythologies*.

Baudrillard, J. (1981) *Simulacra and Simulation*.

BBC News (2017, 23 October) 'UK Diver Swims to Safety after Australia Shark Scare', www.bbc.co.uk/news/world-australia-41717024.

BBC Newsbeat (2015, 9 October) '*EastEnders* Cast Transgender Actor in Transgender Role on UK Television', www.bbc.co.uk/newsbeat/article/34479713/eastenders-casts-transgenderactor-in-transgender-role-on-uk-television.

BBC Trust (2016) BBC Four, www.bbc.co.uk/bbctrust/our_work/services/television/service_licences/bbc_four.html.

BBC Trust (2018) Public Purposes and Purpose Remits, www.bbc.co.uk/bbctrust/governance/tools_we_use/public_purposes.html.

Butler, J. (1999) *Gender Trouble: Feminism and the Subversion of Identity*.

Cahoone, L.E. (2003) *From Modernism to Postmodernism: An Anthology*.

Carr, D. (2013, 25 January) 'Giving Viewers What They Want', www.nytimes.com/2013/02/25/business/media/for-house-of-cards-using-bigdata-to-guarantee-its-popularity.html.

Castillo, M. (2017, 31 May) 'Netflix is Spending $6 Billion on Content this Year and "a Lot More" in Future, CEO Says', www.cnbc.com/2017/05/31/netflix-spending-6-billion-on-content-in-2017-ceo-reed-hastings.html.

Cbronline.com (2018, 26 September) 'Smartphone Penetration Now More than 80% in UK', www.cbronline.com/verticals/etail/smartphone-uk/.

Cohen, S. (1972) *Folk Devils and Moral Panic*.

Comor, E. (2010) 'Digital Prosumption and Alienation', *Ephemera*, 10(3), 439–454.

Constine, J. (2016, 21 December) 'Zuckerberg Implies Facebook is a Media Company, Just "Not a Traditional Media Company"', techcrunch, https://techcrunch.com/2016/12/21/fbonc/.

Cookson, R. (2016, 10 April) 'UK Publishers Look to Consolidate in Print Battle', *Financial Times*, www.ft.com/content/2f0fa2ec-fc9e-11e5-b5f5-070dca6d0a0d.

Delwiche, A. & Jacobs Henderson, J. (2012) *The Participatory Cultures Handbook*.

Digital News Report (2018) 'Overview', www.digitalnewsreport.org/.

Dyer, R. (1998) *Stars*.

Eagleton, T. (1991) *Ideology: An Introduction*.

end_of_audiences_theoretical_echoes_of_reception_amid_the_uncertainties_of_use.

Fenton, G. (2009, 28 October) *The Media Show*, BBC Radio 4.

Fiske, J. (1987) *Television Culture*.

Fiske, J. (1992) 'The Cultural Economy of Fandom', in Lisa A. Lewis (ed.), *The Adoring Audience: Fan Culture and Popular Media*.

Gauntlett, D. (2008) *Media, Gender, Identity: An Introduction*.

Gauntlett, D. (2017, 6 July) '"Theories of Identity" in the New Media Studies A & AS Level', http://davidgauntlett.com/making-media-studies/theories-of-identity-new-media-studies-a-aslevel/.

Gilchrist, M.M. (2010, 1 September) 'The Sad Disappearance of Foreign TV', *Guardian*, www.theguardian.com/commentisfree/2010/sep/01/saddisappearance-foreign-tv.

Gillmor, D. (2004) *We the Media: Grassroots Journalism by the People, for the People*.

Gilroy, P. (1993) *The Black Atlantic: Modernity and Double Consciousness*.

Gilroy, P. (2002) *There Ain't no Black in the Union Jack: The Cultural Politics of Race and Nation*.

Gledhill, C. (2013) 'Genre and Gender: The Case of Soap Opera', in S. Hall (ed.) *Representation: Cultural Representation and Signifying Practices*.

Goldberg, M. (2016, 23 June) 'Exclusive: New "Star Trek" Showrunner Bryan Fuller on Progressiveness, Number of Episodes, Filming Details, and Much More', Collider, http://collider.com/new-star-trek-series-details/.

Goode, E. & Nehuda, B. (1994) *Moral Panics: The Social Construction of Deviance*.

Greenslade, R. (2017, 24 March) 'Am I Alone in Viewing Media Coverage of Westminster Murderer as Disproportionate?', twitter.com/GreensladeR/status/845213916254887937?tfw_creator=NBCNews&tfw_site=NBCNews&ref_src=twsrc%5Etfw&ref_url=https%3A%2F%2Fwww.nbcnews.com%2Fstoryline%2Flondon-parliamentattack%2Flondon-parliament-attack-mediacoverage-triggers-criticism-britain-n738091.

Guardian (2013, 23 May) 'Firestorm', www.theguardian.com/world/interactive/2013/may/26/firestorm-bushfire-dunalley-holmesfamily.

Hall, S. (2013) *Representation: Cultural Representation and Signifying Practices*.

Heritage, S. (2017, 14 July) 'What Happened, Netflix? You Were King of the Hill – Now You're Circling the Drain', *Guardian*, www.theguardian.com/tv-and-radio/2017/jul/14/what-happened-netflixyou-were-king-of-the-hill-now-youre-circling-thedrain.

Herrman, J. (2016, 17 April) 'Media Websites Battle Faltering Ad Revenue and Traffic', *The New York Times*, www.nytimes.com/2016/04/18/business/media-websites-battle-falteringadrevenue-and-traffic.html.

Hesmondhalgh, D. (2012) *The Cultural Industries*.

hooks, b. (1997) 'Cultural Criticism & Transformation', www.mediaed.org/transcripts/Bell-Hooks-Transcript.pdf.

IPSO (2016) *Editors' Code of Practice*, www.ipso.co.uk/editors-code-of-practice/#Privacy.

IPSO (2017) 01032-17 Ward v The Mail on Sunday, www.ipso.co.uk/rulings-and-resolutionstatements/.

Jenkins. H. (1992) 'Textual Poachers: Television Fans and Participatory Culture', *Journal of Fandom Studies*, 2(1), http://williamwolff.org/wp-content/uploads/2015/01/lbennett_1-libre.pdf.

Jenkins, H. (2008) *Convergence Culture: Where Old and New Media Collide*.

Jenkins, H., Ito, M. & boyd, dana (2016) *Participatory Culture in a Networked Era*.

Jenkins, S. (2017, 24 March) 'Media Hype About the Westminster Attack Will Only Encourage Others', *Guardian*, www.theguardian.com/commentisfree/2017/mar/24/coverage-westminster-attack-media-politicians.

Jones, H.D. (2014, 12 November) 'The Circulation and Reception of Foreign-Language European Films in the UK', paper presented at the TFTV Departmental Research Seminar, University of York, http://mecetes.co.uk/wp-content/uploads/2015/06/Jones-Circulation-and-Reception-of-NNE-films-in-UK.pdf

Katz, E. & Lazarsfeld, P.F. (2005) *Personal Influence: The Part Played by People in the Flow of Mass Communications*.

Lévi-Strauss, C. (1974) *Structural Anthropology*.

Levy, A. (2006) *Female Chauvinist Pigs: Women and the Rise of Raunch Culture*.

Lewis, P. (2017, 6 October) '"Our Minds can be Hijacked": The Tech Insiders who Fear a Smartphone Dystopia', *Guardian*, www.theguardian.com/technology/2017/oct/05/smartphone-addiction-silicon-valley-dystopia.

Livingstone, S. & Das, R. (2009) 'The End of Audience? Theoretical Echoes of Reception and the Uncertainties of Use', paper presented at 'Transforming Audiences', University of Westminster, 3–4 September, www.researchgate.net/publication/292135601_The_ruling/?id=01032-17

Loughrey, C. (2017, 2 May) 'Netflix Adds Warnings to 13 Reasons Why After Backlash', *The Independent*, www.independent.co.uk/artsentertainment/tv/news/13-reasons-why-netflixwarnings-criticism-backlash-portrayal-of-suicideparental-controls-a7712696.html.

Lunt, P. & Livingstone, S. (2012) *Media Regulation: Governance and the Interests of Citizens and Consumers.*

Marx, K. (1867) *Das Kapital, Vol. 1, Section 1.*

McCombs. M.E. & Shaw, D.L. (1972) 'The Agenda-Setting Function of Mass Media', *Public Opinion Quarterly*, 36(2), 176–187.

McLuhan, M. (1964) *Understanding Media.*

Mulvey, L. (1975) 'Visual Pleasure and Narrative Cinema', *Screen*, 16(3), 6–18.

Neuman, W.R. & Guggenheim, L. (2011) 'The Evolution of Effects Theory: A Six-Stage Model of Cumulative Research', *Communication Theory*, 21(2), 169–196.

Nichols, B. (1991) *Representing Reality: Issues and Concepts in Documentary.*

O'Halloran, K. (2017, 23 October) '"Hey Dude, Do This": The Last Resort for Female Gamers Escaping Online Abuse', *Guardian* www.theguardian.com/culture/2017/oct/24/heydude-do-this-the-last-resort-for-female-gamersescaping-online-abuse.

Ofcom (2017, 3 April) 'Section One: Protecting the Under-Eighteens', www.ofcom.org.uk/tv-radio-andon-demand/broadcast-codes/broadcast-code/section-one-protecting-under-eighteens.

Office for National Statistics (2017) 'Internet Users in the UK: 2017', www.ons.gov.uk/businessindustryandtrade/itandinternetindustry/bulletins/internetusers/2017.

Perkins, T. (1997) 'Rethinking Stereotypes', in T. O'Sullivan & Y. Jewkes (eds) *The Media Studies Reader.*

Rigby, S. (2011) *Glued to Games: How Video Games Draw Us In and Hold Us Spellbound.*

Rose, D. (2017, 4 February) 'IPSO Adjudication Upheld against MoS Climate Article', *Daily Mail*, www.dailymail.co.uk/sciencetech/article-4192182/World-leaders-duped-manipulated-globalwarming-data.html.

Said, E. (1978) *Orientalism.*

Schatz, T. (1981) *Hollywood Genres: Formulas, Filmmaking and the Studio System.*

Sherwood, H. (2017, 19 October) 'My Week as a Muslim Documentary Sparks Racism Row', *Guardian*, www.theguardian.com/media/2017/oct/19/my-week-as-a-muslim-documentarysparks-racism-row.

Shirky, C. (2008) *Here Comes Everybody: The Power or Organising Without Organisations.*

Shirky, C. (2010) *Cognitive Surplus: How Technology Makes Consumers into Collaborators.*

Smith, T. (2016, 6 November) 'Common Explains Decision to Release "Black American Again" Right before Election Day', hnhh, www.hotnewhiphop.com/common-explains-his-decision-to-releaseblack-america-again-before-election-daynews.25254.html.

Sullivan, J. (2012) *Media Audiences.*

Sweney, M. (2014, 23 February) 'Netflix Gathers Detailed Viewer Data to Guide its Search for the Next Hit, www.theguardian.com/media/2014/feb/23/netflix-viewer-data-house-of-cards.

Sweney, M. (2017, 18 July) 'Netflix Tops 100m Subscribers as it Draws Worldwide Audience', *Guardian*, www.theguardian.com/media/2017/jul/18/netflix-tops-100m-subscribersinternational-customers-sign-up.

Tate, G. (2016, 2 January) 'How Foreign TV Drama Became de Rigueur with UK Reviewers', *Guardian*, www.theguardian.com/tv-andradio/2016/jan/02/foreign-tv-drama-bbcchannel4-netflix.

Tobias, R. (2012) *20 Masterplots: And How to Build Them.*

Turner, G. (2010) *Ordinary People and the Media: The Demotic Turn.*

UNESCO (1982, 22 January) *Grunwald Declaration on Media Education*, www.unesco.org/education/pdf/MEDIA_E.PDF.

USA Today (2014, 5 February) 'Top 10 Internet-Censored Countries', www.usatoday.com/story/news/world/2014/02/05/top-ten-internetcensors/5222385/.

van Zoonen, L. (1994) *Feminist Media Studies.*

Williams, Z. (2017, 26 April) 'Netflix's *13 Reasons Why* and the Trouble with Dramatising Suicide', *Guardian*, www.theguardian.com/tv-andradio/2017/apr/26/netflix-13-reasons-why-suicide.

Wollaston, S. (2017, 9 November) 'Detectorists Review: More Tender Comedy About Men, Middle Age and Metal-Detecting', *Guardian*, www.theguardian.com/tv-and-radio/2017/nov/09/detectorists-review-third-series-tender-comedymen-middle-age-metal-detecting.

Zuckerberg, M. (2016, 13 November) www.facebook.com/zuck/posts/10103253901916271.

Index

13 Reasons Why 124–126

24 Hours in A&E 40

24-hour rolling news 78, 109–110, 114

A

A Series of Unfortunate Events 7

acoustics 223, 228

active audience theories 73

advertising 6, 9, 17, 19–20, 27, 36, 38, 48, 53–54, 57, 66, 68, 78, 80–81, 88, 93, 99–100, 103, 105, 112–113, 115–120, 126, 129, 131–132, 134, 136–138, 140, 158, 171, 174, 197, 207, 211–212, 214, 231, 234, 238, 242

agenda setting 73, 77–80, 97–98

algorithms 110, 112–114, 121

'All That We Share' 36

alternative media 21, 63, 192–194

Althusser, Louis 13, 33, 52

American Gods 16–17

The Archers 20, 104

archetypes 14–15, 21, 31, 57–58

Arctic Monkeys 101–102, 116

audience

    engagement 179–180, 189, 232

    participation 17, 81, 88–89, 91, 93, 135, 195, 203, 231;
        also see participatory media

    theory 73, 94, 97, 202

audio

    codes 7–8

    production 228–230

augmented reality 18, 27, 30

B

back-light 224, 228

bardic function 77, 80, 98

Barthes, Roland 6, 9–10, 13–14, 30–31, 43, 112, 161

Baudrillard, Jean 27–31, 167

BBC 42, 60, 75, 78–79, 85–86, 101, 104, 107–108, 110, 112, 115, 120–121, 126, 135, 144, 171–175, 177–179, 203

BBC4 .... 85–86, 171–179

Big Data 121, 126

billboard 207–209, 214, 238

binge-watch 107, 121–122, 126, 189

binary opposition 9–10, 12–14, 31, 196, 199

Black Mirror 30

Bourdieu, Pierre 84–85, 87, 90–91, 98, 175, 203

brand ambassador 117, 119

bricolage 27, 30–31, 148, 154, 236

brief

    researching 238–249

    selecting 237

    working with 237–238

broadcast 11, 17, 24, 40, 42, 60, 67, 78, 81, 101–102, 104, 106, 108–112, 114, 119–126, 147, 171–175, 178–179, 193, 214, 221, 225, 234

broadsheet 132, 147, 207, 209, 211, 214–215

business model 105–106, 108, 114, 120, 123, 192, 195

Butler, Judith 51–52, 55–56, 63–64, 161, 204

C

cable .... see satellite/cable channels

Cahoone, Lawrence 25

camerawork 7, 12, 39

causality 14, 21, 31

celebrity endorsement 44, 66

Channel 4 .... 24, 40, 42, 79, 104, 115,
121, 126, 171–173, 175

character 7, 14–16, 20–21, 28,
40–42, 49, 55–56, 59–61,
72, 77, 92, 105, 107–108,
125–126, 144, 159–161,
164–168, 172, 175, 178,
181, 183–192, 216, 218,
224–225, 232

Chomsky, Noam 23, 33

citizen journalism 8, 95, 111–112, 114, 130

Citizen Khan 60–61

clawback 77, 80

clickbait 112, 114, 134, 147

climate change 21, 37–38

close-up 7–8, 12, 49, 116–117,
165, 187, 216, 218–219,
221, 225, 227

cognitive surplus 96–97

Cohen, Stanley 74, 97, 156

collective identity 84, 87, 94, 98,
105, 163, 204

colour

    codes 58, 159

    tone 217, 219

colour, use of 7, 58, 145, 150, 154,
159, 182–183, 185, 212–215,
217, 219, 222, 224, 226,
241–242

    editing 219, 226

columns 140–142, 144–145,
201, 206, 209–214, 242

comics 18, 89–90, 107–108, 130, 158

commercial television 85, 120, 126

commercialisation/commercialism ... 100, 102,
197

commodification 30, 38, 51, 62, 88,
100–102, 112, 159,
205, 236

compositional balance 209–210

conditions of consumption 78, 80, 94

consensus 74, 104, 112, 114

conservative views/politics 11, 22–24,
41, 76, 78, 110, 112,
115, 132, 139, 155, 202

constitutive otherness 25, 30

constructed identity 83, 87, 98

construction/constructionist 25, 31, 33–35,
53, 55, 82, 84, 114,
154, 167–168, 215

consumer culture 87, 90, 93, 197

content providers 18, 100–102, 116,
120, 132, 176

continuity 37, 223, 227–228

convergent 99, 235, 237, 245

copyright 111, 114, 227

correspondent 109, 114

counter-representation 38

countertypes 32, 35, 53, 156

crime drama 27, 173, 175, 179–184,
188–189, 191

crowdsourcing 130, 147

cultivation

    differential 76, 80

    theory 35, 66, 73–74, 76–77, 97–98

cultural

    absolutism 61, 63

    capital 84–87, 89–92, 98, 139,
175, 179–180, 196, 203

    categories 17, 21

    change 19, 31

    codes 10, 14, 199

    hegemony ... 23, 31, 41, 52, 73, 192–193

    imperialism 32, 43, 60

    industries 99–102

    myth 33, 43, 75, 77, 199

    poverty 87

    relativism 43, 46

    syncretism 61, 63

cumulative effects theory 73, 80

Cyrus, Miley 51, 118

D

Daily Mail 79, 103, 111–112,
129–130, 132–147, 211

dangling cause 14, 21

dead spots 223, 228

decoding 6, 8, 21, 30, 33,
52, 79, 98, 204

deconstruction 13

demographics 32, 65, 68, 81,
137–139, 163, 177

demotic turn 38–39, 46, 63

design elements 207–209, 211, 214, 242

diaspora 61–64, 155

diegetic 7–8, 36, 185–186, 223

digital

    divide 101–102

    download 105–106, 123

    immigrants 94, 97

    media/video 6, 8, 18–19, 31, 39,
44, 49, 51, 53, 65–69,
71–72, 76, 87, 90–91,
94–95, 97–99, 101–102,
105–108, 110, 112, 115–116,
123, 130–131, 172–174, 178,
193–196, 198, 235, 244

    native 94, 97, 195

    production 115–116

discourse 47, 51–52, 58, 113,
155–156, 168–169, 179

Disney 30, 107

disruption 9, 143, 161, 184–185

distortion 27–28, 52–53, 58

diversification 68, 101–102, 109, 236

documentary 8, 11–12, 28, 38–40,
42–43, 46, 63, 120,
148, 167, 174, 178,
226, 228

    modes 39–40

dominant reading 79, 92

double consciousness 61–64, 155

DTP (desktop publishing) ... 91, 206–207, 214

dub 176, 225, 228

Dyer, Richard 32, 39, 43–46, 84

E

e-media production 231–232
early adopters 101–102
EastEnders 40, 42, 122
echo-chamber 112–114
editorial positions 110, 114
embodied cultural capital 84, 87
encoding 11, 33, 52, 79, 92, 98, 204
end of audience theory 94–97
enunciative productivity 89, 93
equilibrium 8–10, 31, 162, 184
event television 123, 126
expository mode 39, 46
externally sourced light 7
extreme close-up (ECU) 7, 49, 218–219

F

Facebook 72, 108, 111–114, 132,
                                    134–135, 157
fake news 112–114
false consciousness 112, 114
fetishistic scopophilia 49, 58
female gaze 49, 58
feminist theory/feminism 47–50, 52, 55, 58,
                                    61, 63–64, 199
'Find your Magic' 57
Firestorm 8–9
Fiske, John 77, 84, 88–90, 98, 203
fluidity of identity 83, 87, 98, 203
fly-on-the-wall documentary 28, 116, 119
folk devil 74, 76, 97, 156
fonts 210–211
framing (content) 37, 43, 73, 77–80, 97–98
framing (shot) 7, 216–219, 221, 224
free market 100, 124, 126, 131
front cover 68–69, 164, 194, 198–199,
                                    212–214, 241–243

G

game walkthroughs 19, 88, 157, 245
Gap Kids advert 80
gatekeepers 111, 114, 193
Gauntlett, David 23, 32, 47, 81–84,
                                    97–98, 163, 202, 204
genre
    and change 17–20
    conventions 17, 21, 215, 220
    of integration 20–21, 31
    of order 20–21, 31
gender 14–15, 35–36, 41–42,
                                    48–58, 63–65, 68–69,
                                    81, 83, 89, 97, 168–169,
                                    178, 183, 190–191, 198,
                                    201–204, 236
    and crime drama 190–191
    discourse 168
    and gaming 168–169
    identity 49, 53, 83, 201–204
    performativity 63
    representation 41–42, 51–58, 63–64
    roles 48, 57, 168–169
Gerbner, George 35, 74, 76, 97, 112, 188
Giants of the Ocean 40
Gillmor, Dan 95, 98
Gilroy, Paul 61–64, 155
Gledhill, Christine 41
globalisation 18, 30, 32, 43, 60, 66,
                                    100, 102, 124, 172, 236
gossip magazines 44, 212–213
Gramsci, Antonio 23, 33, 52
gratifications 20, 43, 67, 73, 84,
                                    122–123, 125, 161–162,
                                    178–179, 188–189, 202
Green & Black's Velvet Edition
    advertisement 9–10
Guardian 8–9, 37–38, 43, 71, 79,
                                    103, 110, 121, 126, 135,
                                    147, 172, 175, 179–180

H

habitus 84, 87, 98

Hall, Stuart 32–33, 79, 155

hand-held camera 12, 117, 223, 226

hard news 112, 114, 130, 132–133,
141, 145, 147

head and shoulders shot ... 199–200, 218–219

headline 11, 112, 114, 134–136,
139–142, 144, 146–147,
210–213, 225, 241–242

hegemonic 15, 23–24, 31, 37,
40–42, 47, 52, 71, 73,
77, 79–80, 92, 98,
192–193

hermeneutic code 9–10, 14

high-key lighting 199, 218–219, 222

hooks, bell 52, 54, 63–64, 205

HuffPost 18, 110, 135

Hugo Boss advert 58

hyperreality 27–31, 167, 222

I

idents 229–230

ideological reading 13, 20–21

implosion 27, 30–31

in-camera 217–220, 223–224,
227–228

in-group 32, 35–36

independent media 192–193

influencers 117–119

'Inspire her Mind' 53–54

instafamous 118–119

Instagram 18, 100–102, 115,
117–119, 134, 195

institutionalised cultural capital 84, 87

intellectual property 108, 121, 125

intercut 40, 116, 150, 154, 184,
187, 227–228

interpellation 13, 21

interpretative effects theories 73, 98

intersectionality 54, 58, 63–64, 205

intertextuality 13, 26–27, 36, 236

invisible editing 226, 228

IPSO 109, 114, 136–137

J

Jenkins, Henry 73, 87–88, 91–93, 97

The Jeremy Kyle Show 24

K

The Keepers 11–12

The Killing 129, 170, 172–192

L

Labour Party 22–23, 133

lad magazines 68

lead story 141–142, 147, 212

left wing 21–24, 31, 38, 48, 52

Lego experiment 81–82

'Letter to the Free' 129, 147–156

Leveson Inquiry/report ... 109, 114, 136

Lévi-Strauss, Claude ... 9–10, 13–14, 21, 31

Liberal Democrats 22

liberal pluralism 23–24, 31, 33, 37

licensed for broadcast 123, 126

lifestyle

    bloggers 18, 118

    magazines 21–22, 68, 195, 197, 199, 244

light

    fill 218–219

    source 7, 151, 186, 215, 220, 222, 224

Lights Out 116

linear narrative 11, 152

lip-sync 228

lipstick feminism 50, 58

long tail effect 67, 69, 97

low-key lighting 150, 154, 166, 182–183, 185, 187, 218–219, 222

M

magazines 6, 8, 18, 20–22, 43–45, 60, 67–70, 81, 83, 102, 104–105, 115–116, 128–129, 136, 158–159, 167, 170, 194, 205, 207, 209–214, 234, 238, 241–244

mainstream media 19, 46, 60, 192–193, 202

make-up tutorials 88

male gaze 49, 58, 167–168

Marvel 107–108

mass

    amateurisation 95–97

    consumption 107, 114

masterplot 16, 21, 31

masthead 141, 147, 198–199, 212, 241

#MeToo 50

media

    circulation 41, 68, 99–108, 115–116, 119, 121, 126–127, 131, 133–134, 158, 179, 203, 236, 245

    distribution 18, 62, 69, 99–103, 105–106, 108, 115–116, 120–121, 126–127, 130, 135, 158, 171, 174, 193, 196–197, 207, 236, 245

    effects debates 69–73

    language 6, 12, 21, 24–26, 31–32, 35, 39, 63, 128–129, 140–148, 150–151, 157, 160, 170, 173, 180–187, 194, 198–201, 215, 224, 236, 240, 246–245

    literacy 69–72, 80, 97

    production 7–8, 17, 43, 63, 66, 68, 70–71, 80–81, 88, 92–93, 95, 98–103, 107–109, 115–116, 120–122, 124–127, 148, 157–158, 170–175, 192–194, 203, 206–208, 211, 214–221, 224–238, 240–241, 245–245

    regulation 99–100, 102, 109, 123–124, 126, 136, 159, 236, 238, 245

middle-market tabloid 132, 147

mise-en-scène 7, 58, 115, 150–151, 154, 166, 187, 215–218, 220, 224–226, 228

monopoly 100, 102

montage 7, 11–12, 53, 72, 152, 185, 187, 225, 230

    editing 12

moral panic 71, 74–76, 97

moving image production 220–228

music videos 34, 45, 58, 129, 147–156, 226, 234

My Week as a Muslim 42–43

myth 6, 10, 12–14, 21, 31–33, 43, 45, 75, 77, 199

mytheme 14, 21, 31

N

narrative 6, 8–11, 13–17, 20–21, 28, 38, 40–41, 46, 51–52, 55, 57, 59, 75, 82, 92, 104, 107, 125, 141–146, 150–152, 154, 156, 160–162, 164, 167, 173, 179, 183–185, 187–191, 196, 202–203, 215, 220, 225, 227–228, 230, 236, 238

    theory 9–10, 31

narrowcast 122–123, 126

naturalisation 112, 114

Neale, Stephen 10, 17, 21, 31, 41, 63

negotiated identity 83–84, 87, 98

neo-Marxist 24, 33, 37, 84

neo-noir 183

Netflix 7, 11, 15, 55–56, 102, 105, 107–108, 119–126, 148, 172–173, 176

Neuman, W. Russell 73, 97

new media theories 73

news

    agencies 109, 111, 114, 130

    agenda 21, 23–24, 37–38, 66, 76, 111, 114, 135

    aggregators 110, 115

    sources, trust in 78–79

    websites 18, 42, 75, 110, 112, 145, 180

    newspapers 6, 8, 11, 18, 21, 37–38, 42, 44, 60, 74–75, 78–79, 102–104, 109–110, 112, 114–115, 129–147, 150, 172, 180, 207, 209–215, 225, 234

niche

    audience 120, 122, 126, 174, 177, 193, 203–204

    media 60

Nichols, Bill 39–40

non-verbal codes/communication 7, 9, 36, 199, 218–219

Nordic-noir/Scandi-noir 173, 175, 179, 183, 185, 226

O

The OA 56

objectified cultural capital 84, 87, 90

observational mode 28, 39, 46

Ofcom 109, 115, 123, 126

Oh Comely 129, 170, 194–205

Oliver, Jamie 46

opinion leader 19, 117, 119

orientalism 59, 63–64

otherness 25, 30, 59

out-group 32, 35–36, 64

Outlander 17

outros 229–230

P

page

    layout/design 206–214

    proportion 206–208, 211, 214, 227, 248

    weight 142, 209, 214

pan 7, 187, 221, 228

paparazzi 44, 134, 214, 219

paper weight 206, 248

parallax design 8, 12

participatory

    culture 71, 88, 90–93, 95, 97–98

    gap 87

    media 67, 69, 95, 128–129, 157, 234; *also see* audience participation

    mode 40, 46

pastiche 26, 30–31

patriarchy 32, 47, 50–51, 55, 61, 64, 168, 205

performative mode 40, 46

personal brand 118–119

persuasion theories 73

phenomena 25, 86

photography 217–219

photojournalist 214, 219

pick and mix theory 23, 202

play-through 117

plot 14–16, 21, 31, 40–41, 126, 160–161, 180, 188

plugin 8, 195

pluralism 23, 31, 112, 115

plurality 25

podcast 6, 11, 18, 78, 104, 110, 194, 228, 230–231

point-of-view (POV) shot 8, 221

Political Compass Test 22–23

politics 21–24, 27, 31, 33, 35, 37, 42, 46–48, 50, 54, 59, 61–62, 64–66, 69, 71, 73, 77–78, 94, 98, 101, 109–115, 130–133, 137, 139–140, 144, 146–148, 150, 154–156, 184, 190, 192–193, 202, 230

polysemic 33–34, 44, 52, 62, 79

popular culture 26, 53–54, 57, 67, 87–90, 97, 104, 172

post-feminism 48, 50

post-network television 120, 126

post-production 216–221, 225–227, 229–230, 240, 245

post-structuralism 12–13, 25, 30–31, 37

postcolonialism 59–63

postmodernism 13, 21, 25–28, 30–31, 236

potential reach 115, 119

PR 44, 109, 145, 147

pre-production 229, 245

precession of the simulacra 28–31

preferred reading 33, 37, 53, 79, 201–202, 204, 215

press release 145, 147

print

    media 103–104; *also see* magazines; newspapers

    production 206–214

proairetic code (ACT) 9–11, 14

prosumer 88, 93–95, 98, 196

psychographics 66, 81, 139

public domain 111, 115

Q

queer theory 47, 55, 58

quest narrative 16–17, 31, 160, 162

R

racial essentialism 61, 63

radio 6, 11, 18, 20, 78, 81,
85, 102, 104–105, 108,
110, 122, 126, 129, 135,
173, 194, 228, 230–231,
234

reality television 19–20, 28, 38–39,
45, 63

real persona 44–46

reception theory 67, 79–80, 98

recording principles 229

reel persona 44–46

referential code (REF) 9–10, 14

representation 11, 14–15, 25–26,
28–64, 81–84, 87,
94, 128–129, 140–142,
147–157, 159, 165,
167–170, 173, 179, 190,
192, 194, 198, 203–205,
215, 220, 236, 240–241,
246–245

   age 35

   audience 39

   culture 43

   digital media 71–72

   disability 35

   female 34, 47, 50–56, 63–64,
167–169, 192, 203–205

   gender 34, 42, 47, 50–56,
63–64, 167–169, 192,
203–205, 236

   identity 81–84, 87

   and industry 42–46, 64

   magazines 194, 198, 203–205

   masculinity 56–58, 64

   music videos 147–156

   newspapers 42, 128–129, 140–142

   race/ethnicity 35, 54–55, 59–64,
155–156

   and reality 37–42

   religion 35

   sexuality 35, 64

   social class 35, 63

   systems 32–36

   video games 157, 159, 165, 167–169

right wing 21–24, 139

raunch culture 34, 50–51, 58

S

Said, Edward 59, 63–64

satellite/cable channels 18, 109, 115

satirical 18, 28

Saussure, Ferdinand de 6, 13, 30–31

Schatz, Thomas 20, 161, 182

selective representation 142

semantic 9–10, 14, 66, 199

   code 9–10, 14

semiotic

   productivity 89, 93

   theory 6, 12–13, 27, 30,
37, 43, 79, 89, 94

sensationalism 37–38, 44, 76,
110, 112, 115, 147

shadow cultural economy 89–90, 93, 203

shareholders 100, 102–103, 124,
130

shark attacks 75–76

'She's Always a Woman' 53–54

Shirky, Clay 73, 95–98, 100

shooting script 220, 228, 240

shot list 220, 228

signification 6, 13, 15, 26, 30,
33, 43, 45, 52

signifier/signified 13, 28, 35, 84, 91

simulacrum 27–31, 159

simulation 27–31

soap opera 19–20, 40–42, 63,
104–105, 122, 143,
222, 226

Social Context theories 73

social media 8, 18, 30, 36, 50,
56, 66, 68–72, 78,
80, 82–83, 88, 91,
93, 96, 102–104,
108, 111–119, 123,
126, 130, 134–135,
140, 143–144, 155,
162–163, 178, 189,
192, 195, 225,
231–232, 240–241

societal and media theories 73

soft news 45, 112, 115, 130,
132–134, 141, 143,
145, 147

sound-bed 230

soundtrack 7–8, 11, 24, 108, 148,
187, 223, 227

Spectrek 29

spoiler 123, 126

Star Trek: Discovery 55

Statement of Intent 235, 240, 244–245

stereotypes 15, 32, 34–36, 38,
42, 49–55, 58–60, 91,
142, 145, 156, 236

stock character 15, 60

stardom/star image 39, 44–46

streaming of video-on-demand (SVoD)
119–120

structuralism 12–13, 31, 37, 199

subheading 141, 144, 146, 212–214,
241–242

subscriptions 18, 105, 107, 110,
119–121, 123, 132,
194–195, 197

suffragette 48

symbolic code (SYM) 9–10, 14

synergy 20, 101–102, 158

T

tabloid newspapers 20, 37–38, 44–45, 72, 74, 78, 109, 112, 115, 132, 134, 140, 146–147, 207, 209–212, 214–215

teaser 108, 212, 214

technical codes 7–9, 31

technological

    change 17–18, 31, 102–107, 115

    determinism 66, 71–72, 93, 97

Teen Vogue 69, 128

television 6, 9, 11, 16–20, 24, 27–28, 30, 36, 38–39, 44–47, 52–53, 55, 57–58, 63, 67, 74, 76–80, 85, 89, 92, 98, 104–106, 108, 115–116, 119–129, 135, 161, 170–184, 231, 234

textual productivity/poaching 89, 91–93

Todorov, Tzvetan 8–10, 14, 31

Tomb Raider: Anniversary 129, 157–169

tone (content) 20, 30, 125, 150, 182, 210, 215

tone (sound) 7, 150, 228–230

tone (visual) 7, 150, 164, 183, 185–186, 210, 215, 217, 219, 222, 224, 227

transgender 41–42, 47, 56

transnational 60–61, 63, 102, 123, 157, 193

trending 112, 115

trope 14–15, 17, 31, 57, 167

Turner, Graeme 38–39, 63

TV-MA 126

Twitter 102, 108, 111–112, 115, 118, 123, 130, 134–135, 143, 145, 200

Twitter-spats 112, 115

two-shot 7, 222

U

ultra HD 120, 126

unique users 133, 147

US politics 23

uses and gratifications theory 20, 43, 67, 73, 84, 178, 202

utopian solutions 20, 43, 67, 73, 84, 152

V

van Zoonen, Liesbet 51–54, 63–64

verisimilitude 11, 40–41, 63, 226

video games 19, 129, 157–169, 232, 234

video players/recorders 106–107

video-on-demand (VoD) 7, 11, 18, 40, 67, 105, 119–120, 122–123, 126

vinyl records 105

viral 101, 104, 112, 115–117

virtual reality (VR) 18, 103

vlogging 18–19, 44, 68, 101–102, 116–118

voice-over 12, 40, 46, 223, 225, 227

Vogue 68–69

W

'walk and talk' selfie shot ... 117, 119

watershed ... 40, 123, 126

whip pan ... 7

Y

YouTube ... 18–19, 36, 38, 44, 54, 66–67, 72, 75, 88, 93, 100–102, 106, 108, 110–111, 115–117, 135, 157, 167, 172, 231

Acknowledgements

Music acknowledgements
Letter To The Free
Words & Music by Lonnie Lynn, Emmanuel
Riggins & Robert Glasper
© Copyright 2016 Songs Of Reach Music/
Karriem Riggins Music/I Am A Jazzy Guy
Music/Think Common Music Inc.
Kobalt Music Publishing Limited/BMG Rights
Management (US) LLC/Missing Link Music LLC.
All Rights Reserved. International Copyright
Secured.
Used by permission of Hal Leonard Europe
Limited.

Photo acknowledgements
p1 Dinga / Shutterstock; p6 ZOO.BY; p6
alexwhite; p6 MicroOne; p6 alexwhite; p6
BoxerX; p7 (all) Lemony Snicket's A Series
of Unfortunate Events / Official Trailer [HD]
/ Netflix; p8 The Guardian; p9 (all) Green
& Black's – Velvet Edition / Green & Black
/ YouTube; p11 Netflix; p12 (middle) World
History Archive / Alamy Stock Photo; p12
(right) Reproduced with kind permission of
Gosportz Media LLC; p12 (left) Tesco; p13
The Force Manchester / Sky; p14 Olegusk;
p15 (top) Ivy Close Images / Alamy Stock
Photo; p15 (bottom) Designated Survivor,
ABC; p16 American Gods; p17 Facebook /
Outlander; p18 (top) Netflix; p18 (bottom)
Samsung; p19 *Try Not to Laugh Challenge
/ Smosh Pit* / YouTube; p20 (top) Courtesy
ITV; p20 (middle) Courtesy ITV; p20 (bottom)
BFA / Alamy Stock Photo; p22 (top) Grazia;
p23 Political Compass Test; p24 ITV / REX /
Shutterstock; p25 Clay Butler; p26 droopy76
/ Shutterstock.com; p27 (top) Lufthansa; p27
(bottom) rustyjaw; p29 Spectrek; p30 Black
Mirror / Netflix; p22 (bottom) alexmillos;
p30 (bottom) Dinga / Shutterstock; p32
(left) kurhan; p32 (right) Rawpixcel.com;
p33 nednapa; p34 (top) Courtesy Simon &
Schuster; p34 (bottom) Anaconda / Nicki
Minaj; p35 Chris Thomaidis / Image Bank
/ Getty; p36 TV 2 All That We Share / Do
Goodvertising / YouTube; p37 The Guardian;
p37 (bottom Mark Moffett ? Minden Pictures
/ Alamy; p38 AF archive / Alamy Stock
Photo/ Guggenheim Film Company; p39
Spash News / Alamy Stock Photo; p40 24
Hours in A&E; p41 Neighbours; p42 (top) PA;
p42 (bottom) My Week as a Muslim / Channel
4; p44 When JME Met Jeremy Corbyn /
YouTube; p46 © Jamie Oliver Enterprises
Limited; p47 rupaul.com; p48 (top) Heritage
Image Paratnership Ltd / Alamy Photo
Library; p48 (bottom) Neil Baylis / Alamy

Stock Photo; p49 Moviestore Collection Ltd
/ Alamy Stock Photo; p50 subversify.com;
p51 (top) Wrecking Ball / Miley Cyrus / Miley
Cyrus / YouTube; p51 (bottom) Liesbet van
Zoonen; p52 Who is Rupert Murdoch / CNN;
p53 (top) csheezio; p53 (bottom) John Lewis;
p54 Creative commons; p55 Star Trek; p56
Everett Collection Inc / Alamy Stock Photo;
p57 (top) Ian Alexander Tumblr; p57 (bottom)
Lynx Find Your Magic; p58 Hugo Boss; p59
Courtesy Penguin Random House; p60
With kind permission of Asian Media Group
www.amg.biz; p61 Heike Hustage-Koch /
Creative commons; p43 Apex News and
Pictures Agency / Alamy Stock Photo; p45
Allstar Picture Library / Alamy Stock Photo;
p63 (left) kurhan; p63 (right) Rawpixcel.
com; p65 (bottom) William Perugini; p65
(top) goodluz; p66 (left) Fairy Liquid; p66
(right) BMW; p66 (middle) Top Shop; p66
(bottom) Kylie Jenner / Twitter; p67 (top)
The Syndicate; p67 (bottom) Netflix; p68
(top) Post Office; p68 (bottom) Nuts;
p69 (bottom) Oksana Kuzmina; p70 Kim
Kardashian Blog; p71 (top) Everett Historical;
p72 (top) Moby, Are You Lost in the World
Like Me?; p72 (bottom) CBW / Alamy
Stock Photo; p74 Blue House (Republic of
Korea); p75 (top) Reproduced with the kind
permission of The Sun / News Licensing;
p75 (bottom) Surviving a Shark Attack / Sky
News; p76 Tone it Up; p77 ZZTop1958; p78
ABO PHOTOGRAPHY; p79 Ipsos MORI; p79
Diego Cervo; p80 (bottom) Barnardo's; p80
(top) Gap; p81 BARB; p82 Elspeth Stevenson;
p83 (top 3) Elspeth Stevenson; p82 (bottom)
Air Images; p85 (top) Reproduced with
the kind permission of Andy Watt; p85
(bottom) *Cerddi'r Bugail* (1918) / Creative
commons; p86 wavebreakmedia; p88 Easy
Fresh Face Makeup Tutorial / Jaclyn Hill /
YouTube; p89 (top) People's History of Pop
/ historypin; p89 (bottom) Phillip Maguire
/ Shutterstock.com; p90 VM Shpilka; p91
Odua Images; p92 (top) Jim Orr / Alamy
Stock Photo; p92 (bottom) dauntingfire; p94
COOLPIX P510; p95 A–Z Quotes; p96 Game
of Thrones Wiki; p97 William Perugini; p99
Rawpixcel.com; p100 Rockstar Games; p101
(top) Everett Collection Inc / Alamy Stock
Photo; p101 (bottom) Christian Bertrand /
Shutterstock.com; p102 Matt Ellis / Alamy
Stock Photo; p103 The Independent; p104
chrisdorney / Shutterstock.com; p105 (top)
360b / Shutterstock.com; p105 (2nd top)
chrisdorney / Shutterstock.com; p105 (3rd
top) r.classen / Shutterstock.com; p105 (4th
top) dennizn; p105 (bottom) Ldprod; p106

(bottom) Alan Wilson / Alamy Stock Photo;
p107 (top) Marvel Studios; p107 (bottom)
Avengers Assemble / Marvel; p108 (left)
rvlsoft / Shutterstock.com; p108 (right)
mrwebhoney; p110 The Huffington Post;
p111 The Young Turks
p112 (both) Reproduced with the kind
permission of The Daily Mail; p114 Buzzfeed;
p116 Lights Out; p117 (top 2) Proper Fish
and Chips; p117 (middle 3) TheSacconeJolys
- BIG ANNOUNCEMENT!; p117 (middle 3)
Sugg Siblings Early Christmas!; p118 Selena
Gomez / Instagram; p120 House of Cards;
p121 (top) Beaky Blinders; p121 (middle)
Riverdale; p121 (bottom) Sherlock; p122
Dark; p123 (top) Gladiators; p123 (bottom)
Sky Atlantic; p124 Everett Collection Inc
/ Alamy Stock Photo; p125 13 Reasons
Why; p126 Netflix; p106 Ned Snowman /
Shutterstock.com; p109 OpturaDesign;
p113 Everett Collection Inc / Alamy Stock
Photo; p115 SpeedKingz; p119 sitthphong /
Shutterstock.com; p127 Rawpixel.com; p128
pinkonelet; p130 London Gazette; p131 (left)
Audit Bureau of Circulation; p131 (right)
Advertising Association / WARC; p132 FT;
p134 Amaurea / Creative commons; p135
HuffPost; p136 Was Paperchase right to
apologise for advertising in the Dail Mail?
DEBATE - BBC Newsnight / YouTube; p140
Visual Generation; p138 Statista 2018; p137
aklionka; p138 Reproduced with the kind
permission of You Gov; p139 Reproduced
with the kind permission of You Gov; p140
Visual Generation; pp141–147 Reproduced
with the kind permission of The Daily Mail;
p148 (top) 13th / Netflix; p148 (bottom)
Berta, Berta / William Beck / YouTube;
p151 (all) Common – Letter to the Free
ft. Bilal / thinkcommon / YouTube; p152
(top) Michael Jackson / Earth Song; p152
(bottom) Common – Letter to the Free
ft. Bilal / thinkcommon / YouTube; p153
(both left) Common – Letter to the Free
ft. Bilal / thinkcommon / YouTube; p153
(right) Christos Geroghiou; p154 Common
- Black America Again ft. Stevie Wonder /
thinkcommon / YouTube; p155 Reproduced
with kind permission of STARS; p156 (top)
John Gomez / Shutterstock.com; p156
(bottom) Pepsi; p158 Tomb Raider; p159
(top) Lucozade; p159 (bottom) The Face;
p161 Tomb Raider; p163 (both) Reproduced
with the kind permission of You Gov; p164
(top) Reproduced with the kind permission
of YouGov; p164 (bottom) Lara Croft: Tomb
Raider: Anniversary; p165 (top and 2 right)
David Pimborough / Alamy Stock Photo;

p165 (bottom right) Everett Collection Inc / Alamy Stock Photo; pp166–168 Tomb Raider Anniversary HD Walkthrough - Peru - Tomb of Qualopec pt 1 / MahaloVideoGames; p168 (bottom right) Everett Collection Inc / Alamy Stock Photo; p168 Lara Croft; p153 Christos Gerghiou; p170 Arthimedes; p171 (top) The Singing Ringing Tree; p171 (bottom) Moviestore Collection Ltd / Alamy Stock Photo; p172 (top) Monaneko / GFDL / Creative commons; p172 (bottom) Black Panther; p173 (top) The Killing; p173 (bottom) DR; p174 (top) DR; p174 (middle) ZDF; p174 (bottom) BBC4; p175 Detectorists; p176 (top) Walter Presents; p176 (bottom) Netflix; p177 (all) Reproduced with the kind permission of YouGov; p178 Shock and Awe: The Life of Electricity; p179 The Guardian; p180 The Guardian; p184 The Killing; p181 (left) Pictorial Press Ltd / Alamy Stock Photo; p181 (right) The Killing; p182 (left) Everett Collection Inc / Alamy Stock Photo; p182 (right) Granger Historical Picture Archive / Alamy Stock Photo; pp185–188 The Killing; p189 Sarah Lund's Sweater; p190 The Killing; p191 (bottom left) The Bridge (SE); p191 (top) Everett Collection Inc / Alamy Stock Photo; p191 (2nd top) Everett Collection Inc / Alamy Stock Photo; p191 (3rd top) AF Archive / Alamy Stock Photo; p191 (bottom right) The Fall; p192 Den Rise; p193 Gustavo Frazao; p195 (both) Reproduced

with the kind permission of Oh Comely magazine (ohcomely.co.uk); p196 Iceberg Press; p197 (top left) London Loop; p197 (top middle) Heavenly Recordings; p197 (top right) Dash; p197 (bottom) Tick Tock Redbush Tea; pp198–201 Reproduced with the kind permission of Oh Comely magazine (ohcomely.co.uk); p202 (top) AstroStar; p202 (bottom) ESB Basic; p204 Reproduced with the kind permission of Oh Comely magazine (ohcomely.co.uk); p183 Everett Collection, Inc. / Alamy Stock Photo; p205 Arthimedes; p206 Stockphoto-graph; p208 (top) Channel No 5; p208 (middle) Miss Dior; p208 (bottom) j'adore Dior; p209 (top) pashamba; p209 (middle) Katunina; p209 (bottom left) Now; p209 (bottom right) Now; p211 Noci; p212 Daily Mail; p213 (top) Northern & Shell plc; p213 (bottom) Now; p214 stockphoto mania; p215 (top) Dmytro Zinkevych; p215 (bottom) Mayer George; p216 (top) WENN Ltd / Alamy Stock Photo; p216 (bottom) WENN Ltd / Alamy Stock Photo; p217 (top) Noci; p217 (middle) Jon Fletcher; p217 (bottom) antb; p218 (top) Nik Bruining; p218 (middle) Stone36; p218 (bottom) Nik Bruining; p219 (top) AHowden / Alamy Stock Photo; p219 (bottom) Lev Dolgachov / Alamy Stock Photo; p220 Ivelin Radkov; p221 (top) The Guardian; p221 (middle) The Guardian; p221 (bottom) Tangerine; p222 NAPI WAN ALI; p223 Mr Robot; p224 (all) Mr Robot;

p225 AF archive / Alamy Stock Photo; p225 Moviestore Collection Ltd / Alamy Stock Photo; p226 IOvE IOvE; p227 Rawpixel. com; p228 Home Podcast Studio; p230 (top) Serial; p230 (bottom) Georgejmclittle; p231 (top) Meerkat Movies; p231 (bottom) Very; p229 Rawpixel.com; p232 GingerArt; p233 Stockphoto-graph; p239 Drinkaware; p243 (top left) Reproduced with the kind permission of Phoenix Magazine; p243 (top middle) Reproduced from GQ Australia January 2012 issue; p243 (top right) Reproduced with the kind permission of Phoenix Magazine; p243 (middle left) Reproduced with the kind permission of Bauer Media; p243 (middle middle) Reproduced with the kind permission of Bauer Media; p243 (middle right) Reproduced with the kind permission of the BFI; p243 (bottom left) Harper's Bazaar; p243 (bottom 2nd left) Reproduced with the kind permission of Bauer Media; p243 (bottom right) Reproduced with the kind permission of the BFI; p244 (left) Mandy Moore; p244 (middle) Britney Spears; p244 (right) Taylor Swift; pp248-9 Students from Runshaw College; p234 Monkey Business Images; p235 Jahanzaib Naiyyer; p236 Dmitri Ma; p238 Sentavio; p240 Roobcio; p251 Monkey Business Images